RAISING CLAIMS

STUDIES IN EUROPEAN URBAN HISTORY (1100-1800)

VOLUME 56

Raising Claims

Justice and Commune in Late Medieval Italy

SO NAKAYA

BREPOLS

Cover illustration: Ambrogio Lorenzetti, detail of *The Allegory of Good and Bad Government* (1338-39), Palazzo Pubblico in Siena.

D/2022/0095/24
ISBN 978-2-503-59006-6
eISBN 978-2-503-59007-3
DOI 10.1484/M.[illegible]
ISSN 1780-3241
eISSN 2294-8368

Printed in the EU on acid-free paper.

CONTENTS

List of Illustrations

Figures

Maps

Tables

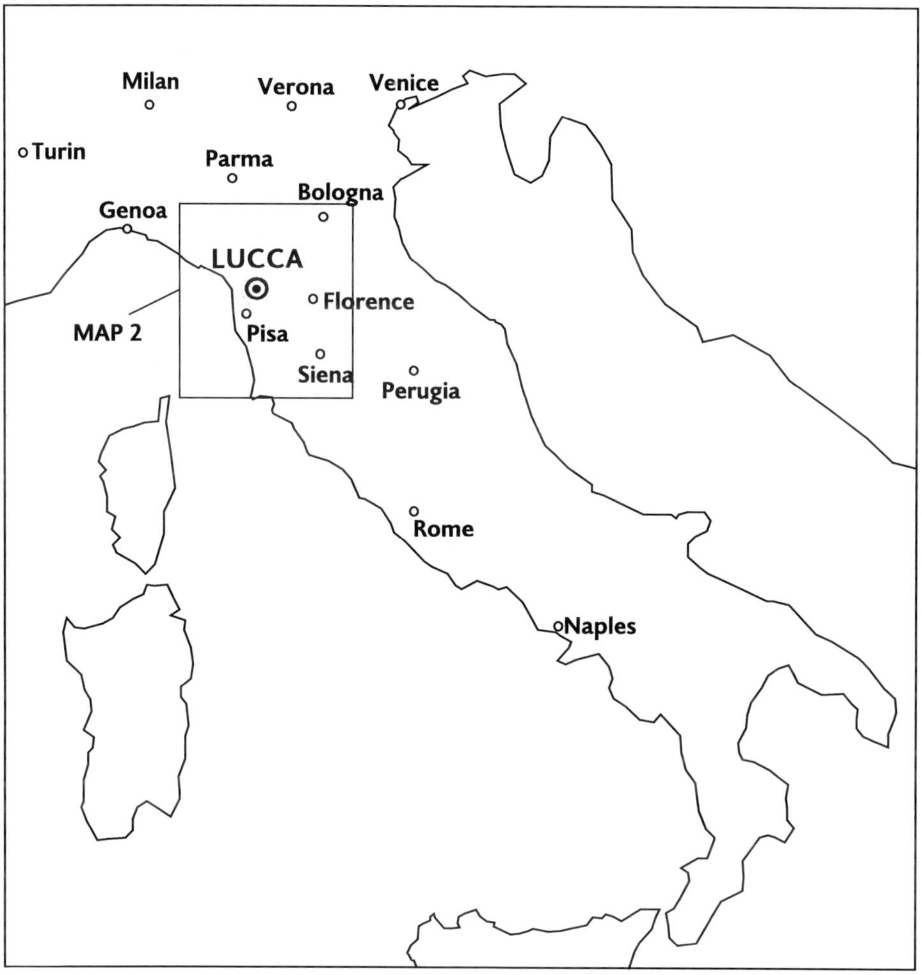
Milan
Verona
Venice
Turin
Parma
Bologna
Genoa
LUCCA
Florence
MAP 2
Pisa
Siena
Perugia
Rome
Naples

Map 1: Italy

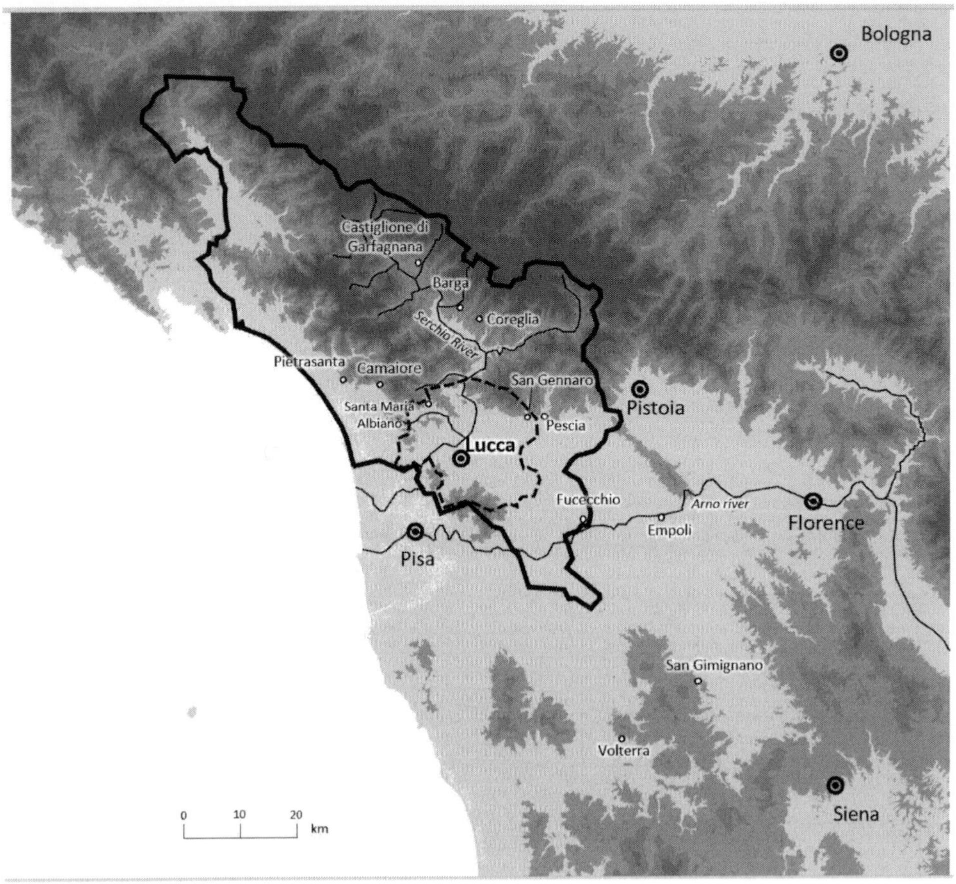

Map 2: Western Tuscany
— Boundary of territory claimed by Lucca in 1308
--- Boundary of Sei Miglia

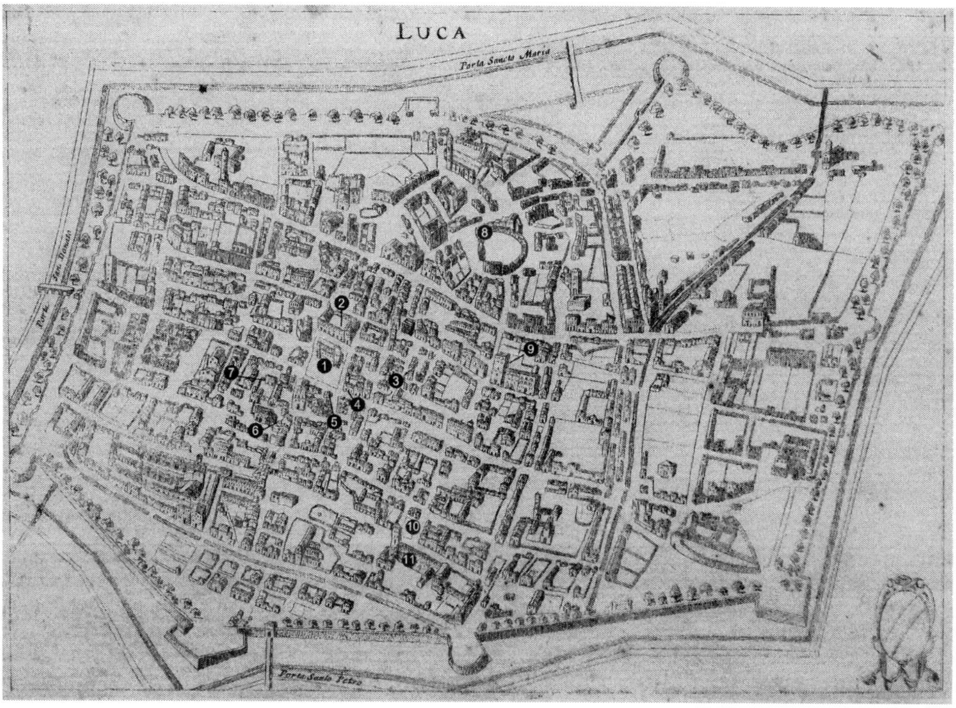

Map 3: Lucca (Hondius J., *Nova et accurata Italiae hodiernae descriptio* [Leiden, 1627], p. 88)
① Piazza of San Michele in Foro
② Communal Palace (the Court of Podestà, the Courts of Consuls, the General Council, the Anziani)
③ Court of San Cristoforo
④ New Court of Justice (in 1336)
⑤ Loggia used by the communal government (the Court of Podestà, the Courts of Consuls in the republican period after 1370)
⑥ Court of Foretani (in the 13th century)
⑦ Court of Treguani (in the 13th century)
⑧ Anfiteatro (used as a prison)
⑨ Guinigi Tower
⑩ Court of Querimonie (in 1344)
⑪ Duomo

Introduction

On 4 May 1336 in the city of Lucca in central Italy, Nicolao, Lanfranco, and Urso, three clerks at the Court of Podestà made their habitual way to the communal palace (Palazzo Comunale), which sits on the north side of the piazza of San Michele in Foro. After taking their seats and opening the ledgers on their desks, they looked up to find several people waiting restlessly, bills of complaint ready in their eager hands.

Recorded in Nicolao's ledger for that day are the claims of one Ceccholo against Nello for six bushels (*staio*) of wheat as compensation for three years of unpaid land rent, of the widow Billa against the heirs of one Pina for 80 *lire* to cover the cost of the latter's food and drink over the previous eight years, and of one Betto against rural community officials for payment of 50 *soldi* as wages for ten days of labour.[1] On that same day, Lanfranco's ledger records a claim seeking restitution of thirty-seven goats that had been seized against a debt, a claim for payment on an iron spear, and a suit requesting a selection of arbiters to settle a quarrel between brothers.[2] Finally, Urso's ledger attests to the existence of claims relating to the restitution of debts and of dotal property.[3] The day's court proceedings also saw progress in trials already underway. From court records of several cases we can glimpse details of the summoning of parties concerned and their pleas, summary orders by judges, the disclosure of testimonies, the handing down of judgements and more, revealing the hectic interactions of judges, clerks, messengers, and litigants.

Another room of the same Palazzo Comunale held the criminal court known as the *Curia maleficiorum*, which also employed court clerks, including one named Guido. These men, too, saw the arrival of angry petitioners. A complaint filed by a man named Jacopo on 2 July that same year accuses one Ciardello of attacking him with a sword and absconding with a large quantity of onions from the latter's food storehouse, along with requests that Ciardello be found guilty and punished.[4] That same month also saw a desperate visit to the court by a certain Andruccio,[5] who had been charged on suspicion of injuring and thereby causing the death of a man named Puccinello. Andruccio denied the charge and laid eight claims of his own before the court, including one to the effect that Puccinello had also borne arms. The clerks summoned witnesses to hear their testimony as to whether Andruccio's claims were veracious.

---

1 Archivio di Stato di Lucca (hereafter ASL.), *Potestà di Lucca* (hereafter *Potestà*), 60, fols. 15r, 17r, 24r.

2 *Potestà*, 58, fols. 8r-v, 11r-12r, 21r-v.

3 *Potestà*, 64, fols. 11r, 12r.

4 *Potestà*, 4726, fol. 1.

5 *Potestà*, 4726, fols. 6v-12v.

In yet another room of the Palazzo Comunale sat Rustico, the Chancellor of the executive council (i.e. the Anziani), before whom various claims against the Anziani were brought. According to Rustico's ledger, on 1 June 1336 the Anziani had deliberated over a petition by a man named Ligo, who wanted special permission to sell land in the Coreglia area, which was normally prohibited.[6] On 8 June the discussion addressed the complaint of a group of bakers, who held that they had been prosecuted by the office of roads based on outdated regulations concerning the management of firewood.[7] On 12 June three men named Jacopo, Giovanni, and Turi, who had been away from Lucca's territory and thus avoided a heavy tax, stated their desire to return to Lucca and entreated for an exemption from the tax.[8] The same day, Ranuccio, a man who had been sentenced to beheading two years earlier, once again argued his own innocence and requested a pardon.[9] As the result of these deliberations, every one of these claims was acknowledged by the Anziani.

These are some of the everyday scenes that unfolded at fourteenth-century Lucca's Palazzo Comunale. Although such claims constitute a motley assortment when seen individually, it is impossible to ignore the enormous profusion of cases – in Lucca, a city of only twenty thousand people, an average of ten thousand claims were filed at the civil court each year.[10] Dozens of people would bring their claims to the Palazzo Comunale on a daily basis. Why were the inhabitants of Italian medieval cities submitting claims to the commune in such numbers? And how was the commune shaped by this daily accumulation of people's claims? This book seeks to consider the historical characteristics of Italian medieval cities by investigating some of their everyday practices – namely the claims brought forward by its people and the response by the communal authorities.

The cities of medieval Italy were notable in terms of both size and density relative to the European context. In addition to the great metropoles of Florence and Milan, the Italian peninsula was also crowded with innumerable smaller and mid-sized cities like Lucca, rich in their own distinctive character. These cities saw the development of manufacturing, as well as of banking and local commerce, which were associated with long-distance trade. Extraordinary developments were also demonstrated in other spheres, such as in religious culture and the fine arts. Yet it must not be forgotten that they were also distinctive in another way; namely, these cities existed in the form of 'communes' (*comune* in Italian, plural *comuni*).

In northern and central Italy, from the end of the eleventh to the beginning of the twelfth centuries, civic collectivities were formed by citizens to resolve problems and maintain the peace in the cities. Civic leaders, working sometimes in concert and sometimes at odds with the bishops and others who had traditionally held signorial power, gradually assumed control of their cities' governing bodies and thus representa-

6 ASL, *Anziani avanti la Libertà* (hereafter *Anz. Av. Lib.*), 10, fol. 13v.
7 *Anz. Av. Lib.*, 10, fol. 18v.
8 *Anz. Av. Lib.*, 10, fols. 20r-21r.
9 *Anz. Av. Lib.*, 10, fols. 21r-v.
10 For details on the number of civil cases, see Chapter 1.

tive authority.[11] The term *comune* first began to be used for such bodies in the 1120s and 1130s, and by the middle of the twelfth century had been formalised as organised institutions with consuls, assemblies, and law courts that oversaw the enactment of legislation, judicial proceedings, and other governmental activities.[12]

Such communes have already attracted scholarly attention by dint of a variety of distinctive features. The classic historical studies by Sismondi and others conceived of the communes from the perspective of *libertas*. Combining the notions of *libertas*, or independence from external constraints, with the republican *libertas* of civic self-government, the communes were regarded as telling the story of a glorious period of Italian history.[13] These idealised images of the independence and self-government of the communes have also exerted a powerful influence on the historiography of political thought.[14]

Since the twentieth century, however, historians have eschewed giving undue emphasis to this idealistic aspect of the communes, tending rather to view them through the lenses of 'rule' and 'governance'. Communes that by rights should have represented cohesive and united citizen collectives were, in historical reality, dominated by a few elites and subject to their rule. This is the premise on which studies of the ruling classes of the communes have been developed. Historiography has paid attention to the origins and characteristics of city leaders and the continuities and changes in their makeup – from military aristocrats with feudal ties to the signorial power at the dawn of the communal age, to a broader military elite that included commercial and judicial actors in the twelfth and thirteenth centuries, to the non-*milites* popular strata (*popolo*) after the mid-thirteenth century, and ultimately to the prominent families whose members subsequently dominated the city as *signori*.[15]

11 C. Wickham, *Sleepwalking into a New World. The Emergence of Italian City Communes in the Twelfth Century* (Princeton, 2015).

12 Initially, such self-governing bodies of citizens were known as *civitas*, while the term *comune* was used adjectivally in the sense of 'communal', 'common', or 'public'. The first use of *commune* as a noun to refer to the city's public organisation has been dated by François Menant to around 1120, and to the 1130s by Alberto Banti, F. Menant, *L'Italia dei comuni (1100-1350)* (2005; Ital. edn., Roma, 2011), p. 12-15; O. Banti, ''Civitas' e 'Commune' nelle fonti italiane dei secoli XI e XII', in G. Rossetti (ed.), *Forme di potere e struttura sociale in Italia nel Medioevo* (Bologna, 1977), p. 217-232.

13 J. C. L. Simonde de Sismondi, *Storia delle repubbliche italiane dei secoli di mezzo* (Capolago, 1831-32). Regarding the definition of political liberty, in particular, as participation in sovereignty by free citizens, see *Ibid.*, vol. XIV, p. 314-315. For a recent assessment of the classic studies by Muratori and Sismondi, see M. Vallerani, 'Il comune come mito politico. Immagini e modelli tra Otto e Novecento', in G. Sergi and E. Castelnuovo (eds.), *Arti e storia nel Medioevo*, vol. iv, *Il Medioevo al passato e al presente* (Torino, 2004), p. 187-206; G. Milani, *I comuni italiani* (Roma-Bari, 2005), p. 159-161.

14 Q. Skinner, *The Foundations of Modern Political Thought* (Cambridge, 1978). On the similarity between Skinner's image of the city-state and the concept of 'communal liberty' among traditional scholars, see E. I. Mineo, 'La repubblica come categoria storica', *Storica*, 43-45 (2009), p. 125-167.

15 For a representative study of the ruling classes, see H. Keller, *Il laboratorio politico del Comune medievale* (Napoli, 2014); J. C. Maire Vigueur, *Cavalieri e cittadini: guerra, conflitti e società nell'Italia comunale* (Bologna, 2004); J. C. Maire Vigueur (ed.), *Signorie cittadine nell'Italia comunale* (Roma, 2013); P. Cammarosano, 'Il ricambio e l'evoluzione dei ceti dirigenti nel corso del XIII secolo', in *Magnati e popolani nell'Italia comunale* (Pistoia, 1997), p. 17-40; A. Poloni, *Potere al popolo. Conflitti sociali e lotte politiche nell'Italia comunale del Duecento* (Milano, 2010); G. M. Varanini, 'Aristocrazie e poteri nell'Italia centro-settentrionale dalla crisi comunale allguerre d'Italia', in

Alongside interest in these ruling elites, it has also been noted that the communes had the character of governmental authority and statehood.[16] As institutions that had emerged as civic assemblages based on collective oaths, the communes developed through the daily judicial and administrative affairs of the consular period in the twelfth century. By the thirteenth century, in the context of a fast-growing economy and an increasingly sophisticated society that brought with it not only various complex problems requiring systematic resolution but also increased social mobility and changes to the ruling class (particularly in terms of the growing influence of the popular strata under the *podestà* and *popolo* regimes), the governing structure of the communes had been considerably institutionalised as a system of governance that resembled statehood.[17] The commune, composed of various specialised institutions that included a chief magistrate, an executive council, councils, courts, and treasury, constituted a ruling body that legitimately governed the population based on established laws and regulations. In addition, the city communes expanded their *iurisdictio* to the surrounding countryside (*contado*) to become city-states with a delimited geographical area, thereby bringing local feudal lords and autonomous rural communities under the umbrella of their rule.[18]

With the revelation of this aspect of rule and governance in historical research, the communes, instead of havens of independence and self-government, now appear to us more as governing bodies led by elite citizens who set laws, gave orders, and imposed obligations on residents within their *iurisdictio*. In this book, which examines the historical realities of the communes of the fourteenth century, the communes likewise appear as governing bodies that ruled their inhabitants through the core institutions of an executive council, councils, and law courts.

Here, I would also like to note that the people at the time recognised another aspect of the commune as an elite-led system of governance; namely, the commune existed as a conceptual authority made up of the residents as a whole.[19] This idea of the commune was evident in the writings of jurists and thinkers of the time, and brilliantly expressed in the famous frescoes that adorn Siena's Palazzo Pubblico.

R. Bordone, G. Castelnuovo and G. M. Varanini (eds.), *Le aristocrazie dai signori rurali al patriziato* (Roma and Bari, 2004), p. 121-193.

16 M. Vallerani, 'Comune e comuni: una dialettica non risolta', in M. C. De Matteis and B. Pio (eds.), *Sperimentazioni di governo nell'Italia centro-settentrionale nel processo storico dal primo comune alla signoria* (Bologna, 2011), p. 9-34.

17 Regarding the structure, institutions and political culture of the communes, see Milani, *I comuni italiani*; L. Tanzini, *Dai comuni agli stati territoriali. L'Italia delle città tra XIII e XV secolo* (Noceto, 2010); E. Artifoni, 'Tensioni sociali e istituzioni nel mondo comunale', in N. Tranfaglia and M. Firpo (eds.), *La storia, 2: Il Medioevo: popoli e strutture politiche* (Torino 1986), p. 461-491.

18 P. Jones, *The Italian City-State from Commune to Signoria* (Oxford, 1997); A. Gamberini, *The Clash of Legitimacies. The State-Building Process in Late Medieval Lombardy* (Oxford, 2018).

19 Here and below, I use the Italian *comune* to refer to the public authority conceptually imagined as underlying the commune as an actual public organisation.

Figure 0.1: Ambrogio Lorenzetti, *The allegory of good and bad government* (1338-39), Palazzo Pubblico in Siena.

In Lorenzetti's *The Allegory of Good and Bad Government* (1338-39, Picture-1),[20] the exceptionally large figure depicted on the right is a personification of the commune itself.[21] The caption below the image reads as follows: 'This holy virtue [Justice], where she rules, induces to unite the many souls [of citizens], and they, gathered together for such a purpose, make the Common Good [*bene comune*] their Lord'.[22] '*Bene comune*' here refers to the enthroned personification of the commune ('*comune*').[23]

20 *Ambrogio Lorenzetti: il Buon governo*. Three murals decorate three of the four walls of the Council Room: *The Allegory of Good Government, The Effects of Good Government*, and *The Allegory and Effects of Bad Government*.

21 N. Rubinstein, 'Le allegorie di Ambrogio Lorenzetti nella sala della pacee il pensiero politico del suo tempo', (1997), now in G. Cappelli (ed.), *Studies in Italian History*, p. 347-364, in particular p. 348-349.

22 E. Castelnuovo (ed.), *Ambrogio Lorenzetti: il Buon governo* (Milano, 1995), p. 383: 'Questa sancta virtu, la dove regge, induce ad unita li animi molti, e questi, a ccio ricolti, un ben comun per lor signor si fanno, lo qual, per governar suo stato, elegge di non tener giamma' gli ochi rivolti da lo splendor de' volti de le virtu che' ntorno a llui si stanno. Per questo con triunfo a llui si danno censi, tributi e signorie di terre, per questo senza guerre seguita poi ogni civile effetto, utile, necessario e di diletto'.

23 N. Rubinstein, 'Political Ideas in Sienese Art: The Frescoes by Ambrogio Lorenzetti and Taddeo di Bartolo in the Palazzo Pubblico', (1958), now in G. Cappelli (ed.), *Studies in Italian History in the Middle Ages and the Renaissance, I, Political Thought and the Language of Politics. Art and Politics* (Roma, 2004), p. 61-98; Q. Skinner, 'Ambrogio Lorenzetti: The artist as Political Philosopher', *Proceedings of the British Academy*, 72 (1986), p. 1-56; R. M. Dessì, 'Il bene comune nella comunicazione verbale e visiva. Indagini sugli affreschi del "Buon Governo"', in AA. VV. *Il bene comune: forme di governo e gerarchie sociali nel basso medioevo* (Spoleto, 2012), p. 89-130; M. M. Donato, 'Il *princeps*, il giudice, il «sindacho» e la città. Novità su Ambrogio Lorenzetti nel Palazzo Pubblico di Siena', in F. Bocchi and R. Smurra (eds.), *Imago urbis: l'immagine delle città nella storia d'Italia* (Roma 2003), p. 389-416. *Bene commune* is a concept that refers to the 'common good' as opposed to respective individual goods. Regarding the idea and practice of *bene comune* in European cities, see Lecuppre-Desjardin and Van Bruaene (eds.), *De bono communi. The discourse and Practice of the Common Good in the European City (13th-16th c.)* (Turnhout, 2010). For Italy, see Andrea Zorzi, 'Bien Commun et conflits politiques dans l'Italie communale', in Lecuppre-Desjardin and Van Bruaene (eds.), *De bono communi*, p. 267-290; AA. VV. *Il bene comune*. Incidentally, intellectuals of the day

This expression of many citizens uniting in spirit to create the '*comune*' – which is to say *bene comune* – reveals the concept of the '*comune*' as something constituted by its citizens.[24] Nonetheless, the '*comune*' is not something to be merely equated with a group of citizens. The '*comune*' existed as something created as the 'ruler' of its citizens, and is depicted as a figure reigning from a throne even in paintings.[25] In other words, the '*comune*', even as something constituted by its citizens, was for that very reason the legitimate power to rule the citizens who were its members.[26]

It is noted that the definition of '*comune*' is posited here purely conceptually.[27] This is consistent with the view, expressed by the jurist Baldus de Ubaldi, that 'properly speaking the people (*populus*) is not men, but a collection of men into a body which is mystical and taken as abstract, and the significance of which has been discovered by the intellect'.[28] This view, which presumes the commune to be a notionally established

---

also used expressions that equated the terms *comune* and *bene comune*. Perceiving the expressions *comune* and *bene comune* to be equivalent was common among thinkers at the time. This is evident from the fact that *bene comune* ('the common good') and *bene del comune* ('the good of the commune') were used interchangeably by Remigio de' Girolami (1247-1319), a contemporary Dominican theologian. In his writings, Remigio frequently cites the good of the commune and the good of the many as being identical to *bene comune* when showing what should take precedence over the good of the individual. See E. Panella, 'Dal bene comune al bene del comune. I trattati politici di Remigio dei Girolami', in *Politica e vita religiosa a Firenze tra '300 e '500* (Pistoia, 1985), p. 24-25, p. 100. This discourse linking the communes with the idea of *bene comune* goes back to Brunetto Latini. In his book *Li livres dou tresor* (1260s), he preaches to government officials that they must preserve the 'peace and honesty of the common good' by acting 'for good of the commune'. See Zorzi, 'Bien Commun', p. 277-278; B. Latini, *Tresor*, ed. P. G. Beltrami (Torino, 2007), p. 284, 253, 408.

24 According to Donato, the 24 citizens depicted in the painting are a visual representation of these 'many citizens'. See Donato, 'Ancora sulle "Fonti" nel Governo di Ambrogio Lorenzetti: dubbi, precisazioni, anticipazioni', in S. Adorni Braccesi and M. Ascheri (eds.), *Politica e cultura nelle repubbliche italiane dal Medioevo all'età moderna. Firenze, Genova, Lucca, Siena, Venezia* (Roma, 2001), p. 43-79, in particular p. 71.

25 Incidentally, this view of the commune is also apparent among contemporary thinkers and jurists. When Marsilius of Padua points out that 'the "legislator" … is the people or the corporate body of the citizens', or when Baldus de Ubaldis says that 'if the *populus* … is the *princeps* of its citizens', the commune – and the 'corporate body' and '*populus*' that are synonymous with it here – comes to personify the 'legislator' and '*princeps*' who obey the citizens. See Marsilio da Padova, *Il difensore della pace*, ed. C. Vasoli (Torino, 1975), p. 171: 'legislatorem… esse populum seu civium universitatem'; J. Canning, *The Political Thought of Baldus de Ubaldis* (Cambridge, 1987), p. 203-204: 'si populus est suorum civium princeps'.

26 Regarding the fourteenth-century development of theories of *universitas* and representation that constitute the crux of this mechanism, as well as their application to Italian cities, see J. M. Najemy, 'Stato, commune e «universitas»', *Annali dell'Istituto storico italo-germanico in Trento*, 20 (*Atti della tavola rotonda tenutasi nell'ambito del seminario su Le origini dello Stato moderno in Italia, secoli XIV-XVI*) (1995), p. 245-263.

27 In the frescoes, the figure of the commune is depicted as being on the upper level alongside the personifications of the other virtues and as having a different size than the *real* citizens lined up below and therefore as belonging to a different dimension than the real world. This kind of commune iconography was not unique to Lorenzetti; it was also depicted on the tomb of Guido Tarlati (Bishop of Arezzo). In the image known as *Il comune in signoria*, the commune is depicted as an enthroned figure holding a sceptre being petitioned for forgiveness by figures below who appear to be sinners. See Pasquini, 'La rappresentazione del bene comune nell'iconografia medievale', in *Il bene comune*, p. 489-515.

28 Here, the term '*populus*' is used as a concept synonymous with the '*comune*'. See Canning, *The Political Thought of Baldus*, p. 187; A. Black, 'Society and the Individual from the Middle Ages to Rousseau: Philosophy, Jurisprudence and Constitutional Theory', *History of Political Thought*, 1-2 (1980), p. 145-166, in particular p. 152: 'populus proprie non dicitur homines, sed hominum collectio in unum corpus mysticum et abstractive sumptum, cuius significatio est inventa per intellectum'. E. H. Kantorowicz, *The King's Two Bodies: A Study in Mediaeval Political Theology* (Princeton, 1957), p. 210.

authority – where an authority is considered to be distinct from both a real governing body or ruler and also from a mere assemblage of citizens – is reminiscent of Thomas Hobbes's view of the 'commonwealth', the mantle of which has been inherited by the phenomenon of the modern state.[29]

The idea of the '*comune*' as being the 'ruler' of its citizens was embodied in the communal institutions (i.e. executive council and courts) and officials (i.e. political leaders and judges) who served as its real-world representatives and purported to act in its name. But even if the concept of the '*comune*' was elaborated only ideologically in the communal political culture, its representations were not inconsequential to the real practice of governance.[30] Lorenzetti's frescoes were painted on the walls of the executive council hall in Siena where the *Nove*, the executive college, convened as the political representatives of the '*comune*'. It was against the backdrop and under the watchful gaze of this image of the '*comune*' that they conducted their deliberations and rendered their decisions.

Keeping in mind the relationship between the abstract '*comune*' and the commune as a real governing body, the character of the commune to which the people brought their claims becomes clearer. It was an authority dominated neither by the private interests and desires of the city elites nor by the institutional powers that governed inhabitants unilaterally from above. The commune was seen as an authority that should act on behalf of the '*comune*' as 'ruler' of the citizens; at least ideally, it was a public power that should govern with one eye focusing on the *bene comune* as the good of the entire citizenry. Understanding the commune in this way will be important for examining the claims people brought before the commune as well as its governing activities.

How should we consider the communes characterised in this way? A focus on the public governmental systems and statehood of medieval communes might bring to mind studies that have considered them as an origin of the modern state. Previous studies have focused on legislation prohibiting private violence in medieval cities and the introduction of inquisitorial trials *ex officio*, seeing therein the development towards a modern statal order that monopolises violence and seeks to build a unified public order.[31] Certainly, medieval cities were the sites of more than a few systems and

---

29 Recent studies in the history of political thought have noted that medieval thinkers and jurists nurtured the pervasive modern view of the state. See Black, 'Society and the Individual'; Igor Mineo, 'La repubblica'; Najemy, 'Stato, comune'; P. Schiera, 'Legittimità, disciplina, istituzioni: tre presupposti per la nascita dello Stato moderno', in Chittolini, Molho and Schiera (eds.), *Origini dello stato. Processi di formazione statale in Italia fra medioevo ed età moderna* (Bologna, 1994), p. 17-48. By contrast, while Skinner finds signs of Hobbes's 'state' in the ideas of Machiavelli and Bodin, he regards this as being characteristically distinct from the medieval commune (Skinner, *The Foundations of Modern Political Thought*, v. 2, p. 349-358).

30 Regarding the political languages of the commune and their persistence, see Gamberini, *The Clash of Legitimacies*, p. 41-60.

31 For a study concerning the monopolisation of violence on the part of public authority in ordinances *antimagnatizie* by the *popolo* in the latter half of the thirteenth century, see G. Tabacco, 'La storia politica e sociale. Dal tramonto dell'Impero alle prime formazioni di Stati regionali', in R. Romano and C. Vivanti (eds.), *Storia d'Italia, II: Dalla caduta dell'Impero romano al secolo XVIII* (Torino, 1974), p. 1-274, in particular p. 223-249. As for inquisitorial procedure, M. Sbriccoli, 'Giustizia criminale', in M. Fioravanti (ed.), *Lo stato moderno in Europa. Istituzioni e diritto* (Roma, 2002), p. 163-205; E. Dezza, *Accusa e inquisizione dal diritto comune ai codici moderni* (Milano, 1989).

philosophies that were handed down to subsequent eras.[32] But if we keep in mind the Weberian view of the state, which develops a monopoly over violence as an index of statehood, it becomes more difficult to portray state phenomena as unique to the era and society of late medieval Italy.[33]

In recent studies of medieval and early modern Europe, the state has been only broadly conceptualised, for example as 'enduringly ordered collective life in a political association'.[34] Exploration of this idea has focused not on the development of the modern state considered *a priori*, but rather on those aspects of states that were embedded in their respective societies and whose principles were concordant (or at least not incongruous) with private social practices.[35] One of the keywords addressed in recent studies is 'practice', taking the viewpoint of comprehending the state through its practices.[36] The state is not a given *a priori*, but only takes shape and begins to function when people confer meaning upon it and reach out to it.[37] In that sense, the state was called into being not only by the rulers who served as its representatives but also by the common people, who did so by raising their claims and through the acts of accessing its

---

32 In the field of the history of political thought, Schiera examines the relationship between command and obedience and the problem of discipline as internal principles leading to the modern state based on the writings of Marsilius and Baldus. See Schiera, 'Legittimità, disciplina'.

33 In these conventional studies, attention is devoted to the constitution and governing systems of the Renaissance period, while the communes are given as negative a portrayal as the world that preceded them. A typical example is a study by Chabod, who views the expansion of the bureaucratic systems of monarchic states during the Renaissance as the ancestral form of the modern state. See F. Chabod, 'Esiste uno Stato del Rinascimento?' in *Opere di Federico Chabod*, II, *Scritti sul Rinascimento* (Torino, 1967), p. 593-604.

34 This is an expression of Otto Brunner's, a definition widely shared also by Chittolini among studies of medieval states. See O. Brunner, *Land and Lordship: Structures of Governance in Medieval Austria* (Philadelphia, 1992), p. 95; Chittolini, '"Il privato", il "pubblico", lo Stato', in *Origini dello stato*, p. 553-589, in particular p. 567-568.

35 One such achievement from the 1990s is Kirshner (ed.), *The Origins of the State in Italy 1300-1600* (Chicago and London, 1995). For reports and discussions from research workshops not included in this collection, see the following collections, *Annali dell'Istituto storico italo-germanico in Trento*, 20 (*Atti della tavola rotonda tenutasi nell'ambito del seminario su Le origini dello Stato moderno in Italia, secoli XIV-XVI*) (1995), p. 233-271. Regarding the Florentine state, W. J. Connel and A. Zorzi (eds.), *Florentine Tuscany. Structures and Practices of Power* (Cambridge, 2000). In recent years, new approaches to political discourse and other aspects of the history of political culture have been introduced to research into the late medieval and early modern state. See A. Gamberini and I. Lazzarini (eds.), *The Italian Renaissance State* (Cambridge, 2012).

36 Here I am considering Pierre Bourdieu's concepts of practice. See P. Bourdieu, *Le sens pratique* (Paris, 1980). Bourdieu's concept of practice often features in historical studies relating to medieval justice. See, for example, C. Wickham, *Courts and Conflict in Twelfth-Century Tuscany* (Oxford, 2003), p. 307; D. L. Smail, *The Consumption of Justice: Emotions, Publicity, and Legal Culture in Marseille, 1264-1423* (Ithaca, 2003), p. 16. The perspective that focuses on the strategy of individual practices at the micro level is a research method established by microhistory. S. Lombardini, O. Raggio, and A. Torre (eds.), *Quaderni storici*, 63 (*Conflitti locali e idiomi politici*) (1986); G. Levi, 'On Microhistory', in P. Burke (ed.), *New Perspectives on Historical Writing* (Cornwall, 1991), p. 93-113.

37 Research conceiving of medieval and early modern states through the practices of people at the micro level has progressed in a variety of fields. For example, in his introduction to *Power Elites and State Building*, published as part of a series on the *Origins of the Modern State in Europe*, Wolfgang Reinhard points to elements within the practices of ruling classes that use the state to encourage the expansion of state power. See W. Reinhard, 'Introduction: Power Elites, State Servants, Ruling Classes, and the Growth of State Power', in Id. (ed.), *Power Elites and State Building* (Oxford, 1996), p. 1-18. In contrast to studies that focus on the use of the state by power elites, another recent publication has focused on the significance of the 'bottom-up' use of the state by the populace. See W. Blockmans, A. Holenstein, and J. Mathieu (ed.), *Empowering Interactions. Political Cultures and the Emergence of the State in Europe 1300-1900* (Farnham and Burlington, 2009).

institutions and invoking its authority.[38] Thus, by focusing on the practices by which the state was used, it becomes possible to see a state characterised by the society to which the people performing those practices belonged, rather than as one that followed the rails of a teleological development toward the modern state.

In the case of medieval Italy, the commune was invoked as a public institution by people in a variety of situations in collective city life.[39] The commune was called upon to deal with matters such as improvements of the urban environment, food supply, security maintenance, and military defence, in response to which officials as representatives of the '*comune*' conducted activities that at least formally were aimed at the public good. In the field of justice, in particular, such as with the resolution of private quarrels and the punishment of crime, as we saw at the beginning, people frequently reached out to the commune's courts and councils so that the communal officials might render their judgments. Recalling the words of Alberico da Rosciate that 'justice is the soul of the city' (*iustitia est anima civitatis*), justice turns out to have been a core element of the state's activities conducted by the commune.[40] In this book I focus on the practices of people in the juridical realm which were unfolding in the law courts as well as in the councils.

Recent historiography has tended to consider the administration of justice and judicial policies in Italian cities in relation to social and political practices.[41] On the basis of these studies, let us examine the characteristics of justice and the communes for each period from the twelfth to the fourteenth centuries.

First, studies of the administration of justice in the twelfth century and the first half of the thirteenth century examine how the communes were established and framed

38 Regarding this view of the state, it is worth attending to the following point by Braddick, quoted in Holenstein's introduction to the collection. A. Holenstein, 'Introduction: Empowering Interactions: Looking at Statebuilding from Below', in *Empowering Interactions*, p. 1-31; M. J. Braddick, *State Formation in Early Modern England, 1550-1700* (Cambridge, 2000), p. 90-93: 'We often read that the state did things and even sometimes that it wanted things […] It is argued here that the state does not want or do things; people want the state to do things, and they have varying degree of success in achieving their ends.[…] The state, as we will see, was useful to all sorts of people in early modern England and far from having to penetrate the localities was frequently invited in – state power pervaded the localities, embodied in the actions of innumerable individuals invoking its authority'.

39 For recent studies on the inhabitants' practice of raising claims before the communal authority in Italy, M. G. Muzzarelli (ed.), *Riferire all'autorità. Denuncia e delazione tra Medioevo ed Età Moderna* (Roma, 2020).

40 M. Sbriccoli, *Storia del diritto penale e della giustizia. Scritti editi e inediti (1972-2007)*(Milano, 2009), p. 116-117.

41 For the proceedings of international conferences on justice and conflict in medieval and early modern European cities, see J. Chiffoleau, C. Gauvard, and A. Zorzi (eds.), *Pratiques sociales et politiques judiciaires dans les villes de l'Occident à la fin du Moyen Âge* (Roma, 2007); F. J. Arlinghaus, I. Braumgärtner, V. Colli, S. Lepsius and T. Wetzsteinand (eds.), *Praxis der Gerichtsbarkeit in europäischen Städten des Spätmittelalters* (Frankfurt am Main, 2006). Moreover, for a study that contextualises and summarises both proceedings within recent research trends, see L. Tanzini, 'Diritto e giustizia nelle città tardomedievali: recenti contributi della storiografia europea', *Archivio storico italiano*, 617 (2008), p. 549-559. As evidenced in the titles of these workshops, in recent studies, justice has been considered in relation to practices inside and outside the courts. Furthermore, Andrea Zorzi is responsible for a chapter on justice in *The Italian Renaissance State*, which summarises the findings of recent studies in medieval and early modern Italy. See A. Zorzi, 'Justice', in A. Gamberini and I. Lazzarini (eds.), *The Italian Renaissance State* (Cambridge, 2012), p. 490-514.

by incorporating the logic and style of infrajudicial social practices into their judicial activities.[42]

Twelfth-century city courts, as Wickham has shown in the case of Tuscan cities, adopted legal mannerisms that had been used in private arbitrations, such as debates involving the swearing of the 'oath of calumny' and the acceptance of repeated and uncontested actions as customary proofs, so that the courts could effectively render judgment even in the absence of necessary forces of the state to carry out their decisions.[43] Moreover, the introduction of Romano-canonical procedure (*ordo iudiciarius*), which regulated methods of confrontation – including the claim system comprising *actio*, citation, debate, and attestation – encouraged people to argue and resolve conflicts before judges in a predictable format, thereby setting up the communes as an authority to formalise the rules.[44]

From the later twelfth century, claims brought before the courts increased not only in volume but also in variety. In addition to the usual property cases, the courts heard more complicated disputes involving leases, debts, inheritance, and dote.[45] Moreover, from the mid-thirteenth century, as Vallerani has revealed based on the court records of Perugia, the court of Podestà administered justice in criminal cases such as homicide, injury, and theft, for which it adjudicated convictions and imposed punishments.[46] Here it is noteworthy that many of these criminal cases were initiated by accusations by the victims or their families and proceeded as confrontations between parties in which the accusers assumed the burden of proof. As this shows, the criminal courts of this period were set up not as a repressive institution but rather as a forum that litigants could use strategically as part of a socially endorsed dispute resolution process.

In this form, the administration of justice of the commune was compatible with other social practices such as vendetta and private peace.[47] The vendetta, based on the value of honour, was widespread among not only the *milites* but also the *popolo* as a legitimate practice for redressing injuries to honour, and was premised on negotiations for a later peaceful resolution with one's adversaries.[48] Communal governments, recognising the vendetta's regulatory function in society, chose not to prohibit it altogether,

---

42 B. Garnot (ed.), *L'infrajudiciaire du Moyen Age à l'époque contemporaine* (Bourgogne, 1996); J. Chiffoleau, C. Gauvard and A. Zorzi (eds.), *Pratiques sociales et politiques judiciaires dans les villes de l'Occident à la fin du Moyen Âge* (Roma, 2007).

43 C. Wickham, *Courts and Conflict in Twelfth-Century Tuscany* (Oxford, 2003).

44 M. Vallerani, 'Procedura e giustizia nelle città italiane del basso medioevo (XII-XIV secolo)', in J. Chiffoleau, C. Gauvard and A. Zorzi (eds.), *Pratiques sociales et politiques judiciaires dans les villes de l'Occident à la fin du Moyen Âge* (Roma, 2007), p. 439-494; Id. 'Tra astrazione e prassi. Le forme del processo nelle città dell'Italia settentrionale del secolo XII', in F. J. Arlinghaus et al. (eds.), *Praxis der Gerichtsbarkeit in europäischen Städten des Spätmittelalters* (Frankfurt am Main, 2006), 135-154.

45 We can see this trend in the court records of Milan and Savona, A. Padoa-Schioppa, 'Note sulla giustizia milanese nel XII secolo', in *Milano e la Lombardia in età comunale. Secoli XI-XIII* (Milano, 1993), p. 66-70; D. Punch (ed.), *Il cartulario del notaio Martino. Savona, 1203-1206* (Genova, 1974).

46 M. Vallerani, *Il sistema giudiziario del comune di Perugia. Conflitti, reati e processi nella seconda metà del XIII secolo* (Perugia, 1991).

47 A. Zorzi (ed.), *Conflitti, paci e vendette nell'Italia comunale* (Firenze, 2009).

48 A. Zorzi, 'La cultura della vendetta nel conflitto politico in età comunale', in R. delle Donne and A. Zorzi (eds.), *Le storie e la memoria. In onore di Arnold Esch* (Firenze, 2002), p. 135-170.

but instead authorised its regularisation by limiting the scope of parties who could participate in order to prevent the escalation of reprisals. This appropriation by the communes of private conflict-resolution practices can also be seen in their attempt to ensure private peacemaking, especially in connection with religious movements.[49] For example, in Perugia in 1260, the city council ordered the judicial magistrate to intervene in private settlements made during the peace movement of Flagellanti in order to oblige the parties to keep the peace, under the threat of penalties.[50]

While the importance of inhabitants' recourse to justice and the interaction between judicial activities and infrajudicial social practices can be seen to have continued in subsequent centuries, the second feature of communal justice began to appear from the latter half of thirteenth century, namely the development of active justice characterised by inquisitorial procedures, based in the idea of '*publicum*'.[51] Recent studies, however, rather than seeing this as a progressive phase of the state, have tended to point out that the emergence of this repressive style of justice was informed by 'politics' as practiced by the *popolo* leaders.[52]

Under the *popolo* regime, which acted based on the culture of institutions, the various political languages of *publicum*, such as public utility and public peace, began to be elaborated and promoted in the political and social sphere, thus providing a basis for the implementation of public justice.[53] This can be seen as an ideological policy by which the *popolo*, as the emerging leaders, sought to legitimise their rule and exclude the traditional powers of the *magnate* (as evident in their enactment of anti-*magnate* legislation).[54] Here, the jurists working under the *popolo* notably played an essential role in the establishment of public justice by providing legal advice during the phase of legislation and the interpretation of statutes and *ius commune*, even though these same jurists were also assumed to be able to check political abuses of power.[55]

---

49 G. Kumhera, *The Benefits of Peace: Private Peacemaking in Late Medieval Italy* (Leiden, 2017); K. L. Jansen, *Peace and Penance in Late Medieval Italy* (Princeton, 2018).

50 M. Vallerani, 'Movimenti di pace in un comune di Popolo: I Flagellanti a Perugia nel 1260', *Bollettino della deputazione Umbria di storia patria*, 101 (2004), p. 369-418.

51 M. Sbriccoli, '*Vidi communiter observari*. L'emersione di un ordine penale pubblico nelle città italiane del secolo XIII', *Quaderni fiorentini per la storia del pensiero giuridico*, 27 (1998), 231-268.

52 Vallerani, 'Procedura e giustizia', p. 440.

53 On the characteristics of the *popolo* period, see E. Artifoni, 'Tensioni sociali'; Id., 'I governi di «popolo» e le istituzioni comunali', *Reti Medievali*, 4-2 (2003), 1-20; A. Poloni, *Potere al popolo. Conflitti sociali e lotte politiche nell'Italia comunale del Duecento* (Milano, 2010); Vallerani, 'Comune e comuni'.

54 A. Zorzi, 'Politica e giustizia a Firenze al tempo degli ordinamenti antimagnatizi', in *Ordinamenti di giustizia fiorentina* (Firenze, 1995), p. 105-147; Id., 'Negoziazione penale, legittimazione giuridica e poteri urbani nell'Italia comunale', in M. Bellabarba, G. Schwerhoff and A. Zorzi (eds.), *Criminalità e giustizia in Germania e in Italia: Pratiche giudiziarie e linguaggi giuridici tra tardo medioevo ed età moderna* (Berlin and Bologna, 2001), p. 13-34; J. C. Maire Vigueur, 'Justice et politique dans l'Italie communale de la seconde moitié du XIII siècle: l'exemple de Pérouse', *Comptes rendus de l'Académie des inscriptions et belles-lettre*, 130-2 (1986), p. 312-330.

55 S. Menzinger, *Giuristi e politica nei comuni di Popolo. Siena, Perugia e Bologna, tra governi a confronto* (Roma, 2006); A. Padoa-Schioppa, 'Sul ruolo dei giuristi nell'età del Diritto Comune: un problema aperta', in D. Segoloni (ed.), *Il Diritto Comune e la tradizione giuridica europea. Atti del Convegno di Studi in onore de G. Ermini* (Perugia, 1980), p. 155-166; M. Sbriccoli, *L' interpretazione dello statuto. Contributo allo studio della funzione dei giuristi nell'età comunale* (Milano, 1969).

As the jurist Alberto Gandino showed in his *Tractatus de maleficiis*, the inquisitorial procedure allowed judges, as the protectors of *res publica*, to punish criminals by proceeding *ex officio*.[56] This ideal of granting *arbitrium* to judicial magistrates from other cities eventually made *popolo* leaders aware of the danger of being subjected to indiscriminate interrogation. City councils dominated by *popolo* by manipulating the scope of crimes and criminals against whom inquisitorial procedure and torture could be applied, thereby prevented foreign magistrates from exercising their privilege to interrogate leading citizens, while still allowing them powerful means to investigate serious crimes against the regime.[57] The chapters of statutes prescribing inquisitorial procedures were framed with such political measures in mind, and can thus be seen as the political product of *popolo* elites' efforts to limit judges' discretionary powers.

Thus, from the second half of the thirteenth century onwards, justice increasingly assumed a political dimension as an instrument by which the new ruling class sought to exclude the old regime and rival factions, with the condition that those who were excluded (the *banditi*) could still be reintegrated by pledging loyalty to the current regime.[58] These political devices of exclusion and reintegration resulted in turning the commune into a homogeneous civic body.[59]

Justice in the fourteenth century, the period that serves as the focus of this book, naturally inherited the characteristics of previous eras as it was continuously reframed by people's practices and the political use to which it was put by successive regimes. Now, however, it also began to be coloured by a new tension within the logical basis of the 'legitimacy' of rulings, and thus in the very nature of justice, between the strict letter of the law and personal discretion (*arbitrium*), with the latter prevailing over the former.[60]

In the fourteenth century, the cities of northern and central Italy underwent a shift toward an oligarchic regime under the leading *popolo*, as well as toward dominance by sole rulers, the *signori*.[61] Under this form of governance, as the civic political authority increasingly gained superiority over the judicial magistrates, rulers came to rely on the ideas of *arbitrium* and plenitude of power to legitimise their governance, rather

56 A. Gandinus, *Tractatus de maleficiis*, ed. H. Kantorowicz, in *Albertus Gandinus und das Strafrecht des Scholastik*, vol. II (Berlin, 1926).

57 M. Vallerani, *La giustizia publica medievale* (Bologna, 2005), p. 211-275.

58 G. Milani, *L'esclusione dal comune. Conflitti e bandi politici a Bologna e in altre città italiane tra XII e XIV secolo* (Roma, 2003); Zorzi, 'Negoziazione penale', p. 21-27.

59 Vallerani, 'Comune e comuni', p. 33.

60 A. Zorzi, 'Justice', in A. Gamberini and I. Lazzarini (eds.), *The Italian Renaissance State* (Cambridge, 2012), p. 490-514.

61 For a study that highlights the similarities and commonalities between signorial and oligarchic regimes without opposing them, see Varanini, 'Aristocrazie e poteri', p. 121-193. *Signorie* with links to the communes in the sense of governance were particularly prevalent in the fourteenth century. From the late fourteenth to the fifteenth centuries and later, *signori* appeared who exerted their rule on the basis of overwhelming force. See A. Zorzi, *Le signorie cittadine in Italia (secoli XIII-XV)* (Milano, 2010). For a recent edited volume concerning the *signorie*, see A. Zorzi (ed.), *Le signorie cittadine in Toscana. Esperienze di potere e forme di governo personale (secoli XIII-XV)* (Roma, 2013); J. C. Maire Vigueur (ed.), *Signorie cittadine nell'Italia comunale.*

than on compliance with positive laws as they had previously.[62] Still, in Italian cities, which fell within the cultural sphere of *ius commune*, rulers' *arbitrium*, reliance on which was supported by the opinions of learned jurists, was not mere arbitrariness or self-indulgence, but rather a discretion accompanied by a sense of equality, justice, and rationality, and thus was seen to be strongly bound by a higher level of natural law, if not by the lower-level realm of positive law.[63] Thus, in the judicial sphere of the fourteenth century, *arbitrium* existed in tension with, and was to some extent defined by, the *ius* embodied in *ius commune* and the statutes. It evolved to become part of the underlying logic of the legitimacy of rulings, taking shape as a new modality of justice as positive law ceased to be the absolute standard of justice and became merely one, albeit an important, element among many.

This change of the grounds of legitimacy can be seen, firstly, in the increasing frequency with which judicial magistrates were granted *arbitrium* that allowed them to render justice at their own discretion, superseding the law as written. The *signori* of Milan, the Visconti, based on plenitude of power, often ordered the judicial authorities to act summarily to mete out punishment, ignoring legal formalities and overruling laws pertaining to crimes against their rule (*laesae maiestatis*).[64] Even in the communal cities, where the executive councils held strong control over the foreign judicial magistrates and so limited their discretionary powers, as we saw above, judges were still permitted *arbitrium* to take extraordinary measures when doing so was considered to be useful and necessary by the governing authorities.[65]

The *gratia* can also be considered as a practice peculiar to this period, one that legitimated the exercise of magistrates' *arbitrium* in the sense of being extra-judicial action on the part of the political authorities to correct at their own discretion decisions by judges that adhered strictly to the statutes. Particular attention has tended to be paid

---

62 J. Black, *Absolutism in Renaissance Milan. Plenitude of Power under the Visconti and the Sforza 1329-1535* (Oxford, 2009); M. Vallerani (ed.), *Tecniche di potere nel tardo Medioevo: regimi comunali e signorie in Italia* (Roma, 2010); Id. (ed.), *Sistemi di eccezione, Quaderni storici*, 131 (2009), p. 299-548. The early fourteenth-century jurist Alberico da Rosciate held that 'while ordinary procedure should be regularly observed in criminal trials or civil trials [...] it is likewise clear that the act contrary to that can sometimes be helped by extraordinary law as well'. In other words, a legal sphere that transcended normal positive law was regarded as *legitimate* and even positioned as an indispensable element to be invoked when it was difficult to achieve the objectives of the legal system as a whole solely by following ordinary rules. M. Meccarelli, 'Le categorie dottrinali della procedura e l'effettivita della giustizia penale nel tardo medioevo', in *Pratiques sociales*, p. 573-594, in particular p. 578: 'In criminalibus et in civilibus regulariter ordo iudiciarius est servandus... Item videtur contra quod dicitur aliquando extraordinario iure subveniri'.

63 M. Meccarelli, *Arbitrium. Un aspetto sistematico degli ordinamenti giuridici in età di diritto comune* (Milano, 1998), p. 3-41, 121-128. As to the fact that the *signori* who ruled the cities sometimes issued extra-legal orders, the learned jurists of the time authorised such orders on the condition that they were based in *iusta causa* or *neccessitas*. See E. Cortese, *La norma giuridica: spunti teorici nel diritto comune classico* (Milano, 1962). Therefore, according to Vallerani, the *arbitrium*-based 'exceptional' measures of the medieval period were different from the 'state of exception', which, in Agamben's terms, signifies a suspension of the entire legal system. See M. Vallerani, 'Premessa', *Quaderni storici*, 131 (*Sistemi di Eccezione*) (2009), p. 299-312; G. Agamben, *Stato di eccezione* (Torino, 2003).

64 Black, *Absolutism in Renaissance Milan*, p. 125-127.

65 M. Vallerani, 'L'arbitrio negli statuti cittadini del Trecento', in Id (ed.), *Tecniche di potere*, p. 117-147; Id., *La giustizia publica medievale*, p. 247-275. In Bologna, the council of *popolo*, responding to petitions (called *querele*) that were brought in regarding disorder in the *contado* caused by outlaws and rebels, authorised the judges to summarily proceed with torture, regardless of existing laws. S. R. Blanshei, *Politics and Justice in Late Medieval Bologna* (Leiden and Boston, 2010), p. 429-455.

to the pardons granted by the *signori*, though the republican governments also exercised extra-judicial remissions.[66] Rulers evaluated the supplications raised by their immiserated subjects and granted them *gratia* on a case-by-case basis.[67] Such exceptional and derogating measures could be justified as a corrective that could recover the legality and equality placed at risk by the excessive rigour of laws.[68]

As the frequency of these policies shows, alongside the increasing subordination of foreign judicial magistrates to a political authority composed of leading citizens, fourteenth-century justice experienced a tension and a shift in the logical basis of the legitimacy of rulings, from literal compliance with laws as written to the exercise of *arbitrium* by judges. In this book, I focus on this shift in the modality of justice that characterised the new nature of the commune and its transformation in the fourteenth century – the same period as that of Lorenzetti's frescoes, which represented Justice as the essential and guiding virtue of the '*comune*'.[69]

Previous studies have examined the change in the nature of justice, focusing mainly on the intentions and actions of rulers as officials (i.e. the executive college and judges) who represented the '*comune*' in fields relating to the interests of the state and regime. As described above, Lorenzetti's frescoes were displayed in the chamber where the members of the executive council held their deliberations. As they raised their eyes to the image of justice, behind which was written the text *Diligite iustitiam qui iudicatis terram* ('Love justice, you who rule the earth'), they would render various interpretations on forms of justice not explicitly expressed.[70] In reality, the executive councils of Siena and Lucca, regarding certain acts and situations as 'crises' that threatened the well-being

66 Black, *Absolutism in Renaissance Milan*, p. 114-144; G. M. Varanini, '«Al magnificho e possente segnoro.» Suppliche ai signori trecenteschi italiani fra cancelleria e corte: l'esempio scaligero', in C. Nubola and A. Würgler (eds.) *Suppliche e 'gravamina'. Politica, amministrazione, giustizia in Europa (secoli XIV-XVIII)* (Bologna, 2002), p. 65-106; C. Gauvard, *«De grace especial.» Crime, état et la société en France à la fin du Moyen Age* (Paris, 2010). As for other studies, see chapter 5.

67 M. Vallerani, 'La supplica al signore e il potere della misericordia. Bologna 1337-1347', *Quaderni storici*, 131 (*Sistemi di eccezione*) (2009), p. 411-441.

68 M. N. Covini, '*De gratia speciali*. Sperimentazioni documentarie e pratiche di potere tra i Visconti e gli Sforza', in Vallerani (ed.), *Tecniche di potere*, 183-206. This exceptional power to 'correct' laws at the discretion of political authorities was later regarded as a principal component of supreme sovereignty in the political thought of Jean Bodin.

69 The connection between the ideal '*comune*' and justice is in fact also expressed in Lorenzetti's frescoes, which would have been very familiar to people during this period. If we follow the rope held by the image of the commune in *The Allegory of Good and Bad Government*, it leads to the hands of the people below and then to the personification of Justice at the left side of the picture. From the depiction of these images and the phrase in the caption reading 'this holy virtue [Justice], where she rules', we find that justice is the essential condition for the establishment of the '*comune*', which is to say *bene comune*.

70 This is obviously the opening passage of the Book of Wisdom, written on the wall behind the figure of Justice in *The Allegory of Good and Bad Government*. If the members of the executive council were regarded as people who rule the Earth, it seems likely that access to justice would have been granted in the first instance to these leaders. Siena's executive council, Nove, just like the Anziani of Lucca, administered *gratia* that imposed discretionary modifications of court decisions, W. M. Bowsky, *A Medieval Italian Commune: Siena under the Nine, 1287-1355* (Berkeley, Los Angeles and London, 1981), p. 104.

of the state, suspended the dictates of laws to make extraordinary decisions based on their own *arbitrium*.[71]

However, records from law courts and executive councils show that a large part of the routine work of government consisted of dealing with day-to-day claims raised by inhabitants involved in ordinary disputes. Therefore, even in the period of increasing oligarchisation, in which the majority of inhabitants failed to participate in the political realm as 'citizens', their practice of turning to the commune in search of communal justice – an area that, except for a few studies, has remained largely unexplored despite the continuing call for research[72] – may have prompted the changes in the nature of justice in the fourteenth century. Even though the mode of inhabitants' claims would have been influenced by new practices of governance, their own strategic use of justice would also have had a significant effect on the governors' practices, thereby shaping the dynamics of justice. As suggested also by the fact that the themes of Lorenzetti's frescoes feature in a sermon preached to the masses by Bernardino of Siena,[73] it seems likely that the general populace also recognised the importance of Justice as the guiding virtue of the '*comune*'. They actively and substantively interpreted justice in line with their own interests, even as they were linked to the *bene comune*, and called on the judges and other governing officials to act without being literally bound by positive law. These claims must have contributed to the establishment of a new mode of justice amidst the dismantling of the absolute character of the law as strictly written, and, therefore, to the constant transformation of the '*comune*' as guided by Justice.

The historical sources enabling us to observe the interwoven practices that brought together inhabitants as 'users' of justice, with officials as their 'providers' in the law courts and on the executive council, are the court records and council registers mentioned at the beginning, documents that reflect the ongoing practices themselves rather than their normative ideals.[74] While there have been many studies of normative and

71 Regarding Lucca, see Chapter 6. In the case of Siena, see L. Tanzini, 'Emergenza, eccezione, deroga: tecniche e retoriche del potere nei comuni toscani del XIV secolo', in Vallerani (ed.), *Tecniche di potere*, 149-181.

72 Gauvard pointed out the need for studies from the point of view of users of justice in the conclusions of the international conference held in Avignon in 2001, C. Gauvard and J. Chiffoleau, 'Conclusions', in *Pratiques sociales*, p. 713-720.

73 Bernardino da Siena spoke of the contents of these frescoes in sermons delivered in Siena in 1427, assuming that the pictures and their subjects were widely known to his audience. Dessì, 'Il bene comune', p. 112; Bernardino da Siena, *Prediche volgari: la predicazione del 1425 in Siena*, II, ed. C. Cannarozzi (Firenze, 1958), p. 266: 'Voltandomi a la pace, vego le mercanzie andare atorno; vego balli, vego racconciare le case; vego lavorare vigne e terre, seminare, andare a bagni, a cavallo… E vego impicato l'uomo per mantenere la santa giustizia. E per queste cose, ognuno sta in santa pace e concordia. Per lo contrario, voltandomi da l'altra parte, non vego le mercanzie, anco uccidare altrui; non s'acconciano case, anco si guastano e ardono; non si lavora terre; le vigne si tagliano, non si semina, non s'usano a bagni ne altre cose dilettevoli, non vego se no'quando si va di fuore. O donne! O uomini! L' uomo morto, la donna sforzata, non armenti se none in preda; uomini a tradimento uccidare l'uno l'altro; la giustizia stare in terra, rotte le bilance, e lei legata, co' le mani e co' piei legati'.

74 Regarding the origin of administrative records in medieval Italian cities, see P. Cammarosano, *Italia medievale. Struttura e geografia delle fonti scritte* (Roma, 1991), p. 125-144; J. C. Maire Vigueur, 'Révolution documentaire et révolution scripturaire: le cas de l'Italia médiévale', *Bibliothèque de l'École des chartes*, 153 (1995), p. 177-185; H. Keller (ed.), *Pragmatische Schriftlichkeit im Mittelalter* (München, 1992); T. Behrmann, 'The Development of Pragmatic Literacy in the Lombard City Communes', in R. Britnell (ed.), *Pragmatic Literacy, East and West 1200-1330* (Woodbridge, 1997), p. 25-41. Regarding court records, see A. Giorgio, S. Moscadelli, and C. Zarrilli

legislative activities based on statutes and council books, there has as yet been little research into judicial practices based on court records, especially those of civil courts, in which the lived realities of people's judicial practices were carefully described.[75] This book examines these court records in depth, as well as notarial registers documenting extrajudicial practices, council registers, and city statutes that record judicial policies. Doing so enables us to capture a sense of how the practices of inhabitants and officials in the courts developed and changed in conjunction with interrelated practices outside the courts.

The only city with extant historical sources allowing us to meet these challenges is Lucca, located in Tuscany. To the extent of my knowledge, there is no other city for which civil court registers enabling us to observe citizens' practices in the first half of the fourteenth century have been sufficiently preserved.

Italian cities are diverse in terms of both scale and political system; the 'average' or 'typical' city does not exist. But when compared to other parts of Europe, a unique environment shared by the cities of northern and central Italy certainly does exist – an environment characterised by a legal culture of *ius commune* and a notary system, with a judicial system shared by each city through the itinerant circuit of the *podestà* and by a political context of republican politics that was disrupted by the advent of the *signori*. The case of fourteenth-century Lucca is no exception (see the table below for an overview of Lucca's political history). Though it faced off against various *signori* and occasionally endured their rule, the city's oligarchic body continued to govern internal affairs, including judicial matters, and inherited communal institutions and republican ideas that were vividly and ideologically reinforced after independence was achieved in 1370.[76] This experience of signorial dominion and the ideology of republican rule naturally exerted an influence on the reframing of judicial practices and the dynamics of justice. Therefore, the characteristics of justice and the commune that are revealed in Lucca's surviving historical sources would seem to be applicable not only to Lucca, but also to a certain extent to many cities across northern and central Italy, especially the

---

(eds.), *La documentazione degli organi giudiziari nell'Italia tardo-medievale e moderna. Atti del convegno di studi* (Roma, 2012); S. Lepsius and T. Wetzstein (eds.), *Als die Welt in die Akten kam. Prozeßschriftgut im europäischen Mittelalter* (Frankfurt am Main, 2008).

75 Mario Ascheri has also lamented the lack of studies of civil justice at the level of practice as compared to the plethora of studies at the legal doctrinal level, M. Ascheri, 'Istituzioni e giustizia dei mercanti nel Tre-Quattrocento', in M. Del Treppo (ed.), *Sistema di rapporti ed élites economiche in Europa (secoli XII-XVII)* (Napoli, 1994), p. 33-61. For exceptional studies that are based on civil court records, D. L. Smail, *Legal Plunder. Households and Debt Collection in Late Medieval Europe* (Harvard, 2016); Id., *The Consumption of Justice: Emotions, Publicity, and Legal Culture in Marseille, 1264-1423* (Ithaca, 2003); V. Colli, '*Acta civilia in curia potestatis*: Firenze 1344. Aspetti procedurali nel quadro di giurisdizioni concorrenti', in Arlinghaus et al. (eds.), *Praxis der Gerichtsbarkeit*, p. 271-303; D. J. Osheim, 'Countrymen and the Law in Late-Medieval Tuscany', *Speculum*, 64 (1989), p. 317-337; T. Dean, 'Wealth distribution and litigation in the medieval Italian countryside: Castel San Pietro', *Continuity and Change*, 17-3 (2002), p. 333-350.

76 A. Poloni, *Lucca nel Duecento. Uno studio sul cambiamento sociale* (Pisa, 2009); L. Green., *Castruccio Castracani. A Study on the Origins and Character of a Fourteenth-Century Italian Despotism* (Oxford, 1986); Id. *Lucca under Many Masters: A Fourteenth-Century Italian Commune in Crisis (1328-1342)* (Firenze, 1995); C. Meek, *The Commune of Lucca under Pisan Rule, 1342-1369* (Cambridge, 1980); Id., *Lucca 1369-1400. Politics and Society in an Early Renaissance City-State* (Oxford, 1978); M. E., Bratchel, *Lucca 1430-1494. The Reconstruction of an Italian City-Republic* (Oxford, 1995); Id., *Medieval Lucca and the Evolution of the Renaissance State* (Oxford, 2008).

republican communes – such as Florence and Siena, the home of Lorenzetti's frescoes – that underwent oligarchisation as they confronted signorial powers.

This book consists of two parts. Part I examines the commune and civil justice. In this sphere, which focuses on rights relationships between private individuals, such as real estates or credit obligations, the aspect emerges of vigorous claims to the commune by people bringing private disputes. Chapter 1 examines the redefining of the commune in society by considering the question of why its inhabitants brought their claims before the communal courts so frequently, even though other means of resolving disputes were available. Chapter 2 considers both these claims brought to the courts as well as those brought before the executive council, revealing that this 'bottom-up' approach by the people constituted an opportunity to create, realise, and alter the communal laws and institutions. While the claims seen here advanced by the inhabitants can be broadly divided into those that seek formal compliance with the law and those requiring action based on the *arbitrium* of the executive council, such as revisions or exemptions to the law, Chapter 3 reveals that the logic underlying the legitimacy of rulings in the civil courts of the late fourteenth century underwent a shift of judicial principle from an emphasis on legal formality to a reliance on the *arbitrium* of judicial officials. Then we will examine how this change in the character of justice took place based on the specific actions of fourteenth-century Lucchese jurists, litigants, judges, and Pisan doges.

Part II deals with criminal justice. Unlike civil justice, which was based on confrontations between parties to a dispute, in criminal justice, in which the commune was actively involved, the actions of the executive college and judges who represented the commune came to the fore. And here, in particular, in the context of the activities of governors occasioned by the claims of the inhabitants, there emerged a movement to relax the strict constraints of existing positive laws so as to render justice according to their own *arbitrium*. Chapter 4 clarifies the practices of Lucca's criminal trials based on court records and sentence books. Herein, we can see not only judges' sentences, but also the figure of political power with the authority to impose fines and, consequently, to grant pardons (*gratia*). Chapter 5 examines such pardons. Pardons are acts by which the executive council exercises its *arbitrium* to alter decisions made by judges on the basis of city statutes, or else actions by which political leaders provided benefits to their 'subjects'. Inquiring into the manner of the introduction and subsequent expansion in Lucca of such pardons, which were incompatible with the principles of the commune, serves to clarify how the commune came to be endowed with a new sense of justice. Chapter 6 considers exceptional judicial instances in which judges rendered summary proceedings without going through ordinary procedures. While this was possible because the political authorities conferred *arbitrium* on foreign judges, from these instances of extraordinary justice it should be possible to see an aspect of the late medieval commune in which political authority subordinated judicial authority to it and elaborated the idea of justice on its own.

From the practices of inhabitants and governors that unfolded in the spheres of civil and criminal justice, we will see a new form of justice that emerged in the fourteenth century at the closing of the medieval era, a figure of justice shaped by everyday practices brought by inhabitants and rulers in the clash between the two mutually contradictory forces of the republican system and the *ius commune* tradition on one hand and the necessity of dealing with actual 'crisis' on the other, and the dynamic figure of the commune with which justice was associated.

CHAPTER 1

Why did People Go to the Courts?

1. The High Volume of Claims Heard by Civil Courts

The first impression that those who research the court books of Lucca gets is the massive volume of civil cases. Estimating the annual number of civil cases – claims, to be precise – from the court books of several civil courts in the 1330s and 1340s yields a total of approximately ten thousand a year (Table 1) in a city and its surrounding *contado* whose overall population accounted for only around forty to forty-four thousand people.

Table 1.1: Annual number of claims

	Actual claims in extant records over a one-year period			Extrapolated number of claims per year		
	Ordinary trials	Summary trials	Total	Ordinary trials	Summary trials	Total
Court of Podestà	826	1,299	2,125	1,239	3,897	5,136
Court of San Cristoforo	108		108	108		108
Court of Querimonie	193		193	193		193
Court of Foretani	655		655	1,473		1,473
Court of Treguani	589		589	589		589
New Court of Justice and the Executor	670		670	670		670
Court of Visconti	147	403	550	147	806	953
Appellate Court	157		157	157		157
Rectors' Court	203	637	840	941	1,274	2,215
Total	**3,548**	**2,339**	**5,887**	**5,517**	**5,977**	**11,494**

(summary trial = claims recorded in the *libri reclamorum simplicium*)

The commune of Lucca provided various judicial options for the inhabitants of Lucca and *Sei Miglia* (the *contado* of Lucca) involved in civil conflicts. The Court of Podestà was a central institution of communal justice and the most popular court in Lucca. The *podestà*, an office usually filled by people from other cities, was the highest-ranking judicial, political, and military magistrate throughout the twelfth and thirteenth centuries, but by the 1330s the office had been reduced to a merely judicial role. Two judges and two notaries accompanied him; one judge was deputed to civil matters (known as the *Curia domini Lucani potestatis*) and another was entrusted to malefactions in the *Curia maleficiorum*.[1] To fulfil his duty, this foreign judicial official also employed 12 *berrovarii* to capture those who had been banished (*banniti*) and 50 *nuntii* as messengers and seizers.[2] This judicial institution was obligated to obey the city statutes, of which the earliest in existence is that from 1308; these statutes were often revised, for example in 1316, 1331, 1336, 1342, 1350, 1360, 1372, and 1392.

Cases tried in this civil court were recorded in three types of court books. The first type were the *libri reclamorum sollemnium* (books of solemn complaints), which contained suits concerning debts or insolvency. The second type were the *libri causarum* (books of cases), which recorded cases regarding estates and assets. These two types included ordinary trials, which followed the ordinary judicial proceedings. The third type of court book, the *libri reclamorum simplicium* (books of simple complaints), registered summary trials without presenting *libello* (bill).[3]

We can calculate an annual value for the number of claims heard in the Court of Podestà by drawing on the court books of ordinary trials produced in the first half of the fourteenth century. According to the records, in the period from May to December 1336 – the only period for which a full series of such court books is extant – the civil court was in session for 115 days. On the remaining 125 days, the court was in recess for various reasons, such as saints' festivals and wars.[4] For this period, we have two *libri reclamorum sollemnium*, containing 458 cases, and two *libri causarum*, containing 442 cases.[5] Subtracting the 74 entries from the *libri causarum* referring to cases initiated previously, a total count of 826 cases were brought to trial in this period. On the assumption that a similar number of claims began during the four months from January to April of the same year (i.e. the period for which no court books exist), we can

1 City statutes from 1308 contain a description of the military aspects of the *podestà*'s duties, but such descriptions disappear almost entirely after 1331. S. Bongi (ed.), *Statuto del comune di Lucca dell'anno MCCCVIII* (Lucca 1867) (hereafter *Statuto 1308*), II, 1 (De electione Potestatis et eius modo et forma, et de feudo et familia et de sindicatu ipsius), p. 51-54; ASL, *Statuto del Comune di Lucca*, 4 (hereafter *Statuto 1331*), II, 20, p. 89-90.

2 *Statuto 1308*, II, 23 (De electione nuptiorum Maioris Lucani Regiminis et Lucani Comunis et eorum numero), p. 85.

3 *Libri reclamorum simplicium* simply recorded cases, noting only the names of the plaintiff and defendant, regardless of whether or not they appeared in court, and a summary of the relevant judicial decisions. Though the cases registered in these books proceeded verbally, departing from the procedure observed in ordinary trials, I include these cases in my calculations, as it was quite true that the parties brought their complaints before the court.

4 ASL, *Potestà di Lucca* (hereafter *Potestà*), 60, fols. 447r-448v: 'Titulus dierum utilium curie domini Lucani potestatis'. *Ibid.*, fols., 449r-450r: 'Titulus dierum inutilium curie domini Lucani potestatis'.

5 *Potestà*, 58, 60, 64, 67.

estimate that 1,239 new cases were brought to trial in the Civil Court of Podestà in 1336.

To this number we must also add the number of cases recorded in the *libri reclamorum simplicium*. For 1340, over eight months, 1,299 entries are recorded in the *libri reclamorum simplicium* for plaintiffs with initials A–J.[6] Assuming that these entries only correspond to half the total number of claims heard, we are able to estimate a count of 2,598 cases for the eight month and a total annual count of 3,897 cases given a summary trial in Lucca.[7] Extrapolating, then, from the 2,125 actual cases counted in the court books over two 8-month periods yields 5,136 cases as an estimated annual count of claims heard in the Court of Podestà.

Next, the residents in Lucca and its surrounding countryside could also bring civil complaints to one of the six different courts of consul, which consisted of the Courts of San Cristoforo, Querimonie, Foretani, Treguani, Visconti, and the New Court of Justice and the Executor. The foundation of these courts dates as far back as the twelfth century, earlier than Podestà, and while the courts of the consul were all abolished and integrated into the Court of Podestà by order of Paolo Guinigi at the end of fourteenth century, the activity of these courts over the preceding century is attested by their records. The consuls, who were appointed as judges among the Lucchese, observed the *Statutum Curiarum Lucane Civitatis* as well as the general city statutes.[8]

We can find details of the cases heard before these courts from two types of court books, namely the *libri libellorum* and the *libri reclamorum*.[9] The Court of San Cristoforo was the principal and earliest court of consul, hearing disputes between citizens for sums of 25 *lire* or more.[10] For 1338, the *libri reclamorum* for this court contain entries for 27 cases, while the *libri libellorum* record 81 cases, yielding a total of 108 for the annual number of trials brought before this court.[11] The Court of Querimonie, in turn, heard disputes involving sums of less than 25 *lire*. Here in the records for the year 1334 we find 170 cases in the *libri reclamorum*, but only 23 in the *libri libellorum*, making a total of 193 cases.[12] The Court of Foretani had jurisdiction over cases involving rural villagers.[13] The *libri reclamorum* for this court contain 491 cases for nine months, from May 1336 to January 1337, for plaintiffs with initials L–V.[14] Additionally, the *libri libellorum* of the year 1337 record 164 cases.[15] Given the incompleteness of the *libri*

6 *Potestà*, 104.
7 The four *libri reclamorum simplicium* in 1345 recorded 1986 complaints, *Potestà*, 164, 168, 174, 177.
8 ASL, *Archivio Guinigi*, 263 (hereafter *Statuto della Curia 1331*).
9 There were actually the *libri causarum*; however, we need to exclude the number of cases recorded in this book, as these cases overlapped with the ones reported in the *libri libellorum*.
10 Provisions in the Statute of Courts from 1331 (which date back to the end of the thirteenth century) restricted cases to those involving claims by urban citizens against each other for amounts of no less than 25 *lire*.
11 ASL, *Curia di S. Cristoforo*, 112, 113, 114.
12 ASL, *Curia delle Querimonie*, 3, 4, 5.
13 D. J. Osheim, 'Countrymen and the Law in Late-Medieval Tuscany', *Speculum*, 64 (1989), p. 317-337.
14 ASL, *Curia dei Foretani o di S. Alessandro*, 15.
15 ASL, *Curia dei Foretani o di S. Alessandro*, 14, 16.

reclamorum, we can estimate that there were approximately 1,473 cases a year.[16] The Court of Treguani had statutory jurisdiction over ecclesiastical matters and, in practice, over suits for damages for breach of contracts and of prior sentences. For this court, 267 cases are recorded in the *libri reclamorum* and 322 in the *libri libellorum* for 1340, bringing the total to 589 cases.[17] The New Court of Justice and the Executor (*Curia Nuova di Giustizia e dell'Esecutore*) reassessed and executed existing sentences, trying offenders against existing judgements and arbitrations and defaulters of obligations stipulated by notaries. For 1338, the *libri reclamorum* for this court contain 75 cases, and along with 595 cases reported in the *libri libellorum*, the total number of cases is 670.[18] Finally, the Court of Visconti had statutory jurisdiction over matters relating to guilds (*arte*), but in practice dealt mainly with claims seeking compensation for real estate damages. For 1346, 147 cases have been recorded in the *libri libellorum*, while the *libri reclamorum simplicium* contain 403 cases (only trials of plaintiffs with initials L–V), from which we can estimate 806 cases per year. Accordingly, we can extrapolate the total number of cases for the year to be around 953.[19]

In Lucca, appeals in civil cases were heard at the Appellate Court.[20] However, this court was not one of final appeal; the statutes of this court assumed further appeals against the Appellate Court's sentences in the Court of Podestà for the cases issued by courts of consuls in first trial, and in the Rectors' Court or before the Anziani for the rulings made in the Court of Podestà in the first trial. In 1335, we find 157 appeals recorded in the *libri appellationum* (books of appeals).[21]

The Rectors' Court (*Curia dei rettori*), which heard both the first and final trials, was outside the communal judicial system.[22] The vicar of the foreign ruler convened the court in Augusta, the fortress inside the city,[23] where the *vicevicarius* presided over the cases as judges. For 1332, we have two *libri petitionum*, one covering 130 cases involving plaintiffs with initials L–Q during the first half of the year and the other reporting 73 cases from March to June. Calculating from these 203 actual cases, we can estimate that a total of 941 cases were heard that year.[24] In contrast, the *libri reclamorum simplicium*

16 Trials of plaintiffs with initials L–V usually correspond to half of all the cases. Accordingly, I simply doubled the 491 cases recorded in the *libri reclamorum* to obtain a yearly estimate. To these 1,309 cases, I added the 164 cases contained in the *libri libellorum*.

17 ASL, *Curia dei Treguani*, 30, 31, 34.

18 ASL, *Curia Nuova di Giustizia e dell'Esecutore*, 38, 39, 40, 41.

19 ASL, *Curia dei Visconti*, 38, 39, 40.

20 A. Romiti, 'Lo «statutum curie appellationum» del 1331', *Actum luce*, 23 (1994), p. 111-151; S. Lepsius, '*Dixit male iudicatum esse per dominos iudices*. Zur Praxis der stadtischen Appellationsgerichtsbarkeit im Lucca des 14. Jahrhunderts', in Arlinghaus et al. (eds.), *Praxis der Gerichtsbarkeit*, p. 189-263.

21 ASL, *Maggior Sindaco e Giudice degli Appelli*, 37, 41.

22 The Rectors' Court operated from 1328 to 1368, when the dominion of Pisa finally ended. S. Bongi (ed.), *Inventario del Reale Archivio di Stato in Lucca*, I (Lucca, 1872), p. 91-121.

23 For example, an entry from 19 February 1334 places the location of the court at the house of Pinelli's sons inside the Augusta Fortress. ASL, *Curia dei Rettori*, 6, fol. 7v.

24 ASL, *Curia dei Rettori*, 3, 4. In this court, two *libri petitionum* were produced in the same period: in 1332, the first book contained the cases of plaintiffs with initials L–Q in the first half of this year (130 cases) and a second book registered the cases of all plaintiffs between March and June (73 cases). As the percentage of cases of plaintiffs with initials L–Q is estimated at 36% of all cases according to other court books, we can presume that the second *libri* would contain 26 cases. The possible number of cases of plaintiff with initial letter between L and Q from March to

contained 637 cases for the six-month period between August 1354 and January 1355, allowing us to estimate 1,274 cases for the year.[25] Thus, we can extrapolate 2,215 cases as an estimate for the number of cases per year, although this is a projection owing to the lack of documents in this court.

Overall, we can find records for 5,887 actual civil claims in Lucca recorded in extant court books over a one-year period. If we include the cases extrapolated for court books that have been lost, the projected total can be estimated at 11,494 cases a year. This seems to be surprisingly high for a small city like Lucca, whose urban population was about 20,500-24,000 citizens in the first half of the fourteenth century, with approximately 20,000 more villagers scattered throughout the surrounding countryside.[26] Approximately 10,000 claims a year means that each adult (about half of the population) would necessarily have been involved in one judicial conflict every two years on average as a plaintiff or a defendant.[27] This large number of civil complaints is an important background factor when considering the characteristics of civil justice in fourteenth-century Lucca.

How do we explain this heavy use of the civil courts? While it is certainly true that civil conflicts arose frequently in medieval society, this explanation is not sufficient on its own. In this chapter, we will consider the details of the complaints, the trial process, the judgements, and the characteristics of civil trials as distinct from other conflict resolutions such as arbitration and reconciliation. This consideration will help us to understand why the people chose communal courts as places to air and settle their grievances. Furthermore, the ways in which communal courts were used will reveal how people saw the commune as an authority in society.

2. Civil Trials

(1) Parties and cases: easy entrance to the courts

Who went to communal courts? What claims did they raise? In this section, I focus on ordinary trials, namely, the 900 cases held in 1336 in the Court of Podestà, as recorded in the court's *libri causarum* and *libri reclamorum sollemnium* for that year.

June is estimated at 113 cases, making up 26 cases in the second *libri* and 87 cases in the first *libri*, if calculating for 4 months. If converted into the number of cases a year, the total number is estimated to be 339 cases; if the number of cases of all plaintiffs is converted, the total number is estimated to be 941 cases.

25 ASL, *Curia dei Rettori*, 18.

26 Green estimates the number of city inhabitants based on the number of individuals who swore an oath of loyalty to King John of Bohemia, L. Green, *Lucca under Many Masters: A Fourteenth-Century Italian Commune in Crisis (1328-1342)* (Firenze, 1995), p. 243-250. For the number of rural inhabitants who lived in *Sei Miglia* and could file a case in the city courts, Leverotti identifies 5853 households based on an *estimo* from 1331. F. Leverotti, *Popolazione, famiglie, insediamento. Le Sei Miglia lucchesi nel XIV e XV secolo* (Pisa, 1992), p. 31-36. Here, I estimate the rural population by multiplying the number of households by average household size (3.29), a value derived from a stocktaking of cereals in 1353, ASL, *Offizio sopra l'Abbondanza*, 379.

27 To calculate the percentage of adults, I use the date of estimation of 1371 in Prato, D. Herlihy and C. Klapisch-Zuber, *Tuscans and their Families. A Study of the Florentine Catasto of 1427* (New Haven and London, 1985), p. 182-201.

The identity of the litigant parties remains unclear because of the shorthand used in the court books. Information is limited to the names of the parties, their parentage, and their provenance, occasionally including surnames and titles ('*ser*' for notaries and '*domina*' for women) with some occupational titles. Overall, the impression given is that people of various social classes filed claims in the communal court, including nobles, jurists, notaries, merchants, widows, artisans – such as shoemakers (*sutor*) and glaziers (*bicchierarius*) – shopkeepers – such as tavern keepers (*tabernarius*) –, unskilled labourers, and rural residents, as well as those defined as *pauper et miserabilis persona*.

Parties involved in trials were required to make their claims and arguments in writing according to a specified format, as well as to know and be able to use statutory provisions to win court battles. It is therefore likely that notaries as legal experts were employed on behalf of such parties. In fact, studies of Bologna and Florence have focused on the activities of notaries who acted as procurators in such trials.[28] The court books of Lucca, however, present a different image of civil trials from that of court battles between legal experts. Of the 900 cases for 1336, trials wherein notaries participated accounted for only 286 (32%), and while 500 of the 1846 litigant parties (27%) appointed a procurator, only 13% (232) delegated notaries to act as such in their trials. Consequently, in Lucca, many ordinary citizens – from prominent families to artisans, labourers, and rural villagers – frequented the courts, filed claims, and argued with each other, using the city statutes.

Let us consider their claims in terms of content (Table 2).[29] In the 900 cases of 1336, we find 197 complaints concerning debt (22%), 157 concerning unpaid land rent (17%), and 52 concerning unpaid house rent (6%). Another 54 involved restitution of dotal property after a husband's death (6%), and 12 concerned repayment in cases of livestock leasing (*soccida*) (1%). These claims, in short, concerned insolvency, and it was these that generally provided the starting point for the cases recorded in the *libri reclamorum sollemnium*. Conversely, the *libri causarum* contained complaints concerning insolvency as well as various other matters. We can confirm 131 complaints opposing previous judicial orders (15%), 73 regarding immovable property (8%), 23 for the restitution of movables (3%), and 22 regarding compensation for damages to farmland (2%). This type of court book also recorded suits for matters such as unpaid wages and breaches of arbitrated settlements.

Some parties were involved in disputes over property or significant sums of money, for example, the restitution of a dowry of 490 *lire* or a debt of 495 *lire*.[30] In many other cases, however, disputes involved quite small sums, for example, a debt of 2 *lire*, unpaid

---

28 M. Vallerani, *La giustizia pubblica* (Bologna, 2005), p. 139-142, 150; V. Colli, '*Acta civilia in curia potestatis*: Firenze 1344. Aspetti procedurali nel quadro di giurisdizioni concorrenti', in Arlinghaus et al. (eds.), *Praxis der Gerichtsbarkeit*, p. 271-303; D. L. Smail, *The Consumption of Justice: Emotions, Publicity, and Legal Culture in Marseille, 1264-1423* (Ithaca, 2003), p. 71-72.

29 We can confirm some definite forms in the petition, which indicates that the parties made a petition referring to the samples recorded in *Ordo iudiciarius*.

30 *Potestà*, 67, fol. 93r; *Potestà*, 67, fol. 15r.

Table 1.2: Claims at the Court of Podestà in 1336

	Cases	%
Debt	196	22
Unpaid land rent	158	17
Unpaid house rent	52	6
Restitution of dote	54	6
Unpaid livestock rent (*soccida*)	12	1
Immovable property	73	8
Restitution of movables	23	3
Compensation for damage to farmland	22	3
Opposition to judicial orders	131	15
Uncertain	148	16
Others	31	3
Total	**900**	**100**

house rent of 1 *lira* and 4 *soldi*, or 1 *lira* for damage to farmland (the plunder of vines and figs).[31]

The cases listed in the *libri reclamorum simplicium* were limited to suits involving small sums. Because the parties did not need to present *libello*, no information is listed as to the specific complaints. However, specific values and contents can be supposed from the descriptions of the amounts seized, usually small sums such as 5 *soldi*, mostly derived from debts and unpaid rents on houses or land.[32]

A major reason for the massive number of claims was that court costs were very low. The primary expenses, which parties were obliged to pay for trials, were those entailed by a legal action for court notaries and criers as well as the costs of having notaries create copies of notarial documents, and of securing legal consultation (*consilia*) by jurists. According to an analysis of statutes and records of revenue from the civil courts, court fees (*datia*) were not collected for claims heard before the courts of consul except in cases of seizure (*preda*), appellation, or *litis contestatio*, especially before 1372.[33]

A review of 15 requests for the losing side to pay court expenses at the behest of the victor after a verdict shows that the court costs ranged from 15 *soldi* to 11 *lire* 3 *soldi* (on average, 3 *lire* 11 *soldi*; 6 cases under 2 *lire*, 5 cases from 2 to 5 *lire* and 4 cases over 5

31 *Potestà*, 67, fol. 103r; *Potestà*, 67, fol. 26v; *Potestà*, 67, fol. 200r.

32 *Potestà*, 104.

33 As for the *datia predarum* see Smail, *Legal Plunder. Households and Debt Collection in Late Medieval Europe* (Harvard, 2016), p. 169-170. As for the *datia* for the case of appellation, *Statuto 1308*, IV, 22 (De causis extimandis coram iudice appellationis et datiis solvendis), p. 262. In the courts of consul, the parties, if they did *litis contestatio*, had to pay the *datia* 2 *denari* per *lira*, *Statuto della Curia 1331*, IV, 11 (De dato tollendo), fols. 51r-v. The Court of Podestà also started collecting *datia* after the addition of the statute in 1372, ASL, *Statuto del Comune di Lucca*, 6 (*Statuto 1372*), fol. 176r: 'statuimus quod quelibet persona, universitas et locus solvere teneatur in futuram in causis et pro causis tam principalibus quam appellationibus…' As for revenue, ASL., *Camarlingo Generale*, 4.

lire).[34] This is the cost of the trials wherein a verdict was reached. Costs for other trials would have been even lower.

In this regard, let us review the prices based on De La Roncière's study of Florence in 1326-1332. He estimates monthly living costs (rent, food, clothes, and other daily necessities) as being 77 *soldi* 1 *denaro* for one-person households and 177 *soldi* for four-person households among wage workers and other members of the lower classes, and 244 *soldi* for members of the upper classes.[35] In addition, average daily wages were 4.6 *soldi* for construction workers and 8.6 *soldi* for a master.[36] In the 1330s, one florin was the equivalent of 62 *soldi* in Florence and 69 *soldi* in Lucca.[37]

To sum up, Lucca's communal courts were open places easily accessed by almost all residents for use in various civil matters. Next, I would like to consider the trial processes and the substance of the arguments heard therein, which also demonstrate the ease with which people accessed the courts.

(2) Process and discussion: the libri causarum *and the* libri reclamorum

Court notaries distinguished between complaints of insolvency (e.g. debts and unpaid rents) and various other complaints, with the former being registered in the *libri reclamorum sollemnium* and the latter in the *libri causarum*. Additionally, the development of cases in each type of court book was different, probably owing to the varied claims (Figure 1).

34 *Potestà*, 58, fols. 105r-112v, 305r-307r; *Ibid.*, fol. 122r; *Ibid.*, fols. 123r-v; *Ibid.*, fols. 144r-v; *Ibid.*, fols. 151r-161v; *Ibid.*, fols. 265r-268v; *Ibid.*, fols. 327r-329v; *Potestà*, 60, fols. 57r-64v; *Ibid.*, fols. 166r-167v, 225r-226r; *Ibid.*, fols. 169r-170r, 219r-220v; *Ibid.*, fols. 244r-247v, 271r-v; *Ibid.*, fols. 273r-277r; *Ibid.*, fols. 190r-v, 202r-v, 361r-v, 471v; *Potestà*, 64, fols. 15r-v, 39r-41v; *Potestà*, 67, fols. 339v-342v, 425r-v.

35 C. M. De La Roncière, *Prix et salaires à Florence au XIVe siècle (1280-1380)* (Roma, 1982), p. 394-395, 402.

36 *Ibid.*, p. 279-281, 326.

37 *Ibid.*, p. 841-843; Green, *Lucca under Many Masters*, p. 254.

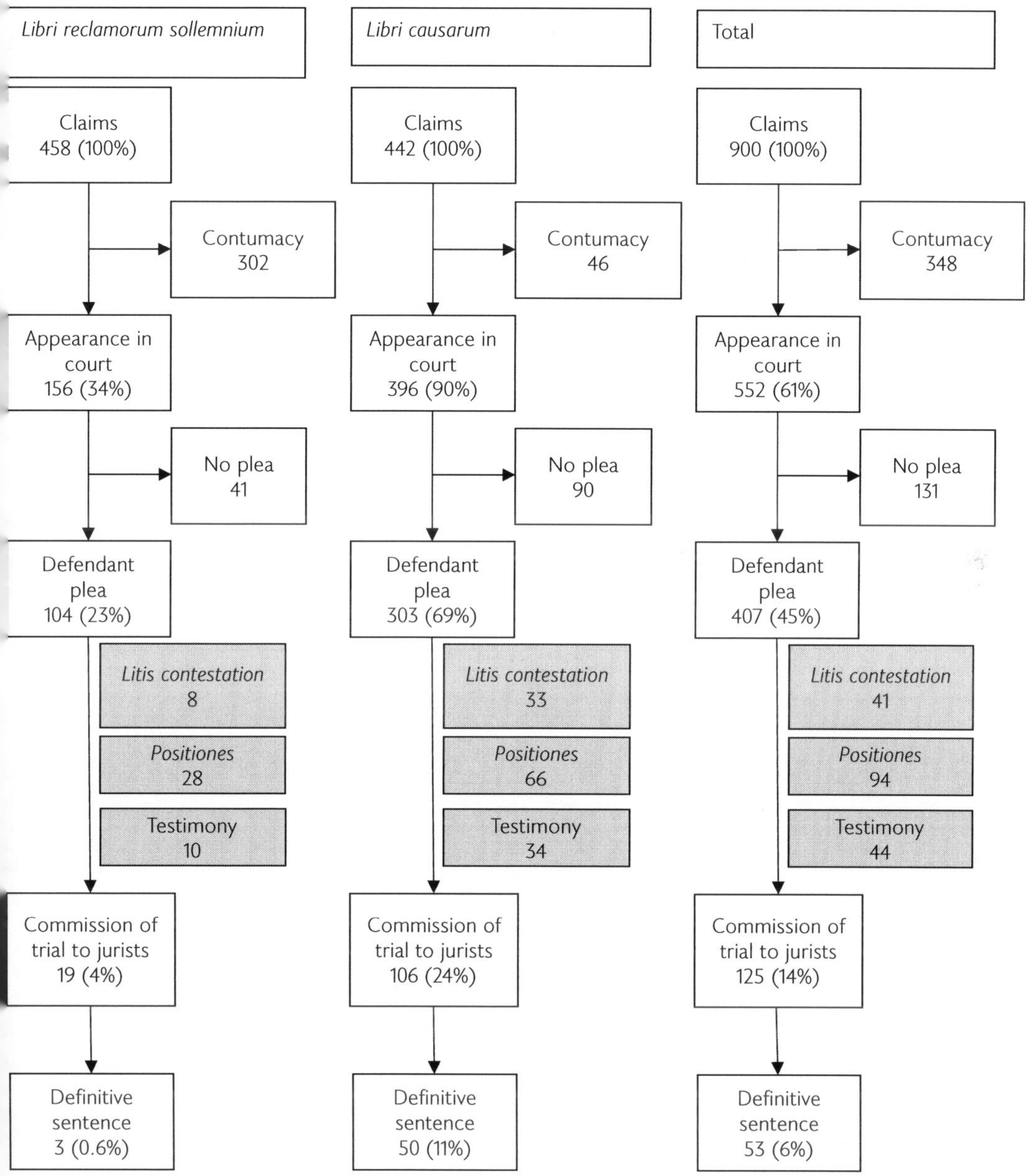

Figure 1.1: The development of civil trials at the Court of Podestà in 1336

i). Cases recorded in the libri reclamorum sollemnium

Almost two thirds of the defendants recorded in the *libri reclamorum sollemnium* (i.e. those involved in insolvency cases) committed contumacy by not appearing in court. This would lead judges to issue judicial orders for various actions, including the seizure of movables (*preda*) or immovables (*tenuta* or *insolutum*), the capture and detention of debtors (*captura* and *detentio*), payment or eviction (*preceptum*), and bans (*bannum*). The margins of the descriptions of these orders include annotations regarding the process of their execution.

In cases where the defendants appeared to present a plea, the parties would proceed to a series of procedures to clarify all the facts, including *litis contestatio* (a process of contesting a suit by statements), *positiones* (the presentation of a detailed list of arguments), and testimony. However, many trials recorded in the *libri reclamorum sollemnium* did not involve these procedures. We find only 8 cases (2%) that include *litis contestatio*, 28 cases (6%) that include *positiones*, and 10 cases (2%) involving testimony. Only a few cases reached the final process of a trial. In 19 cases (4%), the parties commissioned jurists for a legal consultation (*consilium*), and judges pronounced definitive sentences on the basis of *consilia* in only 3 cases.

Therefore, insolvency cases were generally processed quickly, with judicial orders following a defendant's contumacy. Here the communal courts were used by creditors as a means of compelling payments from unwilling debtors.

Defendants likely did not appear in order to respond to the petition because they recognised that they stood no chance of success, owing to the competent evidence presented by plaintiffs in the form of notarial documents (*publicum instrumentum*). Judges, at the sight of a bond (e.g. for rent of immovable property or dowry), would almost automatically issue a judicial order, even if the defendant contested the complaint. In doing so, judges were simply following a provision of the statute, '*De summaria ratione reddenda contra obligatos per publicum instrumentum*', which required them to issue judicial orders based on notarial documents.[38] The absolute primacy of documents in insolvency cases shows that the communal judicial system was based on the system of confirmation of rights by notarial documents.

Nevertheless, defendants were not without means of opposition. One was the exception (*exceptio*), which raised challenges by highlighting formal flaws; this will be considered in detail in Chapter 2. A second option was to provide documentary proof of repayment. The statute stipulated that repayment must be confirmed with notarial documents or documents written by the creditor. This is another example of the primacy with which documents were treated.[39] A third option was simply not to recognise the relation of obligation in the first place. For example, a defendant being sued for unpaid land rent had only to insist that he was the true owner of the land in

---

38 *Statuto 1308*, IV, 3 (De summaria ratione reddenda contra obligatos per publicum instrumentum), p. 250-252; *Statuto 1331*, IV, 3, p. 121-123.

39 *Statuto 1308*, IV, 3, p. 251: 'Quod instrumentum debiti non possit dici vel nullum, nisi de solutione vel satisfatione vel transactione constaret per publicum instrumentum…'

question and the issue of the dispute would then go to the ownership of the land. Such cases were developed in the same way as those recorded in the *libri causarum*.

ii). Cases recorded in the libri causarum

Cases found in the *libri causarum* conjure up a different image of trials than those in the *libri reclamorum sollemnium*. Almost all defendants (90%) appeared in the courts to oppose the initial petition with frequent recondite arguments that led to the prolongation of the trials. We find many trials that involved *positiones*, a procedure whereby the parties presented itemised arguments (*positio*) subdivided into interrogative statements, resorting to testimonies for proving *positio* if they were contested. In this case, we find 106 cases (24%) where jurists were commissioned, 50 of which (11%) arrived at a definitive sentence, a high proportion relative to the number of the insolvency trials found in the *libri reclamorum*.

Conversely, many cases did not reach the point of requiring a judge's final judgement, but alternative solutions were reached after a debate between parties. In 235 cases (excepting nine expressly describing *compromessum*, agreement to arbitration),[40] entries in the court books break off abruptly without detailing the outcomes. For example, trials were interrupted with no further description in various situations, such as after debates between the parties, after scheduling the day on which parties would next appear, after the presentation of evidence, or after committing a trial to consideration by jurists. Such entries undoubtedly indicate contumacy by both parties; without anyone to cover their fee, court clerks would have had no reason or inducement to continue the entry. Conceivably, this shows that plaintiffs abandoned their court case to seek alternate means of resolution outside the communal courts.

Table 3 summarises the duration of cases in the courts, drawing on a sample of 144 cases started in May, June, and July 1336 wherein both parties appeared in court. Almost half the cases (71) either broke off or were finished within a week, while over 80% were finished within one month: 23 cases from 8 to 14 days and 24 cases from 15 days to one month. The few remaining cases involved more lengthy trials: nine cases from 1 to 2 months, seven cases from 2 to 3 months, five cases from 3 to 4 months, one case from 5 to 6 months, and three cases that lasted over a half-year.

The various petitions and discussions were recorded in the *libri causarum*. Ultimately, however, these disparate arguments turned on the issue of the ownership of lands or immovable assets. For example, trials initiated to contest a judicial order often pivoted on the issue of unpaid rents on land or houses, and then on the ownership thereof. Such cases ceased to be suits involving creditors and debtors and became appeals by both parties asserting ownership of immovable assets.

Let us consider how ownership was proven in such trials, which, unlike insolvency cases, involved the presentation not only of documents but also of testimonies attesting

40 The agreements to arbitration were often shown in trials between members of the same extended family (*consorteria*). The city statute prescribed it, *Statuto 1331*, V, 21 (De questionibus vertentibus inter consortes), p. 172-173.

Table 1.3: Duration of contested trials initiated in May, June, and July 1336 recorded in the *libri causarum*

	Cases	%
1 to 7 days	71	49
8 to 14 days	23	16
15 days to 1 month (30 days)	24	17
1 to 2 months	9	6
2 to 3 months	7	5
3 to 4 months	5	3
4 to 5 months	0	0
5 to 6 months	1	1
6 months or more	4	3
Total	**144**	**100**

possession. As both parties often presented documents as well as testimonies, resulting in the debate being prolonged, it is not clear whether the effect of the document or the effect of the testimony prevailed. On the one hand, the parties' near-universal insistence on documentary evidence attests to the evidentiary primacy of documents in Italian society, where a notarial culture prevailed. On the other hand, testimonies of ownership of immovable property were also effective, particularly in cases where both parties were attempting to prove their possession of the same land and were presenting a genealogy of rights along with their documents. In such cases, it was more important for a party to prove the fact of peaceful, longstanding, and lawful possession with testimonies in addition to documents, as we shall see.[41]

iii). Characteristics of civil trials

We can understand how two aspects of a civil court rendered it an accessible place: one was the process of trials characterised by an adversarial system and another was the possibility of discussions not on a legal but on a factual level.[42]

The civil courts of Lucca, as in other cities, adopted the Romano-canonical procedure, which was represented in *ordo iudiciarius*. This procedural system functioned to induce the parties to clarify the facts through discussions moving towards final sentencing. The general process started with the formula of the petition, then to several suceeding procedures: citation; appearance in court; pleading by parties – including

41 As for this theme, P. Grossi, *Le situazioni reali nell'esperienza giuridica medieval* (Padova, 1968).

42 There were no differences between the trials in the Court of Podestà and those in the courts of consul as regards the types and process of trials.

exceptions by the defendant– *litis contestatio*; *iuramentum*; attestations; interrogations with *positiones*; *testes*; *consilia*; and finally to sentencing.[43]

However, a close consideration of the court books reveals the freedom that parties enjoyed with these procedures. The frequent interruption of trials, in fact, signals the intention of the parties to seek resolution outside the courts (*extra iudicium*). In particular, entries that break off after the advice of a jurist had been commissioned for the trial in question suggest that the parties, presumably anticipating the substance of a jurist's advice, opted to forego both the disclosure and confirmation of such advice in the pronouncement of a sentence (thus avoiding the associated expense), choosing instead to seek a resolution outside the court.[44] This can be in fact attested by a notarial contract of 1340, according to which Paulo and Franceschino had filed a case in the Court of San Cristoforo in 1340, and that '[a]lthough the mentioned lawsuit, issue and trial was already being commissioned by consuls of this court to the jurist Simone of Camporeggiano, the parties want to descend from lawsuit, issue and trial and to come to a concord'[45]. After this, the notarial documents proceeded to the description of the reconciliation under the notary. The ease with which procedures could be halted or abandoned established a low threshold of entry to the communal courts.

Another factor contributing to the accessibility of the communal courts for residents was that the courts served as an arena where they could engage in discussions based on concrete facts 'in the raw', such as the fact of possession or of document-based rights relationships. This is easily illustrated by a comparison between Lucca, which still felt to some degree the influence of Langobardic legal culture, with the case of Pisa, a city with a longstanding tradition of Roman law. As early as the twelfth century, concrete facts were already being discussed in the Pisan courts by converting them into a legal idiom using Roman legal concepts such as *actiones* (i.e. the plaintiff's legal entitlement to bring a lawsuit in a law court).[46] For example, a plaintiff who had possessed a certain piece of land could, upon its being occupied by another, bring a suit using the Roman legal concept of '*interdictum uti possidetis*'. This indicates that the fact of occupancy was conceptualised as a 'right' meriting legal protection; in Pisan trials, discussions revolved around whether a plaintiff was worthy of this legal 'right', which was to determine, for example, whether he was the original acquirer (*primitive acquisitor*).

However, in the courts of fourteenth-century Lucca, the parties did not convert real facts into the legal 'rights' of Roman law and discuss them at a legal level. They only

43 As for *ordo iudiciarius*, Agidius de Fuscarariis, *Ordo iudiciarius*, in L. Wahrmund (ed.), *Der ordo iudiciarius des Aegidius de Fuscarariis* (Innsbruck, 1916); A. Engelmann (trans. by R. W. Millar), *A History of Continental Civil Procedure* (Boston, 1927), p. 455-492; G. Salvioli, *Storia della procedura civile e criminale*, P. Del Giudice (dir.), *Storia del Diritto Italiano*, III-1 (Milano, 1925), p. 151-346; A. Giuliani, 'L'*ordo judiciarius* medioevale. Riflessioni su un modello puro di ordine isonomico', *Rivista di diritto processuale*, 43-2 (1988), p. 598-614.

44 The register of Anziani records a petition by *collegio iudicum* against the parties who went towards the Appellate court when they conceived that the advice, unopened, would be disadvantageous to them. ASL, *Anziani avanti la Libertà* (hereafter *Anz. Av. Lib.*), 26, fol. 117r.

45 ASL., *Archivio dei Notari*, 103 (Giovanni Locti), p. 334-339: 'Et iam dicta lis, questio et causa per consulem dicte curie conmissa foret sapienti viro domino Simoni de Camporeggiano iudici. Et dicte partes velint a dicta lite, questione et causa discedere et ad concordiam devenire'.

46 Wickham, *Courts and Conflict in Twelfth-Century Tuscany* (Oxford, 2003), p. 121-134.

discussed, at a factual level, what entitlement parties had to the land (e.g. by virtue of purchase or inheritance), or how they possessed it (directly or through a tenant). Such aspects of the civil courts of fourteenth-century Lucca had been inherited from twelfth-century Lucca, discussed by Wickham.[47] The possibility of discussions based on social realities rather than legal terminology was suitable to and accessible by the broad classes of people who looked to the communal courts as sites of conflict and resolution.

3. Conflict Resolutions *Extra Iudicium*

(1) Arbitration and reconciliation in notarial books

The city courts of Lucca, as we have seen, were easily accessible to ordinary people owing to the freedom of parties to make use of procedures and discussions based on social facts rather than legal terminology. However, these elements were not the immediate reason for such use. Why did people look to the communal courts as sites of conflict resolution instead of resolving conflicts among themselves? To more precisely understand the positioning of communal justice as a means of resolving various conflicts, we need to analyse the notarial record with an eye to *extra iudicium* practices outside the courts.

Broadly speaking, conflict resolution was pursued either between parties on their own or through intervention by a third party (i.e. judge or arbitrator). Parties, in fact, went back and forth between these two modes of resolution. While it was possible that parties, having tried to resolve problems on their own, would leave the resolution to be determined by a judge or arbitrator, compromise between parties was sometimes reached before a third-party decision could be issued, as we see in cases where the disclosure of a jurist's advice was pre-empted.

While it seems likely that such reconciliations between parties were common, they are not easy to verify from documentary sources. Let us consider the example of an agreement between parties concerning the conditional waiving of a debt. While any record of oral agreements between parties is naturally unavailable, it is also impossible to find agreements of debt waiving, as they are potentially masked by spurious documents of repayment or by documents recording where parties made new contracts incorporating existing debts.

Such unlocatable agreements notwithstanding, parties did prefer to confirm agreements by making notarial contracts, especially regarding significant estates, and notarial registers accordingly recorded contracts of arbitration and of reconciliation.

We therefore find that cases of third-party arbitration greatly outnumber those involving unassisted reconciliation between parties. Although arbitration, naturally conducted by individuals who were not communal officials, was considered to be *extra iudicium*, a practice outside the public judicial system, it nevertheless assumed a public

47 *Ibid.*, p. 68-107.

character in the sense that the decisions of arbiters were, like notarial contracts, legally binding, so that the communal courts assured the fulfilment of arbitration settlements.

Two legal acts of arbitration can be found in the notarial books, namely, arbitration agreements (*compromessum*) and arbitration decisions (*arbitratus*). An arbitration agreement was a procedure wherein both parties presented their arbiters and swore to accept their decisions on pain of penalty.[48] This procedure distinguished arbitration from trial and mediation. It was distinct from trial in the sense that the parties selected arbiters and that the arbiter's decision was only binding by virtue of the parties' sworn agreement to accept the decision; and it was distinct from mediation in that decisions by a third party who had been accepted by the parties as an arbiter were legally binding irrespective of the parties' actual acceptance of them.

How many times were arbitration and reconciliation attempted? Unlike in the case of civil trials, the dispersal and loss of notarial records makes it difficult to determine the frequency of these extra judicial resolutions with any certainty. However, eight notarial registers from three notaries, recording a total of 3,542 contracts between 1328 and 1342, provide us with the basis for making a rough estimate.[49] Examination of these documents yields 9 reconciliations, 71 arbitration agreements and 41 arbitration decisions (0.3%, 2%, and 1.2% of all registered contracts respectively).[50] We can identify 242 notaries among men in Lucca who swore allegiance to King John of Bohemia in 1331 and 1332.[51] A survey of existing notarial registers from seven notaries shows that the average number of contracts stipulated for a single notary ranged between 44 and 287 contracts (an average of 168) per annum.[52] These data suggest that the number of arbitration decisions made in a year may be equivalent to the number of final decisions in Lucca's judicial sphere (cases held in the Court of Podestà, for example, reached final decisions in only 6% of ordinary trials, which accounts for half of the total of 10,000 complaints for a year). Thus, arbitration would have been a frequently used instrument – one likely to have been considered a more effective means of reaching third-party resolutions.

---

48 This procedure can be found in arbitrations of the twelfth century, 'Forme di organizzazione giudiziaria delle città comunali italiane nei secoli XII e XIII: l'uso dell'arbitrato nei governi consolari e podestarili', in Arlinghaus et al. (eds.), *Praxis der Gerichtsbarkeit in europäischen Städten des Spätmittelalters* (Frankfurt am Main, 2006), p. 113-134.

49 ASL, *Archivio dei Notari*, 102, 103 (Giovanni Lotti); ASL, *Archivio dei Notari*, 108, 109 (Nicolao Lupori); ASL, *Archivio dei Notari*, 116 (Bartolomeo Buommesi).

50 The reason why the number of arbitration decisions was less than 60% of the number of arbitration agreements is likely because the parties, even after the arbitration agreements had been settled, were able to reach a compromise; either this, or they could not consent to the arbitration decisions and therefore unjustifiably forced the notaries not to inscribe the decisions in the registers. However, in some cases arbitration decisions were made and recorded even when both parties were absent. ASL, *Archivio dei Notari*, 110, p. 33: '... absentibus tunc suprascriptis partibus coram Francesco condam pinaccii Lucano cive...'

51 ASL, *Capitoli*, 52.

52 These values are based on an analysis of the registers of the following seven notaries: Federico Biagi drew up an average of 44 contracts per year over 10 years; Giovanni Lotti, 71 contracts per year over 21 years; Nicolao Lupori, 251 contracts per year over 21 years; Bartolomeo Buommesi, 232 contracts per year over 20 years; Francesco Torringhelli di Rabbio 170, contracts per year over 15 years; Francesco Sembrini, 119 contracts per year over 4 years; and Iacopo Turchi, 287 contracts per year over 36 years. ASL, *Arcivi dei Notari*, 95-97 (Federico Biagi); 102-106 (Giovanni Lotti); 108-115 (Nicolao Lupori); 116-123 (Bartolomeo Buommesi); 124-126 (Francesco Torringhelli di Rabbio); 146 (Francesco Sembrini); 213-238 (Iacopo Turchi).

(2) Advantages of arbitration: rapid procedures and familiar arbiters

Why did people prefer to use arbitration to resolve conflicts? What merits did arbitration have? First, the procedures that arbitration entailed were rapid and direct. Although it was possible that parties spent a long time in designating and commissioning arbiters, the process from that point forward (i.e. after reaching an arbitration agreement) would have progressed rapidly. An arbitration agreement provided for a set schedule; for example, an arbiter was required to reach a decision within eight days.[53] Wording was included in some agreements to the effect that arbiters should decide summarily (*summaria*), signifying that arbiters and parties must rapidly arrive at a conclusion, regardless of the complicated formalities and exceptions that were an inevitable part of the ordinary trials. The rapidity of arbitration had many advantages to trials in terms of expense. This is expressed by the phrase 'parties… want to avoid labours and expenses and proceed in the manner of *extra iudicum* what were forced to do in trial'[54] used in cases of arbitration.

Another advantage offered by arbitration was the directness of procedures such as hearing both parties by arbiters. Among the basis of decisions by arbiters, which are written in the notarial records, we can find such descriptions as: We decide on the basis of 'diligent examination of the petition, response to it, testimony, and hearing parties and their procurators'[55] or on the basis of 'diligent hearing of everything that parties wanted to say'.[56] In the case of trials, the jurists who drew up the *consilia* that served as draft judgements simply consulted the descriptions in the court registers. In contrast, 'hearings' before arbiters seem to have been more desirable for those who wanted to avoid discussions filled with empty formalities and so resolve the substance of their disputes.

The differences between trial and arbitration are apparent not only in terms of procedure but also in the nature and criteria of decisions. It is not easy to ascertain whether an arbitration decision was one-sided or compromised, owing to the general lack of detailed descriptions of petition and examination. However, in 28 of 61 cases, arbiters either totally vindicated one side or imposed obligations against one side. For example, in a case started by a claim of Labruccio (citizen) for the repayment of 100 florins against Rogerio (churchman), the arbiter Simone of Camporeggiano (jurist) ordered Rogerio to pay the stated amount within two months.[57] This distinguished arbitration from mediation wherein a mediator generally decided the case based upon consideration of the intentions of both parties.

53 ASL, *Archivio dei Notari*, 102 (Giovanni Lotti), p. 73-74.

54 ASL, *Archivio dei Notari*, 105 (Giovanni Lotti), p. 36: 'dicte partes… volentes laboribus et expensis parcere et facere extra iudicum quid in iudicio facere cogerentur…'

55 ASL, *Archivio dei Notari*, 103 (Giovanni Lotti), p. 253-257: 'diffinimus, decidimus et terminamus, quia visi set diligenter examinatis dicta infrascripta petitione et responsione ad eam facta per suprascriptum Coluccium Burichelli…, et dictis testium…, et auditis partibus et earum procuratoribus…'

56 ASL, *Archivio dei Notari*, 116 (Bartolomeo Buommesi), p. 166: 'quia auditis diligenter hiis omnibus que dicte partes dire voluerunt'.

57 ASL, *Archivio dei Notari*, 103 (Giovanni Lotti), p. 112-114.

However, we can also find 20 cases wherein arbiters made equivocal decisions that were not given in trials. For example, in a case wherein the hospital of Santa Maria Forisportam raised a complaint about possession of land on the part of Giraldo, the arbiter ruled that Giraldo must abandon the land in exchange for payment of 30 *lire* by the hospital.[58] In other cases of inheritance, the arbiters often decided careful subdivision among disputatious successors.

Such equivocal decisions turn our gaze towards the identity of arbiters and the criteria they used for their decisions. Some arbiters could be identified by their title of '*dominus*' as jurists, as in the case of Simone of Camporeggiano. In 34 of 115 cases, arbitration decisions were entrusted to jurists, who also gave legal advice in the trials.[59] In 31 cases, notaries with certain legal expertise played the role of arbiters (sometimes accompanied by jurists).

Apart from these legal professions, ordinary citizens were also selected as arbiters in 53 of 115 cases. By title, we can identify four as priests (*presbiter*) and eight as master artisans (*magister*). In other cases, we know from their surnames that arbiters were selected from influential families.[60] In other cases, they were unknown people from the same district or village as the parties.[61] In some cases, parties from different villages respectively selected their own *paesani* as arbiters,[62] likely because their familiarity with the circumstances of the conflicts meant they could render convincing decisions.[63]

(3) The criteria for arbitration decisions: arbitrium *and* concordia

What criteria did these arbiters use to base their decisions on? In the texts of arbitration agreements, we find various phrases used to describe such criteria, including 'summarily, in a discretionary manner' (*per via arbitri sommarie*), 'in a discretionary and lawful manner' (*per via arbitrii et iuris*) and 'in a discretionary manner, with rationality, good, equality' (*per arbitrium et ratione et de bono et equo*). The common element in all of

58 ASL, *Archivio dei Notari*, 103 (Giovanni Lotti), p. 576-577.

59 I sampled 115 cases of arbitration agreement and arbitration decisions recorded in the registers of three notaries from 1331 to 1343, ASL, *Archivio dei Notari*, 102, 103, 105 (Giovanni Lotti); ASL, *Archivio dei Notari*, 108, 109 (Nicolao Lupori); ASL, *Archivio dei Notari*, 116 (Bartolomeo Buommesi).

60 The entrusting of arbitration to such individuals can be observed even when rural residents were parties to a dispute. This was in part because the arbitration contract was itself entered into the city, but it was also conceivable that pre-existing socioeconomic links existed between these rural disputants and influential citizens and that these citizens were regarded as actors capable of rendering reliable judgements.

61 ASL, *Archivio dei Notari*, 108 (Nicolao Lupori), p. 250, 278; ASL, *Archivio dei Notari*, 111 (Nicolao Lupori), p. 346; ASL, *Archivio dei Notari*, 112 (Nicolao Lupori), p. 323.

62 ASL, *Archivio dei Notari*, 110 (Nicolao Lupori), p. 299.

63 When we analyse the relationship between the arbiters and the contents of their decision, arbitration decisions by jurists and notaries – people with legal training who were likely expected to exercise their expertise in the context of the arbitration – were somewhat more likely to award one-sided victories, while judgements by general arbiters were comparatively more likely to impose obligations on both parties. While we cannot make any simple distinction, because eclectic decisions imposing obligations on both parties were common even among jurists, as were judgements by general arbiters that cast matters clearly as black and white, there seems to have been a certain relationship between the arbiters and the content of their decisions.

these is *arbitrium* or discretion.[64] Other terms that appeared in the context of *arbitrium* included '*ius*' (law), '*equus*' (equality), '*ratio*' (rationality) and '*amicabile compositio*' (amicable composition),[65] but these all seem to have been regarded as constituent elements of *arbitrium*.[66]

Of these, '*ius*' featured frequently in arbitrations not only by legal professionals but also in those of ordinary citizens. This did not necessarily entail adherence to specific laws, given *ius*' coexistence with *arbitrium*, but seemed simply to indicate a system of law or legal sense in general terms.[67] Arbitration decisions, even those based on *arbitrium* rather than on specific positive laws, could not be selfish and were required to demonstrate good judgement in a legal sense. Therefore, arbitration, even as an extrajudicial act, should be considered in a broad sense as having been collocated with the Roman legal system.

The term '*amicabile compositio*' appeared in various arbitrations as a criterion to be relied on by arbiters. Moreover, in the preambles of decisions, phrases such as '*pro bono pacis et concordie pertium*' or '*ad pace et concordia reducenda*' were used to describe the purpose of arbitration. These elements, which guided arbiters to the results of the decision, distinguished arbitrations from court-based trials. Arbiters, required to make peace, had to consider the various circumstances of a dispute rather than statutory laws. Accordingly, almost all arbitration decisions featuring words such as *pace* or *concordia* were rendered not by legal professionals but by ordinary people, most likely individuals from the same neighbourhood who were well-versed with the relevant circumstances. Arbitration decisions often entailed compromise, not generally seen in a trial, for the simple reason that arbiters had an inside grasp of the situation and made decisions that prioritised concordant relationships over strict adherence to the law. Such arbitration would have been a good solution for parties who urgently desired to resolve their conflicts.

A relatively high proportion of arbitration decisions were actually accepted. Failures to execute arbitration decisions were still possible, despite arbitration agreements and the statutory prohibition against objections. Registers from the Court of Podestà in 1336 reveal eight cases wherein parties brought suits for the nonfulfillment of arbitration decisions by their opponents, appealing the communal courts to compel the

---

64 As for the significance of *arbitrium* in *ius comune*, see Meccarelli, *Arbitrium*, p. XVII-XXXII. As apparent in such terms and phrases as 'summarily' (*sommaria*) and 'whether or not one obeys [the law]', this shows that the arbiter was not bound by any specific law, but was free to make judgments according to common sense. According to Meccarelli, although medieval Roman law was characterised by legal formalism, at the same time such 'discretion' (*arbitrium*) was accorded a certain functional role in the establishment and interpretation of the law.

65 ASL, *Archivio dei Notari*, 108 (Nicolao Lupori), p. 310-311.

66 According to Meccarelli, the concept of *arbitrium* in *ius comune* was interrelated with '*iustitia*', '*aequitas*' and '*ratio*', Meccarelli, *Arbitrium*, p. 3-41, 121-128.

67 The fact that the description of the term '*ius*' in arbitration was substantial, not formal, can be seen in an arbitration case wherein the words '*et iuris*' was expressly added as a postscript to the phrase '*per via arbitrii*' (*per via arbitrii et iuris*).

execution of these decisions.[68] However, these few cases do not seem indicative of incompetence in the arbitration process.

The fact that parties generally accepted arbitration decisions is confirmed in the marginal descriptions found in the notarial registers. Out of 75 arbitration decisions, entries for 31 cases (41%) feature marginal annotations to the effect that the parties either paid the amount specified in arbiters' decisions or accepted the decisions and promised to observe them. As a minimum number of acceptances, those lacking annotations notwithstanding, this is significant in the context of the status quo of frequent objections against judicial orders and constant appeals of earlier decisions in the Court of Podestà.

In sum, arbitration had many merits. It was inexpensive, its proceedings progressed rapidly, it allowed direct debate without being bound by legal formalities, and the decisions of arbiters prioritised mutual satisfaction. These merits resulted in the relatively high acceptance of arbitration decisions. The fact that arbitration was apparently the best choice for the resolution of conflicts is also evidenced by the relatively large number of such cases. The parties who sincerely wanted to settle complicated problems must have moved towards arbitration.

4. The Significance of Judicial Orders

(1) Reasons for using the communal courts

Here, it becomes clear that the traditional relations we have assumed between state and society did not hold true in practice. It was *not* the case that people went to the courts to seek assistance from the state's coercive power when conflicts could not be settled in the local community. Private arbitration represented a better option than the communal courts for parties seeking to resolve their conflicts. We thus return to our initial question, namely, why did people turn to the courts?

We can deduce several reasons. The first was to express their anger and dissatisfaction publicly in the courts so that aggrieved parties could retain their social status. Conflicts could be widely publicised through trial procedures such as issuing summonses in the street and pronouncing sentences. Smail has noted that resorting to the courts would have the effect of disclosing problems publicly so that plaintiffs could attack or humiliate their opponents, thereby displaying their competitiveness.[69] Such actions

---

68 *Potestà*, 58, fol. 285r; *Potestà*, 60, fols. 15r, 65r, 495r; *Potestà*, 64, fol. 198v; *Potestà*, 67, fols. 34r, 386r, 398r; *Potestà*, 58, fol. 193r; *Potestà*, 60, fol. 9r. Moreover, even in the courts of consuls, two requests for enforcement were issued at the New Court over the course of the year. We can also confirm that one complaint appealing an arbitration decision was heard by the Court of Foretani over the course of the year, along with eight at the Court of San Cristoforo. ASL, *Curia Nuova di Giustizia e dell'Esecutore*, 30, fol. 75r; ASL, *Curia Nuova di Giustizia e dell'Esecutore*, 25, fol. 17r; ASL, *Curia dei Foretani o di S. Alessandro*, 16, no foliation, 10 January 1337; ASL, *Curia di S. Cristoforo*, 112, fols. 7r, 40r, 116r, 154r, 156r; *Curia di S. Cristoforo*, 113, fols. 46r, 11r; *Curia di S. Cristoforo*, 115, fols., 17r, 25r.

69 Smail, *The Consumption of Justice*; Smail, *Legal Plunder*; D. L. Smail, 'Violence and Predation in Late Medieval Mediterranean Europe', *Comparative Studies in Society and History*, 54 (2012), p. 1-28; D. L. Smail, 'Debt, Humiliation, and Stress in Fourteenth-Century Lucca and Marseille', in B. Sère and J. Wettlaufer (eds.), *Shame*

Table 1.4: Judicial orders issued at the Court of Podestà in 1336

	Cases
Seizure of movables (*preda*)	71
Seizure of immovables (*insolutum*)	54
Orders of payment or eviction (*preceptum*)	51
Ban (*bannum*)	46
Others	21
Total	**243**

would have been significant in a medieval society that attached importance to fame and reputation. This is why the people filed cases even for small sums, despite the associated costs of proceedings and seizures, etc.

A second motive was that securing a legal advantage would place them in a favourable position for subsequent arbitration or reconciliation. In trials, parties that engaged notaries (legal professionals) as procurators often raised objections against their opponents, focusing excessively on the legal formalities. Such cases, after lengthy discussion, were eventually broken off before any final decisions could be reached. Parties who recognised their disadvantage in terms of substantively arguing their rights would tend to raise procedural challenges in the courts as a precursor to negotiating more favourable terms with an opponent.

Such motives seem to have inspired more than a few people to file suits in the communal courts. Others may have looked to the courts for another reason. The key here is provided by the judicial orders, i.e. orders issued summarily by the judges on the sole basis of notarial documents. Such orders mandated actions such as the seizure of movables (*preda*) or immovables (*tenuta* or *insolutum*), bans (*bannum*), or orders to evict debtors (*preceptum*), as we saw above.[70] In 243 of the 900 ordinary cases brought before the Court of Podestà in 1336, trials were concluded with these orders (Table 4). The actual number of judicial orders was more extensive, as our calculations do not include many other cases wherein trials continued after the issuing of judicial orders with challenges to their validity. Examining the books containing the reports of *preda* by all civil courts, Smail reveals that there were 2,113 acts of predation per year in Lucca in the 1330s.[71]

The supposition that the main aim of the complainants was to obtain the issue of judicial orders is supported by the fact that many trials that eventuated a final ruling (34

---

between Punishment and Penance. The Social Usages of Shame in the Middle Ages and Early Modern Times (Firenze, 2013), p. 247-262.

70 As for summary procedure, Salvioli, *Storia della procedura*, p. 327-346; A. Engelmann, *A History of Continental Civil Procedure*, p. 497-502. This procedure, according to Salvioli, can be seen in the statutes of other cities.

71 Smail, *Legal Plunder*, p. 173-180.

of 53 cases) were initiated in opposition to previous judicial orders. Therefore, even the trials that ended with sentences passed the procedure of judicial order at least once.[72]

A main attraction of the public courts for those who faced opponents, particularly those insolvent, must have been the commune's executive power. This force, which private arbitration did not offer, was employed in judicial orders and could be invoked solely by presenting notarial documents.

The crier-sergeants serving the judges were the agents of the executive power of the judicial courts. Their coercive potential is clearly shown in the case of a criminal trial, wherein a rural villager named Berto, accused of injuring another, contradicted the accusation as follows.[73] Ciomeo, an opponent of Berto and possibly his creditor, had, together with Jacopo, a sergeant of the Court of Podestà, armed with lances, blades and knives, trespassed onto Berto's land in an effort to seize Berto's cattle (i.e. to carry out a *preda*). Berto interrupted the seizure and threatened the two men, arguing that Ciomeo had no legitimate claim to his cattle. Though Berto presented this defence and asked that the sergeant be punished for the illegitimate seizure, his efforts were to no avail and he was punished with a fine of 45 *lire*.

This example demonstrates the violence inherent in such seizures and the expectation on the part of the creditor, Ciomeo, who relied on enforcement by the communal court for the debt collection.[74] This possibility of summary procedure and enforced debt collection was most likely a major reason for citizens to frequent the courts, particularly for those suing insolvents. In fact, complaints against insolvents featured in half of ordinary trials and in many summary trials.

(2) The strategic use of judicial orders

However, it is also worth noting that judicial orders given with a summary procedure were not necessarily used as the means to recover a debt or unpaid rent. This is shown by objections, occasionally expressed violently, as in Berto's reaction above, which were commonly raised against judicial orders. In total, 15% of the ordinary trials in 1336 in the Court of Podestà started with objections to judicial orders. In these cases, parties sought to negate their debts or disprove an opponent's ownership of properties that served as the basis of a judicial order.[75] Let us consider a typical example.

---

72 Furthermore, from the fact that 131 trials in 1336 opened with objections to a judicial order, 26% of these led to final decisions; basing final decisions on advice by jurists can also be seen to have been positioned as a means of resolving objections that might give rise to a judicial order.

73 *Potestà*, 4737, fols. 29r-30v. As for defense and testimony on it, *Potestà*, 4743, fols. 5r-7r, foglio staccato.

74 There are other cases regarding violence by court servants. For example, *Potestà*, 4787, no foliation, 9 January 1344: 'dum ipse Nenus iret eidem simonem ad predandum… ex offitio curie domini potestatis Lucane de presenti mense jannuarii, dictus Simone contendit sibi pingnus et non permisit se predare. Et pingnus et praedam contendit et etiam ipsum nunptium percussit in pectore cum manibus ipsius simonis'.

75 This was due to the confirmation errors on the part of judges conducting the summary proceedings. The stipulation to judges 'De non dando alicui licentiam predandi nisi viso publico instrumento' is included even in postscripts to regulations after 1336. *Statuto 1331*, p. 154.

On 9 July 1336, Giovanni Bottini contested a *preda*, a judicial order permitting creditors to seize a debtor's movables,[76] that had resulted from Petruccio Pucetti's complaint about Biancuccio Nuccori's unpaid rent on the basis of *carta locationis* between them. This *preda* permitted Petruccio, as the landowner, to seize Biancuccio's movables. Giovanni contested the validity of this *preda*, arguing that Giovanni himself had acquired the land in question, which he possessed through collecting rents from a tenant, by virtue of a *tenuta*, a judicial order permitting seizure of an immovable that had found in favour of Giovanni against Lagia Taldini in the Court of San Cristoforo.[77] Contesting this argument, Petruccio asserted that Lagia had never taken possession of the land and that Petruccio had possessed it through collecting rents from his tenant, Biancuccio, who in turn had loaned it to another tenant, Cellone Vitoli.[78]

According to the judicial order from the Court of San Cristoforo we cannot know the further development of this trial, as the entry breaks off. However, we see here that two judicial orders were called into question. One was the *preda* that Petruccio, in a previous trial, had received in the Court of Podestà against his tenant Biancuccio for unpaid rent. Another is the *tenuta* won by Giovanni in his suit against Lagia in the Court of San Cristoforo. In both cases, the judge, upon seeing the documents concerning debts or obligations, would have summarily issued the judicial order authorising the creditors' claims to the contested property, but whether that property actually belonged to their debtors is uncertain.

In their summary issue of judicial orders at the sight of documents regarding obligations such as *carta debiti*, *carta mutui*, and *carta locationis*, judges were following a rubric contained in a statute, '*De summaria ractione reddenda contra obligatos per publicum instrumentum*'.[79] However, such hasty and summary decisions could complicate situations further. It is possible that parties expected this careless attitude from judges, and obtained the judicial orders strategically. They were not being foolish in obtaining these dubious rights, but seeking deliberately to obtain them.

The reason why they would willingly work to secure even questionable judicial orders was that taking possession had strategic importance. In a legal sense, someone who took possession of a property, even by virtue of dubious rights or orders, positioned themselves as a defendant rather than as a plaintiff who had to shoulder the burden of proof, which entailed considerable labour and expense. In addition, in a substantial sense, accumulated facts of possession gave a possessor valid grounds for proving ownership. In the case mentioned above, Giovanni claimed to be the rightful owner

---

76 *Potestà*, 58, fols. 28r-30v.

77 *Ibid.*: 'cum granum predictum pertineat ad ipsos germanos et terra unde ipsum granum habitum et perceptum fuit ex tenuta per ipsam Johanem nomine suprascripto adepta in Curia Sancti Cristofori Lucane civitate contra dictam Lagiam relictam condam Taldini Bonaiuncte… de ipsa terra sint et erant per se et dictum tenitorem in possessionem…' (fol. 28v).

78 *Ibid.*: 'non obstante quod dicatur per dictum Johanem dicto nomine dictam terram elevatam fuisse in tenutam per dictum Johanem tamquam esset de bonis domine Lagie… cum re vera dicta domina Lagia nunquam fuit in possessionem dicte petie terre sed potius dictus Coluccinus fuit et est in possessionem dicte petie terre ex locatione inde facta Biancuccio et Dominico germanis… a quo Biancuccio dictus Cellone habet in locatione dictam petiam terre ad reddendum dicto Coluccino staria.xii. blave grani et mili…' (fols. 28v-29r).

79 *Statuto 1331*, IV, 3 (De summaria ractione reddenda contra obligatos per publicum instrumentum), p. 121-123.

based not only the *tenuta*, which officially permitted him to take possession of Lagia's land, but also through fact of possession based on that *tenuta*.

Another example shows the validity of judicial orders – especially, *tenuta* or *insolutum* – which permitted a creditor to take possession of a debtor's immovable property, in conflicts over ownership. On 24 July 1330, Spinello Lupardi, acting as procurator for a girl named Ghita, appealed the Court of Podestà to protect his possession of land that was also subject to a claim by the widow Mattea. Spinello argued that he possessed said land on Ghita's behalf by virtue of a title of *insolutum* obtained by Ghita's father, Bonagiunta, against Biancuccio from the judge of the Court of Foretani.[80] Against this, Mattea contested that she had a better right to said land because of the title of the dowry of Rosa, which Mattea had obtained.[81] In this case, we can see that a judicial order originally derived from the insolvency of a debtor (Biancuccio), was presented as title to the possession of land against affirmation on the basis of dowry, and that the fact of possession even by virtue of *insolutum* was used as a basis for land rights.

Such use of judicial orders, and the validity of facts of possession based therein, becomes comprehensible if we consider the relationship of property rights at that time and the way in which such rights were perceived. On the one hand, the prevalent culture of notarial contracts in late medieval Italy contributed to an abstract understanding of rights as having a documentary basis, such that claims to possession were regarded as valid only if they were based on a legal title. On the other hand, in Lucca's countryside, where citizens had invested heavily in land from the twelfth century, property rights were excessively subdivided and actively traded in the form of rights to land rents, making it impossible for people to obtain 'perfect' titles to properties.[82] In fact, parties in the public courts repeatedly engaged in discussions not only on transactions of land in notarial documents but also over the final rulings over property rights; therefore, the force of *res judicata* was not absolute.[83] It was effective in this situation for real possession to be established based on certain, if not perfect, titles, which might include judicial orders such as *tenuta* or *insolutum*, resulting in the reinforcement of abstract documentary rights that could help in future legal disputes.

---

80 *Potestà*, 11, fol. 22r: 'Spinellus Lupardi tabernarius actorio nomine pro Ghita filia pupilla et herede condam Bonaiute vinacterius de civitate Lucana exponit coram vobis domino iudice domini potestatis quod ipse habet tenet et possidet pro ipsa herede unam petiam terre… et quam dictus Bonaiuta cepit insoluto contra Biancuccium…'

81 *Ibid.* fol. 22r: 'Macthea relicta condam Ducci Bonaveris de San Martino de Ducentola dicit se habere iura potiora quam habeat dicta Ghita in dicta et super dicta petia terre ex iure eidem Macthee cessso et obuento [obtento] a Roza relicta condam Bellonii… Item allegat et producit cartam dotis dicte Roze…'

82 As for the characteristics of the ownership of land in the twelfth century, see C. Wickham, *Community and Clientele in Twelfth-century Tuscany. The Origins of the Rural Commune in the Plain of Lucca* (Oxford, 1998). For that in the fifteenth century, S. Polica, 'An Attempted «Reconversion» of Wealth in XVth Century Lucca: the Lands of Michele di Giovanni Guinigi', *Journal of European Economic History*, 9 (1980), p. 655-707; for the sixteenth century, M. Berengo, *Nobili e mercanti nella Lucca del Cinquecento* (Torino, 1965), p. 301-320. We can see the same tendency in the fourteenth century from the land tax registers, ASL, *Estimo*, 2.

83 For example, we see some cases wherein decisions in the Rectors' Courts were later brought up for discussion in the Court of Podestà, as well as cases wherein issues for which rulings had previously been issued in the same court were dragged up once again. Judgements only began to demonstrate the recognition of the validity of prior rulings from the late fourteenth century onward, after Lucca came under the rule of Pisa, a city that followed the Roman law.

Possession based in judicial orders was officially approved by the commune and was initiated and maintained in the public eye. The court records describe the public spectacle of owners taking initial possession; for example, when a plaintiff named Guilluccio, who had won a licence to possess land with a house in the court, was introduced to '*corporalem possessionem*' by a communal servant and was publicly proclaimed the new possessor to the surroundings by opening and closing the door of the house.[84] The city statutes, furthermore, prescribed that communal servants should publicly announce changes in ownership in the neighbourhood eight days after the investiture of lands.[85] The testimony confirms the visibility of possession based on judicial order. A witness who was asked 'based on what title Matteo started to possess the lands' responded 'based on *insolutum*, obtained against Vannello or his successors'.[86] Therefore, judicial orders, which authorised new possession officially and publicly, could be effective as a strategic measure in a society wherein the accumulation of possession based on certain, if not perfect, titles had a great significance.

Thus, the strategic use of judicial orders by people could change their original meaning. Originally, judicial orders had been a measure to restore 'rightful' rights relationships on the basis of notarial documents. Now they had been repurposed as a means of gaining a defensible title to possession and could be used socially as a valid public decision. We can see here that people recognised a disconnect between judicial institutions based in a notarial document system and their social reality. Their strategic deployment of judicial orders consequently redefined the communal courts, as well as the commune itself, as functional authorities in society.

5. The Commune within Society

In this chapter, I have considered civil justice in fourteenth-century Lucca from the viewpoint of how the communal courts were used by the people. The court records preserved in Lucca suggest that a massive number of complaints were raised each year. This means that even during the fourteenth century, a period when Lucca experienced considerable political confusion, such as dominion by several foreign rulers, the communal authorities continued to be used and accepted in the judicial sector with respect to civil rights.

However, this does not necessarily mean that the communal judicial system was able to provide a good solution in civil disputes, or that people filed appeals in the court in the expectation that the authorities would settle problems they could not settle themselves. Those who truly desired to resolve complex issues took the more convenient route of seeking arbitration by familiar arbiters who were well-versed with

84 *Potestà*, 82, fol. 218v: 'In corporalem possessionem soprascriptae petiae terrae cum domu super se capiendo eundem Guilluccium dicto nomine per manus destra et mictendo eum in domum et super dictam petiam terram cum domu super se… et aperiendo et claudendo hostium dictae domus…'

85 *Statuto della Curia 1331*, I, 6 (De tenutis denuntiandis infra viii dies post investionem ipsi), fol. 6r.

86 ASL, *Curia di S. Cristoforo*, 9, fol. 7v: 'Interrogatus quo titulo dictus Matheus […] eam incepit possidere / dixit ex insoluto adepto contra vannellum tintorem vel suos heredes'.

the situations in question, who were able to hear allegations directly, and who provided thoughtful decisions that prioritised reconciliation between the parties.

The reasons why citizens resorted to the courts and their real expectations of the commune can be intuited from the judicial orders – issued officially and summarily – that permitted petitioners to recover debts by taking possession of defendants' estates solely on the basis of documentary evidence of insolvency. This coercive power, and the rapidity of judicial orders not available to private solutions, would have been attractive for citizens. It should also be noted that those who wanted judicial orders did not always seek to use this system for its intended purpose, that is, to coerce the realisation of a rights relationship based on documents. Some, and possibly many, people obtained judicial orders strategically to take possession of a property and accumulate facts of possession even on the basis of dubious titles, in order to build an advantage in future conflicts.

In the use of communal courts, we can see a peculiar relationship between people and the commune in medieval Italy. It is through people's strategic use of the commune that it was able to exist as a public authority, flexibly and constantly changing to be acceptable and useful in society. The commune did not insist on the original function of its institutions, namely, the coercive restoration of rights relationships written on paper. If it had acted so rigidly, it would not have been so appealing to the inhabitants, who attached importance to facts and facticity as well as to abstract rights set down in documents. The strategic use of the communal courts, and particularly of judicial orders, continually shaped the commune as a public authority suited to the lived realities of people's social experience.

CHAPTER 2

Realisation of the Commune through Claims

1. Interaction between the Commune and its Inhabitants

What emerged from the civil trials of fourteenth-century Lucca was a commune that, rather than being separate from society, was connected to it. The commune was continuously being redefined, and it functioned as a public authority within society through the uses and practices of its inhabitants. In this chapter, I discuss these aspects of the commune further by focusing on two behaviours on the part of its inhabitants. The first is the exception (*exceptio*) frequently invoked by parties in trials, while the other is the inhabitants' appeals to the governing council to alter the laws.

What I define here as the exception (*exceptio*) are the claims by which parties pursued the formalistic faults of their opponents at trial. In medieval Italy, where a legal culture based on *ius commune* prevailed, emphasis was placed on formal aspects, such as judicial procedures, while the legal qualifications of the litigating parties and systems were put in place through checks by jurists to deal strictly with actions that deviated from laws such as city statutes. In this context, litigants tried to win trials by focusing in court on the pursuit of extrinsic violations and faults that their opponents had made rather than on intrinsic rights relationships. This phenomenon can be confirmed not only in Lucca but also in the criminal trials of thirteenth-century Bologna and Perugia, in the civil trials of Milan in the late thirteenth century, and of Marseille in southern France in the fourteenth century; it was widely observed in areas with an established culture of *ius commune* and a strong tendency in favour of legalism.[1] In Section 2, I investigate litigants' deployment of exceptions in detail to reveal how this practice was in fact indispensable for realising laws enacted by the commune and the substance of its institutions, and how the design of these institutions was premised on the practices of the people.

Whereas the exception activities in the courts functioned to formally substantiate the existing laws and systems, the claims by individuals to the Anziani executive college, which I consider in Section 3, served to shake up the commune's laws and institutions and contributed to the realisation of their *original purpose*. In the record books of

1 M. Vallerani, 'Consilia iudicialia. Sapienza giuridica e processo nelle città comunali italiane', *Mélanges de l'École française de Rome. Moyen Âge*, 123-1 (2011), p. 129-149; M. Vallerani, *La giustizia pubblica medievale* (Bologna, 2005), p. 139-142, 261-268; M. Vallerani, 'Consilia. Un progetto di schedatura archivistica della consulenza giuridica in età comunale', *Le carte e la storia*, 12-1 (2006), p. 24-29; A. Padoa-Schioppa, 'La giustizia milanese nella prima età viscontea (1277-1300)', in *Ius Mediolani: studi di storia del diritto milanese offerti dagli allievi a Giulio Vismara* (Milano, 1996), p. 1-46; D. L. Smail, *The Consumption of Justice: Emotions, Publicity, and Legal Culture in Marseille, 1264-1423* (Ithaca, 2003), p. 60-61, 95-100.

the Anziani, we can see the process by which complaints regarding civil matters were brought before the Anziani, how new legislation was issued on this basis, and how this in turn resulted in amendments to city statutes. These might have been the addition of new provisions, the amendment of existing laws, or the introduction of new legislation that exempted the application of laws to individual cases. As well as complying with the laws, inhabitants strategically lobbied the Anziani in response to their changing social circumstances and with their own interests in mind for legal addenda, amendments, and exemptions, which enhanced the flexibility of the commune's rigid legal system and adapted it to society.

As we examine the involvements of these inhabitants in the arena of the law, the unique character of the Anziani also begins to emerge as a representative body of the commune. Consisting of ten leaders, the Anziani wielded political and administrative authority as a governing council over matters that included the military, finances, and the maintenance of order. Rather than blindly obeying existing laws in the manner of the *podestà* or his judges, the Anziani gave careful scrutiny to the claims of citizens and decided to enact new provisions or apply exemptions to existing laws according to contingent circumstances and in consideration of the good of the commune. From the analysis in this chapter, it will be clear that both the inhabitants and the Anziani, while remaining fully concerned with their own good, collaborated nonetheless to 'rationalise' the laws in the name of the *bene del comune*.

2. Exceptions in the Courts

(1) Exceptions in civil trials

Let us bend our ears to the voices of the people who visited the courts of fourteenth-century Lucca. When we focus on the disputes discussed in the courts, as the trials proceeded, we find that the points of dispute often shifted to trivial matters, such as the qualifications of the opposing parties and formal faults in the proceedings. Let us consider two examples.

[Case A] A trial from 1338 in the Court of San Cristoforo[2]

On 6 June, the plaintiff, Chello Bindi, issued a claim against his brother, Dino Bindi, for a mortgage on land in Dino's possession, suing either for the land or for restitution of the mortgage amount of 58 *lire*. In response, the defendant countered that his possession of the land was legitimate. On 13 June, both the plaintiff and the defendant brought up the fact that the other party had neglected his obligations to stand for the night watch and to pay taxes, each claiming that the other had consequently no right to trial.[3] However, one month later, both sides submitted documents

2 ASL, *Curia di San Cristoforo*, 112, fols. 84r-85v.

3 *Ibid.*, fol. 84v: 'Dinus suprascriptus dicit dictum Chellum audiendum non esse in sua petitione sed potius repellendum, cum ipse Chellus non solverit custodias nocturnas ut alii Lucani cives»; e «Dinus suprascriptus dicit dictum Chellum audiendum non esse, cum non solverit impositam florenorum vel grani secundum formam

proving their payment of taxes and fulfilment of their duties. The point at issue then shifted to the question of from whom Chello had received the mortgage. Dino claims that Chello's rights had been transferred from a (Parmesan) *foreigner* by the name of Jacopino by way of another man named Petro, thus denying the validity of said rights.[4] In response, Chello countered that Jacopino was in fact Lucchese.[5] Afterwards, the discussion unfolded along parallel lines, and the two sides temporarily postponed the court proceedings. Four months later, on 5 December, both parties returned to court, where the defendant, Dino, claimed that because Petro, from whom Chello had received the mortgage, was under *bannum*, his contract was void.[6] However, Chello immediately submitted documentation showing that Petro had been released from the *bannum*. Afterwards, the point at issue shifted once again back to the question of whether or not Jacopino was Lucchese, at which point the record breaks off. In this trial, the plaintiff demands restitution of a mortgage amount and land from the defendant; however, most of the case involves discussions regarding the existence or otherwise of violations of ordinances or proceedings, such as whether both parties have fulfilled their obligations as citizens – that is, legal qualification – and whether foreigners or *banniti* are entitled to the said rights.

[Case B] A Trial from 1336 in the Court of Podestà[7]

On 1 October, the plaintiff, Luporino Bellucci, lodged a claim against the fact that one Donatuccio Betti (the defendant) had been given a judicial order authorising the seizure of Luporino's movables. The order was issued because of land rent that Donatuccio should have paid. However, Luporino claimed that he had already paid the rent to another man by the name of Puccino Cantone. Later, Puccino appeared in court to claim that he had received rent from Luporino because Puccino had previously acquired the right to do so at the New Court of Justice by virtue of a title of *insolutum* (a judicial order for the seizure of immovables). Against this, Donatuccio argued that this judicial order from the New Court of Justice was not valid because it was granted in contravention of the law. Puccino, on the other hand, claimed that Donatuccio was under *bannum* and was accordingly ineligible for trial or to receive the judicial order. Here, the case was entrusted to a jurist and the record breaks off. In this trial, Donatuccio and Puccino were at odds over the rent that Luporino was to pay. From the details, it seems that Donatuccio had acquired a judicial order authorising seizure even though Puccino had previously obtained another judicial order in another court. Here

stantiamenti'; *Ibid.*, fol. 85r: 'Chellus suprascriptus dicit dictum Dinarellum audiendum non esse in dicta sua oppositione, cum ipse Dinarellus non solverit custodias nocturnas'.

4 *Ibid.*, fol. 85v: 'Dinus suprascriptus dicit executionem per dictum Cellum [...] factam non esse et procedere in aliquo non debere, maxime cum iura efficacia non habet vel talia pro quibus agere possit eo modo quo agit, maxime considerata persona dicti Jacopini forensis de Parma a quo dicit dictum Petrum iura quesivisse ex cuius persona dicta iuriscessio est nulla inutilis et inefficax tamquam cessa a forense et non subiecto iurisdictioni Lucani communis'.

5 *Ibid.*, fol. 85v: 'Chellus [...] negat dictum Jacopinum in ipsa oppositione nominatum esse forensem et non subiectum Lucani communis'.

6 *Ibid.*, fol. 119r: 'maxime cum Petrus condam Coluccii Carincionis, a quo dictus Chellus adserit se iura habere in hiis que petit, sit imbanpnitus Lucani communis in libris .xxv'.

7 *Potestà*, 58, fols. 334v-336r.

Table 2.1: Topics of discussion in cases at the Court of Podestà in 1336

	Cases	%
Rights relationship only	126	45
Rights relationship and exceptions	63	22.5
Exceptions only	91	32.5
Total	**280**	**100**

again, the points at issue do not concern the right to land rent itself, but rather aspects such as the legality of the judicial order acquired by the other party and whether or not the other party was under *bannum*.

Thus, in the civil courts of fourteenth-century Lucca, formal matters regarding the legal qualifications of and procedures observed by opposing parties seem to have featured more heavily in court discussions than the substance of the initial claim (e.g. land and debt rights). Such exceptions can be seen in 154 cases, which corresponds to 55% of the 280 cases heard in the Court of Podestà for 1336 for which the details of the discussion were clear. Of these, in 91 cases (32.5%) the trials turned exclusively towards remuneration for exceptions, without any discussion whatsoever regarding substantial rights relationships (Table 1).

When we analyse the 154 trials involving exceptions, we find exceptions relating to various points, which together total 234 separate matters. These individual exceptions can be divided into two categories, namely exceptions that concern the respective legal qualifications and exceptions that concern procedural rule violations (Table 2). Next, I would like us to consider these various exceptions, perceiving behind them the process for realising the laws and institutions of the commune.

Table 2.2: Types of exceptions presented at the Court of Podestà in 1336

	Cases
Exceptions concerning personal qualifications	75
Procurator	29
Tutor	4
Ban (*bannum*)	13
Pronuntia	8
Citizen's default of duty	9
Non-participation in the vigilance group (*bapneria*)	4
Foreigner	4
Minor	4
Exceptions concerning procedure	140
Legal proceedings	58
Format of documents	31
Procedures validating contracts and judicial orders	3
Authority of judges	21
Lite pendente trials	27
Other	19
Total	**234**

(2) Types of exceptions

i). Exceptions concerning personal legal qualifications

The most commonly observed exceptions concerning personal legal qualifications relate to the delegating of tutors and procurators in trials. For example, in one trial, Gea (the widow of the late Coluccio and procurator for Coluccio's heir) sues for the restitution of debts owed on which basis a judicial order was issued. The judicial order, in turn, was refuted by one Puccino Bacciomei, who stated that the judicial order was and had always been void, because Gea was not the rightful tutor, of the late Coluccio's sons. She had not observed the formal procedure for becoming a tutor, and neither the creation of an inventory nor the delegating to her of property management was conducted in a legal manner.[8] As in this case, defendants often looked for formal defects in the procedure by which procurators or tutors were delegated, and occasionally

8 ASL, *Potestà di Lucca* (hereafter *Potestà*), 67, fol. 163v: 'dictum qualequale preceptum nullum esse et fuisse tanquam [...] dicta domina Gea non existente legitima tutrice suprascriptorum filiorum condam Coluccii et, maxime quia non servivit nec conplevit solemnia tutele nec fecit inventarium nec sibi concessa fuit administratio prout debuit de iure'.

succeeded in undermining the validity of contracts or rulings on which their opponents relied.

Exceptions relating to *bannum* were more effective among the qualifications for exceptions, as is also seen in the two cases mentioned above. In the context of medieval Italy, a *bannum* was considered as 'the manifestation of the will of the sovereign power and the penal consequences of its non-observance' though used in multiple senses, including denunciations by the commune, political exile, and punishment.[9] The *bannum* taken up in exceptions in Lucchese trials, rather than political exile, meant a type of punishment for contumacy or any other failure to comply with orders issued by the commune. Persons who were subject to a *bannum* were placed outside the lawful protection of the commune. In Lucca's statutes it was stipulated that violence against criminal *banniti* was lawful, and in civil matters, violence on the part of creditors against *banniti* for debt was also permitted.[10] Moreover, the *banniti* were also stripped of their rights to sue in communal courts.[11] Exceptions presented in the trials illustrate this point. For example, a man named Andruccio, citing the provision of Book 1, Chapter 53 of the city statute, argued that his opponent, Cecco, was subject to a *bannum* by the commune of Lucca for debt and as such was uneligible to bring a case to trial.[12] Additionally, other types of person placed in the same legal status as the *banniti* were those subject to *pronuntia* (*pronuntiati*) issued by the New Court of Justice for insolvency,[13] and exceptions were often raised in this regard as well.

Both *bannum* and *pronuntia* at the New Court of Justice were frequently issued during this period. The record books from 1339 at the New Court of Justice show that *pronuntia* were issued in 130 cases for failing to comply with rulings and breaches of contract. Also, regarding *bannum*, in April 1335, 379 individuals were subjected to *bannum* for non-payment of taxes imposed in January that year.[14] Of these, however, 228 were released from *bannum* for subsequent payment of tax. Even though *bannum* and *pronuntia* were punishments for defiance of the commune, they were relatively easily issued given the possibility of subsequent release. As a result, quite a large number

9 A register of *bannum* for Bologna in the year 1250, for example, lists 1,261 people as having been subject to bans. See Milani, 'Prime note', p. 501-502. For the criminal ban of Siena, P. R. Pazzaglini, *The Criminal Ban of the Sienese Commune 1225-1310* (Milano, 1979).

10 S. Bongi (ed.), *Statuto del comune di Lucca dell'anno MCCCVIII* (Lucca 1867) (hereafter *Statuto 1308*), III, 80, p. 192; *Statuto 1308*, III, 88 (De eo quod imbapniti pro maleficio possint impune offendi), p. 196-197.

11 *Statuto 1308*, III, 80 (De non faciendo rationem imbanpnitis), p. 192; ASL, *Archivio Guinigi*, 263 (hereafter *Statuto della Curia 1331*), V, 9 (De non faciendo rationem alicui imbannito vel pronuntiato), fol. 55v.

12 *Potestà*, 8, fol. 57v: 'Andruccius suprascriptus dicit dictum Ciucchum audiendum non esse in predictis, cum sit bapnitus pro Lucano communi pro debito [...] allegat capitulum statuti Lucani communis libri primi, capitulo LIII, sub rubrica de non faciendo ractionem inbapnnitis'.

13 A provision in the city statutes states that the legal position of those subject to *pronuntia* was similar to that of *banniti*, which tells us that such individuals were not eligible to bring a case to trial. *Statuto della Curia 1331*, V, 9, fol. 55v.

14 This is a list of *banniti* inserted into the record book of the Anziani. ASL, *Anziani avanti la Libertà* (hereafter *Anz. Av. Lib.*), 8, fols. 28r-55v: 'Hec sunt bapna et bapnimenta data lata [...] Qui infrascripti cives Lucani qui contumaciter culpa et dolo non solvunt et solvere cessaverunt et cessant presens mutuum nuper factum ipsis civibus'.

of people ended up being placed under *bannum*, albeit only temporarily. This is the background in which exceptions were raised both frequently and effectively.

Exceptions for citizens failing to fulfil their obligations were also presented in connection with their eligibility for bringing a case to trial, as we saw above in Case A. At the Court of Podestà in 1336, the defendant, Bonagiunta Lupori, who had been accused of not paying rent on a house, claimed that the plaintiff, Sardella Luti, was not qualified to bring the case to trial because he did not observe his duties to the commune, either personal or material; this exception was ultimately successful.[15] This exception was consistent with a provision of the 1331 city statutes entitled 'On the punishment of those who have not joined a vigilance group (*bapneria*) and who have not assumed their civic duty (*honera*)'.[16] At the time, extraordinary taxes and military obligations were frequently, though irregularly, imposed in conjunction with increased wartime spending.[17] These circumstances, which resulted in many people failing to meet their obligations, were the background behind the high frequency with which these exceptions were raised.

The policy of stripping away the eligibility of *banniti, pronuntiati,* and defaulters of civic obligations to sue in the courts was something that had been carried out as a sanction against those who had flouted public authority since the mid-thirteenth century, during a period when the commune was being established as a public government. A result of this governance policy, however, was the creation – albeit temporary – of large numbers of people who no longer possessed the right to trial, which in turn created an opportunity for the strategic leveraging of exceptions in trials.

As a final example of exceptions concerning qualifications, let us look at those pertaining to foreign citizens. Here, 'foreigners' refers to people who are not affiliated with the Lucchese jurisdictions. In Case A, Dino presents an exception that the rights claimed by the Chello derive from a foreigner.[18] Also, in another case brought before the Court of Podestà in 1338, the plaintiff, arguing against the rights claimed by the defendant, points out that *ser* Giovanni, who had drafted the contract document, was from Fucecchio, a town outside Lucchese territory and argues that the contract is therefore void.[19] Here, the defendant counters that *ser* Giovanni's native territory of Fucecchio was Lucchese territory in 1323, when the contract was stipulated. To this, the plaintiff offered the rebuttal that following the revolt of 1314, Fucecchio had been

---

15 *Potestà*, 58, fols. 147v-148r. '... super dicta sua petitione procedi non debet nec ei ius fieri cum dictus Sardella non subeant honera realia et personalia pro Lucani communis...'

16 ASL, *Statuto del Comune di Lucca*, 4 (hereafter *Statuto 1331*), V, 10 (De pena illorum qui non fuerint in bapneria et honera civitatis non subierint), p. 164.

17 Accord to the record book of the Anziani, such obligations were mandated fully 56 times in the nine months from July 1331 to March of the following year alone. S. Nelli and G. Simonetti (eds.), *Anziani avanti la libertà (Lucca, 1330-1369)*, I (Lucca, 2007), p. 260-277.

18 Provisions prohibiting contracts with foreign citizens. *Statuto 1308*, I, 25 (De possessionibus civium, qui sunt cives alterius civitatis non permittendo alienari), p. 23; *Statuto 1308*, IV, 73 (De eo quod venditiones facte non subiecto iurisdictioni Lucani Comunis sint casse), p. 289.

19 *Potestà*, 82, fols. 15r-18v: '... dicit quod cartas dicti quondam ser Johannis non est fides adhibenda cum dictus quondam ser Johannes non fuerit subiectus iurisdictione Lucanis communis ...', fol. 18v. The statute also stipulates that contracts shall only be executed by notaries belonging to the jurisdiction of Lucca. *Statuto 1308*, II, 56 (De cartis faciendis manu notarii subiecti iurisdictioni Lucani Communis et non per alium), p. 110.

outside Lucca's jurisdiction. The discussion continues, and the record unfortunately ends part way through the testimony. In fourteenth-century Lucca, just as in other Italian cities, territorial boundaries were changing constantly. Along with the many foreigners working inside the city, this border volatility was another factor contributing to litigants presenting exceptions.

ii). Exceptions concerning procedure

Next, let us look at exceptions that concern procedure. The most frequently appearing in trials are exceptions concerning negligence in terms of litigation procedure. For example, defects in the filing of summons and petitions were presented to invalidate prior rulings and judicial orders. While mostly invoked as a stalling tactic, we also see exceptions in several cases that had a concrete effect, such as those that invalidated judicial orders issued on feast days or highlighted that an opponent's argument was not carried out within ten days of a complaint.[20] These various exceptions that related to the procedural elements of lawsuits could be described as the activities of parties capitalising on the complexities of the litigation procedure of the Romano-canonical laws that were introduced since the twelfth century.

We often see exceptions raised against documents submitted by opposing parties. Many notarial documents were submitted to the court as evidence of contracts, such as of sale or dowry. In most cases when certificates were submitted, the opposing party almost always requested a copy. They then attempted to find fault with the format and content of the document. During this period, when notarial contracts were becoming more widespread, certificates submitted to the courts were copies from notarial registers, but exceptions might be presented alleging these to be counterfeit, requiring that the originals be submitted. While many of these challenges were also strongly informed by bargaining elements intended to buy time or increase the cost burden on the other party, on occasion, specific and accurate exceptions were also raised, as in the case of inconsistencies in dates, times, named witnesses, or the signatures of notaries.[21]

The validation of notarial contracts or communal decisions necessarily entailed procedures such as the payment of indirect taxes (*gabella*) and the filing of reports to the commune (*denuntiatio*), and defects in these became subject to exception.[22] For example, in a case brought to the Appellate Court in 1335, the plaintiff, Jacopo,

---

20 *Potestà*, 64, fols. 21r-v: '... lapsus est terminus ... decem dierum infra quem debuerit hostendere de omni suo iure ...'; *Potestà*, 67, cc. 206r-209v: '... preceptum non ... fieri potuerit obstante dicta die feriata'.

21 *Potestà*, 60, fols. 239r-241v: 'Henrighectum, qui dicitur scripsisse dictum instrumentum et quedam alia de quibus infra fit mentio, fuisse et esse personam incognitam, unde debuit fieri fides de suo privilegio et officio tabelionatus et notariatus'; 'in subscriptione dicti instrumenti non sunt apposita prenomen et congnomen Henrighecti' (fol. 239v).

22 The declaration to the commune was statutorily mandated for various contracts as well as for judicial orders and judgements. *Statuto 1308*, II, 58 (De quinque notariis eligendis, qui sint super denuntiationibus contractuum venditionum, alienationum recipiendis et registrandis), p. 111; *Statuto 1308*, IV, 16 (De insolutis et tenutis denunptiandis notariis imbanpnitorum), p. 258-259. Similar reporting systems are also apparent in Bologna and other cities, and exceptions regarding deficiencies in declaration have also been confirmed for Bologna. G. Tamba, *Una corporazione per il potere. Il notariato a Bologna in età comunale* (Bologna, 1998), p. 199-257.

appealed that, concerning the dowry rights claimed by the defendant, Dino, the indirect taxes arising from the dotal contract had not been paid within the time limit stipulated by the statutes, nor had any report been filed, and thus the contract was null and void.[23] Dino argued against this by citing statutes to the effect that the judicial order on which the plaintiff based his claim was also invalid, since the indirect taxes had not been paid.[24] Jacopo countered this by arguing that the provision relating to indirect tax had not been in effect when the judicial order was issued.[25]Dino rebutted this in turn by stating that the provision was in fact in effect.[26] This case shows that the procedure for the validation of contracts or communal decisions, and their repeated changes, ended up creating a large number of violators, thus providing opportunities for exceptions.

Finally, there are exceptions derived from the pluralism of the Lucchese courts. For example, there are exceptions that argue to the effect that certain judges lacked the authority to rule on the issue at hand.[27] While most such exceptions were thrown out, in trials at the Court of Podestà, specific exceptions were accepted, such as those arguing to the effect that a trial should be held at the episcopal court because the party in question belonged to the clergy, or that a trial should be held at the Court of Foretani because one of the parties was a villager from the surrounding countryside.[28] In addition, exceptions are often seen objecting to the issue of judicial orders at other courts, regardless of whether the trials were *lite pendente*. For example, at a trial in the Court of Podestà, we find a man named Giovanni, whose movables were seized by a judicial order, arguing that 'the order of seizure issued by the Court of Podestà has to be canceled and revoked, and the seized property must be returned on the grounds that a lawsuit between the same parties had been *pendente* in the Court of San Cristoforo'.[29] In support of this claim he submitted a copy of the court record book. Underlying such exceptions was the plural character of the Lucchese courts, especially their overlapping jurisdiction. Although at the Court of Podestà, the six courts of consuls and the Rectors' Court each had their own competence, these spheres of authority were not clearly discrete but rather overlapped to varying degrees. For this reason, it was possible for parties to a dispute to make use of multiple courts for the same case. In this context, rather than solely imputing negligence on the part of an opponent, the exception also entailed a defence against activities by the other party to strategically make use of a court's particular environment.

---

23 ASL, *Maggior Sindaco e Giudice degli Appelli*, 42, fols. 2r-4v, 11r-12v.

24 *Ibid.*, fol. 11v: '…quia dicta instrumenta et contenta in eis et eorum contractus non fuerint denunptiata Lucane gabelle, nec ex eis aliqua gabella soluta, prout debuit secundum formam statuti'.

25 *Ibid.*, fol. 11v: '…non obstat dicta oppositio, cum tempore quo dictum insolutum datum fuit non vigebat aliquod statutum per quod deberet solvi aliqua gabella de aliquo insoluto…'

26 *Ibid.*, fol. 12r: '…tempore dicti insoluti dati vigebant statuta que dicebant quod insoluta non denunptiata Lucane gabelle et de quibus non erat soluta gabella non valerent, nec de rebus in ipsis insolutis contentis ius fieri non deberet…'

27 *Potestà*, 58, fol. 128v: 'vos non esse iudicem conpetentem in predictis'.

28 *Potestà*, 64, fols. 124r-125r; *Ibid.*, 82, fols. 139r-140v. In these cases, the consent of the other party existed and the lawsuits ceased immediately following the complaint.

29 *Potestà*, 11, fol. 32v: 'preda predicta facta ex offitio curie domini Lucane potestatis […] cassari et revocari debere, et bona in predam elevata restitui debere […] quia facta fuit lite pendente inter ipsas partes, quae pendet in curia Sancti Cristofori'.

In the foregoing, we have looked at the various exceptions that dominated the trials of fourteenth-century Lucca. Such exceptions, which were not apparent in the twelfth or early thirteenth centuries, could be described as by-products of the complexification of governance policies, laws, and regulations of the commune in the thirteenth and fourteenth centuries. During this period, when the commune was developing and changing as a highly organised government, the various ordinances and regulations issued created a large number of violators, with the result that litigants were provided with a means of strategic action.

(3) The spade work of exceptions: from the Guinigi family archive

We have a set of historical documents that illustrate the spade work of such exercises of the exceptions brought by parties, namely a copy of court records compiled within a series of '*Libro di processi*' among the documents of the Guinigi family. While copies of court records were usually kept by the winning party to prepare for subsequent rehashing, the records in question were held by the Guinigi family, who were on the losing side. These would have been used for reviewing a trial that the family lost, with the intention of finding procedural faults and raising exceptions.

The trial in question began at the New Court of Justice in 1336 when the plaintiff, one Alderigo Franceschini, demanded the repayment of a debt of 120 florins from the heirs of the defendant, the late Diabello Ballori (from the Guinigi family).[30] At the trial, the defending party raised an exception regarding the qualifications of the plaintiff, and of the notary who drafted the debt certificate; but ultimately Alderigo's complaint was recognised in the judgement.

In the copy of the court records, the margins have been heavily annotated, with memoranda in handwriting differing from that of the main body of the text. For example, in the margin of the section recording the complaint, we find that someone has written 'the statutes say that when a claim is made to more than one person, [the *libellus*] must be submitted for each person, but here, although there are multiple heirs, only one *libellus* has been presented'.[31] Also, the margin of the record of the summons features annotations to the effect that 'the summons and all subsequent matters are invalid because the summons was issued on a feast day of San Giovanni Battista', 'it is not clear that a report of the summons was given by the messenger', and 'no commission has been given to the messenger'.[32] These memoranda were clearly made to prepare for presenting exceptions.

The heaviest concentration of such marginalia is found in the section recording the judgement itself (Figure 1), where they summarise the reasons why the judgement is invalid, listing the following points supporting the exception. First, the filing of

30 ASL, *Archivio Guinigi*, 73, fols. 34r-51v. Both parties belonged to the Antelminelli family.

31 *Ibid.*, fol. 34v: 'statutum dicit quod quando fit porrectio de pluribus qui unicuique debeat porrigi unus, sed hic videtur adserere quod plures sunt heredes et quod unus solus libellus est porrectus'.

32 *Ibid.*, fol. 41v: 'Ista citactio et per consequens omnia ex ea subsecuta videntur non valere quia facta die feriata in honorem dei videlicet decollactionis sancti Johannis Battista'; 'Item non videtur per nunptium ipsius citationis facta relatio'; 'Item non est commissio facta nunptio'.

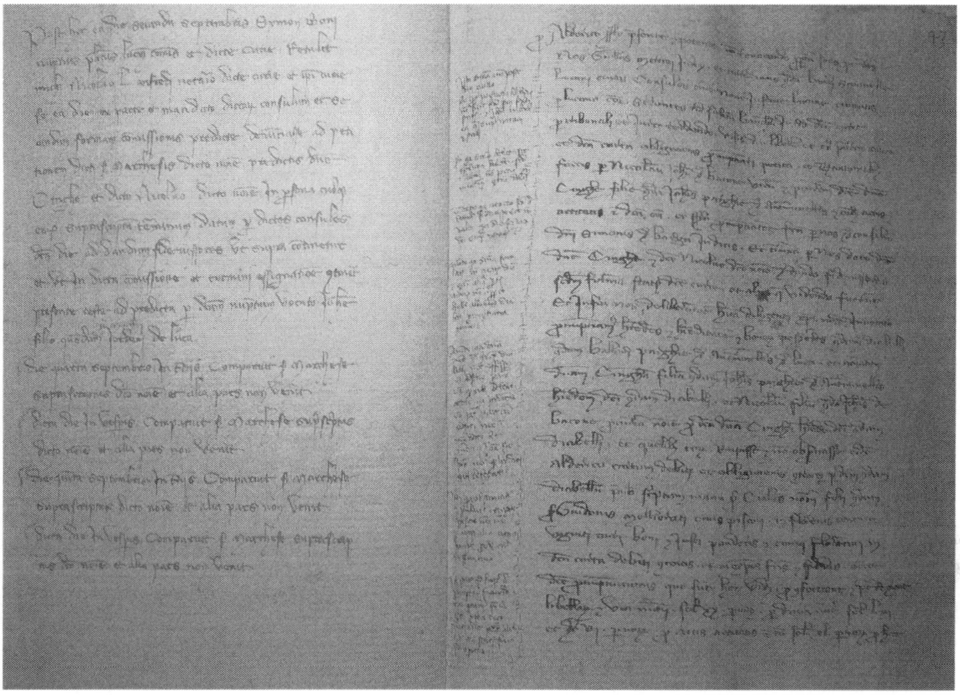

Figure 2.1: Marginal annotations to a book of *Processi* kept by the Guinigi family (ASL, *Archivio Guinigi*, 73, fol. 43r)

the *libellus* was not entered according to the statutory format. Second, although the judgement must be consistent with the letter of complaint, in the document a *pronuntia* was not requested of the 'madame (*domina*)' [referring to Cinga, daughter to the late Giovanni]. Third, the summons issued to the guarantor was invalid because it was made on a holiday, as above. Fourth, the judgement was issued to a 'madame' who was not summoned, and the heirs of Diabello are nowhere in the record listed as being subject to a *pronuntia*. Fifth, Cinga was not Diabello's heir, and the confessions and assertions of the procurator were not considered obstacles because the estate was not committed to the procurator, and the mandate of the procurator makes does not refer to Cinga as the heir or mention that the estate is entrusted to the procurator. In addition, because the presented exception was pending, the procedure could not proceed to final judgement without issuing a further summons. Finally, even though the city statutes stipulate that when a defendant does not appear in court within three days of filing of a letter of complaint, said defendant should be subjected to a *pronuntia*, in this case preparations were made for the judgement (*sententia*).[33]

33 *Ibid.*, fol. 43r: 'Ista sententia videtur posse dici nulla primo quia porrectio libellorum non fuit facta secundum formam statuti. Et ideo vediantur ea que supra notavi et statui'; 'Secundo quia sententia debet esse conformis libello, sed in libello non petit pronunptiam nominatam contra dominam'; 'Tertio quia citactio facta de dando fideiussores non valet quia die feriata ut supra notatum est'; 'Quarto quia sententia fuit lata non citata domina et

While the identity of the person who wrote these annotations is unclear, from here, a picture begins to clearly emerge of how the defendants' party, who lost the trial, used a copy of the court records as a basis from which to re-examine the process of the lawsuit, and was successful in finding noteworthy or procedural faults in the lawsuit to raise exceptions. It seems likely that appeals and claims concerning a retrial would have been conducted based on this memorandum.

(4) Judges, jurists and litigants as seen in exceptions

I would like to consider the background context of exceptions, examining the actions of the judges, jurists, and litigants, so that a picture will emerge of the people who ultimately enforced the laws and regulations via exceptions, thereby supporting the governing activities of the commune.

Exceptions were commonplace in other cities besides Lucca. Vallerani, revealing the large numbers of exceptions that were presented in criminal courts in thirteenth-century Bologna, singles out the driving factor of how the content of judicial decisions was followed by jurists' legal advice (*consilium sapientis*), which had formalist tendencies.[34] In Lucca, also, legal advice was sought when discussions entered a cul-de-sac due to the reciprocal exchange of exceptions, whereupon jurists dispensed advice in accordance with the statutes as members of the Lucchese *collegium iudicum*.[35] It was precisely due to this legal environment that litigants would seek out formal flaws and present exceptions by scrutinising the other party's conduct in light of the law.

It is certain that the existence of formalistic jurists constituted a major impetus for exceptions. Nevertheless, what I wish to note further here is that jurists, far from intervening actively and giving advice in trials, were able to become involved in trials only after their advice was requested. The learned jurist Bartolus de Saxoferrato stated in his litigation manual that judges who oversee a trial should request jurists' advice whenever there is any doubt about the legitimacy of the procedure.[36] However, from the Lucchese court records we know that litigants, not judges, took the initiative in seeking jurists' *consilia*.[37] In other words, whether the advice of a jurist who was a stickler for legal formulae would be delivered, and whether various formulae would

---

quia in aliqua parte actorum non apparet heredes Diabelli pronunptiatos contrarium'; 'Quint quia domina non est heres Diabelli nec confessio vel adsertio procuratoris videtur quod sibi debeat obstare, quia hereditas non potest procuratorem adhiri nec in mandato fit mentio quod ipsa sit heres nec quod hereditas sibi deferatur'; 'Item quia obstantibus et pendentibus exceptionibus propositis non videtur quod absque alia citatione potuisset procedi ad diffinitivam'; 'Item statutum loquitur de pronunptiatione facienda reo contrarium quando non comparet infra tres dies a die porrectionis libelli sed ora sententie fuit facta comparactio'.

34 Vallerani, *La giustizia pubblica*, p. 139-142; Vallerani, 'Consilia iudicialia'.

35 The fact that the jurists who provided legal *consilium* were simultaneously compilers of the statutes presumably created a trial environment in which the provisions of the statutes were strictly observed. For example, the editor of a 1331 court statute appears in a 1336 trial as a legal adviser. *Statuto della Curia 1331*, fol. 4r; *Potestà*, 60, fol. 307v; *Potestà*, 60, fol. 342r; *Potestà*, 58, fol. 319r.

36 Padoa-Schioppa, 'Profili del processo civile' p. 598-599; Rolandino, *Summa totius artis notariae*, fol. 355r: 'Quoniam hanc causam cum consilio sapientum decidere volo…'

37 In several cases, it is clearly stated that judges commissioned jurists for certain problems according to the wishes of the litigating parties. For example, *Potestà*, 67, fols. 120v: 'dominus Petrus iudex et assessor predictus pro tribunali

be followed in a Lucchese trial, depended on the actions not of the judge but of the litigants.

Judges adopted a passive attitude in civil trials and often committed minor errors. As we saw in the previous chapter, many claims were lodged against the judicial orders issued by these judges and many of the judicial orders were overturned. This shows that when the judge received a complaint or issued a judicial order, their decision was rendered hastily without them having scrutinised the details of the complaint or the qualifications of the plaintiff, or having checked for any omissions in the documents filed by the plaintiff. Exceptions to the effect of *lite pendente* were presented because judges failed to confirm whether the same dispute was being conducted in other courts or even in their own court, prior to the filing of the letter of complaint or before issuing an order.[38] The presentation of many exceptions relating to *bannum* shows that judges sometimes overlooked the fact that a trial was initiated by *banniti*, and occasionally even issued them with favourable judicial orders. A *bannum* issued as punishment for defiance of the commune was a symbolic institution showing that the commune was a public authority. Furthermore, the city statutes even forbade the *podestà* and his judges from exchanging words with those under *bannum* or admitting them into the courts and, in the event of violation, prescribed the imposition of a steep fine from the *maggior sindaco*. Nevertheless, this did not stop judges from inadvertently conducting trials in their favour.[39]

This passive attitude on the part of judges to leave checking to the litigants and to allow them to bring the question of whether to correct formal faults before the court is clearly evident in the following example. At a 1336 trial at the Court of Podestà, the plaintiff, Bonagiunta Lupardi (procurator for Vanna), sued Giovanni Gualtrotti (procurator for the rural commune of Corsena) for unpaid land rent. Giovanni received an interlocutory judgement in their favour, and Bonagiunta responded by requesting that the plaintiff's party bear the cost of the lawsuit.[40] The costs of the lawsuit were supposed to be offset by the *bannum* penalty issued to the commune of Corsena in the previous case between Vanna and the rural commune at the New Court of Justice: 'if the opponent's party does not satisfy with this, it is argued that Giovanni and this rural community should not be heard in their petition and that the trial (*ius*) should not be held at their petition, because the rural commune is under *bannum* on account of its

et iure reddendo sedens ad solito bancum iuris dicte curie de voluntate dictarum partium comisit questionem predictam in dominum Guillelmum Mercati iudicem'.

38 In a trial at the Court of Podestà, regarding the judicial orders against him (orders of detention and seizure of property), a plaintiff argued to the effect that 'regarding the case for which the order of detention has been issued, the lawsuit is pendent in your court, and due to this nothing new should be carried out'; and he submitted a copy of the relevant court records. *Potestà*, 82, fol. 69v: '...de predictis, unde detentus est, lis pendet in vestra curia; et lite pendente nulla fieri po[te]st novitas...' Such disinterest on the part of judges to check court records can also be seen in Marseille. D. L. Smail, 'Aspects of Procedural Documentation in Marseille (14th-15th centuries)', in Lepsius and Wetzstein (eds.), *Als die Welt in die Akten kam*, p. 139-169.

39 *Statuto 1308*, IV, 1, p. 249. As for control of officials, S. Lepsius, 'Dixit male iudicatum esse *per dominos iudices*. Zur Praxis der städtischen Appellationsgerichtsbarkeit im Lucca des 14. Jahrhunderts', in Arlinghaus et al. (eds.), *Praxis der Gerichtsbarkeit*, p. 189-269; S. Lepsius, 'Kontrolle von Amtsrägern durch Schrift. Luccheser notare und Richter im Syndikatsprozeß', in Lepsius and Wetzstein (eds.), *Als die Welt in die Akten kam*, p. 389-473.

40 *Potestà*, 60, fols. 137r-142v, 239r-241v e 290r-292v.

debt to Vanna'.[41] Afterward, the lawsuit dragged on for three months, after which point the record breaks off. This case shows that even in a case where one party lacked the necessary legal qualifications to proceed with a lawsuit, so long as the other party did not seek the withdrawal of the lawsuit, a judge would deliberately not interfere, thereby allowing the trial to continue unhindered.

The fact that compliance with legal provisions was left up to the litigating parties was true not only for civil trials but for criminal trials as well. The city statutes dealing with criminal trials provided that *as long as the accused proved*, using official documentation, that a victim had been banned, then the lawsuit should be discontinued. To prove a *bannum*, at the request of the offender [the accused], the *podestà* and his judges should ask the notary who managed the '*Libri bannorum*' to issue a copy.[42] While those under a ban could lawfully be attacked by anyone at all, this provision suggests that a case was still tried as a normal criminal case unless the accused knew the victim to have been under a ban.

In fact, at a criminal trial in 1344, two men named Fancelotto and Viviano were prosecuted for killing a third man named Pante. Because they were going to be placed under a *bannum* for contumacy for the second time, their procurator, Jacopo, appeared in court where he reported and produced certificates attesting that the victim, the late Pante, had been subject to a *bannum* for theft. This exception caused the hearing to be called off.[43] Even in criminal trials, judges were aware of the facts of a *bannum* and applied the provisions of the statutes, based on the initiative of the parties involved. Incidentally, cases similar to this one can also be found among the criminal trials of Bologna.[44]

(5) The legal system as realised through the practices of inhabitants

Exceptions instigated by litigants could be said to have been strategies employed by parties attempting to highlight formal faults and to incline developments in their own favour, where contending solely on the basis of a rights relationship would be unfavourable. It might also be described as conduct by which parties attempted to protect themselves from strategic actions on the part of opponents who sought to profit from the carelessness of the courts. Seen from another standpoint, however, we find that such activities were also important for the realisation of the communal legal system in actual practice. An exception was inherently the act of pursuing rule violations made by an opponent based on statutes. Therefore, the conduct of litigants using communal

41 *Ibid.*, fol. 290v: 'si de hoc adversa pars non contentatur, dicit dictum Johanem dicto nomine et dictum commune in dicta sua petitione audiend(os) non esse, nec ei ius fieri debere super ipsa eius petitione, cum dictum commune sit exbanditum pro debito dicte domine Vanne'.

42 *Statuto 1308*, III, 88, p. 196-197: 'Et teneatur Lucanum Regimen et eius iudex maleficiorum mandare notariis super imbapnitis deputatis, ad petitionem offendentis contra quem procederetur, seu eius procuratoris vel defensoris, occasione offense seu iniurie que diceretur facta in personam imbanpniti, ut copiam bapni persone offense faciat sive ipsi iudici sive offendenti vel eius procuratori vel defensori, ad hoc ut de ipso banpno iudici fiat fides'.

43 *Potestà*, 4790, fols. 12r-13v: 'pro defensionem et excusationem predictorum Fancellecti et Viniani dicit et proponit quod predictus Pante vivoli de nothani est inbannitus Lcani communis'.

44 Vallerani, *La giustizia pubblica*, p. 261-268.

legal provisions was something that contributed, even if unintentionally, to the practical expression of the commune's legal policies. For example, parties desiring to raise an exception would draw focus specifically on the legality of the lawsuit proceedings. This became a power to direct the trial towards something rigorously based on procedural rules for lawsuits, even in circumstances where judges were careless or passive. In addition, an exception had the potential to alter the behaviour of citizens even outside the trial context. Exceptions that related to *bannum* and defaulting on civic obligations made *banniti* and defaulters less inclined to attempt to engage in legal activities (e.g. contracts and trials) in such circumstances and thus incentivised them to fulfil their obligations and return to the fold of communal law.

Of course, it is also obvious from the frequency with which exceptions were invoked that this did not necessarily result in the elimination of legal infractions or procedural shortcomings in lawsuits. Nevertheless, exceptions seem to have contributed in a significant way to the progress of trials in accordance with legal procedures and the realisation of communal policies in spite of carelessness on the part of judges. It was not the ruling representatives of the commune but rather the common people who acted as litigants, fully aware of their own interests, thereby realising the Romano-canonical procedure introduced to the commune in the twelfth century, as well as the penalty policy of stripping violators of their legal status which had been established in the thirteenth and fourteenth centuries for the sake of social governance.

It was necessary that litigants had at least two capabilities to be able to present these exceptions and activate the functioning of the communal legal system. One was legal knowledge sufficient to determine whether the conduct of the court or the other party was compliant with laws and regulations, while the other was the ability to gather information, such as whether the other party was *banniti*.

Legal knowledge, and knowledge pertaining to city statutes in particular, was possessed primarily by members of the legal profession, such as notaries and jurists. In fact, notaries in particular appeared in the courts as experts on legal problems, presenting large numbers of legal exceptions and conducting abstruse discussions on behalf of the parties. Incidentally, exceptions conducted by notaries serving as procurators have also been examined in studies focusing on Bologna, Florence, and Marseille.[45] Nevertheless, as pointed out in the previous chapter, in Lucca notaries participated in approximately three out of every ten trials, and most discussions in court were carried out by common people who did not bear the title of either notary or jurist.

Let us consider an exception raised by a scrap metal dealer (*ferrovecchio*) by the name of Masseo Massini at the Court of Podestà in 1336 as an example of an exception raised by a commoner who was neither a notary nor even a member of a notable family. Regarding a judicial order of detention he had previously been issued, Masseo argued that 'the license [to issue the detention] and capture [actually be carried out]

45 As for Bologna, Vallerani, *La giustizia pubblica*, p. 139-142, 150; In case of Florence, V. Colli, '*Acta civilia in curia potestatis*: Firenze 1344. Aspetti procedurali nel quadro di giurisdizioni concorrenti', in Arlinghaus et al. (eds.), *Praxis der Gerichtsbarkeit*, p. 271-303, in particular p. 284-292; For Marseille, Smail, *The Consumption of Justice*, p. 71-72.

are invalid for several reasons… In Book 4, Chapter 3, *de summaria ractione reddenda*, of the Statutes of the Commune of Lucca it is stipulated that no one can be captured and detained for a sum of less than 100 *soldi*'.[46] Even those like Masseo, who hailed from the middle or lower classes, could conduct discussions by citing city statutes, which were publicly available at the desk of the *maggior sindaco* and in the communal archive (*Camera Librorum*). It was also possible to gain legal knowledge through routine contact with notaries or by relying on influential families that could offer patronage.[47]

A second ability possessed by inhabitants was the capacity to gather information. For an exception, it was necessary to obtain certain information, such as whether an opposing party was a *bannito* and whether or not the notary who drafted the contract on which the other party depended was foreign to Lucca, and then to prove these in court. In the courts, documents were frequently submitted by parties to prove the contents of exceptions, especially copies of the record books prepared by the custodian of the communal archive.[48] As in other Italian cities, a communal archive had also been established in Lucca in the thirteenth century and was frequently visited by citizens who would request and receive copies of the record books stored therein.[49] The city statutes also stated that 'in the *Camera*, where the court record books, council registers, records of decrees, and other documents of the commune of Lucca are stored, copies would be made for those who desired them'.[50] It was precisely due to the accessibility of this information that litigants were able to raise exceptions and engage in discussions concerning matters such as *banniti*, tax defaulters, and procedural faults in their lawsuits on the basis of clear-cut facts.

---

46 *Potestà*, 58, fol. 221r: 'dictam licentiam et capturam non valere nec tenere pluribus ractionibus [...] et per formam statuti Lucani communis de summaria ractione reddenda libro .iiii., capitulo .iii. in quo loquitur quod nullus potest capi vel detineri a soldis centum infra'.

47 For example, in a trial at the Court of Podestà wherein the plaintiff Tubia was suing villagers for land rent, one Pessuccio was appointed procurator for the defendants. Afterwards, one Ciardello joined the dispute between the plaintiff and the defendants, arguing that the defendants were his tenants, and that the complaint against them was unjust. It is notable that the defending procurator, Pessuccio, had the same surname – Malzardi – as Ciardello, who appeared later on. Here, we see a situation where the villagers, at the time they were sued, commissioned a procurator from the Malzardi family, with whom they had previously established a patronage relationship. *Potestà*, 67, fols. 288r-299r.

48 When proving that an opponent was *banniti*, litigants would submit copies from a register of *bannum* (e.g. *Potestà*, 60, fol. 222v: 'Item allegat et producit apodixam banpni dati contra Nucchorum suprascriptum publicatam manu Marchi de Camporeggiano notarii'), and copies of court records when proving that a case was *lite pendente* (e.g. *Potestà*, 60, fol. 55v: 'Item allegat et producit acta actitata in curia querimonie inter dictum Ubertum et dictum Biagium et ipsum ser Paganum publicata manu ser Guidi Luti Mai notarii dicte curie'). Also, when seeking to dismiss an exception by an opposing party regarding non-payment of taxes, litigants would submit proof of payment issued on the basis of financial records (For example, ASL, *Maggior Sindaco e Giudice degli Appelli*, 42, fol. 11v: 'allegaverunt et produxerunt quandam apodixam solutionis gabelle dotis dicte condam domine Balduccie'). Writings by the custodian of the *Archivio pubblico* were signed 'proof published by the hand of *ser* Tedaldino Lazari Gay, notary and custodian of the *Archivio pubblico* of the Commune of Lucca' ('apodixam publicatam manu ser Tedaldini Lazarii Gaii notarii et custodis librorum Camere Lucani communis'), *Potestà*, 60, fol. 141v.

49 For the case of Bologna, Cencetti, 'Camera actorum'. For Archivio pubblico s of the other cities, Koch, 'Die Archivierung', p. 43-49.

50 *Statuto della Curia 1331*, fol. 68r: 'in camera ubi morantur libri actorum curiarum et consiliorum et stantiamentorum et aliorum Lucani communis ita quod volentibus videre copia fiat et fieri possit'. For provisions regarding the copying of the *bannum*, see *Statuto 1308*, III, 78 (De faciendo exemplari nomina et pronomina inbanpnitorum maleficiorum), p. 190.

The information necessary for raising an exception also included details relating to the identity of individuals, such as whether they were foreigners, their age, and their kin relations. This information was not inherently within the purview of the communal administration and thus could not be obtained at the communal archive.[51] This kind of information was commonplace in society and thus 'stored' therein, so to speak.[52] At a trial in the Court of Podestà in 1338,[53] the plaintiff, Guiduccio Soldi, demanded that the defendant, Bartolomeo Ceci, should pay him the cost of repairing a certain house, to which Bartolomeo responded that the man, Gubbino, from whom Guiduccino had purchased the house, was a foreigner, noting that 'the late Gubbino was known as "Gubbino of Pistoia" by those who knew him'; he attempted to prove this with supporting testimony.[54] In Case A, summarised at the beginning of this section, it was similarly pointed out that Jacopino was a foreigner from Parma living in Lucca and that this was known to his acquaintances and so constituted *publica vox et fama*.[55] In this case, because it was common knowledge to the inhabitants that the man was a foreigner, it was being argued as evidence, demonstrating the certainty of the information. Undocumented information about uncertain or ambiguous personal identities was stockpiled in society and became 'truth' recognised as *fama publica* by those in the community.[56] Naturally, this kind of common social information is likely to have been more accessible to the litigants themselves than to the *podestà* – a six-month post held by an official from another city – or his judges.

This sort of information also applies to the information managed by the commune's archive. At a trial in the Court of San Cristoforo in 1304, it was proven by several witnesses that one Lamberto was under the ban. One of these witnesses, a man named Panello, testified to the effect that 'it is public knowledge and notorious in the *contrata* of San Benedetto in the porta of San Cervagio and the surrounding *contrata* that Lamberto was absent from the city and territory of Lucca and that he had already been *bannito* from the commune of Lucca for debt for eleven years'.[57] Others also testified that Lamberto's ban was a matter of *fama publica*.[58]

---

51 However, in Lucca, books for managing foreign citizens began to be prepared from the mid-fourteenth century, and these eventually came to be used as the basis of evidence. For example, in a criminal trial in 1363, one Augustino, who was being charged on suspicion of injury, submitted a copy of a book of foreigners (the *liber forensium*) to show that he was himself from another city. *Potestà*, 4887, fol. 29r.

52 Smail illustrates the ubiquity and public nature of information within the society on the basis of Marseilles case, Smail, *The Consumption of Justice*, p. 207-241.

53 *Potestà*, 82, fols. 38r-41v, 91r-92r.

54 *Potestà*, 82, fol. 40v: 'Item qualiter dictus condam Guibbinus fuit nominatus a cognoscentibus eum, Gubbinus de Pistorio'.

55 ASL, *Curia di San Cristoforo*, 112, fol. 85v: 'Item qualiter de predictis est publica vox et fama in civitate Lucana inter hominess et personas dictum Jacopinum cognoscentes'.

56 To the question of what is *fama publica*, one witness testifies that 'it is the truth'. *Potesta*, 37, fol. 6r: 'Interrogatus quid est dicere publicam vocem et famam-- dixit quid est verum'.

57 ASL, *Curia di San Cristoforo*, 9, fol. 30v: 'publicum et notorium est in contrata Sancti Benedicti porte Sancti Cervagii, et in aliis partibus circumstantibus ipsius contrate quod dictus Lambertus absens stetit a civitate Lucana et eius districtu, et inbanpnitus Lucani communis pro debito iam sunt anni xi'.

58 *Ibid.*, fols. 31r: 'dixit quod publica fama est in dicta contrata Sancti Benedicti et in porta Sancti Cervagii quod dictus Lambertus stetit inbapnitus et absens a civitate Lucana pro debito annis decem et ultra'.

The fact that many communal activities were conducted on the principle of openness underlined the wide spread nature of the information in society. For example, when messengers passed letters of complaints to defendants and summoned them to court, following the statutes, they often did so not only at the defendants' places of residence but also in the defendants' local neighbourhoods through a proclamation with *publice et alta voce*.[59] The *bannum*, too, after the *pronuntia* was declared before a judge, was read with *publice et alta voce* by a crier before the General Council.[60] In such an environment, inhabitants would gather information by listening carefully and making their preparations in order to raise an exception.

(6) Inhabitants' participation in the commune

The commune's activities provided inhabitants with information by virtue of their public nature, enabling litigants to raise an exception to pursue rule violations committed by their opponents. It seems possible that communal institutions became established on the premise of the people's *participation* therein. From this perspective, when we cast an eye over communal policy, we find that participation anywhere on the part of inhabitants, particularly in their use of denunciations, was recognised as having had an essential influence on the effectiveness of the policy (as has also been shown in another recent study that takes note of the significance of inhabitants' denunciations).[61]

For example, on 27 September 1333, the commune issued an official notice with the aim of managing public documents, as follows: 'Any person of any condition, to whom it came, or who had or knew, that anyone had any book, documents or something of any official, should denounce and present them before the *maggior sindaco* and his officials in the palace of San Michele in Mercato, today or by the end of the day tomorrow. Knowing one to be in possession of the aforesaid and having failed to denounce them would be regarded as theft'.[62] Here, denunciation by citizens is regarded as an indispensable means for collecting the communal records. In addition, according to a study by Geltner, in July 1347, prior to an outbreak of the Black Death, Lucca's communal office of roads issued an official notice regarding matters of urban hygiene, such as cleaning the area in front of one's own house and prohibiting animal slaughter near wells. At the end of this notice, it is explicitly stated that anyone was permitted to

---

59 ASL, *Curia di San Cristoforo*, 9, 64, fol. 58v: 'in vicinia publice et alta voce cum proclamatione ipsius nuntii'. The same thing is stipulated in the statutes. *Statuto della Curia 1331*, I, 3, fol. 4v: '[…] fiat citatio et libelli porrectio apud domum et publice in vicinia cum proclamatione nuntii'.

60 For example, *Potestà*, 67, fol. 56r: 'die viii novembris in simili banno positi fuerunt suprascripti rei debitores, mandato eiusdem domini iudicis in consilio generali congregato in palatio S. Michaelis in foro publice et alta voce per Francuccium Franceschini preconem publicum Lucani communis'; *Statuto 1308*, p. 184-188: 'Et quod elapsis ipsis terminis possit in banno ad bancum gridari. Et quod etiam nullo temporis intervallo interveniente, ipsa persona citata et non conparente, possit preconizari et inbanniri in Consilio generali'.

61 M. G. Muzzarelli (ed.), *Riferire all'autorità. Denuncia e delazione tra Medioevo ed Età Moderna* (Roma, 2020).

62 S. Bongi (ed.), *Bandi lucchesi del secolo decimo quarto* (Bologna, 1863), p. 12: 'Qualunqua persona di qualunqua conditione sia, alla quale fusse pervenuto o avesse, u sapesse che alcuno avesse alcuno libro, u scriptura, u alcuna cosa d'alcuno officiale, oggi e dimani per tutto die, li debbia avere denuntiati e presentati in palazzo di san Michele in Mercato, dinanthi al dicto messer lo Sindico et a suoi officiali, e serali tenuto credentia. Sappiendo chi le predette cose avesse e no le denuntiasse, u vero presentasse, si come di sopra è dicto, li sarebbe apposto per furto'.

denounce persons who violated the law and would be entitled to gain a reward from the resulting fine.[63] The most prominent example of this mandatory denunciation is likely the provision that the leaders of the *contrata* district were obliged to bring the ones who had committed malefactions before the *podestà*.[64] The issue of denouncing malefactions is also touched on in Chapter 4.

Official notices like the one described above were delivered throughout the city by official criers. The fact that the records of such notices, unlike other public records, were all written in the vernacular evokes the image of criers actually holding these texts in hand as they made their proclamations. Criers would attract attention by blowing their trumpets on street corners and then loudly announcing the contents of the ordinances in a language that residents would be able to understand.[65] In addition, as has already been pointed out in reference to existing laws, city statutes were attached by a chain to a desk at the *maggior sindaco*, where they were kept open so that they could be read and copied by anyone who wished to do so.[66] Thus, the commune amplified the power of inhabitants' denunciations, which were necessary for realising policy in practice, by promoting their legal literacy.

Seen in this way, exceptions, by which litigants discovered and pursued their opponents' violations of law in the courts and any misconduct of the court by checking them against city statutes, began to emerge very much as a typical example of the institutional management of the commune at the time. That is, in the context of a communal judicial arena in which the administrative laxity of judges and officials was notorious, the realisation and maintenance of order in the civil commune was supported by the participation in judicial administration activities on the part of the people themselves with their own interests in mind.

---

63 G. Geltner, 'Healthscaping a Medieval City: Lucca's Curia Viarum and the Future of Public Health History', *Urban History*, 40 (2013), p. 395-415, in particular p. 408; Id., *Roads to Health. Infrastructure and Urban Wellbeing in Later Medieval Italy* (Philadelphia, 2019).

64 *Statuto 1308*, III, 45 (De pena contrate non capientis et persequentis malefactores et non clamantis post eum), p. 164. The duties of neighbouring residents are also pointed out in 1342 statute. ASL, *Statuto del Comune di Lucca*, 5, I, 111 (De maleficiis denuntiandis per consules contratarum et brachiorum, et de pena vicinorum non capientium malefactores), fols. 35v-36r.

65 For example, *Potestà*, 64, no foliation, 6 May 1336: 'per Guiduccium Loppellie preconem publicum Lucani communis, bannitum et preconizatum fuit, ut supra per omniam continetur, in civitate Lucana burgos et suburgos, in locis et angulis consuetis, sono tube premisso'.

66 *Statuto della Curia 1331*, V, 57, fol. 68r: '… statutus fiat quod moretur ad banchum sindici cum catena litigatus…'; *Statuto 1308*, I, 16, p. 18-19: '…Statutum non debeat reculudi … quominus possit haberi et legi a quolibet volente ex inde copiam et ipsum exemplare'.

3. Speaking out to the Anziani

Table 2.3: Matters considered in this section

Dates	
1330, Jul. 30	Provision: Prohibition of detention due to debt
1330, Aug. 8	Supplement: Complaint: Tax defaulters should be no longer eligible to civil trial ⇒ becomes a statutory provision
1330, Aug. 14	Provision: Prohibition of detention due to debt
1330, Sep. 30	Deregulation: Complaint: Eligibility for trial can be restored by a citizen's payment of outstanding tax ⇒ Authorised
1330, Sep. 30	Provision: Prohibition of detention due to debt
1331	Revision of the City Statute
1333, Dec. 20	Provision: Prohibition of detention due to debt
1334, Jan. 29	Exemption: Complaint by Micheluccia regarding the validity of documents
1334, Feb. 11	Supplement: Addition of cases concerning livestock leasing to those subject to summary justice
1334, Nov. 28	Exemption: Complaint by Ciardello regarding the validity of documents
1334, Nov. 28	Provision: Prohibition of detention due to debt
1335, Jan. 25	Exemption: Complaint by Coluccio regarding the validity of contracts with foreigners
1335, Oct. 10	Supplement: Complaint: Those who do not belong to vigilance group are no longer eligible to civil trial ⇒ Addendum
1335, Oct. 22	Provision: Extension of the prohibition on detention due to debt
1336, Jul. 20	Official notice seeking the views of citizens when supplementing City Statutes
1336, Dec. 3	Revision of the City Statute
1336, Jun. 1	Exemption: Complaint by the foreigner Bacciano regarding the validity of contracts
1339, Dec. 8	Exemption: Complaint by the foreigner Vannuccio regarding the validity of contracts
1342	Revision of the City Statute
1342, Sep. 21	Provision: Prohibition of detention due to debt (for farmers)
1353	Deregulation: Complaint: Measures to the fraudulent refuse of inheritance by peasants ⇒ Amendment to provisions

(1) Inhabitants' involvement in legislation

In 1336, the vicar of the *podestà* issued citizens with an interesting official notice, as follows:

> Any person from the city of Lucca, the *contado*, or surroundings, who wishes to express any good and useful matter to be placed in and added to the Statutes of the Commune of Lucca, which are presently under revision, or else who wishes to express anything that should be withdrawn or struck from the aforementioned statutes for the sake of their improvement, is to make their case in writing before the statute compilers in the House of the Anziani within three days.[67]

This notice still exists in the form of a scrap of paper, which states further that '[the notice] was given by the crier Pecchino Benetti on 20 July'. As noted above, this leads us to imagine that the crier was actually reading out the above announcement in the city streets, carrying this piece of paper in his hands.[68] The year 1336 fell during the period of the rule of Mastino and that of Alberto della Scala, and it seems to have been a year when many changes and revisions to the statutes were carried out on their orders.[69] Looking at city statutes from 1331, we find provisions written under the title 'Addendum given on 3 December 1331' at the end of each chapter.[70] It seems that that the statute compilers tasked with revising these statutes set about their task by listening to the voices of the common people and not only to the governing council.

The legislative activities of the medieval Italian cities included revisions of their statutes,[71] which were irregularly observed every few years, sometimes once a decade, and the promulgation of provisions or *stantiamentum* regularly done by the Anziani and their council. The latter had in itself the same legal effect as the city statutes, were frequently cited in trials, and were often incorporated into the city statutes. These legislative activities were the exclusive arena of jurists, who served as the statutes' compilers, and members of the city's influential families, made up of the Anziani and the council. Particularly in Lucca, the Anziani, comprising ten men for every two-month term, was a powerful executive institution. An election method was adopted wherein

---

67 *Potestà*, 64, no foliation, 20 July 1336: 'Da parte del Vicario di messer lo Podestà; Bandisce che qualunco persona della città di Lucca o del contado o borghi e soborghi, volesse dire e mostrare alcuna cosa buona e utile a mettere e agiungere in nelli Statuti del Commune di Lucca, li quali presentialmente si fanno, o volesse dire o mostrare che alcuna cosa de' detti Statuti per lo milliore si dovesse traere o cassare, diano per scripto dinanzi alli statutari sopra ciò diputati, li quali domorano in casa de' signori Antiani, infra il terzo die'. S. Bongi (ed.), *Bandi Lucchesi*, p. 37.

68 *Potestà*, 64, no foliation, 20 July 1336: 'factum per Pecchinum Benecti preconem die xx Julii' This scrap of paper was found tucked in a court record book from the Court of Podestà. Aside from this scrap of paper, the same content was recorded in the record books of the notices of Anziani (the *liber preconiationum*).

69 S. Bongi (ed.), *Inventario del Reale Archivio di Stato in Lucca*, I (Lucca, 1872), p. 31.

70 *Statuto 1331*, p. 150.

71 Revisions to Lucca's city statutes were sometimes sweeping, sometimes minor. In 1308, under the regime of the Guelph and *popolo*, in 1316, under the rule of Castruccio, in 1331, under the rule of John of Bohemia, in 1342, under Pisan rule, in 1372, when Lucca recovered its sovereignty, and so on – the sweeping revisions that were carried out with each change in regime were accompanied by the compilation of new statutes. By contrast, revisions could sometimes be only additions and amendments to existing statutes, such as those of 1336, or else in other years minor additions or amendments deriving from decrees issued by the Anziani as appropriate.

the preceding Anziani nominated their successors, and the Anziani also selected the councillors; direct participation in the political activity of enacting laws was restricted to the oligarchic members of certain influential families.[72] In that sense, although the Italian cities enjoyed a certain autonomy, they were still a long way from being democratic institutions based on our own current standards.[73]

Nevertheless, the official notice mentioned above shows that the common people took part indirectly in the context of the revision of city statutes. And in fact, we find many other cases in which inhabitants engaged in pleading with the Anziani, which in turn led to the enactment of provisions that were incorporated into the city statutes.

Those exceptions raised in the courts which the parties used to pursue the legal violations of opposing parties based on city statutes and the provisions, had the effect of realising the contents of the communal legal system in *substantive* terms. This might be said to have been a practice that in judicial settings placed an emphasis on formal compliance with the law. In contrast, in this section I examine the complaints of inhabitants presented in a separate room of the same communal palace that also housed the Court of Podestà, the room where the governing council of the Anziani met as the political representatives of the commune. There, complaints were raised by people seeking not compliance with existing laws but rather extensions or revisions of laws – or else exemptions from their application – regarding the issues of civil rights matters. The inhabitants not only complied with previously established rules but also 'corrected' laws and regulations in accordance with their own interests and circumstances. In this sense, their behaviour also had the effect of shaking up the communal legal system. Here, it will become clear that complaints to the political sphere by people had the effect of 'rationalising' the law in a different form than exceptions in the courts and attempting – at least outwardly – to orient it towards the *bene del comune*.

72 The election of the Anziani employed a method that gave considerable influence to their predecessors in office. A statute from 1342 states that every November, the Anziani then in office and the ten *sapientes* chosen by the Anziani and the vicar would choose one hundred electors (twenty for each ward). Then, these electors and the Anziani in office would choose the Anziani candidates (six groups of ten men) for the following year. Electors each had the right to nominate one individual, after which the sixty future Anziani candidates would be chosen by voting. Grouping was done so that no fathers, sons, or siblings would be in the same group. The names of the future Anziani listed in each group were placed in a bag, and then, eight days before the end of the term of each Anziani, a child under the age of ten would randomly pick the next Anziani group from the bag. An interval of one year was deemed necessary before someone could be appointed as a member of the Anziani again. Although this method of selection might seem to have ensured fairness through indirect election and lottery, in practice, candidates still had to be nominated by their Anziani predecessors and by the electors chosen by them.

73 According to Zorzi, political participation was only realised by approximately twenty percent of the citizenry, even in cities that had adopted representative systems like the districts or *arte*. See A. Zorzi, *Le signorie cittadine in Italia (secoli XIII-XV)* (Milano, 2010), p. XII.

(2) Inhabitants' claims and the revision of statutes

i). Revision of statutes

Looking at the city statutes for 1331, we find not only the addition of laws enacted at the time of large-scale revisions in 1336 but also several minor annotations in the margins of the texts of the existing statutes (Figure 2). This shows that the day-to-day provisions issued by the Anziani resulted in occasional updates to the city statutes. And these Anziani decrees were motivated by the complaints of inhabitants. Let us consider some examples of additions and amendments to the city statutes.

An Anziani provision dated 11 February 1334 was motivated by the following complaint submitted before the council. The complainants were inhabitants of Lucca and its surrounding territory who loaned out livestock in exchange for a rental fee. They complained that insolvent cases of livestock rent should be dealt with using the observance of summary justice proceedings at the Court of Podestà, as was the case for unpaid rent for immovables. According to them, while summary procedures had been customarily applied in the past on livestock leasing matters, the judges of the current *podestà* did not follow this custom on the grounds that the statutes made no explicit mention of applying summary procedure to such cases. This meant that those who contracted out livestock were no longer able to have their clients arrested for non-payment on the authority of the *podestà* and as such were suffering major losses.[74]

In response to this complaint, the Anziani ruled that the judges of the current *podestà* should observe summary justice even in insolvency cases concerning livestock leasing and should issue orders to detain insolvents and have their property seized. Most likely in response to this ruling by the Anziani, in the margin of a provision in the 1331 city statutes discussing summary justice, alongside a mark indicating '*additio*', we find an annotation to the effect that summary justice should also be applied in connection with livestock leasing matters (*collaris et soccitis*).[75]

Book 5, Chapter 10 of the 1331 statutes, 'On the punishment of those who have not joined a vigilance group (*bapneria*) and who have not assumed their civic duty (*honera*)', which we saw in the previous section, also seems to have been issued from

74 *Anz. Av. Lib.*, 5, p. 54: 'Coram vobis dominis… Antianis Lucani communis reverenter exponitur pro parte civium Lucanorum et districtualium habentium bestias ad collariam quod consuetum est de soccitis et collariis fieri summarium ius prout fit de affictibus et redditibus per iudicem et curiam potestatis Lucane modo vero iudex presentis potestatis non vult cognoscere questiones soccitarum et collariarum neque signare cartas soccitarum prout consuetum est, dicens non esse sibi et suo officio concessum per statutum de summaria ratione reddenda et quod semper pro soccitis et collariis homines fuerunt capti ex officio potestatis et carte fuerunt signate prout carte affictuum et pensionuum qua occasione Lucani cives et comitativi habentes bestias ad collariam in maximum damnum devenerunt pro eo quod nullus capitur nisi officio potestatis…'

75 *Statuto 1331*, p. 123: 'Et etiam quod potestas possit se intromictere de questionibus viduarum, pupillorum et miserabilium personarum et etiam de redditibus et affictibus, [collariis et soccitis], pensionibus et livellis retentis et pro eis redditores et affictuales, pensionarios et livellarios personaliter capi facere et detineri quam diu solverint [dum tamen de predictis redditibus, affictibus, pensionibus, collariis et soccitis appareant publice scripture seu dactiones vel confessiones secundum formam statutorum salvis semper eorum defensionibus]'. The text in brackets here corresponds to marginal notations that were interpolated into the main text at a later date.

and been amended by Anziani decrees based on citizens' complaints.[76] The central concern of this clause, which cannot be confirmed in the 1308 statutes and is only apparent for the first time in the 1331 statutes, was on stripping tax defaulters of their right to receive a civil trial. Behind the issue of this provision seems to be the taxation carried out between July and September of 1330 and the sanctions implemented against tax defaulters. In particular, a complaint by inhabitants resulting from a decision dated 8 August, noting that individuals who had fled Lucca to live in Pisa continued to collect rent on houses and lands regardless of the fact that they were not taxed and did not pay tax, asked, for the benefit of the commune of Lucca, that only taxpayers who have paid their taxes should have the ability to bring suits in civil courts.[77] In response, the Anziani issued a decree in line with the content of the complaint. The provision in Book 5, Chapter 10 of the 1331 Anziani seems to have been created based on this 1330 Anziani decree, in the form of supplementing the content with the ruling that participation in the vigilance group was a type of civic duty.

The same chapter of the city statutes contains a supplementary note in the margins of a certain page. First of all, whereas the original text of the statute stated that *of those who have joined* a vigilance group, those who have not fulfilled their personal or material obligations (*honera realia et personalia*) are not entitled to trial, there is no provision here regarding the rights of individuals who have never been enrolled in the vigilance group. Then, following a statement to the effect that *those who have not joined* a vigilance group should be fined, a note has been added in the margin to the effect that the trial (*ius*) is not held for them in civil cases in the city of Lucca, which was marked to be inserted into the text (Figure 2.2).[78]

This addition was a consequence of an Anziani decree dated 10 October 1335 based on complaints from the people.[79] The complaint from the 'subjects and faithful' to the Anziani and the vicar held that because so many citizens were absent from the city, the burden of material obligations on the citizens who remained was that much greater, and they therefore sought to have defaulters – absentees and residents alike – rendered ineligible to bring cases to civil trial. It seems likely that these absentees would have been people not registered with the vigilance group. In response to the complaint, the Anziani directed that the statutes should be supplemented with an addendum. The margins of this Anziani decree in the book of Anziani are annotated to the effect that 'this addendum has been made to the city statutes with reference to those who are not subject to the orders of the commune of Lucca and those who have not enlisted in the vigilance group of city districts'.[80]

76 *Statuto 1331*, V, 10 (De pena illorum qui non fuerint in bapneria et honera civitatis non subierint), p. 164.

77 Nelli and Simonetti (eds.), *Anziani*, p. 112.

78 *Statuto 1331*, p. 164: 'Et qui se sic scribi non fecerit condempnetur per potestatem in libris .x. denariorum Lucanorum omni appellatione cessante [main text]'; 'add. ei ius non fiat in causis civilibus in aliqua curia Lucane civitatis [marginal notation]'.

79 *Anz. Av. Lib.*, 9, fol. 42r.

80 *Ibid.*, p. 83: 'quidam additio suprascripta statuto Lucani communis contra non respondentes Lucano communi nec scriptos in banneriis contrate et brachii civitatis'.

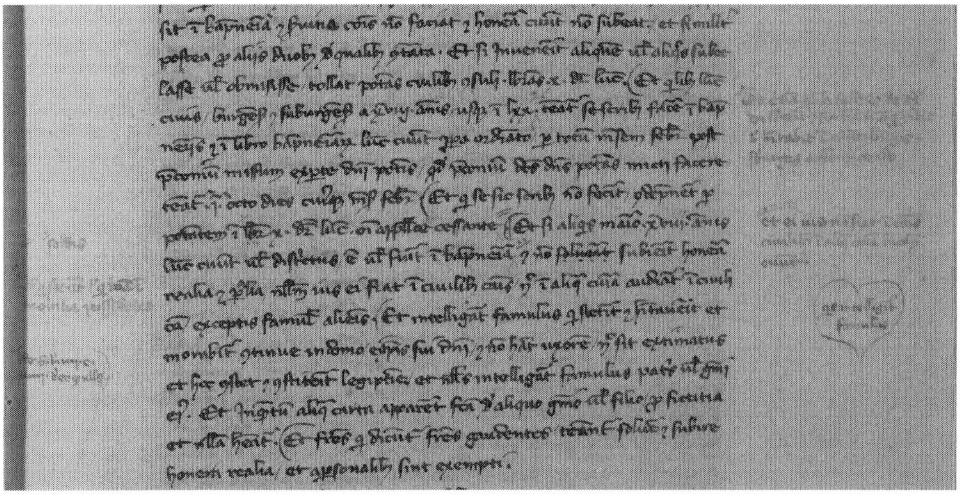

Figure 2.2: Text of the 1331 city statutes with marginal annotations (*Statuto 1331*, p. 164)

Such minor amendments and additions are apparent here and there in the copy of the 1331 statutes. These were the result of various problems that arose when the legal provisions were put into actual practice. In the above case, we can conceive of a situation in which, because the text of the original clause was ambiguous, a formal exception was presented in court, whereupon a detailed rule was added to prevent a recurrence. However, even were the law to be strictly enforced, the possibility remained that it could be rendered toothless by an exception from one of the parties. As we shall see next, in such cases measures were taken to relax laws or limit the scope of their application.

ii). Relaxing the conditions of application and setting exemptions

On 21 June 1353, a citizens' complaint to the Anziani was brought before the Council of Fifty.[81] According to the complaint, a certain statutory provision had been issued as a measure against individuals who sought to evade the payment of land rent by fraudulent means. This provision stipulated that upon the death of a tenant farmer, in the case that a son aged eighteen years or older refused to inherited their father's estate, then the son must notify the court of Lucca in writing with regard to the land on which his father had paid rent. At present, however, cases were appearing of individuals who, despite their refusal to inherit the estates of tenant farmer fathers, were not making notifications and moreover were attempting to evade the payment of rent. As the statute stipulated that the provision would be effective *only if it were proven* that the land rent had been paid in the past, actually proving this was difficult. Many citizens would lose their land rent as the result of such fraudulent refusals to inherit, and the intended effect of the statute

81 *Anz. Av. Lib.*, 35, fols. 58r-59v.

would be null. Having explained the situation thusly, the complaint requested that the statutory provision should be applied if it could not be proven in writing that land rent had been paid, stating that 'attention should be paid to the spirit, not the wording, of the statute and of those who enacted the statutes and laws'.[82]

The members of the Council of Fifty passed an amendment, as suggested in the complaint. From here, an image emerges of the circumstances in which a statutory provision that had been issued to deal with cunning peasants lost its effectiveness in court when confronted with an exception raised by peasants on a formal matter (i.e. proof of rental payments). Therefore, citizens complained to the governing council to request that the strictness of the law be relaxed in light of its original purpose. This request for the 'rationalisation' of the law was accepted by the council and the Anziani.

Whereas the above example called for the relaxation of a law as a measure against an exception raised in terms of formal compliance with that law, the next example is one in which the abuse of a statutory provision by exceptions resulted in the limitation of the same provision's scope of application and the setting of an exception. This provision is one we also saw in the previous section, that is, Book 3, Chapter 10 'Regarding that the trial should not be held for those subject to *bannum*'.[83] This was set as a sanction against defiance of orders by the commune and led to a situation in which many people lost the right to trial. For peasants, however, this proved to be an excellent means by which to render ineffective the complaints of landowners who found themselves under *bannum*. For citizens whose main source of income was rent from rural villages, this provision was fraught with great danger.

As a measure to avoid this danger, already from the statutes of 1308 a provision limiting the scope of application of the same rule had been issued separately. This was the provision in Book 4, Chapter 10, 'On exception concerning *bannum* that should not be presented against [one's] own landlords', which stipulated that peasants were not allowed to raise an exception relating to *bannum* against their own landlords and that judges must not pay heed to such claims even if such were to be made.[84] We can imagine a process by which, in response to cases in which insolvent peasants cited the *bannum* of their landlords in an attempt to stall trials, landowning citizens might raise their concerns, resulting in the establishment of an exception to the statutory provision that had led to the suspension of the trial eligibility of *banniti*.

Earlier, I noted how the provision stipulating that tax defaulters, like *banniti*, lost their eligibility for trial was incorporated into the city statutes in 1331 after its inception in the Anziani decrees between July and September 1330. Against this provision, however, a move was soon afoot to set exceptions to its application. On 30 September 1330, in order not to give peasants who were behind with rent payments further opportunity to dodge their obligations, a citizens' claim requested that, even if they paid the tax arrears later, the deferred payer's activities in court should be rendered effective just as

82 *Anz. Av. Lib.*, 35, fol. 59r: 'mens statuti et condentium statuta et leges debeat attendi potius quam verba…'

83 *Statuto 1308*, III, 80 (De non faciendo rationem imbanpnitis), p. 192.

84 *Statuto 1308*, IV, 10 (De exceptione imbanpnimenti vel alia non opponenda contra dominum suum), p. 256-257.

if payment had been made before the trial began.[85] Behind this claim, clearly, would appear to be a situation in which a trial brought by a landowner to sue for delinquent land rent had been thwarted by an exception raised by a defendant peasant taking aim in turn at the tax arrears of the landowner. In response, the Anziani, after conferring with jurists, issued a decree in line with the substance of the claim. This case may be counted as an example of a complaint by citizens confronted with an exceptions that resulted in a decree setting an exception to the application of a statute.

(3) Individual exemptions

i). Subjects of the claims

What we have seen so far, either in the form of additions to the text of a statute or as restrictions to the scope of a provision's application, has concerned new decrees issued on the basis of requests from the inhabitants – in other words, the establishment of rules and laws *that applied to all inhabitants*. Here, interestingly, the subjects of such complaints are recorded not as specific individuals, but as the citizenry as a whole or a group of people with an interest in a specific issue, 'on the part of the citizens of Lucca',[86] or for the 'subjects and faithful', or else 'on the part of citizens of the city and territory of Lucca having livestock in livestock leasing contract'. Just how many inhabitants were actually involved in bringing claims cannot be determined, and the possibility remains that the 'voice' of the citizenry was arbitrarily taken up by the Anziani to be converted into a generalised request to the commune. In any case, it seems certain that the Anziani and their clerks had an awareness that the enactment of laws to be applied to the citizenry as a whole should be done based on the complaints of unspecified inhabitants rather than of specific persons.

In contrast, many of the decrees of the Anziani can also be seen to concern individual complaints raised by specific people. What was being requested in these cases was not the enactment of new laws but individual exemptions from the application of existing provisions. While this also applies to the claims seeking pardons (*gratia*) in the criminal cases I examine in Chapter 5, in this section, regarding individual claims in the civil sphere, I would like to look at matters pertaining to the authenticity of documents and to transactions with foreign citizens.

ii). The exceptional recognition of copies in the absence of original registries

On 29 January 1334, a woman named Micheluccia, the widow of the late Coluccio, brought a complaint before the Anziani.[87] According to the complaint, a man named Bendinello had also brought a suit against Micheluccia at the Court of San Cristoforo for a debt of 331 *lire* incurred forty years earlier. The debt in question had been paid

85 Nelli and Simonetti (eds.), *Anziani*, p. 130-131.
86 *Anz. Av. Lib.*, 35, fol. 58v.
87 *Anz. Av. Lib.*, 5, p. 44-45.

thirty years previously. However, the certificate of restitution had been in the registry of a notary named *ser* Guglielmo, and all that the widow now possessed as proof of restitution was a copy taken from the same registry by Enrico, Guglielmo's son. Her opponent, Bendinello, argued that the copy should not be trusted unless it could be verified against the original registry, and that, as Guglielmo's registry had since been lost, and Guglielmo and Enrico were themselves no longer in Lucca, having been exiled in 1314, verification against the original record was not possible. Micheluccia thus requested that the copy proving that the debt had been paid should be trusted as if it were a certificate verified against the original register. In response to this complaint, the Anziani decided to have five experts verify the document in accordance with the procedure for restoring a lost dotal certificate,[88] whereupon the trial was suspended with the litigants agreeing to adhere to the results of the verification. The text of the decision is appended with the note 'any matters arising contrary to statute, *stantiamentum*, ordinance, law or *ius* notwithstanding'.[89]

In another, similar example, the Anziani were unable to take the measure of making an individual exception. In the case of a complaint on 28 November 1334, in which one Ciardello requested validation of a document of debt for which the original had been destroyed in a fire, the Anziani sought advice from three jurists.[90] Here, one jurist argued in favour of conducting the procedure of validating the deed as per the complaint, while another argued that the copy should be considered to possess the same validity as the original, given that the copy clearly resembled the original, which was lost in a fire. However, the Anziani chose to adopt the view of the final jurist, who argued solely that the statutes of Lucca should be upheld. No new measures were taken in the end. While a different decision was rendered here than in the case we saw earlier, the reasoning in the previous case was most likely that the complainant was a widow, and so it would have been easy to apply the existing procedure used for restoring a dotal certificate. Even so, I would like to draw attention to the fact that, although their views were not adopted, this case also featured jurists arguing in favour of procedures that would have departed from the city statutes.

The record of decisions by the Anziani for the 1330s contains many decrees concerning loss of documents. On 5 October 1334, a decision was taken that would prohibit exceptions from being cunningly deployed, in a case where the indirect taxation records necessary for validating sales contracts had been destroyed in a fire.[91] Also, in a claim heard on 27 February 1338, *ser* Giovanni requested that copies taken from a 1275 communal register containing confessions from tenant farmers that had since been lost

---

88 One record book containing cases of the restoration of *dote* remains extant. See ASL, *Sei deputati sul reintegrare le doti*, 1. According to Bongi, this is based on a 1317 decree stipulating the recovery of documents pertaining to women's rights from among documents destroyed by fire during the sacking of Lucca in 1314. Bongi (ed.), *Inventario*, II, p. 333-334.

89 *Anz. Av. Lib.*, 5, p. 45: 'statuto, stantiamento, ordine, lege vel iure aliquo contrario non obstante'.

90 *Anz. Av. Lib.*, 6, p. 46-47. According to the complaint, the document of debt had been copied by the notary, *ser* Opizzo, from an original ledger belonging to *ser* Spalla. As *ser* Spallaa had been a custodian of the communal *Archivio pubblico*, his original had been destroyed in the burning of the *Archivio pubblico*.

91 *Anz. Av. Lib.*, 7, fol. 42v. This is a decree that was applied to the citizenry as a whole.

should be granted the same authenticity as the original, with the result that the claim was authorised.[92]

Several political shifts took place during the decade of the 1330s, which saw the frequent banning and migration of notaries and the disappearance of documents. At the same time, this caused the problem of the loss of originals and the authenticity of copies frequently becoming the subject of exceptions even in the courts. In these circumstances, simply following the basic principles of the notary system, in which the validity of notarised certificates was ensured by verification against original documents, was no longer a guarantee of the rights system by the commune. This was the reason why the Anziani authorised individual exceptions.

In this context, perhaps stimulated by the large numbers of individual complaints, in the city statutes after 1336 a provision was added entitled 'On notary papers to be rendered in public form'.[93] The provision stated that in a case where a paper prepared by a notary who has since died is found and is not in a public format, a notary holding the authority to render the paper of the deceased notary into a public form shall be able to prepare a notarised certificate from that paper, and also if it is determined that the memorandum in question should be seen as trustworthy based on an inquiry conducted by a vicar of the *podestà*, the head of the city's jurist association (*collegium iudicum*), and four notaries selected by the vicar. Although this provision relates to scraps of paper and thus differs from the case of the certificate presented earlier, we see here the introduction of a procedure that seeks to confer credibility (pursuant to an inquiry) on papers that had not been deemed trustworthy in previous statutes.

iii). The exceptional legalisation of contracts with foreign citizens

Contracts with foreign citizens from other cities, especially contracts relating to land transactions, were already prohibited by Lucchese statutes. In the courts, exceptions were frequently raised attempting to void contracts by pointing out that the other party's rights were derived from contracts with foreigners or from contracts drafted by foreign notaries.[94] During the exact same period, claims were also being raised in the room where the Anziani gathered, in the same palace as the Court of Podestà, seeking to have contracts with foreign citizens recognised as valid on an exceptional basis.

On 25 January 1336, a Lucchese citizen named Coluccio Matteo, having had difficulty paying his taxes, expressed his desire to sell his house in Lucca to a notary named *ser* Lando from Santa Maria in Monte (located outside the territory of Lucca) and requested that the sale be rendered valid, unhindered by any of the provisions in the city statutes.[95] In response, deeming that agreement between the two parties would be to their mutual benefit, the Anziani permitted the house to be sold at a price agreed by

92 *Anz. Av. Lib.*, 13, p. 13-14. This is an individual decree based on an individual complaint.

93 *Statuto 1331*, p. 155: 'De cedulis notariorum redigendis in publica forma'. This provision was carried over to the new statutes compiled in 1342.

94 *Statuto 1308*, IV, 73 (De eo quod venditiones facte non subiecto iurisdictioni Lucani Comunis sint casse. Et quod omne augmentum dotis factum uxoribus fictitium presumatur in maleficiis), p. 289.

95 *Anz. Av. Lib.*, 9, fols. 6r-v.

both parties. And at the end of the decision, a phrase was added to the effect that the decision should not be hindered by any other decrees or statutes. On 1 June 1336, a man named Ligo, a native of Bacciano (also outside Lucchese territory), expressed his wish to sell his land and rent-collection rights. To this, as well, the Anziani decided to recognise the legality of the sale of land unhindered by any statutes or decrees.[96]

While these complaints sought the exceptional validation of contracts with foreigners that had yet to be concluded, complaints were also brought requesting the retroactive validation of past contracts and legal actions. According to a 1339 complaint addressed to the rector's vicar, Guglielmo, by a man named Giovanni Pieri, following the latter's father's death, as heir he had brought a complaint of default on debts owed against one Franchuccio in the foreign prince's court in 1330 and had won property from said Franchuccio in the form of collateral.[97] However, although Giovanni had been born and raised in Lucca, his father had been a foreign citizen (a native of Brescia), and Giovanni expressed fears that this fact might invalidate his collateral right to the property. Moreover, the certificate granting him the property as collateral had been drafted by a clerk in the foreign Rectors' Court that hailed originally from Pistoia (outside the territory of Lucca). These collateral rights had been granted at the direction of the rector's vicar; at the time, Giovanni had been quite young and ignorant of any statutory provisions. He now hoped that his collateral rights and his rights certificate could be rendered legally valid by special favour of the Anziani, even if this seemingly ran contrary to Lucca's city statutes. In response to this complaint, the Anziani and the rector's vicar, after confirming the relevant certificates, and in consideration of the fact that Giovanni had been born in Lucca, that he had been a minor when he acquired the property as collateral, and that a child's legal actions should be handled in favour of the child, issued a decision to the effect that the rights were valid and that his property could be legally bought and sold.[98]

On 8 December 1339, a petition was issued regarding the purchase by Vannuccio Betti and two others, from the rural village of Calci in Pisa, of property in the territory of Lucca from Rosa, widow of the late Bono, a native of Pistoia. Both parties desired an exception to be made to have the purchase (which had taken place on 26 October 1338) treated as valid.[99] Vannuccio and his partners argued that they were now ready to pay the communal tax that had been imposed on Rosa for the property and that therefore the transaction could be undertaken without any injury to the commune of Lucca. In response to the complaint, the Anziani authorised the exception from the application of the relevant statutes and recognised the legality of the purchase on

96 *Anz. Av. Lib.*, 10, fol. 13v.

97 *Anz. Av. Lib.*, 14, fols. 9r-10r.

98 Here again, the special exemption of this case from the application of the relevant statutes, etc., has been explicitly noted. *Anz. Av. Lib.*, 14, fol. 10r: '...statutis, ordinamentis aut capitulis Lucani communis in contrarium apperentibus non obstantibus quibuscumque quibus auctoritate presentis stantiamenti quantum ad dictum insolutum et bona et iura contenta in eo et ad personam ipsius Johannis oriundi de civitate Lucana ut dictum est intelligatur et sit specialiter derogatum'.

99 *Anz. Av. Lib.*, 14, fols. 88r-v.

condition that the rights of those who held claims against Rosa would be reserved, and that Vannuccio and his partners would fulfil their obligations to Lucca.

(4) The enactment of laws by the Anziani and exemption criteria

i). The bene del comune *and the protection of individual rights*

The decrees issued by the Anziani were frequently appended with a phrase meaning 'statute notwithstanding'. To put it another way, decrees with such wording highlight the fact that they were inconsistent with existing statutes. The activities of the Anziani, then, were free, and not strictly bound by positive law. However, if that were the case, or precisely because that was the case, the Anziani must have felt the need to justify any decisions they took to amend laws or to allow exemptions to laws' application.

When we look for reasons justifying the decisions described in the records, we find that they were provided first of all by the inhabitants. For example, in the complaints brought in 1330 and 1335 against the legal provision stripping those who had not fulfilled their obligations to the city of their eligibility to receive trial, the reasons given were that this would be 'for the utility of the commune of Lucca'[100] and 'for more useful treasury of Lucca'.[101] Also, in the claim brought in 1330 requesting that earlier legal activities should be considered valid with the payment of taxes, the reasoning provided was that this was done in order not to give tenant farmers an excuse to dodge their rental payments.

In claims requesting individual exemptions from the law, with regard to the validity of (copies of) documents an extraordinary situation was taken up concerning the unforeseen destruction of an original ledger. In the context of contracts with foreign citizens, matters such as tax payments, being a widow, having a foreign citizen as a parent but being born Lucchese oneself, and being a child at the time of receiving a transfer of rights, were all cited by the Anziani as reasons for making the claims admissible. Anziani, when accepting claims, also mentioned their reasons for doing so, for example because the foreign buyer would pay the taxes on a property.[102]

However, even summarising in this way the kind of reasoning that obliged them to make decisions that ran counter to existing laws, it seems that the reasoning would vary from case to case, without any sort of consistency. One even begins to think that any claim at all might have been accepted, as long as the need and motive to issue a decision were stated.

Did any criteria exist for screening claims by the Anziani and the council, or any criteria of justice that legitimised certain decisions than ran counter to the law? Assuming such to have been the case, what might they have been? Finding an answer to this question is not easy, because the record of Anziani resolutions basically contains

100 Nelli and Simonetti (eds.), *Anziani*, p. 112: 'pro utilitate Lucani Communis'.

101 *Anz. Av. Lib.*, 9, fol. 42r: 'pro utiliori Lucani fisci'.

102 *Anz. Av. Lib.*, 14, fol. 88r: '... considerato quod ipsi Vannuccius, Boninus et Bectuccius volunt et se offerunt pro ipisis bonis substinere onera Lucani communis que ipsa domina Rosa substinet et substinebat'.

only the complaints that were ultimately approved and the decrees that were issued on that basis, so the nature of the citizens' complaints that were rejected remains unclear. However, if we look very carefully and extensively at the decrees issued by the Anziani, the presence emerges of an ultimate goal, 'the utility of the commune', and an uncrossable line, 'the protection of the rights of individuals'.

In one decree noted above, issued on 30 September 1330, stipulating that, if they paid their taxes, the prior legal activities of tax defaulters would be rendered valid, the Anziani received advice from the jurist Simone de Camporeggiano to the effect that 'this petition is lawful and brings no damage to the commune of Lucca'.[103] Here, from the context, 'damage to the commune' would seem to mean injury in a financial sense. Furthermore, in the claim brought in 1339 by Vannuccio and Rosa requesting the validation of a contract of sale of property to a foreign citizen, it was argued by virtue of the payment of taxes to the commune that the contract was carried out 'without injury to the commune of Lucca'.[104] In this case, both claimants were attempting to convince the Anziani by drawing attention to the fact that the payment of taxes would not injure but contribute to the communal finances.

What the Anziani had in mind as 'damage to the commune of Lucca' when scrutinising citizens' claims, however, was not injury to the commune in the narrow sense of an impact on the communal treasury; decisions that were deleterious to the finances of the commune, at least over the short term, are repeatedly seen in the records of the Anziani, as in the case of tax reductions or exemption measures and the conferral of tax exemption privileges. Instead, might it not have been that the Anziani, as the political leaders of the commune, had in mind not just the interests of the commune in the narrow sense, as a governing institution, but the good of the commune in the broad sense, implying the whole citizenry body?

In their consideration of the *bene del comune* in this broad sense, they paid scrupulous attention to the protection of individual rights. Looking over the record of Anziani decrees, we find none that would seem in any way injurious to the rights of any specific individual. Even in the examples we have seen thus far, when issuing decisions that were inconsistent with existing laws, consideration was still given to the fact that doing so would be injurious to the rights of specific individuals. In the Anziani decision of 1339 that legalised, on an exceptional basis, the purchase of land from Rosa by the foreigner Vannuccio, a reservation condition was attached so that 'this would and could not cause injury to anyone to whom Rosa was obligated until this day'.[105]

The Anziani took pains to ensure that their discretionary decisions, in forms that ran counter to positive law, did not end up infringing on the rights of private individuals. This principle of not infringing on the rights of individuals is also suggested from the fact that the Anziani did not make decisions that might have favoured one party over

103 Nelli and Simonetti (eds.), *Anziani*, p. 130-131: 'habito colloquio cum domino Simone de Camporeggiano iudice et advocato Communis Lucani qui sic nobis respondit videlicet "videtur mihi Simoni advocato Communis quod dicta petitio sit iuridica nec redundat in dapnum Lucani Communis"'.

104 *Anz. Av. Lib.*, 14, fols. 88r-v: '...absque preiudicio Lucani Communis'.

105 *Anz. Av. Lib.*, 14, fol. 88r: 'Salvo etiam quod hec non preiudicent nec preiudicare possint alicui cui dicta domina Rosa foret obligata usque ad hanc diem'.

another during times of civil strife.[106] It seems probable that the Anziani of this period recognised that civil matters belonged outside the remit of government activities, and were instead in the jurisdiction of the jurists who carried on the *ius commune* and its legal system and the city courts grounded in that legal culture.

ii). Was the detention of debtors appropriate?

How could the protection of the *bene del comune* be compatible with the principle of not infringing on the rights of individuals? This was the greatest challenge confronting the commune's governing council. The best case for thinking about this problem is the handling of legal customs and legal provisions that enabled creditors to personally detain debtors (or to have them detained). Already in 1308 it had been stipulated in a clause pertaining to summary justice in Book 4, Chapter 3 of the Statutes of the Commune of Lucca that creditors who brought their claims before the *podestà* with a certificate showing their claim would be allowed to have debtors with overdue payments arrested and detained until they were provided with a guarantor.[107] Seemingly, the detention of debtors by creditors was not only the statutory provision but also the legal custom, which was accepted as a matter of course in society, because this provision is not necessarily referenced in other decrees dealing with this matter.

For the city of Lucca, this legal custom was fraught with major problems. In the register of the Anziani in 1330s, decrees had already been issued three times, on 30 July, 14 August, and 30 September, to the effect that 'no one can be arrested or detained for any debt'.[108] Such decrees were meant to suspend the legal custom of detaining debtors while setting a fixed period of effect; for example, a decree issued on 30 September became effective until 1 January of the following year.

But what was the reasoning behind the suspension of this legal custom? In a decree issued on 20 December 1333, the following sorts of reasons were shown. 'In the hope that the city will be replenished with citizens who could not pay their creditors and were being forced to take flight and become vagabonds, owing to the war and its bad after-effects suffered by the city, we prescribed that no one in the city and its territory

106 A 1331 statute of the Appellate Court authorised complaints to the Anziani in a third trial in the event of dissatisfaction with the appeal decision in a second trial for a civil case. A. Romiti, 'Lo «statutum curie appellationum» del 1331', *Actum luce*, 23 (1994), p. 111-151, in particular p. 139: 'Et quotiens contigerit appellari a processibus civilium causarum Curie Potestatis Lucani, in casibus permissis, ad iudice appellationis Lucani Communiset per ipsum iudicem appellationis contingat infringi vel annullari processum seu sententiam Curie Potestatis, quod possit infra .X. dies a tempore late sententie appellari a dicta sententia iudicis appellationis ad Collegium Antianorum…'. Even so, it is not evident from the records of the Anziani that complaints were actually brought as in a civil trial. One exception, however, is the record of the complaint by Cosuccio in 1330 and the resulting judicial order of seizure of immovables (*insolutum*). Nelli and Simonetti (eds.), *Anziani*, p. 104-105.

107 This provision was intended for the Commune to be able to forcibly rectify distortions in debt claims and obligations arising from non-payment of debts and to protect the rights of creditors. This was frequently cited in actual trials. *Statuto 1308*, IV, 3 (De summaria ratione reddenda contra obligatos per publicum instrumentum), p. 250-252. This provision also survives in city statutes from 1331 onwards.

108 Nelli and Simonetti (eds.), *Anziani*, p. 130: 'nullus possit capi vel detineri pro aliquo debito contracto usque ad kalendas ianuarii proxime futuri'.

shall be arrested or detained'.[109] Lucca had been embroiled in a great many battles during this period, including clashes with the neighbouring states of Florence, Pisa, and Pistoia, as well as the assault on Lucca by the armies of the Holy Roman Emperor Louis IV (Ludwig the Bavarian) in September 1329. The extraordinarily high level of taxation levied intermittently throughout the 1330s was also something that emerged in this context. Many people were forced to default on their debts and flee from the city, fearing forcible collection by their creditors. This was a major loss for Lucca, and this decree temporarily prohibiting the detention of debtors was issued as a means of stemming this outflux of citizens.[110]

The stated reason for the decree prohibiting detention, which was issued on 28 November 1334, was that it was 'fructuous and necessary for *res publica*'.[111] In a decree issued on 22 October 1335, the Anziani also mentioned a claim by 'an indebted citizen of Lucca' who requested that the detention prohibition order be extended 'for the utility of *res publica*',[112] stating that many citizens and people in the territory, unable to pay their debts, were leaving their homes. The outflux of citizens was a matter of grave import that had an impact on the city's public activities, most importantly leading to a decrease in direct and indirect tax revenues.

However, if priority were given to the interests of the commune as a whole by prohibiting the legal custom of detaining debtors, would this not infringe on the rights of individual creditors? Naturally, the prohibition on detaining debtors did not mean that the loans themselves were extinguished; but even so, this restriction on an avenue of debt collection for a certain period surely amounted to an infringement of their rights – rights that had previously been recognised by legal custom. Firmly aware of this, the Anziani sought to overcome the problem by using certain rhetorical strategies. A decree on 22 October 1335 that extended the detention prohibition by one year pointed out that 'the public utility is being harmed' by the situation caused by the outflux of inhabitants, and furthermore that 'the condition of creditors is also deteriorating'.[113] And, 'Regarding both of these harms, we hope to prudently reach a

109 *Anz. Av. Lib.*, 5, p. 10: '...volentes circa replendam civitatem suis civibus qui propter guerras et malum statum civitatis quibus est agitata diutius non potuerunt eorum creditoribus respondere sed velint profugi peregrinari cogiuntur... stantiamus et ordinamus quod nulla persona civitatis, comitatus, districtus et fortie Lucani possit personaliter capi vel detineri'.

110 The General Council of Siena in 1339 also issued a decree prohibiting the custom of restraining debtors indefinitely. Piccinnni sees this decree as being informed by a political and economic conflict between the traditional banking class and the emerging lenders. G. Piccinni, 'Il sistema senese del credito nella fase di smobilitazione dei suoi banchi internazionali. Politiche comunali, spesa pubblica, propaganda contro l'usura (1332-1340)', in Id. (ed.), *Fedeltà ghibellina, affari guelfi. Saggi e riletture intorno alla storia di Siena fra Due e Trecento* (Pisa, 2008), p. 209-289.

111 *Anz. Av. Lib.*, 7, fol. 56r: '... fructuosa et quasi necessaria esse pro re publica'.

112 *Anz. Av. Lib.*, 13, p. 147: 'Visa quadam petitione porrecta pro parte civium Lucanorum debitorum coram dicto domino capitano et nobis per eum commissa continente in effectu quod terminus provisionis et stantiamenti facti anno preterito die .xxviii. novembris quod nulla persona posset personaliter capi labitur eadem .die xxviii. novembris proximi futuri. Et placetur pro utilitate rei publice dictum terminum seu aliam provisionem et stantiamentum de novo concedere'.

113 *Anz. Av. Lib.*, 13, p. 147 (continuing from the above note): 'Et examinatis predictis considerantes quod propter laboriosa guerrarum dispendia que cives et comitatini Lucani diutius passi sunt et quotidie patiuntur, non nulli ex eis ad solutionem debitorum suorum impotentes effeci patriam relinquere compelluntur, per quod et utilitas publica leditur et deterior efficitur conditio creditorum'.

situation that debtors will personally assist in the protection of the public, and earning profit through their labour will [show themselves] worthy to respond suitably to pay duties to Lucca territory and respond suitably to their creditors'.[114] Here, the rationale for the prohibition of detention is seen to be the benefit not only of the communal treasury, but of creditors seeking to recover their debts as well.

From the above, we can see an awareness on the part of the Anziani, whose discretionary decision to suspend a legal custom took into account both the public interest and private rights, and sought to avoid infringing on either: the hurdles that their decisions had to overcome.

iii). Was the detention of indebted peasants appropriate?

With regard to rights in rural villages, the decrees of the Anziani and the city statutes basically prioritised the interests of citizens as landowners while evincing a callous attitude towards tenant farmers in the surrounding territory. Even in the decree, discussed above, prohibiting the detention of debtors, the truth is that in most cases debts relating to rent on land, houses, or livestock were treated as exceptions, resulting in a situation in which farmers remained subject to detention, just as before. Nevertheless, the same was true for farmers who struggled with the depredations of war. When we look at the many petitions submitted to the Anziani by rural communes, we find that rural areas were devastated by the ravages of war, which left them in far more desperate straits than those in the city. In 1342, in particular – a year of great misfortune caused by the escalation of the struggle with Pisa – we find many complaints that were delivered to the Anziani from rural areas. As a result, on 21 September of that year, the Anziani issued a decree to the effect that rural inhabitants should not be detained for debt until the following January.[115] Also, on 17 October, with regard to a complaint that lands had been damaged by the war, making rent payments impossible, a decision was rendered that exempted interest on unpaid land rent. And again, on 27 December the following year, a decree was issued to the effect that the payment for land rents for the previous year would be exempted.

This series of decrees would have been insupportable for citizens for whom revenue from land represented an economic base, and would thus appear to have undermined their rights to a significant degree. Even here, however, the Anziani underlined that these decrees would benefit not only the peasants suffering the ravages of war but their creditors as well. The 21 September 1342 decree prohibiting detention stated that 'because during next whole October, farmers will work their own lands and possessions that they have rented from others according to their possibility'. In so doing it justified its suspension of a legal custom that would otherwise have risked adversely affecting the

114 *Anz. Av. Lib.*, 13, p. 147 (continuing from the above note): 'volentes quod in hoc utrique danpno sic prudenter occurrere quod debitores ipsi defensioni publice cum personis assistant, et, per industrie sue labores emolumenta captantes Lucani comitatus honeribus suisque creditoribus valeant habilius respondere…'

115 *Anz. Av. Lib.*, 18, fol. 27r: 'pro foretanis et comitatinis quod non possint capi'.

harvest with detentions during the busy farming season.[116] Also, the 17 October decree stipulating the exemption of interest on unpaid land rents expressly stated a desire to set a provision that will satisfy tenants and landowners alike[117] When it was decided that this October decree would be extended to 1345, the grounds for the decision exempting interest were explained in the decree as being 'in hopes that debtors will quickly be guided toward payment and that a middle path will be chosen for this issue'.[118]

As governing council, the Anziani demonstrated an attitude of pursuing the *bene del comune* while giving due consideration to 'the good of individuals' when changing legal provisions and legal customs in this way, or when allowing exemptions to their application. From the ways in which decisions by the Anziani that ran counter to positive law were justified, we can suppose how the people of the time thought about the actions of the governing council.

That is, namely, although the governing council was under the sway of certain influential families, it was ultimately a body that embodied and acted as the representative of the notional '*comune*' as a sovereign constituted by its citizenry, and was therefore obliged to aspire not to pursue the private interests of the powerful, but the general interest of the *bene del comune*.

And while this *bene del comune* was occasionally in conflict with 'individual goods', the fact that the former was a composite bundle made up of such individual goods meant that it was called upon to achieve both of these aims at the same time. The Anziani and the people, when they sensed that the achievement of this ultimate goal was unfeasible in the literal application of positive law – or when they felt they could reasonably argue that such a difficulty existed – would exercise their *arbitrium* and act to amend or temporarily suspend laws as necessary.

4. The Creativity of Claims

In this chapter, in the form of claims to the commune by its inhabitants, we have examined conduct with two disparate personalities – namely requests for compliance with the law on the one hand and for amendments or exemptions to the application of the law on the other – that were carried out respectively in the twin spaces of the commune's judicial and political arenas.

---

116 *Anz. Av. Lib.*, 18, fol. 27r: 'inquantum per totum mensem octobris proxime futuri, laboraverint seu laborari fecerint eorum terras et possessiones seu quas tenent ab aliis in locationem secundum possibilitatem eorum'.

117 *Anz. Av. Lib.*, 18, fol. 41v: '… volentes eorum suplicationibus annuere et in predictis taliter providere quod redditores et domini communiter valeant contentari, stantiamus, providemus et ordinamus quod pro blado vino et oleo quomodocumque rationabiliter debitis cuicumque per quoscumque cuicumque conditionis existentes de civitate comitatu districtu et fortia Lucana vel habitantes in eis pro temporibus preteritis videlicet a kalendaris octobris presentis retro tam pro reddita affictus perpetui vel ad tempus quam pro collaria et soccita seu alia quacumque causa, reddatur solum starium pro stario bladi currus vini pro curru et libra olei pro librain quibus legiptime tenerentur…'

118 *Anz. Av. Lib.*, 18, fol. 41v: 'volentes igitur debitores ad solventionem citius faciendam invitare, et in predictis quodammodo viam mediam eligere'.

In the context of Italian cities, city statutes were laws that sought to benefit orderly governance and social life; laws that sought to achieve the *bene del comune*, so to speak. However, once they were enacted and promulgated, they were not necessaryily able to function automatically. The unceasing activities of the Anziani and the inhabitants of the communes were indispensable for the expression of their specific content and the realisation of their original purpose and underlying 'spirit (*mens*)' in the context of a changing society.

The formal realisation of the law was promoted by inhabitants in the form of exceptions. Inhabitants raised exceptions in the courts to pursue formal faults and violations on the part of both judges and their opposing parties. As these were arguments based strictly on the city statutes, they can be considered to have heightened a concern with legalism in the parties and their associates and thus ultimately have played a certain role in the formal realisation of the law.

Moreover, some of the appeals to the law by the people had the effect of rendering the law more flexible for the sake of achieving its original purpose. When inhabitants felt that a law's original intention would not be realised through its literal application, they looked to the Anziani as governing council and appealed to it to motivate the creation of laws, or amendments of and exemptions from existing laws, making them consistent with the complexities of the real world – but simultaneously with their own interests.

It is difficult to judge whether this involvement on the part of inhabitants in these two types of realisation of laws served to steer the commune in a 'good' direction. The inclination towards excessively strict compliance with the law, that the practice of exceptions brought about, would have hindered the operation of laws in line with social reality and the realisation of due rights. Conversely, the repeated legal amendments and exemptions also had the potential to erode the stability of the legal system and undermine the social order. However, what I wish to emphasise here is that it was not the members of the communal governing bodies (i.e. the judges and the Anziani) but the people living outside those institutions that played an important role in realising the commune and its legal system. The policies of the commune were steered by their practice of two interpretive approaches to the law – namely compliance with the law and the flexibility of the law.

These practices of interpretation of forms of justice on the part of inhabitants intersected with their interpretation by the judges and the Anziani. While I will turn to the examination of the practices of interpretation carried out in the courts by judges and litigants in Chapter 3, in this chapter we have been able to see how the attempts of both parties to 'rationalise' the law intersected in the political arena in the form of claims on the part of inhabitants and their acknowledgement by the Anziani. Here, individual claimants and the Anziani, while retaining their respective interests and objectives at heart, would both cite the common goal of the *bene del comune* that served as a justification framework for their claims. And here, the *bene del comune* was conceived of something that was realised by maximising the rights of individual inhabitants that served as its constituent elements, rather than as the kind of thing that could be achieved by infringing on those individual rights. Therefore, the interpretation of justice by the Anziani and by the inhabitants was conducted in line with the principle of not penalising specific victims.

While the appeals to the commune on the part of inhabitants that we have examined in this chapter were almost exclusively found in sources from the early fourteenth century, this is no coincidence. The changes and amendments to the civil law resulting from the Anziani and exceptions in the courts were phenomena specifically characteristic of the 1330s and 1340s. A division of roles was in place in which the courts were sites where the law was strictly observed, and the governing council was a space in which the law was treated more flexibly and was subject to changes or even exemptions. Conversely, by the latter half of the fourteenth century, claims by inhabitants requesting legal amendments or exemptions in the civil matters for the most part disappear from the Anziani's records.

The key to understanding this change over the fourteenth century was to be found in another room in the same palace, namely the law court. As I shall discuss in the next chapter, the civil courts in the latter half of the fourteenth century underwent a shift, from an attitude of strict conformity with the law to one more disposed to rendering decisions freely based on contingent interpretations of laws. Specifically, this became apparent in the courts in the form of a decline in exceptions and an increase in the number of cases in which judges and jurists rendered judgements based not on formal legal compliance but rather on interpreting the 'spirit (*mens*)' of the law. From this point on, the role heretofore fulfilled by the Anziani of 'rationalising' the law was entrusted to the civil courts. The changes that can be seen in the Lucchese courts can be situated in the context of a shift in the underlying logic of justice from formalism to discretion (*arbitrium*) that is broadly apparent in medieval Roman jurisprudence and the judicial sphere more generally. Next, I would like to proceed with the discussion by examining how this shift took place.

CHAPTER 3

A Shift of Judicial Principle: from Formalism to *Arbitrium*

This chapter examines the process of a shift of judicial principle over the fourteenth century, focusing on the practice of civil justice in the courts of Lucca. By a 'shift of judicial principle', I refer to the change in the logical basis of the legitimacy of judicial decisions from a strict observance of laws to the discretionary criteria of *arbitrium* on the part of judges, for whom positive law was merely one standard of reference among many.

This shift from legal formalism towards *arbitrium* (or an expanded reliance on *arbitrium*) can be seen clearly in the growing importance of judges' decisions based on their own '*motus animi*' and the declining significance both of exceptions on points of form and of jurists' opinions in civil proceedings. The appearance in Lucca of such proceedings, which were extraordinary with reference to the Romano-canonical trial model, corresponded to a series of fundamental changes in the procedural laws elaborated by learned jurists in response to the decree issued by Pope Clement V authorising a judge's *arbitrium procedendi*. Close consideration of the practices of civil trials in Lucca should enable us to clarify the concrete processes by which this significant legal shift was engendered and developed at the local court level at the end of the Middle Ages.

First, I examine changes that occurred in fourteenth-century judicial practices based on court records from 1336, 1365, and 1396, paying particular attention to changes in the characteristics of court rulings from the formalistic decisions of jurists that adhered excessively to positive law to the decisions of judges who, in contrast, relied on their own *arbitrium* (Sections 1 and 2). Second, I clarify the significance of this change in civil justice by observing the various changes that took place over the same period in the procedural laws elaborated by learned jurists (Section 3). Finally, I reveal the specific manner of this transformation of judicial principle in the Lucchese courts and the characteristics of justice in the new judicial context by considering three aspects of Lucca's experience under Pisan rule, namely changes in legal circumstance, changes in people's intentions, and the intervention of the Pisan doge (Sections 4, 5 and 6).

1. Changes to Civil Trials over the Fourteenth Century

Examination of court records from 1336, when Lucca was under a foreign master, from 1365, when the city was under Pisan rule, and from 1396, during the Republican period reveals some changes to have taken place in the civil trials of fourteenth-century Lucca.[1]

The first thing to notice is the decline in the number of trials. The annual number of cases (or of claims, to be precise) heard in the Court of Podestà declined from 900 cases in 1336, to 305 cases in 1365, and 192 cases in 1396. We see the same trend in the courts of consuls. A major reason for this was certainly the population decrease caused by the Black Death in 1347-1348. In Lucca and its surrounding territory, half the population was eradicated. The population declined from about 40,000 in 1330s to about 19,000 in the 1370s and 1380s.[2]

Let us examine the substance of the complaints brought before the courts. While claims concerning insolvency (e.g. debt and unpaid land rents) remained major causes for complaints even in the second half of the fourteenth century, other kinds of claims, such as those regarding immovable property and the restitution of dowries, became less common. In particular, attention must be paid to the decrease in the number of oppositions to judicial orders. Such exceptions, as we saw in the previous chapter, had resulted from mistakes in orders summarily decided by judges. They were more representative of civil trials in the first half of the fourteenth century, which were characterised by negligent and passive judges and frequent exceptions by parties in courts dominated by jurists' formalism, so their decline suggests the change of the pre-existing system.

The decline in the rate of defendants' appearances in court and in the popularity of exceptions did not mean the disappearance or decline in the proportion of the cases wherein the parties engaged in lengthy discussions over topics such as ownership or credit relations. Indeed, the percentage of procedures of *positio* and of the presentation of testimonies, as an indicator of long and intense debates, was actually steady throughout the fourteenth century.[3] Therefore, we find that parties that used the communal courts like forums of discussion remained a constant presence in Lucca during this period.

These long trials, often involving intense arguments, ended in different ways over the course of the fourteenth century. Judges in 1336 were used to committing cases to jurists for advice (*consilium*) on which to base formal final judgements. The percentage of such commissions, and accordingly of judgements based on *consilia*, decreased in

1 The court records of the *podestà* in 1336, ASL, *Potestà di Lucca* (hereafter *Potestà*), 58, 60, 64, 67. Those in 1365, *Potestà*, 421, 422, 423, 424, 426, 427, 428, 430, 431, 432. Those in 1396, *Potestà*, 703, 704, 705, 706, 707, 708, 709, 710.

2 C. Meek, *Lucca 1369-1400. Politics and Society in an Early Renaissance City-State* (Oxford, 1978), p. 21-26.

3 The procedure followed by *positio* involves the presentation of an argument by a party by breaking it down into detailed points which are then accepted or rejected by an opponent. If a *positio* elicits an objection, the side presenting the *positio* must prove the allegation with testimony. The presentation of *positio* and testimonies is labour-intensive, thereby demonstrating that the litigant is sufficiently committed to arguing the dispute. Regarding the procedure involved in a *positio*, see A. Engelmann (trans. by R. W. Millar), *A History of Continental Civil Procedure* (Boston, 1927), p. 471-478.

Table 3.1: Shift in the substance of complaints

	1336		1365		1396	
	Cases	%	Cases	%	Cases	%
Debt	197	22	82	27	32	17
Unpaid land rent	157	17	36	12	40	21
Unpaid house rent	52	6	4	1	20	10
Restitution of dote	54	6	16	5	2	1
Immovable property	73	8	19	6	3	1.5
Restitution of movables	23	3	5	2	6	3
Compensation for damage to farmland	22	2	32	10	32	17
Opposition to judicial orders	131	15	11	4	3	1.5
Other	148	16	77	25	40	21
Uncertain	43	5	23	8	14	7
Total	**900**	**100**	**305**	**100**	**192**	**100**

1365 and 1396. While this change gives the impression that the court ceased to play as much of a role in making decisions in civil conflicts in the second half of the fourteenth century, this is not the case.

In the trials of 1365 and 1396, we often find judgements made by judges independently, relying not on jurists' advice but on their own sense of the issues and their own discretion. If such decisions are added to the number of final judgements, the percentage of cases ending in judgements accounted for 6.7% of all cases in 1336 (60 cases), 6.6% in 1365 (20 cases), and 5.7% in 1396 (11 cases). Thus, although we find some decline in the proportion of cases for which the defendants responded to summons in the late fourteenth century, litigants who stayed on to obtain final decisions did remain a constant presence.

This suggests that the shift that occurred in the civil courts during the fourteenth century did not happen in practices on the part of litigants, but rather on the part of the courts; that is, from judgements based on *consilia* by jurists to those rendered by judges according to their own discretion. Such a change in the locus of decision-making to the courts is far from trivial. It relates to the characteristics of justice on which the communal courts and commune based their decisions.

2. A Qualitative Shift in the Identity of Decision Makers

The change of decision-maker brought a qualitative change to the judgements. Let us examine closely the judgements based on *consilia* and those rendered independently of such advice in 1336 and 1365.

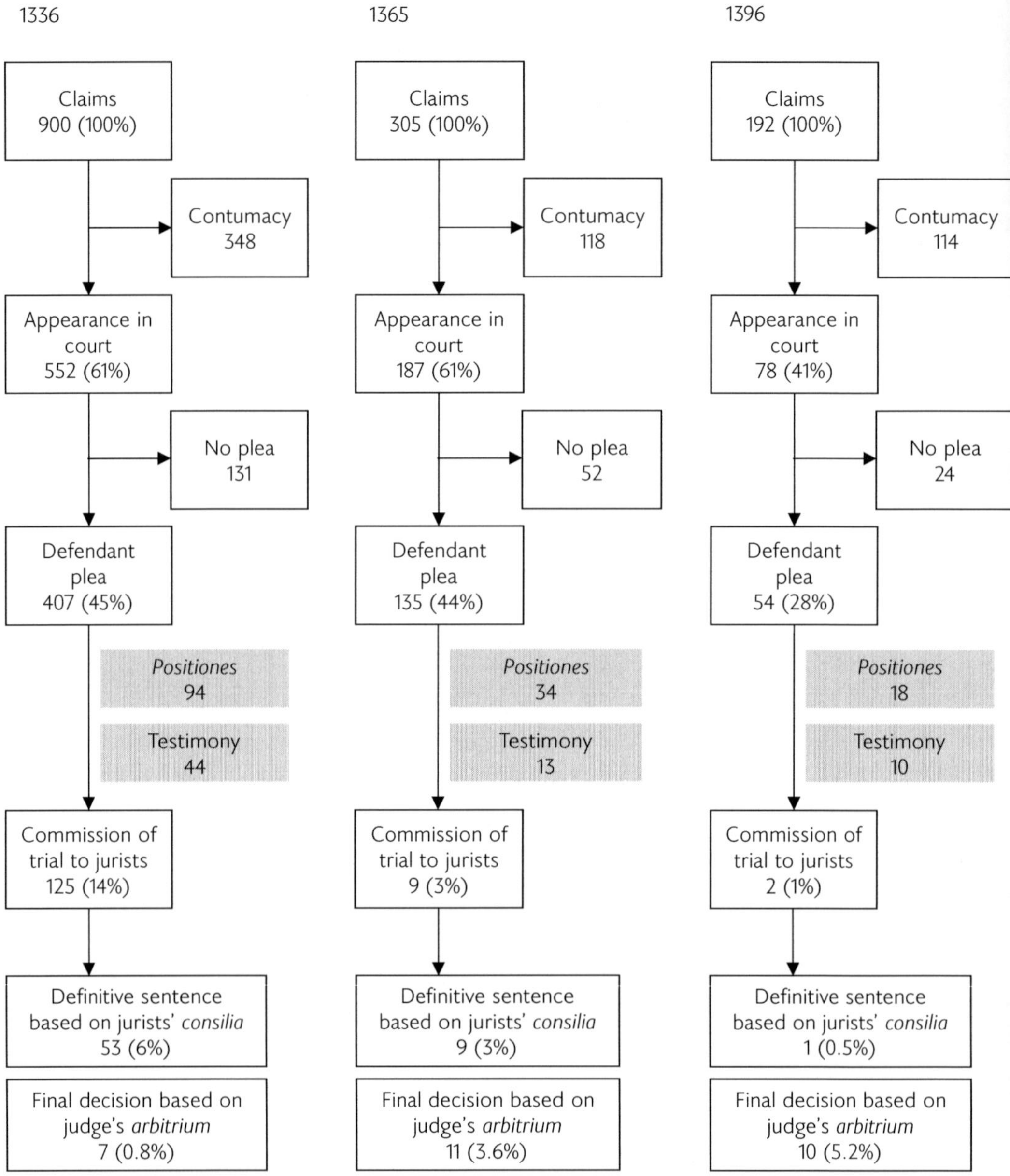

Figure 3.1: The development of civil trials at the Court of Podestà in 1336, 1365, and 1396

In 1336, we find 53 judgements based on jurists' advice in the Court of Podestà. The characteristics of a *consilia* could have a bearing on what criteria the jurists applied it. We frequently see in the *consilia* references to the statutes or to the deliberations: for example, '*viso statuto Lucani communis quid incipit quod nullus tenitor et cetera, posito… rubrica de exceptione inbannimenti non opponenda contra dominum suum capitulo.viii. libri.iiii*'.;[1] '*viso statuto Lucani communis loquente de pena illorum qui non fecerint se scribi inbapneria, et stantiamento postea facto*'.[2] Most of these cited laws are classified as procedural laws, which prescribed judicial proceedings and the qualifications of parties, rather than substantive laws regarding rights. Jurists' advice in 1336 tended to focus on such legal formalities.

Such *consilia* stemmed from the fact that jurists at the time were also involved in the compilation of statutes as '*statutarii*'. Hence, the issues entrusted to jurists' *consilia* were often derived from parties' exceptions regarding procedural formalities. Of trials that culminated in sentences, 34 of 53 cases were initiated in opposition to judicial orders, which often skipped legal formalities. This suggests a process wherein parties receiving unfavourable judicial orders would raise exceptions that took issue with procedural flaws, whereupon formalistic jurists would be commissioned to provide legal advice as drafts of judgement. Exceptions and legal advice relating to formal matters exerted considerable influence on the courts' decisions.

In the court of 1365, only nine judgements are recorded that were based on legal *consilia*: four discussing procedures or qualifications[3] and, interestingly, five concerned with substantial rights relationships.

An example of the latter case is a *consilium* prepared by Lapo Conte, a Pisan jurist, and delivered in reference to the inheritance of the late Puccinello's property. Succession rights claimed by the plaintiff, Coluccio Franchini, as a nephew of the late Puccinello, were contested by the notary, Bartholomeo Bomensis, acting as procurator for the defendant, Jacoba, allegedly the granddaughter of the late Puccinello. Here, the dispute turned on the matter of the legitimacy of Jacoba's filiation with Margarita, Puccinello's daughter. In this case, Lapo Conte ultimately counselled that Jacoba was the legitimate granddaughter, which meant that the plaintiff, Coluccio, as a collateral relation of the late Puccinello, was not in the primary line of succession.

The basis of Lapo's advice is provided in his statement of motive (*motus animi*). Citing the *Digesta* and other legal codes,[4] he explained his reasoning as follows: 'taking testimonies presented by both parties into consideration, it is said that testimonies of the defendant's side are predominant due to their large number and had more sufficient reasons. Therefore, the movement of my *animus* is concordant with them'.[5]

1 *Potestà*, 60, fol. 225r.

2 *Potestà*, 58, fols. 359r-360v.

3 *Potestà*, 428, fols. 23r-26v, 51r-52r.

4 Lapo cites doctrines such as those in the *Digesta* or written by learned jurists such as Cino da Pistoia to show the legal basis of his own legal advice.

5 *Potestà*, 430, fols. 25v-26r: 'consideratis depositionibus testium utriusque partis inter eos qui aliquid dicunt preponderant depositiones testium rei propter numerum et quia magis sufficientem causam reddunt ideo *motus animi* mei cum eis concurrit…'

The reasoning behind the jurist's advice, based on '*motus animi*', contrasts with the formalistic aspects that the jurists of 1336 considered as primary reasons. This new criterion for judgement, distinct from the observance of positive laws, could be said to have begun to spread among jurists after the mid-fourteenth century.

Next, let us consider final decisions taken by the judge not based on jurists' advice. The actual number of such decisions increased from 7 cases in 1336 to 11 cases in 1365, although the total number of trials had been decreasing for 30 years.

Decisions made exclusively by judges, which had normally been referred to as *pronuncia* in 1336, began to be referred to as *sententia*, a term previously reserved for formal judgements based on *consilia*.[6] Besides this terminological change, the format used in the court records for the judges' decisions also converged with that used for formal decisions based on *consilia*; descriptions of judges' decisions were no longer simple but were listed in more detail, for example, enumerating the references, such as testimonies and allegations, on which the judgements were based.

As for the contents of the judges' decisions, in 1336 judges normally had competence to decide only on simple matters wherein there was no room to exercise their own consideration, as in validating documents attesting repayments of debt. In 1365 we can find many decisions made by judges after closely examining the parties' assertions of rights. For example, one judge, Antonio de Cecchiis, in 1365 decided on his own authority to order the restitution of a dowry in a *sententia* after his 'mature and diligent deliberation' on the parties' pleas, testimonies, and testaments.[7]

Judges in 1365 began to make decisions on their own authority not only on substantial matters but also in reference to formalities that had been exclusively entrusted to jurists in 1336. Judges, even on their own accord, recognised the legality of contested judicial orders,[8] which was a different situation from the trials in 1336 in which jurists had assessed the validity of the judges' decisions as the custodians of legal formalism.

The shift in the character of civil justice from 1336 to 1365 can be summarised as follows. First, regarding the original locus of final judgements: whereas judges' sentences in 1336 were wholly determined by jurists' advice, by 1365 judges' independent decisions, no longer reliant on jurists' opinions, had become mainstream and were formally treated as official rulings. Second, and in parallel with the first shift, legal formalism, as represented by exceptions on points of form and jurists' subsequent *consilia* which in 1336 had dominated the civil courts, became much less significant as a logic for decision-making by 1365. Conversely, decisions based on '*motus animi*' (and thus *arbitrium*), followed by a substantial discussion on rights relationships became more common over the fourteenth century. This change seems to suggest a shift in

6 *Potestà*, 426, fols. 7r-11v, 24r-33v, 53r-55v, 76r-79v, 101r-104v. Also, in such cases, before sentencing, the presiding judge would declare 'pronuntiavit conclusum esse in causa et questione predicta' (fol. 78v) to bring the discussion to an end and guide it to a final ruling on his own initiative.

7 *Potestà*, 426, fols. 101r-103r.

8 For example, a monk named Simone sought to extinguish a judicial order that he be detained for debt, regardless of the fact that, as a monk, he was outside the jurisdiction of the Court of Podestà. Therefore, based on the city statutes, the presiding judge ruled to extinguish the judicial order that had been issued previously by the same court, releasing Simone. *Potestà*, 423, fols. 33r-34r.

the logic and characteristics of the justice that underpinned communal decisions. I will consider the reasons and circumstances of this important shift below, beginning in Section 4.

When we examine court records from 1396, we can see a continuation of the trend of the changes that occurred between 1336 and 1365. Whereas the Court of Podestà issued only one sentence based on a *consilium* in 1396, final decisions rendered by judges without relying on jurists became more common (10 cases). Jurists could no longer claim to be the custodians of formal procedures. In fact, one *consilium*, delivered in 1396, concerned problems with the execution of testaments and the validity of the transfer of rights, which required substantial arguments based on the Roman legal concepts of *usufructuarius* (usufructuary right) and *possessio* (possessory right).[9] Then, unlike the jurists, the judges by 1396 were occupied with problems concerning both formalities and rights relations. They closely examined allegations by the parties and rendered final decisions relying on their own *arbitrium*.

3. A Shift in Judicial Principle in the Realm of Procedural Law

We have seen the shift that occurred in the civil courts of fourteenth-century Lucca, both in civil trials and, further, in the underlying logic of justice. This shift can be expressed as a transition from a rigid judicial system dominated by jurists' formalism to a flexible justice system wherein the prime decision-makers were judges reliant on their own *arbitrium* and who were liberated, at least to some degree, from adhering to the strictures of positive law. This shift from formalism towards *arbitrium* (or an expansion of the use of *arbitrium*) in Lucca corresponded to a series of changes in the procedural laws elaborated by learned jurists in the late Middle Ages.

Ever since the age of the glossators, debate had existed about whether judges were bound to the letter of the law or should be given latitude to privilege unwritten principles of equity over a strict interpretation of the law.[10] In the thirteenth and fourteenth centuries, when commentators, seeking the *ratio* of norms not expressed in the text, came to interpret the law more flexibly, procedural theories began to be elaborated that allowed judges to proceed on their own discretion. Below I would like to survey these general changes in civil and criminal procedural laws in order to highlight the significance of the shift in the judicial principle of civil justice in fourteenth-century Lucca.

---

9 *Potestà*, 706, fols. 4r-9v, 19r-25v.

10 A. Padoa Schioppa, *A History of Law in Europe. From the Early Middle Ages to the Twentieth Century* (Cambridge, 2017), p. 193-197.

(1) Criminal procedures

We can see the expansion of judicial *arbitrium* in the criminal legal procedures in the thirteenth and fourteenth centuries, particularly in the shift from accusatorial procedures to an inquisitorial process.

Vallerani's study of criminal records from 1257 in Perugia revealed that the criminal courts used mostly accusatorial procedures that adopted an adversarial system based on *ius commune*, wherein the accuser shouldered the burden of proof, just as in civil procedures. Here, judges played a merely minor role as judicial coordinators and did not intervene actively in the examination of evidence.

In contrast, an inquisitorial procedure, which originated in the papal decrees of Innocent III, required judges to take the initiative, *ex officio*, in order to seek the truth by questioning the accused and collecting evidence through testimony.[11] This legal procedure, according to the jurist Alberto Gandino, writing in the second half of the thirteenth century, was extraordinary in its violation of *ius commune*. Nevertheless, after the second half of the thirteenth century it rapidly came into wider use in secular courts in various Italian cities.[12] In fact, as we will see in the next chapter, by the mid-fourteenth century, Lucca's criminal courts had already adopted an inquisitorial procedure in almost all trials. As defenders of the state's interests, judges were induced to rely on their *arbitrium* in various ways, for example, with prosecutions without *accusa* and torture procedures initiated solely based on indirect evidence.[13]

This increasing reliance on judges' *arbitrium* is evident in not only in the procedural aspects of trials but also in the discovery phase of fact-finding and evidence assessment. Tommaso di Piperata, a learned jurist who played an important role in the second half of the thirteenth century, asserted that judges could issue sentences based on their own *arbitrium* even in cases where the required conditions for evidence were lacking (e.g. wherein witnesses did not fulfil certain necessary conditions), as long as the judges'

---

11 R. M. Fraher, 'The Theoretical Justification for the New Criminal Law of the High Middle Ages: *Rei publicae interest, ne crimina remaneant impunita*', *The University of Illinois Law Review*, 3 (1984), p. 577-595; R. M. Fraher, 'IV Lateran's Revolution and Criminal Procedure: The Birth of Inquisitio, the End of Ordeals, and Innocent III's Vision of Ecclesiastical Politics', in R. I. Castillo Lara (ed.), *Studia in honorem eminentissimi cardinalis Alphonsi M. Stickler* (Roma, 1992), p. 96-111; K. Pennington, 'Innocent III and the Ius Commune', in R. H. Helmholz et al. (eds.), *Grundlagen des Rechts: Festschrift für Peter Landau zum 65. Geburtstag* (Paderborn, 2000), p. 349-366; M. M. Vallerani, 'Modelli di verità. Le prove nei processi inquisitori', in *L'enquête au Moyen Âge: études réunies par Claude Gauvard* (Roma, 2008), p. 123-142; M. Vallerani, 'Procedura e giustizia nelle città italiane del basso medioevo (XII-XIV secolo)', in J. Chiffoleau, C. Gauvard, and A. Zorzi (eds.), *Pratiques sociales et politiques judiciaires dans les villes de l'Occident à la fin du Moyen Âge* (Roma, 2007), p. 439-494, in particular p. 460-462.

12 According to Gandino in *Tractatus de maleficiis*: 'sed hodie de iure civili iudices potestatum de quolibet maleficio cognoscunt per inquisitionem ex officio suo… et ita servent iudices de consuetudine, ut notat dominus Guido et ut vidi communiter observari, quamvis sit contra ius civile'. This shows that the inquisitorial procedure was considered to be an extraordinary and illegal process, even though it was much diffused as a customary one in the courts. Albertus Gandinus, *Tractatus de maleficiis*, in H. Kantrowicz, *Albertus Gandinus und das Strafrecht der Scholastic* (Berlin, 1907), p. 39; Vallerani, *La giustizia pubblica medievale* (Bologna, 2005), p. 211.

13 M. Sbriccoli, '*Vidi communiter observari*. L'emersione di un ordine penale pubblico nelle città italiane del secolo XIII', *Quaderni fiorentini per la storia del pensiero giuridico*, 27 (1998), p. 231-268; Padoa Schioppa, 'La coscienza del giudice', p. 271: 'quando potestas habet arbitrium, etiam si non essent indicia plura sed unum tantum, posset ad tormenta procedere'.

animus coincided with the proofs.[14] This could be read as a sign of transformation from legal formalism towards a free evaluation of the evidence.

Furthermore, the 'extraordinary' quality characterised justice wherein *arbitrium* played an important role, as we will see in Chapter 6. From the second half of the fourteenth century, actions endangering the state or regime in Italian cities were considered as extraordinary crimes in the criminal courts, where they were judged to be under the control of political authorities in a summary and informal manner. Justice based on the logic of *arbitrium* would have been inconceivable in the courts of the thirteenth century, where judges' discretion was rigidly circumscribed by Romano-canonical legal procedure.

(2) Civil procedures

Although civil justice was traditionally dominated by the Romano-canonical procedure *ordo iudiciarius*, we can see a trend moving away from traditional practices after the fourteenth century. This was reflected in the introduction of summary procedure, as per the phrase 'plainly, without clamour and the form of ordinary trial procedure (*de plano sine strepitu et figura iudicii*)'. This allowed judges to proceed and make decisions relying on their own *arbitrium*, without being exclusively bound by rigid procedural norms.

In Lucca, at least, summary procedures can be broadly categorised into three types. One is the procedure concerning compulsory seizure owing to debts, which originated in Langobardic law.[15] We see this in civil cases where judges summarily and without opportunity for independent thought issued orders of executions, relying solely on documents attesting the debts.[16] The second was a procedure adopted in the summary trials, recorded in the *libri reclamorum simplicium* in the Lucchese courts, which were distinguished from ordinary trials. These summary trials seem to have accepted oral rather than written petitions, which were applied in trials involving claims for small sums. These two summary procedures were executed automatically and did not leave any room for judicial *arbitrium*.

The third summary procedure, significant in terms of its role in the expansion of the *arbitrium* in civil justice, was used *de facto* in court practice as early as the thirteenth century, and was subsequently established with the issuance of the decree '*Saepe contingit*' by Pope Clement V in 1312-14.[17] Faced with repeated exceptions by parties, the decree was promulgated so that the trials could proceed simply and plainly

14 Padoa Schioppa, 'La coscienza del giudice', p, 271: 'secure per arbitrium quod habent, si tamen conscientia et animus cum probatione concurrit'.

15 Engelmann, p. 497-502.

16 This procedure had already been stipulated in the 1308 city statute, and is also evident in city statutes for other cities See S. Bongi (ed.), *Statuto del comune di Lucca dell'anno MCCCVIII* (Lucca 1867) (hereafter *Statuto 1308*), IV, 3 (De summaria ratione reddenda contra obligatos per publicum instrumentum), p. 250-252; G. Salvioli, *Storia della procedura civile e criminale*, P. Del Giudice (dir.), *Storia del Diritto Italiano*, III-1 (Milano, 1925), p. 327-346.

17 O. Descamps, 'Aux Aux origines de la procédure sommaire: Remarques sur la constitution Saepe contingit (Clem., V, 11, 2)', in Y. Mausen, O. Condorelli, F. Roumy, and M. Schmoeckel (eds.), *Der Einfluss der Kanonistik auf die europäische Rechtskultur*, IV (Prozessrecht) (Wien, 2014), p. 45-63; K. Pennington, 'Introduction to the Courts', in W. Hartmann and K. Pennington (eds.), *The History of Courts and Procedure in Medieval Canon Law* (Washington,

without the clamour and the form of ordinary trial procedure and to settle any doubt about how to proceed in the canonical and secular courts. The decree instructed the judge not to exact the *libellus*, demand the *litis contestatio* and remove occasions for delays by refusing dilatory and frustrating exceptions. However, the judge could not abbreviate the suit by eliminating necessary proofs and defences or other procedures that introduced the truth into a trial.[18]

The last part of the decree decisively set the condition, 'if the parties do not present the contradiction'. This seems to have given the parties the opportunity to take the initiative in the proceedings. However, the canonical jurists who originally commented on the decree neutralised this obstacle as follows. In a commentary on the *Saepe contingit* around 1322 or 1326, the canonist Giovanni d'Andrea noted that cases entrusted to parties would only be those wherein the judge could not proceed based on their own *arbitrium*. Otherwise, in cases of a public nature above all, as noted in the *Clementina Dispendiosam* of 1314, the initiative of proceedings had to remain in the judges' hands.[19] Another canonist, Bonifatius Vitalini (pseudo-Vitalini), also commented on the last phrase of the decree in favour of increasing judicial *arbitrium*, arguing for his interpretation that the parties could object not to summary progression but only to a judge's intention *to proceed using ordinary procedure*.[20] In this way, the *Saepe contingit* and its canonical commentators deprived parties of the procedural initiative and handed the judges '*arbitrium procedendi*'.

This summary procedure had to be 'not a restricted cognizance of the matter in dispute' but 'a cognizance that, though stripped of formality and rendered expeditious, was still materially *complete*'.[21] On this point, this summary procedure, while also expeditious, could be distinguished from the other two summary procedures, which were not considered to involve 'complete cognizance'. Hereinafter, I use the term 'summary justice' to refer to this new type of summary proceeding.

2016), p. 3-29; C. Donahue, Jr., 'Procedure in the Courts of the Ius Commune', in *The History of Courts and Procedure*, p. 74-124, in particular p. 116-117.

18 Clem. V. 11. 2: "Saepe contingit, quod causas committimus, et in earum aliquibus simpliciter et de plano, ac sine strepitu et figura iudicii procedi mandamus, de quorum significatione verborum a multis contenditur, et qualiter procedi debeat dubitatur. Nos autem dubitationem hujusmodi quantum nobis est possibile decidere cupientes, hac in perpetuum valitura constitutione sancimus, ut judex cui taliter causam committimus, necessario libellum non exigat, litis contestationem non postulet, in tempore etiam feriarum ob necessitates hominum indultarum a jure procedere valeat, amputet dilationum materiam, litem quanto poterit faciat breviorem, exceptiones, appellationes dilatorias et frustratorias repellendo, partium, advocatorum et procuratorum contentiones et jurgia testiumque superfluam multitudinem refrenando. Non sic tamen iudex litem abreviet quin probationes necessariae et defensiones legitimae admittantur. Citationem vero ac praestationem iuramenti de calumnia vel malitia, sive de veritate dicenda, ne veritas occultetur, per commissionem huius modi intelligimus non excludi[...] Si tamen in praemissis casibus solennis ordo in toto vel in parte non contradicentibus partibus observetur: non erit processus propter hoc irritus, nec etiam irritandus." Engelmann, p. 495-496.

19 M. Meccarelli, *Arbitrium. Un aspetto sistematico degli ordinamenti giuridici in età di diritto comune* (Milano, 1998), p. 265: 'quando sic procedere non est in iudicis potestate [...] secus si sic procedere voluntati iudicis relinquatur ut in constitutionem Dispensadiosam'.

20 Meccarelli, *Arbitrium*, p. 266-267.

21 Engelmann, p. 497; Pennington, 'Introduction to the Courts', p. 28-29.

(3) How did the shift in the logic of justice come about?

We can summarise the characteristics of a series of changes that occurred in the circle of learned jurists and in the procedural practice of civil and criminal justice at the end of the thirteenth and fourteenth centuries as follows. While formalism and the initiative of parties based on the adversarial system, as principles of the Romano-canonical procedure, grew weaker, *arbitrium* on the part of judges gathered momentum in its decisional and procedural aspects. What instigated and drove this shift in the logic of justice from formalism to *arbitrium*?

In terms of ideology, it has been noted that theological and philosophical reflections emphasised the moral certainty and *arbitrium* of the judges.[22] Furthermore, we know that the jurists who elaborated the concept of *publicum* contributed to the introduction and development of inquisitorial procedures in the thirteenth century, and that Clement V and the canonical jurists invented civil summary procedures through their promulgation and interpretation of the *Saepe contingit*.

The decree and the jurisprudential interpretations certainly influenced the practice of the communal courts. However, it is also worth noting the practices by which the new principle they provided was introduced into and accepted by the secular courts, to the extent of eclipsing longstanding and deep-rooted legal principles. We know that the new summary procedure was adopted by the Visconti's reform in Milan and its subject cities in the second half of the fourteenth century, and also spread to and became a normal procedure in the civil courts of other Italian cities in the sixteenth and seventeenth centuries.[23] However, the concrete processes that drove the decline of ordinary procedures of *ius commune* and the subsequent introduction and diffusion of summary procedures originating in *Clementina Saepe* have yet to be satisfactorily elucidated at the level of actual court proceedings. Mario Ascheri has lamented the extremely meagre interest that existing studies have shown toward civil procedures, above all toward summary procedure. By contrast, medieval jurists took a more serious view of 'the legality of the process', giving us numerous studies on *ordines iudiciarii*.[24]

Lucca is the only city in Italy, perhaps in Europe, where court books, city statutes, and council records survive from multiple points in time throughout the fourteenth century. This allows us to reveal the concrete processes by which summary justice was introduced and which represented a shift in the logic of justice, based on practices in the local courts. In the following sections, I examine this shift in judicial logic,

---

22 Padoa Schioppa, 'La coscienza del giudice'.

23 J. Black, *Absolutism in Renaissance Milan. Plenitude of Power under the Visconti and the Sforza, 1329-1535* (Oxford, 2009), p. 117-118. It is pointed out that these were new summary procedures in the civil courts of Torino and Venezia in the sixteenth and seventeenth centuries. S. Cerutti, 'Giustiziae località a Torino in età moderna: una ricerca in corso', *Quaderni storici*, 89 (1995), p. 445-486.

24 M. Ascheri, 'Il processo civile tra diritto comune e diritto locale: Da questioni preliminari al caso della giustizia estense', *Quaderni storici*, 101 (1999), p. 355-387, in particular p. 361-364; Ascheri 'Istituzioni e giustizia dei mercanti nel Tre-Quattrocento', in M. Del Treppo (ed.), *Sistema di rapporti ed élites economiche in Europa (secoli XII-XVII)* (Napoli, 1994), p. 33-61, in particular p. 39-40. This consternation, as expressed by Ascheri and cited by Colli, remains valid today. V. Colli, '*Acta civilia in curia potestatis*: Firenze 1344. Aspetti procedurali nel quadro di giurisdizioni concorrenti', in Arlinghaus et al. (eds.), *Praxis der Gerichtsbarkeit*, p. 271-303, p. 271.

from the traditional formalistic justice strictly influenced by the Romano-canonical procedures toward a mode of justice more reliant on judicial *arbitrium* in three political and social contexts from fourteenth-century Lucca, limiting my discussion simply to the level of procedures without addressing the level of substantive laws. First, I examine Lucca's changing legal environment, as reflected in jurists' *consilia* (Section 4). Second, I address a change that took place in the practice of raising exceptions, which had been a vector in civil proceedings for formalistic jurists, as well as in judges' ways of responding to them (Section 5). Third, I discuss the intervention of the Pisan doge, which in fact contributed to the expansion of judges' *arbitrium* (Section 6). Close consideration of court practices, from these viewpoints, reveals that the new logic of justice emerged gradually on the basis of practices in the local courts as the unexpected and contingent consequence of collaborative action by litigant parties, judges, local jurists, and political authorities like the doge, each of whom acted strategically in pursuit of their own interests.

4. The Decline of Local Jurists

(1) Breaking the monopoly of the collegium iudicum

I would like to pay attention here to the local jurists who dominated civil justice and reinforced its formalistic aspects in the first half of the fourteenth century, as it has been supposed that the decline of their influence *preceded* the rise of judicial *arbitrium* in the latter half of the fourteenth century.

The jurists who delivered *consilia* belonged to the *collegium iudicum* in Lucca. In 1333, this college was composed of 17 jurists, and all of them came from Lucca and its territory.[25] A 1301 register from the Court of San Cristoforo, the oldest extant book of proceedings in Lucca, lists six final judgements, all based on separate *consilia* by local jurists.[26] Afterwards, during the first half of the fourteenth century, advice by local jurists belonging to the *collegium iudicum* provided a degree of legal uniformity to Lucca's various civil courts by effectively guiding court decisions, including in the Appellate Court and the Curia of Rettori.

Members of the *collegium iudicum* not only delivered *consilia* to judicial courts but also were appointed as judges in the courts of consuls and courts in the vicariates. Moreover, they acted in the political sphere as members of the Anziani and its councils and as the editors of the city statutes.[27] Their ability to give legitimacy to communal institutions was derived from extra-communal authority, namely, the *ius commune*. These local jurists managed to maintain constant influence as custodians of civil and

---

25 ASL, *Anziani avanti la Libertà* (hereafter *Anz. Av. Lib.*), 5, p. 112; L. Green, *Lucca under Many Masters: A Fourteenth-Century Italian Commune in Crisis (1328-1342)* (Firenze, 1995), p. 205.

26 ASL, *Curia di San Cristoforo*, 7.

27 Sara Menzinger clearly reveals the importance of jurists for the legitimacy of council activities in the case of Bologna and Perugia, S. Menzinger, *Giuristi e politica nei comuni di Popolo. Siena, Perugia e Bologna, tra governi a confronto* (Roma, 2006).

political order in Lucca throughout the thirteenth and the first half of the fourteenth centuries, a politically turbulent age under the successive rulership of the Lucchese Popolo, Uguccione di Pisa, Castruccio Castracani, and several other foreign masters.

Local jurists' monopoly over providing legal advice to the courts was already prescribed in the 1308 statutes. The provision '*de questionibus commictendis iudicibus collegii Lucane Civitatis*', which came into force also in the 1331 statutes, prohibited judges from committing suits to jurists who did not belong to the *collegium iudicum*, on penalty of a 100 *lire* fine.[28]

However, this monopoly was undermined by Pisan rule from 1342 to 1368. A 1350 proviso to a 1342 statute contained the interpretative comment '*ad declarationem et coreptionem statutorum*' stipulating the rule regarding commission to the *collegium iudicum*: if judges belonging to the *collegium iudicum* were not able to reach an accord among themselves, the *collegium* must transmit the matter to be consulted to the jurist, not suspected by parties, whom the *collegium* wanted to elect or to have colloquium from inside or outside of the city of Lucca.[29] It is certain that this proviso – in particular, 'the jurist to be committed from inside or outside of the city' –, was intended to permit foreign jurists to intervene in the city's civil justice.

The 1372 statutes, enacted after Lucca won its independence, expanded the possibilities for commissioning foreign jurists. The provision '*De commissionibus faciendis*' authorised judges in the moment of the final judgement to commit cases to jurists resident within 40 miles of Lucca, a distance that encompassed Pisa, Pistoia, and Florence but not Siena or Bologna. Legal advice for intermediate judgements could still only be commissioned from the members of the Lucchese *collegium iudicum*.[30]

The period of Pisan rule in the middle of the fourteenth century proved to be the tipping point for the decline of local jurists in Lucca. I would like to closely examine two points about what happened in the jurists' world during this time, namely, the increased influence of Pisan jurists and the deterioration of the legal environment in Lucca.

(2) Intervention by Pisan jurists

Pisa, located 16 kilometres from Lucca, was a city where the Justinian code was rediscovered and then studied assiduously.[31] In the fourteenth century, it ranked alongside

28 *Statuto 1308*, IV, 25 (de questionibus commictendis iudicibus collegii Lucane Civitatis), p. 263.

29 ASL, *Statuto del Comune di Lucca*, 5 (hereafter *Statuto 1342*), fol. 129r: 'Et si iudices omnes dicti collegii non essent concordes in consilio dando super dicta questione eis comissa, quod dictum collegium teneatur et debeat consulendam transmittere alicui iurisperito partibus non suspecto quem eligere voluerint vel colloquium habere cum quo voluerint de intus civitatis Lucane vel extra'.

30 ASL, *Statuto del Comune di Lucca*, 6 (hereafter *Statuto 1372*), IV, 36 (De commissionibus faciendis), fols. 98v-99r.

31 While the two codes compiled by Pisa in the 1160s (*Constitutum legis* and *Constitutum usus*) were initially based on Lombard law, Roman legal concepts and provisions were subsequently appended in the later twelfth century, so that by the start of the thirteenth century they had come to incorporate many elements of Roman law. C. Wickham, *Courts and Conflict in Twelfth-Century Tuscany* (Oxford, 2003), p. 114-116.

Bologna and Perugia as a base of *ius commune*. Bartolo da Sassoferrato started teaching there in 1339. His student, Baldo degli Ubaldi, taught at the University of Pisa in 1357.[32]

Although the hostile relations between the two cities prior to 1342 prevents us from satisfactorily confirming exchanges of legal personnel between Lucca and Pisa during this time, Pisan rule from 1342 to 1368 brought considerable intervention in the Lucchese judicial sphere by Pisa, where *ius commune* was more entrenched. It is particularly noteworthy that Pisan jurists intervened in civil justice as the providers of *consilia*. Whereas in 1345, all jurists who were entrusted with 21 cases were Lucchese, one of the 12 commissions awarded in 1356 resulted in the delivery of a *consilium* by a Pisan jurist. In 1365, 4 out of 10 *consilia* (including intermediate judgements) were delivered by Pisan jurists. This confirms that Pisan jurists were gradually infiltrating the Lucchese legal sphere, reflecting the proviso permitting the commissioning of *consilia* from non-citizen jurists.

A November 1347 petition by the Lucchese *collegium iudicum* to the Anziani illustrates the circumstances of the arrival of Pisan jurists. The petition stated that the litigant parties, in the event they anticipated that the advice given by local jurists would be disadvantageous to their case, would turn to the Appellate Court to have the case entrusted to a foreign jurist.[33] The Lucchese jurists decried this troublesome strategy by litigants, arguing it to be a waste of labour and expense that tarnished the 'honour' of the Lucchese *collegium iudicum*. They asked the Anziani to instruct the Appellate Court to disclose the advice of local jurists. This petition, whose demands were accepted by the Anziani, shows that the introduction of foreign (specifically, Pisan) jurists into Lucchese civil justice was instigated by strategic action on the part of litigants, and shows the displeasure felt by Lucchese jurists whose advice was blocked by the commission of cases to foreign jurists.

The *consilia* delivered by Pisan jurists occasioned a shift in the content of *consilia*. Whereas legal advice in the 1330s focused on procedural formalities, *consilia* in 1365 and 1396 discussed more substantive points with reference to legal texts and the concept of *ius commune*. The *consilium* of Lapo, mentioned previously, referred to the *Digesta* and a text by Cino da Pistoia. It also used the concept of '*motus animi*', which Baldo had emphasised as a criterion for judicial decisions. According to Baldo, judges must interpret the allegations with their own *arbitrium* and specify the truth of them according to their '*motus animi*'.[34] Lapo's *consilium* obviously drew theoretically on the ideas of Baldo, who taught in Pisa from 1357-1358. Thus, the ideas of the commentators exerted an influence on the practice of civil justice in Lucca.

---

32 E. Spagnesi, 'L'insegnamento di Baldo degli Ubaldi a Pisa e Firenze', *Atti e memorie dell'Accademia toscana di scienze e lettere La Colombaria*, 69 (2004), p. 127-155.

33 *Anz. Av. Lib.*, 26, fol. 117r. In fact, in one 1365 trial we find a scenario in which, as a jurist's advice was about to be disclosed to the court, the other party visited the Appellate Court to halt the disclosure. *Potestà*, 428, fols. 23r-26v, 50r-51r.

34 A. Padoa Schioppa, 'La coscienza del giudice', in Id. (ed.), *Italia ed Europa nella storia del diritto* (Bologna, 2003), p. 251-292; Baldo degli Ubaldi, *Consilia* (Lugduni, 1543), vol. I, cons. 310: '[si] motus iudicis cum confessione concurrit, de suo motu animi debet stani eius verbo, quia iudex non presumitur immemor salutis eterne: statur iudici asserenti de conscientia sua…, quia mentes hominum non possunt depingi in pergameno, lex commisit nonnulla iudicantis arbitrio et religioni'.

The introduction of the Pisan jurists' *consilia* and the accompanying concepts of *ius commune* acted in turn to influence the legal activities of parties, a few of whom began discussing judicial matters and about making use of '*actio*' and legal texts in the second half of the fourteenth century. Conceivably, demand for local jurists who specialised in traditional formalities would have declined in this situation.

(3) The deterioration of the legal environment

Next, let us consider the deterioration of Lucca's legal environment as a contributing factor in the decline in the number and influence of local jurists. This change in circumstances was already underway before the introduction of Pisan jurists.

Lucchese jurists had traditionally travelled to Bologna to study *ius commune*. In a case in 1338, Dino Maulini supplicated the Anziani to waive a custody tax for his son Bartolomeo, a notary who would eventually become a *iudex* in 1350s, on the grounds that Bartolomeo was studying *ius commune* in Bologna.[35] On 17 September 1347, the Lucchese Anziani established a scholarship of 10 florins a year for five years for those who wanted to study *ius civile vel canonicum* or *ars medicinalis* in Bologna.[36] It is worth noting the stated motivations of this scholarship. The preamble said that 'it was wished that the city of Lucca would be replete with virtuous people, above all those who had *artibus liberalibus*, for which the city now lacks because of the poverty of citizens'.[37] The impression given in the preamble about the poor state of legal studies in Lucca can be confirmed when reading an appeal to the Anziani presented by a group of citizens composed of one jurist, three notaries, and eight other city residents on 17 December 1347, three months after the scholarship decree.

> They have long desired, and still eagerly desire to be led to the knowledge of the *ius civile* by the grace of God and your lordship. But the lack of faculties, due to immediate urgency and infested necessities and events, does not allow to make our way to Bologna or any other centre of jurisprudence for study. It is for this reason that the city of Lucca is so deprived of plenty of legal experts. No citizen of Lucca is found studying the *ius civile* in Bologna or any other place, as your prudent wisdom can see. If the remedy is not beneficially applied by your lordship, only few, or none at all, legal experts, those currently lacking, will be found in the city of Lucca. So, at the request of those who wish to study the *ius civile,* Martino has begun reading and teaching the codes. And although he wishes to continue his lecturing with God's

---

35 *Anz. Av. Lib.*, 13, p. 52. It should be noted that Bartholomeo later returned to Lucca as a jurist, where he went on to play an important role in the Lucchese politics of the later fourteenth century. In addition, in 1339 the notary Lanfranco Pellori received a tax exemption because he was studying the *ius commune* in Bologna. *Anz. Av. Lib.*, 14, fol. 2r.

36 *Anz. Av. Lib.*, 26, fol. 90r. It was also decided that five-year scholarships of 6 florins per year would be awarded to those wishing to acquire notary skills. Incidentally, scholars were obliged to dedicate themselves exclusively to their studies and to submit proof of this to the Anziani from their host instructor.

37 *Anz. Av. Lib.*, 26, fol. 90r: 'volentes quod civitas Lucana virtuosis hominibus repleatur et maxime in artibus liberalibus, de quibus expoliata est in presenti propter paupertatem civium et alia, que bono statui dicte civitatis concurrerunt contraria in preteritis'.

> blessing, lack of faculties prevents him from totally completing his lectures. [...] So, it is supplicated that, considering the utility and necessity of *res publica* and *bonum commune*, you provide Martino with the material resources that would allow him to continue to offer his teaching better. This is in order to prevent scholars and those with a desire to study jurisprudence from being deprived of good foundation.[38]

In answer to this complaint, the Anziani rendered a decision as follows:

> We consider the individual contents included in the petition, and of how much a plenty of legal experts certainly contribute to the honour and prestige of *res publica* of the city of Lucca and to the benefit of the citizens of Lucca, and desire to give material resources which would allow the aforementioned students, others wishing to study the *ius civile*, and to their doctor Martino to continue to do this study... Thus we provide that Martino must receive a stipend of 100 *lira* paid by the commune of Lucca from the treasurer of Lucca for a period of two years beginning from 1 January to come. This is contingent upon Martino's regular reading and teaching the above codes, as he should.[39]

A variety of circumstances come to mind as possibly underlying these two decisions, both handed down by the Anziani in 1347. Perhaps having witnessed and been inspired by the excellence of Pisan jurisprudence, the Anziani moved actively to train and cultivate jurists of their own. However, the complaint and the Anziani decree described above are strongly redolent of a sense of crisis over the actual shortage of jurists and potential successors. Underlying this deterioration in the jurisprudential environment seems to have been the fact that urban society was exhausted from the famines and wars that had recurred so often around this time (on the eve of the Great Plague), and the

---

38 *Anz. Av. Lib.*, 26, fol. 130r: '...quod ipsi cupierunt diutino tempore iam elapso et nunc avidius cupiunt ad iuris civilis scientiam provehi Dei et vestra gratia procedente, sed facultatibus eisdem deficientibus propter ingruentiam temporum et infestos necessitatis eventus nequiverunt et adhuc nequeunt Bononiam vel ad alia studia proficisci, propter quam causam civitas Lucana est destituta iuris copia peritorum. Nec in Bononia vel alibi aliquis civis Lucanus reperitur in iure civili studere, prout hec vestre prudentie patere possunt. Et nisi per vestram prudentiam remedium salubriter apponatur pauci aut nulli iurisperiti reperientur in civitate Lucana, hiis deficientibus qui modo sunt. Cumque dominus Martinus ad petitionem quorundam in iure civili studere volentium, legere codicem incohavit et in eius lectura intendat dei gratia perseverare, nec possit impotentia facultatum dicte lecture totaliter superesse... supplicatur qualiter attenta tam utilitate quam necessitate rei publice et communis boni placeat providere dicto domino Martino taliter quod super dicto studio habeat materiam perseverandi et dietam de bono in melius procedendi, ut predicti auditores et ceteri studere volentes in dicta scientia tanto bono principio non fraudentur'.

39 *Anz. Av. Lib.*, 26, fols. 130r-v: 'Nosque attendentes ad singula in dicta petitione contenta et quantum ad honorem et exornationem rei publice civitatis Lucane suorumque civium commoda redundet indubie copia peritorum, desiderantesque dare materiam quantum in nobis est studentibus suprascriptis, ac etiam aliis studere volentibus in iure civili et suprascripto domino Martino eorum doctori in ipso studio perseverandi... stantiamus providemus et ordinamus quod predictus dominus Martinus a kalendis januarii proxime futuris ad duos annos tunc proxime secuturos videlicet singulo anno durante dicto termino duorum annorum habeat et percipere debeat et consequatur de avere introitus et pecunia Lucani communis a camerario dicti introitus pro tempore existenti libras centum denariorum Lucanorum parvorum, si et inquantum dictus dominus Martinus ordinate legat ut debet librum codicis supradicti...'

fact that many jurists who had been part of the former leadership had been banished under enemy rule by Pisa.[40]

Yet, the attempt to re-establish a jurisprudential environment proved ineffective. The number of Lucchese jurists continued to decline steadily in spite of government assistance; although the precise number of jurists who belonged to the *collegium iudicum* is not clear, owing to the absence of any definitive accounts from the latter half of the fourteenth century, we find only three local jurists who appear in the court records and books of the Anziani from this period.[41]

The decline of local jurists that stemmed from the deterioration of the jurisprudence environment in Lucca in the middle of the fourteenth century is noteworthy as having *preceded* the decline of legal advice by local jurists, the commissioning of legal advice from Pisan jurists, and the increase in rulings by judges that all became apparent in the late fourteenth century. Of course, while the influence of Pisan jurists and, as we shall see, the intentions of litigants, and the increasing authority of judges, might conceivably have accelerated the decline in the influence and number of Lucchese jurists, this trend's starting point was the deterioration of the jurisprudence environment in Lucca and the decrease in the number of local jurists against the backdrop of the political, social, and economic crises leading up to the middle of the fourteenth century.

Pietro d'Anzola, a jurist from this period, in his commentary on a chapter in Rolandino's *Summa totius artis notariae* entitled 'On advice that should be given', explains that the commissioning of jurists arose in circumstances 'where judges cannot competently examine the content of evidence or the details of an argument because they are occupied in other works'.[42] In late fourteenth-century Lucca, another, diametrically opposed phenomenon emerged that could be explained by the same logic. That is, in circumstances where the number of local jurists in the region was decreasing and the few remaining jurists were very busy providing political advice and performing judicial administration, local jurists became distanced from the task of providing legal advice in civil trials. It seems highly likely that the actual circumstances of this decline among local jurists began with the decline of legal advice, as well as with the shift in judicial principle in Lucca.

---

40 For example, on 13 June 1347 a Lucchese jurist named Giovanni Sbarre, who had been active in the 1330s, asked the Anziani to be allowed to return to Lucca, after which his request was approved along with a tax exemption. *Anz. Av. Lib.*, 26, fols. 61r-62r.

41 Bartholomeo Maulini, Lodovico Mercati, Simone de Barga.

42 Rolandino Rodulphini Bononiensis, *Summa totius artis notariae* (Venezia, 1546), fol. 355r: 'Et quia iudex aliquando dubitat de quaestione coram agitata, vel quia quandoque in aliis negociis est in tantum occupatus: quod non potest conpetenter examinare probationes, neque audite allegationes'; A. Padoa Schioppa, 'Profili del processo civile nella Summa artis notariae di Rolandino', in Tamba (ed.), *Rolandino e l'Ars notaria*, p. 583-609, in particular p. 599.

5. Exceptions among Litigants and *Arbitrium Procedendi* among Judges

(1) Persons seeking legal advice

A provision in the 1308 statute stipulated that judges could only commit their cases to local jurists. It must be noted, however, that this provision did not necessarily obligate judges to commit their cases to jurists; it merely stipulated that in the event they did so, cases should be committed to local jurists. In fact, this point of not obligating judges to receive legal advice is consistent with the views of the learned jurist who wrote the *Ordo iudiciarius.* According to Tancred of Bologna's *Ordo iudiciarius* (completed in 1216) and the *Speculum iudiciale* of Guillaume Durand (first compiled in 1271, and later updated in 1286 and 1291), judges were required to render a decision based on their own judgement *or otherwise* after hearing from a legal adviser.[43] Nor is there any statement to be found in Rolandino's *Summa totius artis notariae* (1255) obligating judges to receive legal advice.[44]

However, a certain postscript appended to Lucca's 1331 statute and not found in the provisions of the 1308 statute states that 'officials [judges] of the commune of Lucca must commit civil cases [to jurists] at the request of the parties'.[45] The fact that this phrase was written in different ink suggests that it was added sometime after the statutes were compiled in 1331 (but prior to 1342). With this addition, when and if they were requested to commit their case to a jurist by the litigant parties, judges were now under obligation to commit cases to a *local* jurist. Incidentally, the city statutes of places like Siena and Pisa also included provisions for commissioning jurists based on requests from the parties, and accounts of the commissioning of cases to jurists 'at the request of the parties' have also been confirmed from judicial records in Milan.[46]

In *Summa totius artis notariae,* Rolandino places the initiative to commit cases to jurists with judges and restricts the roles of the parties solely to providing the names of jurists they consider suspicious or untrustworthy.[47] However, the contemporary jurist Pietro dei Boattieri offers a broad interpretation of Rolandino's view, reading it to mean that the parties should be able to provide judges with both the names of jurists they

43 Engelmann, p. 484-486.

44 Rolandino, *Summa totius artis notariae,* fols. 355r-356v (De consillis dandis). Rolandino notes that 'in some lands' judges issued their decisions on their own authority without relying on the jurists' advice. According to Padoa Schioppa, this suggests that it must have been typical for judges to base their rulings on jurists' advice in mid thirteenth-century Bologna, where this book was written. However, it cannot necessarily be said whether this was a customary practice or one that was mandated by law. Padoa Schioppa, 'Profili del processo civile', p. 598-601. While the earliest surviving sentence books for a Bolognese civil trial are from 1336, approximately eighty years after Rolandino's work, the sentences are not based on a jurist's advice. Archivio di Stato di Bologna, *Curia del Podesta, Atti, decreti e sentenze,* 2. Conversely, legal advice was customary in Milan. A. Padoa Schioppa, 'La giustizia milanese nella prima età viscontea (1277-1300)', in *Ius Mediolani: studi di storia del diritto milanese offerti dagli allievi a Giulio Vismara* (Milano, 1996), p. 1-46, in particular p. 19-30.

45 *Statuto 1331,* p. 128: 'Et teneatur quilibet officialis Lucani communis questione civiles ad petitionem partis comictere eo modo quo dictum est supra sub dicta pena'.

46 Padoa Schioppa, 'La giustizia milanese', p. 19-25.

47 Rolandino, *Summa totius artis notariae,* fol. 355r: 'quoniam hanc causam cum consilio sapientium decidere volo…'.

find suspicious and of those they find trustworthy. The act of providing the names of trustworthy jurists opens up the possibilities for the parties' active involvement in the selection of jurists.[48] In Lucca, as well, on occasions of commissions to jurists during actual trials, the names of trustworthy and suspicious persons were conveyed to judges by the litigants.[49]

(2) Exceptions and legal advice

The phrase appended to the 1331 city statute that a judge 'must commit civil cases [to jurists] at the request of the parties' suggests that legal advice would have become more common if requests for legal advice by the litigants were more frequent, and vice versa. The intentions and strategies of litigants had the potential to be problematic as factors affecting the increase and decrease of advice by jurists, which is key to understanding the shift of judicial principle that took place in the fourteenth century.

An important action by parties to elicit jurists' advice was the exceptions, which have already featured repeatedly in these pages before now. While exceptions in which disadvantaged litigants attempted to reverse their prospects by challenging the legal qualifications of opponents and identifying procedural faults were frequently raised in the early fourteenth century, most of these cases were entrusted to the advice of local jurists as a result. In other words, the high volume of exceptions raised by parties elicited lots of advice from local jurists, thereby situating the courts as arenas that placed an emphasis on correctness of form.

Looking at the transition of exceptions over the fourteenth century, we find that while the proportion of exceptions presented by litigants (i.e. the combined total of 'essential issues and exceptions and 'exceptions only' in Table 2) experienced a slight decline, it can be confirmed that a certain number remained in the late fourteenth century as well. However, the proportion of parties attempting to cut their way through trials exclusively by searching for formalistic faults on the part of their opponents ('exceptions only') had dropped significantly.

---

48 Padoa Schioppa, 'Profili del processo civile', p. 601.

49 *Potestà*, 423, fol. 53v: 'Et quaesito per dictum dominum iudicem ab ipsius partibus de earum confidentibus et suspectis et eis habitis et in scriptis receptis idem dominus iudex de dictarum partium voluntate et ipse hedem partes lites et questiones… commiserunt in sapientem virum ambabus partibus confidentem dominum Lodovicum legum doctorem filium domini Guilielmum Mercati de Luca'. Also, in a 1365 case, a Lucchese rather than a Pisan jurist was admitted as a 'trustworthy person' because the parties felt that the problem at issue should be committed to a Lucchese lawyer knowledgeable on the subject of Lucchese statutes, laws, and consuetude. *Potestà*, 423, fol. 53r: 'ex quo partes ambe sunt Lucane, et de foro Lucano ipsa questio comicti debent in iudicem Lucanum et quia facilius statuta brevia et iura Lucana et consuetudines ut praticus ipsorum scire et habere poterit. Et dat pro confidentibus omnes iudices Lucanos neminem exceptando nisi solum advocatum partis adverse'.

Table 3.2: Topics of discussion at trials
(*figures in the table represent number of cases; percentages indicate the proportion of trials in which discussions were held)

	1336		1365		1396	
	CASE	%	CASE	%	CASE	%
Essential issues only	126	45	68	56	33	61
Essential issues and exceptions	63	22.5	27	22	17	32
Exceptions only	91	32.5	26	22	4	7
Total	**280**	100	**121**	100	**54**	100

Next, looking at changes to each type of exception (Table 3), we find a decline among them to the effect that opponents lacked legal qualifications, being subject to *bannum* or *pronuntia,* and among exceptions concerned with the format of documents. In 1336, these exceptions frequently impeded discussions and had the effect of extinguishing trials and even rights themselves, and were a problem often committed to the care of jurists. In particular, the problems that were the subjects of the exceptions relating to *bannum* and *pronuntia* were caused when judges inadvertently commenced trials or issued summary judicial orders against individuals who were not eligible to stand trial. Accordingly, the disappearance of these exceptions could be conceived of as a sign of the emergence of a more conscientious attitude on the part of judges and an active attitude toward trials on the part of judges in the latter half of the fourteenth century.

Still, one other factor may explain the decline of exceptions relating to matters such as *bannum*. Namely, this was the introduction of fines for cases where exceptions pertaining to such matters could not be proven, as indicated in a clause entitled 'On the punishment for those claiming but being unable to prove exceptions in relation to *bannum* and *pronuntia,* and so on'.[50] Although it is unclear exactly when between 1331 and 1372 this provision, which we first see in the 1372 statutes, was added,[51] the effects of this provision seem to have caused litigating parties to cease the practice of raising exceptions regarding *bannum* and *pronuntia* indiscriminately.

Even though the number of cases involving the presentation of exceptions declined over the period between 1336 and 1365, the relative proportion of each type of exceptions did not decrease significantly. In comparison, the number of exceptions dropped significantly in 1396. This was due to the existence of a new provision added on 24

50 *Statuto 1372*, IV, 155 (De pena opponentis et non probantis exceptionem inbannimenti seu pronunciamenti vel aliam), fol. 120r. The provision stipulates that in the event that proof cannot be supplied, the offenders will be subject to a summary fine of up to 100 *soldi.*

51 While this provision appears in its complete form in the 1372 city statute, the fact that it derives from the 'court statute' rather than the city statutes makes it impossible to determine exactly when it was added between 1331 and 1372. Looking at the court statute for 1331, we find the same title as that of the 1372 provision in the margins of a provision concerning exceptions. The city statute and court statute were first consolidated in the 1372 city statute.

Table 3.3: Changes in the subject of exceptions
(*figures in the table represent number of cases; percentages indicate the proportion of total **exceptions**)

	1336	1365	1396
Exceptions concerning personal qualifications	75 (8.3%)	20 (6.5%)	5 (2.6%)
Procurator	29	12	4
Tutor	4	3	
Ban (*bannum*)	13		
Pronuntia	8		
Citizen's default of duty	9	1	
Non-participation in the civil defence group (*bapneria*)	4	1	
Foreigner	4	1	1
Minor	4	2	
Exceptions concerning procedure	140 (16%)	57 (19%)	18 (9%)
Legal procedures	58	26	9
Format of documents	31	4	
Procedures validating contracts and judicial orders	3	1	
Competence of judges	21	22	6
Lite pendente	27	4	3
Other	19		1
Total	**234 (26%)**	**77 (25%)**	**24 (13%)**

October 1381 by the Anziani and those responsible for revising statutes. This was a provision entitled 'On exceptions that obstruct litigation', in which a restriction was placed on exceptions in general as follows:

> Because trials and their proceedings are delayed every day as the result of exceptions that impede the development of the trials, we desire that no exception should be presented to impede proceedings, unless the exception regards matters already judged (*res iudicata*), giuraments, and the payment of debts that can be proven with public documents.[52]

Also, a supplemental provision added on 18 December 1381 stipulated that lawsuits that had been procedurally stalled for a period of four months must not be obstructed by an exception to the effect that litigation was pending (*lite pendente*).[53] The attitude on the part of the Anziani and statute reformers in their attempt, evident in these two

52 *Statuto* 1372, fols. 158r-v. 'Et quia cotidie per exceptiones que ad impediendum processum processus et expeditio retardatur, volumus quod nulla exceptio processum impediat nisi exceptio rei iudicate transactionis et iurisiurandi et solutionis debiti quod petitur de quibus appareant publica documenta…'

53 *Statuto* 1372, fol. 164r: 'Item quod exceptio litis pendentis solet in causis occurrere volumus quod si in causa dicte litis pendentis fuerit cessatum procedi per quatuor menses tunc exceptio litis pendentis non obstet'.

provisions from 1381, to prevent the strategic deployment of exceptions that would prolong litigation in a meaningless fashion, seems to be the highly significant factor given that litigants in 1396 no longer engaged in the indiscriminate raising of exceptions to the degree they did before.

Even so, why was it that laws that deviated considerably from the prior legal traditions of the court – to the extent that they were able to reject even exceptions that raised doubts about the legal legitimacy of trials – ended up being enacted in 1381? To reflect on this question, indeed, we will have to look at prior conditions in the sites of practice, meaning in this case the practices of the courts in 1365.

(3) The fate of exceptions

When we compare 1336 with 1365, we find that the proportion of cases in which exceptions were raised had not significantly decreased. In fact, some even showed an upward trend, such as exceptions concerning legal procedures and exceptions concerning the qualifications of judges. However, as we look at the trial process (see Figure 1), cases for which the legal advice of jurists was commissioned had dropped by half. Why did this happen? Anticipating my conclusion, the answer is that the way of handling exceptions brought before the courts had changed. That is, formalistic issues arising from the exceptions of litigants were no longer entrusted to jurists, but had instead started to be adjudicated or rejected by judges.

A good illustration of this trend is the reduction in the number of interlocutory judgements based on legal advice issued mid-trial when exceptions introduced complications. Whereas 19 cases were committed to jurists mid-trial for exceptions in 1336, leading to interlocutory judgements issued based on legal advice, only two such cases arose in 1365, while absolutely none at all can be confirmed for 1396. And instead of being handled by jurists, exceptions were now handled independently by judges. How did this situation come about? I would like to think about this by looking at a few cases.

On 13 November 1365, in a trial involving a claim brought by one Nicolozo (acting as procurator for Paupo) seeking the restitution of real property from one Francesco, upon Nicolozo's submission of his procurator's certificate the defendant, Francesco, countered that Nicolozo did not have a valid contract to represent his client.[54] At this, Nicolozo insisted that he had been commissioned as a legitimate representative. Here, the judge instructed the parties in attendance that the issue would be committed to a jurist. Shortly thereafter, however, both parties requested the judge to adjudicate justice (*ius*) in this matter. In response to this request, the judge investigated the procurator's contract certificate and declared that Nicolozo's qualifications as procurator were legitimate.

As with this one, other cases can be found in which the parties elected to have judges rather than local jurists act as referees on matters of procedural form.[55] Most likely, the parties would have expected such decisions to be carried out quickly and inexpensively.

---

54 *Potestà*, 432, fols. 63r-65v.

55 *Potestà*, 424, fol. 40r; *Potestà*, 426, fol. 7r

Even so, we find few cases in which parties confronted with such exceptions are clearly shown to have entrusted matters to adjudication by a judge. In most cases, either no indication was given or a request was made to commission a jurist. What is interesting is the responses given by judges at such times.

In a trial that began on 11 July 1365 at the Court of Podestà between the plaintiff, Moccio (procurator acting for Benedetto, the abbot of Santo Cristiane monastery), and the defendant, Giovanni de Poggio,[56] Giovanni argued that Moccio had not been appointed as a formal procurator and was thus ineligible to bring the case to trial. In response, on 15 July Moccio claimed that his appointment was bona fide and indicated his desire for the judge to issue a declaration to this effect. The same day, Giovanni deployed a new exception, this time saying that 'Your lordship [the judge] does not have the competence to rule on this matter'. On 21 July, the judge examined the mandate of the procurator submitted to the court and declared Moccio to be a legitimate procurator. On 24 July, Giovanni continued his exception, citing a clause entitled 'On the *podestà*, not conducting trials against certain persons'. On 28 July, the judge referred to the items pertaining to summary proceedings in the statutes and declared that he possessed authority in the case at hand. Giovanni tenaciously persisted, and on two occasions – on 2 August and again on 4 August – he deployed exceptions concerning Moccio's qualifications as procurator and questioned the judge's competence, requesting that legal advice be given if his opponent objected. On 21 August, in a letter from the Pisan doge, the judge received direction to conclude the trial with a summary judgment. Perhaps because of this directive, the judge subsequently continued the lawsuit on his own recognizance, without commissioning a jurist. In October, the plaintiff's party proceeded with the presentation of a *positio,* and the judge asked the defendant to respond to the same. Giovanni was still not satisfied, and on 5 November presented another exception regarding the procurator's contract and the judge's competence. The judge rejected Giovanni's argument and ordered him to respond to the *positio* presented on the part of the plaintiff. At this, Giovanni responded to the *positio* while making plain his disagreement, and the trial at last proceeded.

Had it been 1336, Giovanni's persistent exception would have been promptly passed on to a local jurist. But in 1365, judges rendered their own decisions. Moreover, this was despite the fact that Giovanni was *requesting* the commission of a jurist. The provision appended to the 1331 statute that a judge 'must commit civil cases [to jurists] at the request of the parties' was in this case ignored.

As another example, in a trial in which the Pisan jurist Lapo presented legal advice for a final judgement, the defendant raised an exception midway through the trial to the effect that an affidavit submitted on the part of the plaintiff had missed the deadline for bringing evidence and was therefore inadmissible and, furthermore, had requested the advice of a jurist. Ignoring both requests, the judge decided on his own to allow the testimony.[57]

56 *Potestà*, 432, fols. 2r-11v, 80r-84r.
57 *Potestà*, 422, fols. 61r-61v.

Despite the occurrence of a certain number of exceptions in 1365 as well, the reason for the decline in the incidence of the commissioning of jurists and the seeking of legal advice was specifically the increased initiative on the part of judges to move trials forward by cutting short exceptions and making decisions on their own. In the legal terminology of the day, judges possessed a large degree of *arbitrium procedendi* (procedural discretion). The closure of the route from exceptions on the part of litigants to the solicitation of the advice of jurists led to a decline in the number of cases ending after a jurist had given advice on their legitimacy as well as a rise in the number of cases in which judges exercised discretionary freedom in their rulings on issues of substantive rights.

Therefore, it was judges' gaining of *arbitrium procedendi*, a power that existed in a separate dimension from either the intentions of litigants or the circumstances of local jurists (i.e. whether or not the parties placed any trust in local jurists) which was another important key to explaining the motive behind the shift from formalism to *arbitrium* in the civil courts of fourteenth-century Lucca. This is where our final problem emerges. Namely, how was it that judges in Lucca were able to acquire such *arbitrium procedendi*?

6. The Doge and 'Proper' Summary Justice

(1) Permission from the doge for judges to dispense summary justice

i). Letter from the doge

The concept of *arbitrium procedendi* is in direct opposition to the adversarial system that served as a fundamental principle in the Romano-canonical procedure. It finds legal justification in Clement V's *Saepe contingit,* which established summary justice as well as commentaries on this text by canon law jurists, a fact that would also have been known in Lucca during the latter half of the fourteenth century. One litigant involved in a trial at the Court of Podestà in 1367 stated that 'even in the trials which must proceed summarily, the ordinary procedure which is prescribed in the chapter in the *Saepe contingit* and in other laws must be followed'.[58] The circumstances by which the courts and people of Lucca came to know of these theories of jurisprudence remain unclear. It is conceivable that Pisan jurists may have introduced them, but the exact reasons are unknown. However, the issue here is how this new theory or these new procedures came to be introduced and disseminated throughout Lucca, whose juridical practice had been deeply ingrained with formalism. Certainly, declining numbers of local jurists and increasing requests to judges by parties in the mid-fourteenth century were the context in which judges were gradually conferred with greater powers of

58 *Potestà*, 450, fol. 143v: '...respondet quod etiam in causis in quibus procedi debet summarie sequi et servari debet ordo iuris traditus in preallegato capitulo saepe contingit... in clementina et in aliis iuribus'.

initiative. Therein, however, we find that there existed another powerful motive that promoted judges' discretionary powers.

Surveying the court records for 1365, one notices several curious entries that do not conform to the court record format. These are copies of letters to the *podestà* of Lucca and his judges from the Pisan doge, Giovanni dell'Agnello, who was a *signore* of Pisa and ruled Lucca during this period.[59] The existence of a total of 23 such letters has been confirmed for 1365, 19 in the proceeding books and a further four in the *Liber memorie*. These letters were not limited to 1365 but were issued multiple times between 1364 and 1368 as Giovanni established his signorial rule in Pisa as doge.

Moreover, intervention by a political actor such as the Pisan doge in trials, and above all in civil trials, was quite unusual in the Lucchese courts, which followed the Romano-canonical procedure. Even under the rule of the Pisan Anziani and other foreign masters in the first half of the fourteenth century, political actors had never intervened in individual cases in the civil courts; trials in which only jurists and judges could participate, were supposed to be an inviolable sphere for politics. In the late 1360s, this principle was temporarily shattered. The intervention of an extrajudicial element in the person of the doge was in itself an important factor enabling the expansion of the *arbitrium* of judges in Lucca.

The doge's instructions to the Court of Podestà were frequently neutral or general in terms of their content, and for the most part refrained from favouring individual parties in litigation.[60] We frequently encounter instructions encouraging the elucidation of relevant facts and the rapid advancement of a trial, urging '[the *podestà*] to discover the truth with regard to the content of the petition and to conduct a summary trial quickly and expeditiously, without clamour and the form of ordinary trial procedure'.[61] In some cases, the letters specify a deadline for the resolution of a trial along with instructions that the lawsuit in question 'should be brought to completion without delay within 20 days'.[62] Moreover, while we find instructions for the commissioning of arbitrators or to hasten decisions by arbitrators (5 cases),[63] these could also be said to be instructions aimed at promptly resolving cases brought before the courts without the fuss of a trial.

The implications of instructions on the part of the doge encouraging the discovery of the truth and ensuring a rapid resolution of a trial are easily understood when we consider the alternative. What the doge sought to eliminate, as is evident from his

---

59 The signore of Pisa, Giovanni dell'Agnello de' Conti, established his control of Pisa on behalf of the *popolo* regime from August 1364, simultaneously governing or perhaps reigning as the ruler of Lucca, a state of affairs that continued until the Holy Roman Emperor Charles IV's visit to Lucca in August 1368. Meek, *The Commune of Lucca under Pisan Rule, 1342-1369* (Cambridge, 1980), p. 105-118.

60 Although specific instructions do exist, such cases do not recognise the interests of any one side. E.g. *Potestà*, 426, 65r: '... volumus quod ... informes... si prefatus Gerius ipsum ronzinum de florentia duxit ante pacem factam vel postea...'; *Potestà*, 432, 69r: '...volumus tibi mandantes quatenus diligenter inquiras si pacta predicta inita et facta fuerunt de consensu et voluntate partium'.

61 *Potestà*, 421, 79r: 'Volumus tibique mandamus ut reperta veritate de contentis in petitione[...] ius summarium expeditum et celere sine strepitu et figura iudicii facias et ministres'.

62 *Potestà*, 423, fol. 16r; *Potestà*, 423, fol. 41r; *Ibid.*, fol. 43v; *Potestà*, 424, fol. 5r; *Potestà*, 424, fol. 10r; *Potestà*, 426, fol. 7r; *Potestà*, 426, fol. 34r; *Potestà*, 426, fol. 80r.

63 *Potestà*, 421, fol. 5r; *Potestà*, 423, fol. 3r; *Potestà*, 423, fol. 52r; *Potestà*, 424, fol. 55r; *Potestà*, 430, fol. 27r.

explanation that 'these frivolous and expense cavilings in trials are most odious to us',[64] was a situation in which trials would be senselessly drawn out by a exception as a vile practice obscuring the essential issues of complaints and hindering the discovery of truth.

At the root of this lay the traditional Roman legal principle of formalism and an adversarial principle that imposed obligations on judges. The doge's instructions of summary justice were intended to allow judges to focus on the discovery of truth and to proceed freely from the legal binding. These instructions from a higher political authority provided a direct opportunity for the Lucchese judges to acquire *arbitrium procedendi.*

In the trial, discussed earlier, between Moccio, the procurator for the Santo Cristiane monastery, and Giovanni de Poggio, a major reason why the judge could ignore the persistent exception raised by Giovanni regarding the judge's competence and the qualifications of the procurator for the other party and so abstain from commissioning legal advice, was the directive he received from the doge on 20 August to, 'in consideration of the rights of both parties, ...we order [judges] to conduct summary trial and dispense justice without delay'.[65]

ii). The litigants motivating the doge

It was complaints from parties that made the doge issue these instructions, which served to strengthen judges' *arbitrium*. In almost all cases, instructions from the doge were issued in the form of answers to petitions by litigants. Letters sent from the doge to Lucca would be accompanied by petitions submitted to the doge by litigants, and the clerks of the Court of Podestà who received them transcribed the letters into the court records along with the content of petitions. Because the parties would sometimes be forced to carry letters from the doge to the *podestà* to the court, one can imagine how the litigant parties could sometimes visit the Pisan doge to make their complaints in person, there to acquire a letter directly that they would carry to the court in Lucca.[66]

Petitions to the doge were an effective litigation strategy for litigants. The parties would often visit the doge in the midst of a trial in an attempt to influence the trial to their own benefit. For example, in the trial mentioned earlier between Moccio and Giovanni, Moccio, the procurator for the monastery, who continued to be annoyed by exceptions, visited the doge to file the following complaint.

---

64 *Potestà*, 423, fol. 16r: 'Quia litigantium cavillationes frivole qui sunt expensarum materia nobis sunt plurimum odiose [...]'

65 *Potestà*, 432, fols. 7v.: 'mandamus quatenus visis et auditis iuribus partium [...] ius summarium et iustitie complementum tribuas sine mora'.

66 Even in the instructions from the doge, it is indicated that the complaint is being sent together with the letter, and that the instructions are being given in connexion with the same. *Potestà*, 423, fol. 53r: 'Mictimus tibi praesentibus licteris inclusam petitionem super qua volumus quod[...]'. In other examples, the doge sends a letter to a party, instructing them to visit him. *Potestà*, 423, fol. 17r: '...vogliamo che sensa indugio veduta la presente lectera vegni a Pisa alla nostra presentia... provido viro Pacino Martini civi nostro Lucano nobis dilecto'.

> It is supplicated that the monastery and its procurator not be led into and held in disputes in this way, but that the lawsuit be done and be brought to a conclusion summarily, plainly, without clamour and the form of ordinary trial procedure, without protraction, in consideration of the rights of the parties on principal fact and adherence to the truth. Also that the strict procedures and delays that were specifically deemed to be exempted by your lordship [the doge] be eliminated … and without being hindered by dilatory and declamatory exceptions or other evasive words and cavilings….[67]

In response to this petition, on 20 August the doge issued the aforementioned instruction to the judge 'in consideration of the rights of both parties … to conduct summary trial and dispense justice without delay'. From this point, we can confirm how, in situations where trials had become bogged down in stalemate as the result of exceptions raised by their opponents, parties would visit the doge in an attempt to direct proceedings their way, whereupon the doge would grant a judge permission to proceed summarily. The canonist, Giovanni d'Andrea, explained that while the decision whether or not to invoke Clementina Saepe, which authorised a judge's *arbitrium procedendi*, was made by judges themselves in cases concerning to public law, it was made by parties for matters pertaining to rights in relations between individuals.[68] Indeed, this principle would become apparent in Lucca as well, in the form of the parties' petitions to the doge.

(2) In search of a 'proper' trial: interpretations by parties and the judges

i). Rapid trials as complete cognizance

In specific terms, then, let us consider the development of summary justice which began with the intervention of the doge. While it is certain that the instruction 'to discover the truth…and to conduct a summary trial quickly and expeditiously, without clamour and the form of ordinary trial procedure' permitted judges to break away from formalism and the adversarial system, what that entailed in specific terms remains vague. How quickly did judges proceed with their trials, and to what extent did they ignore trial formats and exceptionsargued by the parties?[69] Something that we should recall first is that this summary justice, grounded in *Saepe contingit* and beginning with instructions from the doge, did not aspire to be a summary trial as an alternative to a normal trial,

---

67 *Potestà*, 432, fols. 7r-v: 'supplicatur quod… ne dicte monales vel earum sindicus et procurator taliter ducantur vel teneantur in litigio sed summarie et de plano sine strepitu et figura iudicii et sine protelatione videantur iura partium super facto principali et terminetur veritate respecta sine temporis intervallo, obmissis solepmnitatibus et dilationibus quibus intelligatur ex vostro restricto generaliter et specialiter derogatum […] non obstantibus aliquibus exceptionibus dilatoriis et declamatoriis vel aliis suffugiis et cavillationibus […]'

68 Meccarelli, *Arbitrium*, p. 265-266.

69 In the case of Bologna's criminal trials, judges listened to the defendant's exceptions and adopted a cautious attitude even to supporting evidence, despite having received permission to conduct summary trials from the executive council. S. R., Blanshei, *Politics and Justice in Late Medieval Bologna* (Leiden and Boston, 2010), p. 484-497.

but rather to a 'cognizance that, though stripped of formality and rendered expeditious, was still materially *complete*'.[70]

Even the doge issuing the instruction to expedite the trial seems to have been conscious of not infringing on the legal legitimacy of trials grounded in legal procedures and statutes. In the aforementioned trial between the plaintiff, Moccio, the procurator for the Santo Cristiane monastery, and the defendant, Giovanni de Poggio,[71] the doge, having received a complaint from the plaintiff, Benedetto, issued orders to the *podestà* on 20 August and 9 December to 'conduct a trial on the issue addressed by the complaint without spending a lot of time and increasing expenses with frivolous cavilings'.[72] However, in a letter from the doge dated 19 November and submitted by Giovanni to the Court of Podestà on 11 December, the doge, who had received a complaint from Giovanni requesting that the trial should be conducted based on Lucchese law, directed the judge to observe legalities and adhere to the mandate of justice.[73] Most likely the doge, too, had no wish for the trial itself to lose legal legitimacy owing to excessive curtailment on account of a judge's aggressive timetable.[74]

ii). Litigants' interpretations of 'summary justice'

Therefore, the task of concretely rendering the doge's abstract instructions to carry out the trial expeditiously but with complete cognizance in accordance with individual cases, was entrusted to the people in the actual courts – namely to litigants and judges. Here, the issue was frequently that of determining whether exceptions argued by the respective parties were 'frivolous excuses' that should be dismissed as stalling tactics or else matters that should be heeded as fundamentally determining the legitimacy of the trial and the rights at issue.

In a trial that began on 19 December 1365,[75] the judge, based on summary instructions from the doge, dismissed an exception raised by the defendant, Paccino Martini, against the appointment of the procurator representing the plaintiff, Teccina (daughter of the late Ugolino). On the other hand, the judge did listen to another exception raised

70 Engelmann, p. 336.

71 *Potestà*, 432, fols. 2r-11v, 80r-84r.

72 *Potestà*, 432, fol. 80v: 'mandamus quatenus qui in dicta petitione continentur omni mora temporis sublata de medio facere studeas cum effectu ne dictum monasterium cavillationibus frivolis protrahatur in longum et expensarum profluviis fatigetur'.

73 *Potestà*, 432, fol. 81r: '…volentes tibique tenore presentium commictentes quatenus de predictis facias quid est iuris et ad debitum iustitie noveris pertinere'.

74 It is difficult to ascertain the extent to which the doge's instructions reflected his intentions and judgements. When the complaints of the litigant party are compared with the instructions from the doge that were to be carried out in response, in many cases, the doge's instructions are in line with the substance of the complaint. However, cases do exist in which the complaints of the parties were not accepted wholesale. For example, in one case, the doge, having received a complaint from a party requesting recognition of their rights, issued instructions for a summary trial. This shows that rather than merely accepting the complaints, the doge was conscious to adopt a stance of neutrality when issuing his instructions. *Potestà*, 426, fol. 7r.

75 A trial in which Teccina (procurator Nicola) was suing Paccino for being molested in connection with land ownership. *Potestà*, 415, no foliation, 19 December 1364; *Potestà*, 423, fols. 13r-17v, 35r-39v; *Potestà*, 432, fols. 38r-40v.

by the defendant to the effect that a certificate submitted by the plaintiff had not been drafted by a notary but was in fact a private document, despite the plaintiff's criticisms of this as a 'frivolous exception'. The courts had by now become a site for the application of summary justice as a procedural rule with some latitude for interpretation. Here, litigants interpreted 'summary justice' for themselves, discussing with each other and appealing to judges regarding the extent to which this new summary justice should accept an exception. Let us consider some examples.

(a). Case 1: On the speed of trials and legitimacy of procedure

In a trial in which the plaintiff, Giovanni, a priest of the church of Santo Stefano (Simone, a notary, acting as procurator for the plaintiff) argued his claim to the estate of the late Cuccino, which was in the possession of the defendant, Biagio (Filippo, a notary, acting as procurator for the defendant), the plaintiff brought a complaint to the doge, and secured an instruction from the doge to the judge to 'conduct summary justice, discovering the truth, while avoiding frivolous exceptions and judicial cavilings '.[76] Immediately after this order was given, Filippo, the procurator for the defendant, deployed an elaborate discussion that gave a definition of summary justice.

> Even in trials which have to proceed summarily, the complaints that are submitted must be clear and certain, their copies must be handed to the opposing parties, terms must be set that can be deliberated and provided with a response, the oath of calumny must be taken by parties, and term must be assigned by the judge to the parties to present *positiones,* interrogations, and responses, and to conclude the trial. This is shown in the chapter of the *Saepe contingit, de verborum significatione,* in the laws of Clement and others that have ruled on this issue. And if the order or the form of the procedure are perverted or omitted, then matters undertaken will no longer have legal value.[77]

Here, we find in Filippo's definition an overlap with the orientation towards 'complete cognizance', as observed in the *Saepe contingit.* After his argument, Filippo argued that the plaintiff's *positiones* did not merit a response because the points were vague and too open to interpretation. In response, Simone, as procurator for the plaintiff, responded that the defendant's exceptions should be dismissed as per the doge's letter. However, Filippo attached his own interpretation to the doge's summary instructions, namely that 'by virtue of the letter from the eminent doge, no legitimate exceptions and defences should be removed nor should the form of the statute be removed. Rather the truth

76 *Potestà*, 450, fols. 142r-146v: '... iuridicis cavillationibus exceptionibus frivolis subterfugiis et protelationibus sunptuosis veritate reperta ius summarium tribuas' (fol. 142r).

77 *Potestà*, 450, fol. 142v: '...dicit quod etiam in causis ubi procedi debet summarie debet fieri certa et clara petitio et parti adverse debet inde offerri copia et terminum statui ad deliberandum et respondendum, item debet prestari iuramentum calumpnia per partes et terminum per iudicem partibus assignari ad probandum et positionibus et interrogatis et responsionibus et in causa concludenda ut hoc nam probantur in capitulo sepe contingit, extra, de verborum significatione, in clementis et aliorum iuribus et legibus de dicta materia disponendis. Et si ordo et forma iuris perverteretur vel omitteretur non valerent de iure ea qui actitarentur'.

must be discovered not by *de facto* and *ex arrupto* [*abrupto*] but by legal mode and procedure'.[78] In view of this argument, the judge ultimately elected not to reject the defendant's exceptions but to proceed with the trial carefully and meticulously, such as by allowing sufficient time for submitting evidence.

(b). Case 2: On methods for the discovery of truth

At issue in this next case was the method of 'discovering the truth' indicated in the doge's instruction to observe 'summary justice'. In a trial at the Court of Podestà, the plaintiff, Franceschino, sought compensation for damages to his lands from the defendant. In this trial, the rural commune of San Giorgio[79] contested an order that the defendants pay compensation of 6 *lire* that had been issued by a previous judge based on an oath by Franceschino (attesting the truth of his complaint). At issue was the question of whether to apply the provisions of the city statutes, which recognised the efficacy of oaths in cases involving small sums. If the defendants' side had appealed to the doge to make it clear that no damage had been done, they could not have been held liable. Moreover, they requested another evidentiary method – one that was not an oath – and especially a thorough clarification of the facts. In response, the doge instructed the *podestà* to find out the truth about the issues in the petition, and to observe justice in a summary manner without regard to anything that was not the singular, clear truth, and to ensure that no one could make a grievance, dispute, or resistance against the truth.[80] Whereas Franceschino continued to demand the execution of the prior judgement, the rural commune appealed to the judge by interpreting the doge's instruction as follows.

> In consideration of the doge's letter, what the doge intends, and has ordered your lordship [the judge] to do, is to investigate and discover the truth about the allegations, and then to conduct a summary trial in consideration of that singular, clear truth – not for your lordship to allow your mind to dwell on imagination or oaths [...] without being obstructed by Franceschino's oath or statute enacted regarding oaths.[81]

Franceschino did not remain silent. He, too, visited the doge to make the following complaint: 'Franceschino's side has validly proved the case, with much labour and

78 *Potestà*, 450, fol. 146r: '...dicens quod per licteras magnifici et excelsi domini ducis non tolluntur exceptiones et defensiones legiptime nec tollitur statuti forma set debet reperiri veritas modo et ordine iuridico et non de facto et ex arrupto ut alia pars petiit'.

79 *Potestà*, 424, fols. 5r-6v, 18r-21v, 29r-31v, 64r-65v.

80 *Potestà*, 424, fol. 6r: 'volentes tibi quod stricte mandantes quatenus de comprehensis in petitione predicta, veritate comperta, ad nichil aliud habendo respectum, nisi ad solam et lucidam veritatem summarie facias quod est iuris, ne quisque lamentari possit contra veritatem opporri vel gravari'; *Ibid.*, fol. 6v: 'Mictatur potestati, et reperta veritate faciat quid iuris est, ad nichil aliud habito respectu nisi ad solam veritatem'.

81 *Potestà*, 424, fol. 18v: '...respondet quod consideratis licteris domini nostri ducis... sue intentionis est et vult ac mandat prefatus dominus dux quod vos investigetis et inveniatis veritatem de narratis. Et quod secundum veritatem et habito respectu ad veram et lucidam veritatem, ius summarium faciatis [...] quod non ad afictionem vel ad iuramentum vostrum animum firmentis [...] non obstante iuramento dicti franceschini vel statuto per quid dispensatur quod iuramento stetur...'

expenses, in accordance with Lucca's city statutes. They [the rural commune], sensing that they would be defeated in law in the case, have brought the exposition and petition before your lordship, keeping silent about the truth of the matter. [...] By virtue of a letter from your lordship [the doge], Franceschino is hindered from prosecuting the case and his rights'.[82] With this complaint, Franceschino succeeded in winning instructions from the doge to, as before, order the *podestà* to discover the truth and conduct a summary trial, but this time with additional wording 'in accordance with *forma statutorum Lucani communis*'.[83]

Although the judge's subsequent response on this matter is unfortunately unavailable, after the above letter in support of Franceschino was delivered from the doge on 29 January, the rural commune, perhaps sensing a ruling to their disadvantage, immediately informed the court that they had received information on the concerned individuals, thus changing their strategy of claiming that they had not known this earlier. In this case, on the question of whether the discovery of the truth should be based on a statutory provision concerning oaths, we can see how the litigants interpreted the contradictions in the doge's attitude towards 'the discovery of truth' and 'observing the law' in their own favour and attempted to convince the judge while securing letters from the doge to clarify his instructions.

(c). Arbitrary interpretations by judges and their consequences

Judges who, having received instructions to observe summary justice, appear to have been liberated from the fetters of the law and gained *arbitrium*, must have been very confused in the face of litigants' interpretations of 'summary justice' – that is, interpretive arguments on the part of those who sought to apply ambiguous instructions from the doge to their specific cases. We frequently find scenarios in which judges acted on their own discretion to dismiss exceptions raised against the appointment of procurators, exceptions pertaining to their competence as judges, and exceptions with reference to legal procedure. Exceptions that anyone – particularly other judges – could see reflected 'frivolous excuses' intended to draw out proceedings were easily dismissed by judges.

However, for subtle problems where judgements might differ depending on the individual judge, the forced advancement of trial procedures could result in subsequent appeals or a rehashing of the problem. In consideration of this danger, as we saw earlier, regardless of instructions from the doge to pursue summary justice, judges would hear and consider litigants' exceptions and conduct trials in accordance with laws and statutes. Even so, cases can be confirmed in which trials were pushed through by force.

82 *Potestà*, 424, fol. 19v-20r: 'Et pro parte dicti franceschini facte fuerunt probationes legiptime in causa, secundum formam statutorum Lucani communis cum multo labore et expensis. Et quod ipsi videntes se de iure subcumbere in dicta causa fecerunt expositionem et petitionem coram dominatione vostra, tacita veritate, infamantes dictum franceschinum indebite et iniuste,[...] misit dicto potestati vostris licteris interclusam, quarum vigore dictus franceschinus impeditur in prosecutionem dicte cause et sui iuris'.

83 *Potestà*, 424, fol. 19v: 'facias et fieri facias ius summarium et expeditum veritate reperta, secundum formam statutorum Lucani communis'.

In cases where parties felt that they had been unfairly treated and judged, and would even have to bear the trial costs, they must have secured a more favourable decision by bringing their complaints before a different judge; the routes of petitioning the doge and appealing to the Appellate Court, as well as bringing their complaints before a later-appointed judge were still available. Let us consider two cases.

In a trial involving a complaint by Caterina, widow to the late Nicolao, requesting the restitution of her dotal property,[84] the plaintiff's party acquired an instruction from the doge to the *podestà* 'to discover the truth in a summary fashion by investigating the rights of the parties so as to proceed with the trial and finish it'. Perhaps because of this instruction, the judge subsequently brought the trial to a conclusion, ruling in favour of Caterina. The defendant, Donato, was not satisfied with the judge's high-handed management of the trial, however. Immediately after the ruling, Donato went to the doge, arguing that he had not been given time to present his allegations and requesting that the issue be delegated to a neutral judge. In response, the doge instructed the judge to allow an appeal within the scope allowed by the Lucchese statutes, and the case was passed to the Appellate Court.

A similar appeal can be seen in a trial that has already come up repeatedly, that between Moccio, the procurator for the Santo Cristiane monastery, and Giovanni de Poggio. This trial actually began on 10 July 1365, after which it continued through many twists and turns until at least 12 August 1367. During this period, summary instructions were issued by the doge on three occasions, until eventually a final judgement based on legal advice was given in favour of the monastery on 17 June 1366, with an order that Giovanni surrender the land at issue. Giovanni subsequently would bring his complaint before the Appellate Court, but, according to Moccio, the trial ended when Giovanni abandoned his appeal.

However, on 8 January 1367, Giovanni brought his complaint before a subsequently appointed judge of the *podestà*, stating that new evidence had come to light in connection with his land rights and reopening the issue by submitting several documents. Moccio naturally protested, deploying the notion of *res iudicata* to argue for the execution of the prior ruling. He then insisted that in the event of opposition by the other party, the case should be committed to a jurist. Taking exception to this, the judge examined the filings and the exception without commissioning a jurist and ended up issuing a decision on his own initiative to stop the execution of the earlier ruling.

Moccio naturally protested and immediately brought his denunciation to the Appellate Court. His letter of complaint claimed that the *podestà* and his judges were harassing him, that the ruling issued in June 1366 had not been executed in accordance with the statutes and, moreover, that no attempt had been made to commission a jurist who could give legal advice on the case. Then, citing numerous laws, such as provisions in the city statutes dealing with commissions and chapters in the *Codex constitutionum* of the *Corpus Iuris Civilis* 'on matters already judged' (*de re iudicate*) and 'on the execution of matters already judged' (*de executione rei iudicate*) as comprising

84 *Potestà*, 426, fols. 7r-11v, 24r-33v, 53r-55v, 76r-79v, 101r-104v, 128r; *Potestà*, 432, fol. 22r.

the laws and statutes violated by the judge of the *podestà*,[85] he asked the Appellate Court's judges to order the *podestà* and his judges to extinguish the decision with which they had suspended the execution of the ruling. Unfortunately, we do not know the further developments of this case from the surviving records.

Here we can see the consequences arising when judges, seemingly freed from the ordinary constraints of the law upon receiving summary instructions from the doge, then took a high-handed approach to pushing their trials forward. 'Summary justice' was to be defined only insofar as it was interpreted as such by litigants in the respective cases. It follows, therefore, that judges were not the only ones who obtained freedom after being liberated from the law. Parties were likewise freed from the formal strictures of the law, whereupon they joined in the task of creating a kind of justice through their own interpretations. When ordinary procedure was suspended at the instructions of the doge in the quest for summary justice, the regulatory lacuna that was produced as a result was filled by the task of arriving at a joint interpretation by litigants and judges over what constituted a 'legitimate' trial or 'justice'.

(3) Confirmation of summary justice as the 'normalisation' of exceptional experience

Instructions from the doge to judges to pursue summary justice undoubtedly had a major impact on the shift from a formalistic order supported by local jurists to a legal order based on judges' *arbitrium*. This exceptional experience of the five years (1364-1368) of continued intervention in trials by the political authorities would have firmly engendered among people the legal sense that it was possible to 'legitimately' free judges from the strict confines of ordinary procedure encoded in the *ius commune*.

After Lucca gained independence from Pisa in 1370, judges' *arbitrium* expanded in scope as city statutes were enacted that could be applied to lawsuits in general, rather than solely at the level of individual cases. A supplementary clause prohibiting exceptions adopted on 24 October 1381 includes a provision 'On summary justice which should be observed in civil cases.[86] The provision stipulates 'in order to end disputes rapidly that all judicial officials should, in civil cases over which they have jurisdiction, follow procedures and conduct hearings summarily and plainly, without clamour and the form of ordinary trial procedure'.[87] This provision was part of revisions to the statute of 1372 by the incumbent Anziani together with six *sapientes* (including one jurist). This could be described as a landmark provision in Lucca giving legal recognition to judges' *arbitrium procedendi* for all civil lawsuits. The provision, however, was not an introduction of summary justice but merely a legal imprimatur for the

85 *Potestà*, 450, fol. 44r: '...contra infrascripta iura et statuta videlicet contra statutum Lucani communis libro .iiii. sub rublica de questionibus commictendis [...] Item contra Lex .fi. codicem de executione rei iudicate et contra Lex .i. codicem de re iudicate et[...]'

86 *Statuti 1372*, fols. 156v-157r: 'De summaria racione reddenda in litibus civilibus'.

87 *Statuti 1372*, fol. 156v: 'Ut finis litibus celerius imponatur volumus quod in omni causa civili seu que civiliter intentatur, procedatur, cognoscatur et detinetur per quemcumque officialem prout causa ad suam iurisdictionem pertinuerit summarie et de plano sine strepitu et figura iudicii, nulla iuris et aliorum statutorum solemnitate servata...'

practices of summary justice that had been worked out in the courts by litigants and judges during and after the previous decade, which had marked the latter period of Pisan rule. Although summary justice had until this point been in widespread use as an exceptional practice, it was herein 'normalised' in terms of the law.

Looking at court records from 1396, we see clearly the effects of summary justice in the significant reduction of needless exceptions on matters of form. However, regardless of the considerable expansion of judges' discretion by summary justice and the fact that a provision placing a general prohibition on exceptions had been issued in 1381, some types of exceptions continued to be raised by the parties, specifically exceptions concerning the appointment of procurators, legal procedure, the competence of judges, and *lite pendente*. This shows how, even at the end of the fourteenth century, and in the face of the priority given to expediting the clarification of truth, there were still some judges and litigants who wanted to ensure the underlying legal legitimacy of the trial procedure, and it demonstrates how the lacunae in procedural rules produced by the summary provisions were filled by these actors in the ongoing search for 'summary justice' in the form of complete cognizance.

From the above cases, we see that the evolution from formalism to *arbitrium* that arose in fourteenth-century Lucca was not simply a shift from an adversarial system to a judge-led model. Instead, it was a shift from trials conducted by jurists and litigants in strict compliance with the law to trials contingently realised by litigants and judges through their repeated interpretations of the nature of a 'legitimate' trial or 'justice'.

7. The Commune's Appropriation of the Realm of Civil Law

The shift from formalism to *arbitrium* in civil trials in fourteenth-century Lucca occurred neither naturally nor as the intended outcome of some powerful extrinsic force. Rather, it was an unintended result of practices on the part of litigants, jurists, judges, and a doge, each pursuing their respective goals, which unfolded against the backdrop of specific political and social conditions. And in circumstances where the letter of the law no longer provided an absolute standard of reference, the idea of what constituted a 'legitimate' trial or 'justice' was jointly interpreted time and again by judges and litigants.

I have already mentioned that this shift of judicial principle in the civil courts corresponded to a series of changes in contemporary procedural laws, both criminal and civil. Finally, as another shift that was taking place behind this shift in judicial principle, I would like to look at the juridical field engendered by communal authority at the end of the Middle Ages, particularly towards the appropriation of the realm of civil law.

The realm of civil law in the Italian context had for a long time been administered by jurists and notaries based on ideological and universal authorities such as the *ius commune* and emperorship. The commune, which emerged as a *de facto* political power in the eleventh and twelfth centuries, needed their influence as well as their mantle of traditional authority, and heightened its own legitimacy by incorporating their activities.[88] As the commune grew in influence, however, it began to move to exert its rule over the field of civil law on its own, without having to rely on universal authority. This process is lucidly illustrated in the declining influence of the Lucchese jurists and notaries of the fourteenth and fifteenth centuries.

Looking first of all at jurists, we can see a retrenchment in terms of the scope of their activities in the courts. The civil courts of the latter half of the fourteenth century, in parallel with the shift in judicial principle from formalism to *arbitrium*, saw a decrease in jurists' advice and, concomitantly, an increase in independent rulings by judges. This shift signified a shift in the realm of civil law, from the charge of jurists, who drew their influence from the *ius commune* and therefore acted independently – to a certain degree – from the commune, into the hands of the *podestà* and his judges as representatives of the commune. While the judicial officials were also jurists holding degrees in jurisprudence, they were hired as administrators who had been invited from other cities, and their authority depended on an appointment from the communal council.

The decline of the jurists' influence in the realm of civil law is also seen in the selection of judges for the courts of consuls, which in its traditional form had existed since the earliest days of the commune. Until the first half of the fourteenth century, these courts had been strongholds of local jurists who had served as both judges and providers of legal advice. However, after the mid-fourteenth century, when the numbers and influence of local jurists began to decline, the individual consular courts began to be successively abolished. In the case of the Court of San Cristoforo, local Lucchese jurists were replaced as presiding officials by appointees from other cities after 1371, and by those who held the title of vicar of the *podestà* after 1381. Finally, in 1400, all of the consular courts were quietly abolished by the *signore*, Paolo Guinigi, and consolidated under the jurisdiction of the *Communal* Court of Podestà.

This move by the commune to assert exclusive control over the field of civil law also swept aside the scope of activities of the notaries who, like the jurists, had depended on universal authorities for their legitimacy. Italian notaries, who based the '*publica fides*' on the emperor or the pope, were originally kept at a certain remove from the commune. Even in Lucca, signatures included the title 'notary by authority of the emperor'.[89] Also, in the first half of the fourteenth century, the authority to *make* notaries (*potesta creandi et faciendi notarios*) was held not by the commune but by the descendants of count palatine, the Avvocati family.[90]

---

88 Regarding the commune's relation with notaries at the time of the commune's establishment, see G. G. Fissore, *Autonomia notarile e organizzazione cancelleresca nel Comune di Asti. I modi e le forme dell'intervento notarile nella costituzione del documento comunale* (Spoleto, 1977).

89 For example, 'Ego Taddeus quondam Nicolai Malpilli de Luca, imperiali auctoritate notarius'. Tirelli, 'Il notariato a Lucca in epoca basso-medievale', in M. Montorzi (ed.), *Il notariato nella civiltà Toscana* (Roma, 1985), p. 241-309, in particular p. 263.

90 Tirelli, 'Sulla crisi istituzionale del comune a Lucca (1308-1312)', in *Studi per Enrico Fiumi* (Pisa, 1979), p. 317-360. According to the 1308 statute, the requirements for acting as a notary were stipulated as being at least eighteen years old, having spent five years in the study in grammar, and having been examined and approved by members of the Avvocati family and by consuls of the *collegium iudicum*. *Statuto 1308*, II, 61 (De eo quod nullus posit esse notaries nisi studuerit quinque annis), p. 113.

However, after the commune of Lucca was granted *potesta creandi et faciendi notarios* in 1369 by the Holy Roman Emperor Charles IV, the description 'imperial authority' disappears from the signatures of several notaries, and examples begin to appear of signatures written simply as 'Lucchese citizen'.[91] After this, the commune of Lucca continues to strengthen its control over the notaries, and in 1434 goes so far as to interfere with the criteria and screening process for admission into the *arte* of notaries.[92]

This intervention by the commune into the notarial sphere of activities is also evident in the notarial registers, which served as contract ledgers and were kept by notaries as their own private property. Those in possession of registers from other notaries were already obligated to report this to the commune under the 1308 city statute's terms, to prevent their scattering and loss.[93] However, the management of notarial registers through such reporting was promoted in the 1372 statute and in a 1388 provision in the form of stricter regulations and an expansion of the scope for such reporting.[94] Ultimately, in provisions enacted in Lucca in 1446 and 1448 – earlier than in other cities – it became mandatory for the registers of deceased notaries to be stored in the commune's official *Archivio pubblico*.[95] These attempts by the commune to directly manage the notarial registers, which had been held as the private property of notaries as independent professionals, show how profoundly the commune had appropriated the realm of civil law.

Thus, the shift from local jurists to the judges of the *podestà* as the judicial agents in the civil trials of the latter half of the fourteenth century could be positioned as part of a larger transition in the civil world of late medieval Italy. This transition was especially clear regarding the commune's intervention into and appropriation of the realm of civil law, which until then had been served by jurists and notaries who based the legitimacy of their activities on universal authorities external to the commune.

---

91 For example, 'Ego Gregorius Gilius olim Andreucci Arnaldi notarius, civis Lucanus', *Ibid.*, p. 263. *Statuto 1372*, III, 17 (De modo et forma probandi aliquem esse notarium).

92 In fact, the Avvocati family are not mentioned in the 1434 collective statute for jurists and notaries. A. Romiti and G. Tori (eds.), *Statuti e matricole del Collegio dei Giudici e Notai della città di Lucca* (Roma, 1978).

93 *Statuto 1308*, II, 55 (De sacramento notariorum et aliis quam pluribus diversis circa eorum exercitium spectantibus), p. 108-110: 'omnes notarii Lucane Civitatis, districtus et sex miliariorum presentes et fucturi, habentes libros aliquorum notariorum vel alicuius notarii, teneantur et debeant denunptiare in Camera Lucani Communis cuius et quorum notariorum habeant libros…, notarii et custodes librorum Lucani Comunis… teneantur et debeant ex inde unum librum facere, in quo predicta describant'. The fact that reports were actually made to the custodian of the *Archivio pubblico* can be confirmed from a custodial memorandum dated 1367. ASL, *Archivi pubblici*, 13.

94 However, the permanent storage of such registries was incomplete. Meyer points out the scattered state of registries in fourteenth-century Lucca, as well as the fact that they were frequently sold off. A. Meyer, 'Hereditary Laws and City Topography: On the Development of the Italian Notarial Archives in the Late Middle Ages', in A. Classen (ed.), *Urban Space in the Middle Ages and the Early Modern Age* (Berlin, 2009), p. 225-244. Also, in 1389 there is a record of a custodian of the *Archivio pubblico* lamenting the illegal sale, scattering, and loss of these registries. E. Lazzareschi, 'L'Archivio dei Notari della Repubblica lucchese', *Gli Archivi Italiani*, II-6 (1915), p. 175-189, in particular p. 179-180.

95 In Florence, registries were held by the notary guild. In Lucca, however, the influence of the notary guild was not as great, and the commune undertook direct custody from an earlier time than in other cities. A. D'addario, 'La conservazione degli atti notarili negli ordinamenti della Repubblica lucchese', *Archivio storico italiano*, 109 (1951), 193-226, in particular p. 206.

Lucca at the end of the Middle Ages also witnessed significant changes internal to the commune itself in the form of the expanding influence of political authorities over judicial institutions. This is a phenomenon that was particularly evident in the sphere of criminal justice, which we will see in the following chapters. In criminal trials after the mid-fourteenth century, we find that the governing council exercised its *arbitrium* to alter guilty verdicts issued by judges that were based in statutes, or which would grant judges license to be escape the strict shackles of positive law.

Considering the interventionist trends of the political authorities in the sphere of criminal justice, it is also clear that the degree of their intervention in the administration of civil justice was relatively minor. The intervention by the doge, which was exceptionally apparent in civil trials in the 1360s, did not go so far as to broach the content of the rulings. Behind this lack of intervention by the political authorities into civil matters may also have been the lack of motivation for involvement in the civil sphere – of the balancing of rights between individuals – as compared to the criminal sphere, which was concerned with the maintenance of public order. Moreover, what seems to have been even more influential was the existence of a certain shared recognition that the sphere of civil justice – the realm of private rights – was inviolable for the political authorities, a field where their intervention would not have had any legal legitimacy.

The search for a mode of justice in the administration of civil justice that did not see such an intervention by the political authorities, but which was not necessarily completely reliant on positive law, was – to repeat the point once again – left to collaborations between litigants and communal judges. Questions on the nature of justice in this civil sphere – how strictly to adhere to a legal procedure that guaranteed the 'legitimacy' of a trial's outcome, and whether to focus on discovering the truth or on observing the laws – were left to the discretion and interpretation of the judges and litigants in the courts, from whom answers would be derived, time and again.

CHAPTER 4

Criminal Justice in Fourteenth-Century Lucca

1. The rise of criminal justice

Until the twelfth century, the communal courts mainly judged civil matters, such as those concerning properties and debts. Only from the thirteenth century onward did the communes begin judging *maleficia* or 'evil acts' committed in society. A criminal register from Perugia in 1258 studied by Vallerani includes 636 cases of *maleficia,* such as injuries and homicides tried in the Court of Podestà.[1] However, the boundary between civil justice and criminal justice in the mid-thirteenth century was unclear. In Perugia, where a civil court operated, the criminal court also heard cases involving property damage or insolvency. It mainly adopted an accusatorial procedure (560 of 636 cases), wherein the burden of proof fell on the victims as the accusers. As a result, criminal judges issued convictions in only about 10% of cases (68 of 636).[2] In other words, thirteenth-century criminal courts did not necessarily involve the commune's judgement of *maleficia*; rather, we might call it simply a forum wherein parties involved in conflicts confronted each other to discuss, negotiate, and resolve their problems, similar to the practices of civil courts.

In the mentioned 1258 criminal register from Perugia, 76 cases followed an inquisitorial procedure, originally derived from a decree by Pope Innocent III in the early thirteenth century and adopted in the 1220s and 1230s for the secular courts.[3] From the outset, this procedure provided an *ex officio* prosecutorial initiative to the judge for seeking proof of *maleficium*. The confrontation between the commune (represented by the judge) and a defendant in this inquisitorial procedure ran contrary to the principle of the adversarial system favoured by the *ius civile*.[4] While the inquisitorial procedure was first introduced as an exceptional recourse in the city courts, the procedure's use persisted until it was finally given theoretical legitimacy by Alberto Gandino in the 1280s in the *Tractatus de maleficiis,* with his use of Innocent III's legal maxim '*ne*

1 M. Vallerani, *Il sistema giudiziario del comune di Perugia. Conflitti, reati e processi nella seconda metà del XIII secolo* (Perugia, 1991).

2 *Ibid.*, p. 60-62, 116-122.

3 R. M. Fraher, 'IV Lateran's Revolution and Criminal Procedure: the Birth of Inquistio, the End of Ordeals, and Innocent III's Vision of Ecclesiastical Politics', in R. I. Castillo Lara (ed.), *Studia in honorem eminentissimi cardinalis Alphonsi M. Stickler* (Roma, 1992), p. 96-111; M. Vallerani, 'Modelli di verità. Le prove nei processi inquisitori', in *L'enquête au Moyen Âge: études réunies par Claude Gauvard* (Roma, 2008), p. 123-142; M. Vallerani, 'Procedura e giustizia nelle città italiane del basso medioevo (XII-XIV secolo)', in Chiffoleau, Gauvard and Zorzi (eds.), *Pratiques sociales*, 439-494, in particular p. 460-462, p. 467.

4 M. Vallerani, *La giustizia pubblica medievale* (Bologna, 2005), p. 211; A. Gandinus, *Tractatus de maleficiis*, ed. H. Kantorowicz, in *Albertus Gandinus und das Strafrecht des Scholastik*, vol. II (Berlin, 1926), p. 39.

maleficia remaneant impunita'.[5] Gandino interpreted the 'victim' on whom a *maleficium* inflicted loss to be not the actual injured party but the public (*publicum*), and that a judge as the public's representative could legitimately restore the damage by punishing the perpetrators.[6]

So, how did criminal justice, now differentiated from civil justice by inquisitorial procedure, develop in the fourteenth century? Among those who have studied the criminal justice system that prevailed in this period, Vallerani has revealed indications of a marked decrease in the use of the accusatorial procedure in registers from early fourteenth-century Bologna. This decrease owed not to the increase in the number of inquisitorial procedures but rather to an overall decline in Bologna of the importance of public justice during this period, caused by inherent problems in the accusatorial procedure such as its high cost and excessive formalism, as well as by political intervention in public justice.[7]

By the middle of the fourteenth century, as we shall see in Lucca, inquisitorial procedure had become the primary procedure in criminal courts. This period saw the clarification of judges' active approach to punishing *maleficia*. Zorzi has noted a change in how the commune policed *maleficia* in Florence in the latter half of the fourteenth century.[8] Prior to the middle of the fourteenth century, the urban public order had been maintained by city districts, parishes, and other local organisations. However, amidst the social changes that arose owing to the Black Death and the political changes signified by the development of oligarchic regimes, the commune began to exert a state-like control of public order in the later fourteenth century, using a centralised police system acting in response to the anonymous denunciation of malefactors to communal officials.

Recent studies have revealed the experience of criminal justice in smaller and mid-sized cities based on criminal records. These include Dean's survey of crimes in Bologna, Savona, Mantova, and Lucca;[9] Graziotti's account of public justice in the small town of San Gimignano in the first half of the fourteenth century;[10] Kumhera's study of criminal justice and private peacemaking in Siena in the fourteenth century;[11] Carraway Vitiello's exposition of various aspects of criminal justice in Reggio Emilia under the

---

5 For example, Gandinus, p. 5: 'quia expedit rei publice, ne maleficia remaneant sine pena'; R. M. Fraher, 'The Theoretical Justification for the New Criminal Law of the High Middle Ages: *Rei publicae interest, ne crimina remaneant impunita*', *The University of Illinois Law Review*, 3 (1984), p. 577-595; K. Pennington, 'Innocent III and the Ius Commune', in R. H. Helmholz et al. (eds.), *Grundlagen des Rechts: Festschrift für Peter Landau zum 65. Geburtstag* (Paderborn, 2000), p. 349-366.

6 M. Sbriccoli, '*Vidi communiter observari*. L'emersione di un ordine penale pubblico nelle città italiane del secolo XIII', *Quaderni fiorentini per la storia del pensiero giuridico*, 27 (1998), p. 231-268.

7 Vallerani, *La giustizia pubblica*, p. 113-166.

8 A. Zorzi, *L'amministrazione della giustizia penale nella Repubblica fiorentina: aspetti e problemi* (Firenze, 1988); A. Zorzi, 'Ordine pubblico e amministrazione della giustizia nelle formazioni politiche toscane tra Tre e Quattrocento', in *Italia 1350-1450: tra crisi, trasformazione, sviluppo* (Pistoia, 1993), 419-474.

9 T. Dean, *Crime and Justice in Late Medieval Italy* (Cambridge, 2007).

10 T. Graziotti, *Giustizia penale a San Gimignano (1300-1350)* (Firenze, 2015).

11 G. Kumhera, *The Benefits of Peace: Private Peacemaking in Late Medieval Italy* (Leiden, 2017).

Visconti at the end of the fourteenth and fifteenth centuries;[12] and Blanshei's research into criminal justice and politics in Bologna in the fourteenth century.[13]

In this chapter, I would first like to present a picture of Lucca's criminal court by considering the volume of cases heard, the ways in which *maleficia* were brought before the court, the types of criminals, the procedures adopted in the court, and the conclusion of trials, as recorded in the criminal registers. I will also pay attention to the post-sentencing stage by examining marginal notes in the sentence books. To what extent did those convicted serve their sentences, and how might these penalties have been lifted? Such questions, in turn, will necessitate consideration of political interventions into judicial decisions, as in the case of *gratia*, by which penalties were waived or commuted, a matter that I discuss further in Chapter 5.

2. Volume of *Maleficia* Brought Before the Criminal Court

(1) Number of criminal cases

Here, as Lucca's criminal Court of Podestà, I discuss the *Curia maleficiorum*, where the *podestà* and his assistant judges interrogated and condemned those who committed *maleficia*, including homicide, injury, insult, theft, and arson, all proscribed as crimes in the communal statutes.

First, let us estimate the annual number of *maleficia* brought before the criminal court of Lucca in the fourteenth century. The court's jurisdiction extended to the city and the surrounding countryside, Sei Miglia, which had a population of 40,000 in the first half of the fourteenth century and 19,000 in the second half of the fourteenth century, after the Black Death.[14] For serious crimes only, this jurisdiction encompassed the vicariate area as well. This court's criminal registers from the 1340s yield 238 cases for 1344,[15] 267 cases for the twelve-month period from July 1355 to June 1356,[16] 155 cases for 1363,[17] and 244 cases for 1392.[18] Therefore, an estimate for the annual number cases of around 230-270 seems reasonable, despite the small number in 1363. Interestingly, the number of cases did not decline even after a decrease in the population owing to the Black Death.

This number might seem small in comparison to our estimated annual number of civil cases (10,000), but that is not the case, especially if we consider the 636 cases in

12 J. Carraway Vitiello, *Public Justice and the Criminal Trial in Late Medieval Italy: Reggio Emilia in the Visconti Age* (Leiden, 2016).

13 S. R. Blanshei, *Politics and Justice in Late Medieval Bologna* (Leiden, 2010).

14 As for the population in Lucca and Sei Miglia in the first half of the fourteenth century, see Chapter 1, Section 1. Meek has estimated the population of these areas in the 1370s and 1380s; C. Meek, *Lucca 1369-1400. Politics and Society in an Early Renaissance City-State* (Oxford, 1978), p. 21-26.

15 ASL, *Potestà di Lucca* (hereafter *Potestà*), 4785, 4787, 4788, 4790.

16 *Potestà*, 4846, 4847, 4848, 4849.

17 *Potestà*, 4901, 4902, 4903, 4904.

18 *Potestà*, 5076, 5077, 5078, 5079, 5080, 5081, 5082.

Perugia in 1258 (1285 population between 23,000 and 28,000), which included civil cases such as the damage of property (116 cases) and insolvency (63 cases).[19]

Hereafter, we will primarily pay attention to the period from July 1355 to June 1356, which is the first year-long consecutive period in Lucca for which both court and sentence books are available in their entirety. During this period, the criminal court prosecuted 267 cases and called 518 defendants in front of judges.

(2) *Routes to the criminal court:* accusa, denuntia, fama publica

Maleficia were brought before the Court of Podestà by three principal routes. The first of these was via accusations by victims or their families.[20] Criminal proceedings initiated via accusations were similar to civil trials in the sense that they adopted an accusatorial procedure wherein the accuser confronted the accused, but they differed in the sense that accusers sought punishment rather than compensation. The second route to the court was denunciation by local officials.[21] We find many perpetrators of *maleficia* being denounced to the central court by local officials, such as the consuls of city blocks (*contrata*), the consuls of rural communities, and the vicars of the vicariates. Third, the communal court could be notified by *fama publica, clamosa insinuatione,* or anonymous reports.

Of the 267 cases in 1355-1356, 48 (18%) were initiated by accusation, 158 (60%) by denunciations by officials, 52 (19%) by *fama publica* or similar indirect routes, and 9 by other means (i.e. trials for failed accusations).

Whereas many criminal trials in fourteenth-century Lucca were initiated by denunciations by officials or *fama publica,* almost all the cases from Perugia in 1258 began with accusations by the victims or their families. Many accusations in criminal trials in the thirteenth century reveal that prosecutorial initiative rested with the parties involved in the conflict, rather than with court officials. In other words, the criminal court was incorporated as part of the dispute resolution process within local society. Conversely, the fact that accusations accounted for only a minority of the criminal trials in fourteenth-century Lucca shows that the communal court was not a passive institution: rather than waiting for accusations from victims, it actively sought out *maleficia* in society for prosecution.

---

19 Vallerani, *Il sistema giudiziario.*

20 For example, Coluccio, who was insulted by Juntone, came to the court and demanded that the court punish Juntone according to the statute. *Potestà*, 4790, fols. 10r-11r: 'Coram vobis domino Johanne de civitate castelli iudice curie malleficiorum Lucani communis, Coluccius bonturi pannarius Luccanus civis suo iuramento accusat Juntonem condam bacciomei de communi capelle sancti donati de domezano vallis ottavi in eo de eo et super eo videlicet quod dictus Junctone irato animo et malo modo, et in dispectu et dedechus ipsius Coluccii dixit eidem Coluccio et contra ipsum Coluccium in facta verba iniuriosa… Quare petit eum puniri et condepnari secundum formam statuti…'

21 For example, Aguilante, a consul of the San Tomei block, denounced Bartolomeo for committing *maleficium* against Ripa, i.e. a cutting her with a knife. *Potestà*, 4787, non foliation, 15 March, 1344: 'Coram vobis domino Johanne iudice curie maleficiorum Lucani communis et vostra curia, Aguilante guidi consul contrade sancti tomei in coaria porte sancti donati consulatus nomine pro dicta contrada denusiat[denuntiat] Bartholomeum gucii…'

Table 4.1: Routes by which *maleficia* were brought before the criminal court in 1355-1356

	CASES	%
Accusation by victims or their family members	48	18
Denunciation by officials	158	60
Fama publica	52	19
Other	9	3
Total	**267**	**100**

In fourteenth-century Lucca, this system of denunciation by local officials gained popularity at the expense of accusations by victims. In Lucca, 60% of the cases were initiated by official denunciations, which were almost unknown in mid thirteenth-century Perugia. Communal statutes obligated city blocks and the rural communes to denounce *maleficia* committed in their own territories.[22] In fact, in some instances, rural consuls were condemned for their failure to denounce criminals.[23]

Looking at other cities, we find that while denunciations by local officials were not common in San Gimignano in 1319 and 1325-1326 (accounting for just 9%, or 7 of 77 cases),[24] they were more evident in Florence in 1343-1345 (50% of cases)[25] and in Reggio Emilia from 1373-1408 (58%, or 555 of 951 cases).[26]

Apart from such policing by local officials, *maleficia* were also brought before fourteenth-century central courts via *fama publica* or anonymous reporting.

The proportion of trials initiated by *fama publica* increased during the second half of the fourteenth century. They accounted for 15% of all criminal trials in 1344, 19% in 1355-1356, and 48% in 1396. The introduction and popularisation of this route to the courts allowed the commune to take prosecutorial initiative away from victims and local officials in the sense that the communal central court could access information directly through *fama publica* when deciding whether an act deserved to be prosecuted. This increased use of *fama publica* indicates not only the central court's growing intervention in society but also the exploitation of information from below, because a close analysis

22 As for the *maleficium* that the consuls of city blocks should denounce, ASL, *Statuto del Comune di Lucca*, 5 (hereafter *Statuto 1342*), I, 111 (De maleficiis denuntiandis per consules contratarum et brachiorum, et de pena vicinorum non capientium malefactores), fols. 35v-36r. As for the obligation for rural communities to denounce, *Statuto 1342*, I, 34 (De pena communitatum sex miliariorum non denuntiantium maleficia, et de pena recipientium pecuniam vel obligationem pro maleficiis non denuntiandis et non denuntiantium maleficia), fol. 15v.

23 For example, in a case that started on 12 October 1338, a consul of Santa Maria de Lappelle was convicted of not catching criminals who committed *maleficium*, *Potestà*, 4739, fol. 11r. Moreover, based on the sentence books of 1344, we can see consuls of rural communities who were convicted of not denouncing criminals or of not handing over the criminals to the court, ASL, *Sentenze e bandi*, 13.

24 Graziotti, *Giustizia penale*, p. 70-83.

25 Zorzi, 'Ordine pubblico', p. 427-428.

26 Carraway Vitiello, *Public Justice*, p. 54-66.

on each case shows that the victims or related parties were involved in originating anonymous *fama* even in cases that were brought with *fama publica*.[27]

A similar tendency can be seen over the same period in Florence. While Zorzi noted that this process reflected the oligarchic centralisation of governmental power,[28] as we will see in Chapters 5 and 6, the shift towards oligarchy and the empowerment of political institutions can also be seen over the same period in Lucca.

3. *Maleficia*

Let us consider the details of the individual *maleficia* prosecuted in the court by examining three examples, which I will also refer to in the next sections on trial procedure and sentencing.

Table 4.2: *Maleficium* in the trials of 1355-1356

	Cases	%	People	%
Homicide/Injury resulting in death[29]	41	15	79	15
Accomplice to homicide	2	1	39	8
Theft/Robbery	14	5	57	11
Incendiarism	6	2	32	6
Kidnapping	4	1	11	2
Rape	1	0	1	0
Injury	144	54	179	35
Accomplice to injury			12	2
Joining in a free fight			1	0
Throwing (no harm done)	2	1	11	2
Threat	6	2	21	4
Verbal abuse	7	3	9	2
Civil issue	6	2	18	3
Other damage	4	1	6	1
Neglect of order (officials or community)	20	7	25	5
Neglect of order (individuals)	6	2	13	3
Failure of accusation	4	1	4	1
Total	**267**	**100**	**518**	**100**

27 See also, S. Nakaya, '*Fama Publica* and Informants in the Judicial Records of Lucca in the 14th Century', in G. M. Muzzarelli (ed.), *Riferire all'autorità. Denuncia e delazione fra medioevo ed età moderna* (Rome, 2020), p. 79-95.

28 A. Zorzi, 'Contrôle social, ordre public et répression judiciaire à Florence à l'époque communale: éléments et problèmes', *Annales ESC.*, 5 (1990), p. 1169-1188.

29 There was no distinction between homicide and injury resulting in death in prosecutions recorded in the court books.

(1) Case A (homicide)[30]

Date of prosecution: 7 September 1355
Initiated by: A denunciation by the consuls of Santa Maria Albiano, a rural commune
Accused: Cellottoro, Bertocho, Piero, Coluccino Paruei, Guido, Puccinello Butelli, Giovanni Menichelli (all of Santa Maria Albiano), and Giovanni Puccinello (from Orbicciano, now a resident of Santa Maria Albiano)
Allegation: Cellottoro and Bertocho, rampaging and armed with a scythe, shield, spear and knife, threatened Giovanni Mateo of Santa Maria Albiano. The suspects struck Giovanni six times: twice on the head, once on the waist, once on the right leg, once on the finger of the left hand, and once on the body. Giovanni bled severely and eventually died as a result of these attacks. Piero, Coluccino Paruei and five others joined Cellottoro and Bertocho to aid in this homicide.
Date of the alleged crime: 8 June 1355
Place of the alleged crime: On a public road in a rural commune, Santa Maria Albiano

During the period in question, 1355-1356, 79 suspects were prosecuted for homicide or injury resulting in death in 41 cases, with 39 suspects prosecuted in two cases as accomplices. Many of these were committed jointly, as in the cited example above (22 cases). In one case, more than ten people were tried for a crime. These cases seemed to be premeditated and intentional homicides rather than accidents. For example, in a trial prosecuted on 18 December 1355, Bonuccio Celli and four others, armed with weapons, were alleged to have broken into the house of Stefano one night and then stabbed him in his throat and face, killing him. After that, the intruders kidnapped Stefano's wife and son. Those convicted of homicide or bodily injury resulting in death were generally condemned to be beheaded or hanged as per the city statutes.[31]

Homicides or injuries resulting in death were mostly committed beyond the city walls, on public roads, in piazzas, in the forest, or in houses. Of these, 4 cases occurred in the city, 31 in the countryside, and 6 in the vicariate. The period 1355-1356 saw the countryside in a state of unrest, corresponding to the time when the security of the countryside began to be policed by the office of the *bargello*, as we shall see in more detail in Chapter 6.

Aside from homicide, the criminal registers of 1355-1356 record several other serious crimes: 14 cases of theft or robbery, 6 cases of arson, 4 cases of kidnapping, and 1 case of rape. These crimes were committed jointly outside the city by rural villagers.[32] For example, in a trial initiated on 4 February 1356, Junctino and five other 'master thieves' (*publici latrines et derobbatores*) were prosecuted for the theft of a donkey and a knife worth 14 florins from Giovanni Lemmi.[33] The suspects disobeyed the summons twice and were then convicted to be hanged and required to return their loot. Generally,

30 *Potestà*, 4846, fols. 83r-84v.
31 An exceptional case was a conviction against Bartolomeo: decapitation or a fine of 750 *lire*. *Potestà*, 4847, fol. 31r.
32 On 18 November 1355, 14 suspects who lived in a vicariate were prosecuted for incendiarism, *Potestà*, 4846, fols. 214r-215r.
33 *Potestà*, 4849, fols. 44r-45v.

those who committed such serious crimes were sentenced to death or fines of more than 500 *lire*.

(2) Case B (injury)[34]

Date of prosecution: 12 October 1355
Initiated by: A denunciation by the consuls of San Pietro Somaldi, a city block
Accused: Giovanna (wife of Ambrogio Amerigo; originally from Florence and now *habitator* of Lucca) and Landello from Lucca
Allegation: Giovanna and Landello approached each other, quarrelling violently. Landello landed a blow with his fist on Giovanna's breast. For her part, Giovanna punched Landello and threw a stone at him, hitting him in the face, and he started to bleed
Date of the alleged crime: 7 October 1355, nones (three o'clock in the afternoon)
Place of the alleged crime: On a public road in San Pietro Somaldi, a city block

Injury was a popular *maleficium* that comprised more than half (144) of the crimes prosecuted in the Lucchese criminal court. Judges tried 179 people for injury, 12 as accomplices to injury, and one other for participating in a melee. Of these, 32 cases involved multiple accused: in some cases against a single victim and in others (as in example B) against each other.

Indictments in cases of injury are very descriptive, with details about whether the crime was committed with weapons, what types of weapon were used, the locations of the injuries, and whether there was bloodshed – all factors that would be considered by judges in determining fine amounts, as I discuss below. Injuries with bare hands (27 cases) occurred less frequently than with weapons (117 cases). Stones, sticks, spears, knives, and swords were used as weapons. Of 144 injuries, 129 cases involved bloodshed. This could suggest that word of bloodier *maleficia* was more likely to reach the courts, while scuffles not involving bloodshed were more likely to be overlooked by local officials.

Injuries were committed in both the city (58 cases) and the countryside (86 cases). The majority of these violent acts happened openly on the public roads and in the piazzas, which is likely why they were, in most cases, denounced by local officials (44 by the consuls of city blocks and 71 by the consuls of rural communes).

Maleficia involving the throwing of stones or spears (2 cases), threats (6 cases), or verbal abuse (7 cases) were considered equivalent to injury.[35] In the case of threats, it was important to describe whether assailants were armed and whether they had drawn their swords. As for verbal abuse, phrases such as '*puttana* (prostitute)' for women,

34 *Potestà*, 4846, fols. 147r-148r.
35 Here I have counted threats and verbal abuse which were committed concomitantly with injury as equivalent to injuries, which means that the number of instances of threats and verbal abuse was actually larger.

and '*ladro* (thief)' or '*traditore* (rebel)' for men were commonly prosecuted as the *maleficium* of defamation.[36]

(3) Case C (theft pertaining to a civil matter)[37]

Date of prosecution: 21 October 1355
Initiated by: A victim's accusation
Accused: Jacopo (son of the late Michele Sigheri)
Allegation: Jacopo trespassed into the house of Margarita, widow of the late Bonucci, and removed three beds with wool covers worth over 100 florins, which had been used by Junctorino (another son of the late Michele Sigheri), his wife Giovanna, Margarita, and the late Bonucci. Jacopo must be punished according to the statutes and return the stolen goods
Date of the alleged crime: From July to September 1348
Place of the alleged crime: In a house in the commune of Batone

At first glance, Case C, which seems to have been a theft of goods worth 100 florins, was not so different from the case mentioned above of robbery by the master thief Junctino. Here Jacopo proclaimed his innocence throughout the trial and was found not guilty. However, had he been found guilty, his crime would still not have merited the death penalty, as the 'theft' was committed in the context of a civil matter. Jacopo took away the beds that he assumed to be his property. The accusation was presented in court seven years after this 'crime' was committed. It was possible that the relationship between the two parties, which had previously been amicable, had deteriorated to the point that the accuser brought up the past deed of the accused as a 'crime'.

We can find six other cases similar to Case C. In one, a citizen, Ceo, was accused by Francesco of having intruded onto land owned by Francesco, and then expelled tenants. In this case, both parties discussed and proved their respective rights to the land, as they would have done in a civil trial.[38]

Other types of *maleficium* also existed aside from those mentioned above. We can see 20 cases concerning negligence by officials regarding communal orders. For example, in 16 cases, the consuls of rural communes were prosecuted for failing to denounce *maleficia* committed in their territory to the Podestà. Two other cases involved false denunciations, and the remaining two cases concerned disobedience of the summons.

Individuals were also prosecuted for disobeying communal rules (6 cases). These included the prosecution of merchants for using scales that did not have an official mark, of witnesses for contumacy of summons, and of various people for carrying out communal work without certification. Trials in such cases, including those of

---

36 *Potestà*, 4849, fol. 91r: "Pucttana, puttana vergognati che tu ai facti figliuoli daltrui"; *Ibid.*, fol. 95r: "tu se furo et ladro"; *Potestà*, 4848, fol. 41r: "traditore che tu se ladro".

37 *Potestà*, 4846, fols. 175r-178v, 190r-191v.

38 *Potestà*, 4848, fols. 35r-37v.

negligence by officials, were initiated by *fama publica* or/and denunciation by *fide dignis personis* (reliable people).

Finally, four people (4 cases) were prosecuted for failure to prove an accusation, which was tantamount to false accusation.

The sample year, from July 1355 to June 1356, was a year wherein serious crimes were committed comparatively frequently. In 1363, for example, of a total of 155 cases, serious crimes (for which the death penalty would be imposed) were prosecuted in only 14 cases: homicide or injury resulting in death in nine cases (6%), and kidnapping in five cases (3%). Of the 116 cases of injury (75%), 90 involved bloodshed.[39] In other cases, throwing (with no harm done) was prosecuted in two cases, threats in three cases, verbal abuse in four cases, and cases involving a civil matter in four cases.

Let us compare the criminal cases of mid fourteenth-century Lucca with those of mid-thirteenth-century Perugia.[40] In Perugia, while homicides were prosecuted in 17 cases (3%), injury was also the main crime (229 cases, 36%). Notably, crimes involving civil matters accounted for more than half of the crimes in Perugia: theft in 156 cases (25%), damage to property in 116 cases (18%), and non-payment in 63 cases (10%). Whereas the criminal court in thirteenth-century Perugia was used strategically by parties involved in civil conflicts, such usage was no longer prevalent in fourteenth-century Lucca, where the criminal court was a forum less for conflict resolution between parties than for the punishment of those who violated communal laws.[41] This becomes evident when we look at trial procedures and sentencing.

As the court clerks did not describe the social standing of the accused, we know only their names and places of origin. From 1355 to 1356, the criminal court prosecuted 95 citizens (*cives*),[42] 392 rural villagers, 25 foreigners (e.g. from Firenze or Pisa), and 6 persons of unidentified origin. Apart from 5 unidentified cases, 80 crimes were committed in the city, 164 in the countryside, and 18 in the vicariate. Citizens and rural villagers generally committed *maleficia* in their respective territories. In some cases, the accused and victims came from the same province, while others might involve villagers assaulting citizens or vice versa. Such cases indicate the strict social and economic relationship between city and countryside. As we shall see, the city statutes prescribed relatively heavy fines on villagers who committed crimes against citizens, presumably to prevent such crimes taking place in the countryside.

---

39 *Potestà*, 4901, 4902, 4903, 4904.

40 Vallerani, *Il sistema giudiziario del comune di Perugia*, p. 50-60, 98-99.

41 The proportion of crimes prosecuted in Lucca was not dissimilar to that reported by Kumhera for crimes prosecuted in Siena's *contado* in 1343 and 1345: 13 cases of homicide (3%), 263 cases of injury in (62%), 36 cases of theft and robbery (9%), 73 cases of insults and threats (17%), and 15 cases of property damage (4%), Kumhera, *The Benefits of Peace*, p. 71-87, 264-265.

42 Here I exclude those who simply resided in Lucca (qui moratur Luce) from the category of citizen (*cives*).

4. Procedures

Let us consider how cases A, B, C proceeded after prosecution.

Case A:

Dates	
Sep. 9	The judge ordered a messenger to summon Cellottoro and the others to appear in court within two days to respond to the denunciation.
Sep. 10	The messenger reported that he had done so.
Sep. 15	The judge ordered the messenger to issue a second summons.
Sep. 15	The messenger reported that he had done so.
Oct. 14	The crier pronounced bans on Piero, Coluccino Paruei, and five others, fining them 300 *lire* each.
Oct. 14	Cellottoro and Bertocho were sentenced to *bannum*. They were to be brought to the place of execution to put to death and to have their property confiscated by the commune. Then, after securing in advance fair proportions of the amount to be distributed among the sons and daughters of Cellottoro and Bertocho, the family of the victim would be eligible to receive 100 *lire* of the confiscated sum.

After the prosecution, the eventual success of a trial would depend on the intention of the accused to appear in court. In medieval cities such as fourteenth-century Lucca, it was difficult to arrest suspects owing to the absence of systematic police forces.[43] After failing to respond to a summons for appearing in court twice (*contumacia*), the accused would be considered to have admitted to the charges and thus would be placed under *bannum*.

From 1355 to 1356, 286 accused (55%) and 114 cases (43%) failed to respond to their summons and were placed under ban. Similarly, high percentages of contumacy can also be seen in other fourteenth-century cities: 57% (133 of 234 accused) in San Gimignano in the first half of the fourteenth century[44] and 48% in Reggio at the end of the fourteenth century.[45] In Bologna, 52% were in 1372 and 44% in 1393,[46] and in Florence, 58% in 1352-1355 and 56% in 1380-1383.[47] Those who were pronounced as *banniti* in the criminal court were removed from the protection of the commune, not only in the matter of properties but also in the matter of their person, so that everyone,

---

43 As for the staff of courts concerning enforcement, see Chapter 6, paragraphs 3 and 5.

44 Graziotti, p. 70-83. The percentage of cases of contumacy varied depending on the year in San Gimignano. While in 1319, 38 of the 108 accused were banished, in 1325-1326, 95 of the 126 accused were placed under ban.

45 J. Carraway Vitiello, 'Contumacy, Defense Strategy, and Criminal Law in Late Medieval Italy', *Law and History Review*, 29-1 (2011), p. 99-132.

46 Carraway, *Public Justice*, p. 151.

47 L. I. Stern, *Criminal Law System of Medieval and Renaissance Florence* (Baltimore and London, 1994), p. 229.

especially the victim's family, could freely harm the accused with impunity.[48] Therefore, the medieval ban was a system that checked the disobedience of communal orders by applying the threat of a vendetta by victims or communities, not by of state policing power.[49]

Let us consider cases wherein the accused appeared before the court. From 1355 to 1356, 223 accused (43%) were brought to the court. Moreover, the trials of nine accused individuals were broken off without any sentences after contumacy because of the transfer to other courts like the episcopal court, which had jurisdiction over them (see Figure 1).

Case B:[50]

Dates	
Oct. 16	The judge ordered the messenger to summon Landello and Giovanna to appear in court within two days to respond to the denunciation.
Oct. 16	The messenger reported that he had done so.
Oct. 17	Giovanna appeared in court and swore an oath of truth on the Bible.
	Giovanna, who was interrogated by the judge, denied the suspicions set out in the indictment entirely. She insisted that she certainly had thrown a piece of lime against the face of Landello, but she did not admit to having bloodied his face.
	The judge recognised Ambrogio, husband of Giovanna, and Giovanni Curradi as guarantors.
Oct. 19	Landello appeared in court and swore an oath of truth on the Bible.
	Landello confessed that the content of the indictment was true, but that Giovanna attacked Landello first.
	The judge recognised a master woodcutter, Butinus Buti, as a guarantor.
Oct. 22	A witness, Datuccio Vanne, testified that the content of the indictment was true, but that it was not a stone but a small piece of lime that Giovanna had thrown at Landello. Datuccio responded to the question of how he knew this fact to the effect that he had witnessed it.
	A witness, Francesca, wife of Ciao, testified that the content of the indictment was true. Francesca, questioned as to how she knew this fact, responded that she had witnessed the scene. Furthermore, she testified that Giovanna had inflicted harm on Landello, first in

48 As for Lucca, *Statuto 1342*, I, fol. 24r: 'De eo quod imbanniti pro maleficio possint impune offendi'. In other cities, Carraway Vitiello, *Public Justice*, p. 155-157.

49 Carraway Vitiello notes the various functions of bans, such as public assertions of authority by the government, and identifies the practices of parties followed by bans. Carraway Vitiello, *Public Justice*, p. 151-157; Carraway Vitiello, 'Contumacy, Defense Strategy'.

50 *Potestà*, 4846, fols. 147r-148r.

	the face with fist and lime, and that Landello afterwards had hit Giovanna in the chest.
	A witness, Nutina, the wife of Datuccio, upon being questioned, testified that she did not know anything about the suspicion.
	A witness, Bartolomea, wife of Guccini, upon being questioned, testified that she did not know anything about the suspicion.
Oct. 22	The judge ordered a messenger to summon Landello and Giovanna to be present in court at the presentation of testimony and to be given a set term within which to make a response.
	A messenger reported to the court clerk that he had done so.
Oct. 22	The judge, in the absence of the accused, opened the testimony and gave them eight days to reply to the witnesses.
Oct. 30	Ambrogio, husband of Giovanna, as a procurator of his wife, and Landello, appeared in court and presented the peace agreement in the instrument between Giovanna and Landello, dated on 27 October 1355, so that they could enjoy the remission stipulated by the statute.

Criminal trials in fourteenth-century Lucca proceeded within the framework of judge versus accused, which differed from the procedure adopted in thirteenth-century Perugia. Now the judge conducted criminal trials, following the article of the statute *De maleficiis inquirendis et modo procedendi super eis*.[51] Let us reconstruct the process of criminal trials based on this article and on the actual court and sentence books.

As Case B shows, the accused were permitted to leave the court after presenting a guarantor. If the accused fled and defaulted on their fine, their guarantors would have to pay it on their behalf. The statute, therefore, prohibited the accused who had committed a vicious crime warranting corporal punishment from presenting a guarantor and leaving the court.

The city statutes assumed three ways to ascertain the truth, namely, voluntary confession, confession obtained by torture, and testimony.

Voluntary confession was the principal basis upon which the judge considered the truth of the allegations. In the trials of 1355-1356, 124 accused (83% of convicted) confessed to their crimes and were found guilty. An accused who confessed to a crime could have his or her fine reduced or mitigated, in general by a quarter.[52]

51 *Statuto 1342*, I, 2 (De maleficiis inquirendis et modo procedendi super eis), fols. 4v-6r.

52 The city statute prescribed the reduction by one fourth of a fine because of confession, *Statuto 1342*, I, 10 (De pena minuenda confitenti maleficium in prima examinatione), fol. 8r; ASL, *Statuti del Comune di Lucca*, 6 (hereafter *Statuto 1372*), II, 122, fol. 41v. The sentence book also indicates the reduction of fines owing to confessions, ASL, *Sentenze e bandi*, 13, non foliation, 31 January 1344: 'remissa ei quarta parte dicti condemnationis propter eius confessione quam fecit in prima eius examinationi'.

The statutes permitted the judge to torture only those who committed theft, blasphemy, or other crimes incurring fines of more than 50 *lire*.[53] Though the criminal court and sentence books do not show any evidence of the use of torture,[54] it is possible that other judicial officials, such as the bargello, did use such method, based on the petitions to the Anziani wherein the convicts explained the rigorous use of torture by the judge as the reason for their contumacy. We will see these petitions in detail in Chapter 5.

Testimony was taken from witnesses in cases of the denial of allegations by the accused, as in Case B. The statutes prescribed that the judge should interrogate witnesses and that the court clerk should write down the testimonies both inside and outside the court. In 1355-1356, testimonies were presented in the trials of 52 accused.

There were two types of testimony. The first, '*testes ad defensam*', were presented by defendants in order to refute the suspicion, as we shall see. The second, '*testes ad offensam*', which we see in Case B, were used by the judge to determine the veracity of the suspicion. In the examination, the witnesses had to answer whether or not they knew the facts. A relatively large number of witnesses responded '*nichil scire*'. Those who were aware of the facts further responded on how they came to have such knowledge, for example as an eyewitness, through hearsay (witness by *fama publica*), or through communication from a certain person.

As seen above, the criminal court of fourteenth-century Lucca adopted an inquisitorial procedure wherein the judge was given the initiative to interrogate the accused and witnesses and to ascertain the truth of the allegations. According to the statutes, cases brought to the court following the accusation of victims also proceeded in this inquisitorial fashion.[55] However, as exceptions, we can also see cases in the court books wherein the accuser assumed the burden of proof and the trial proceeded as a confrontation between accuser and accused, as in Case C.

Case C:[56]

Dates	
Oct. 21	The judge ordered the messenger to summon Jacopo to appear in court within two days.
Oct. 21	The messenger reported that he had done so.

53 The city statutes also prohibited the torture of pregnant women, and imposed a fine on any judge or *podestà* who implemented torture that resulted in the death of suspects, *Statuto 1342*, I, 2 (De maleficiis inquirendis et modo procedendi super eis), fol. 5r; *Statuto 1372*, II, 9 (De modo torquendi et in quo casu prohibita et seu promissaex tortura), fol. 22r.

54 The city statutes prescribed that torture must be carried out in the presence of the judge and a notary, who was obligated to record the nature of the torture. *Statuto 1342*, fol. 5r; *Statuto 1372*, II, 10 (De eo quod torture debeat esse unus notarius maleficiorum), fol. 22v.

55 *Statuto 1342*, I, 2, fol. 5v: 'et quelibet accusa et denuntiatio possit poni et describi per notarium malleficiorum in modum inquisitionis, et ea via super ipsa procedi in his tamen maleficiis et excessibus super quibus potest procedi per viam inquisitionis'.

56 *Potestà*, 4846, fols. 175r-178v, 190r-191v.

Oct. 24 Jacopo, the accused, and Duccio, the accuser, appeared in court. Jacopo asked the court to receive a copy of the written accusation and a term for his response.

Oct. 26 Jacopo appeared in court and swore an oath of truth on the Bible. He denied the accusation as follows:

The accusation does not have to be accepted and the trial does not have to be started, as the formula of the written accusation was imprecise and Duccio was not competent enough to bring an accusation on this matter. Furthermore, Jacopo denied the contents described in the accusation.

Duccio responded that the trial must proceed according to this accusation and that he would like to make clear the colour of the bed cover, which had been not declared in the accusation.

Oct. 27 Jacopo and Duccio appeared in court. The judge gave Duccio ten days to prove the accusation.

Duccio presented to Jacopo the following statements [*positiones*] on which he asked Jacopo to respond. Duccio can prove the contents of these statements:

positio 1	Duccio was a son of the late Tofano Christofani.
Jacopo's response	believe (*credit*).[57]
positio 2	Duccio was a legitimate child.
Jacopo's response	believe (*credit*).
positio 3	The late Margarita was the daughter of the late Tofano.
Jacopo's response	Acknowledges that the late Margarita was the daughter of the late Tofano, but disagrees that Margarita died after the death of Bonuccio, her husband.
positio 4	The late Margarita was a legitimate child.
Jacopo's response	believe (*credit*).
positio 5	The late Margarita died without leaving any sons.
Jacopo's response	believe (*credit*).
positio 6	The late Bonuccio died in June of 1358. If Jacopo denies it, he has to indicate another death day.
Jacopo's response	believe (*credit*).
positio 7	The late Junctorino Michelis died in June of 1358. If Jacopo denies it, he has to indicate another death day.
Jacopo's response	believe (*credit*).

	Duccio asked Jacopo to respond to the above statements. Jacopo asked the court for a copy of the statements.
Oct. 29	Jacopo appeared in court and responded to the above statements.
Oct. 31	Duccio presented the following allegations (*titulus et intentio*).

titulus 1	The late Margarita died after the death of Bonuccio.
titulus 2	Clothes, a bed, a frying pan, and other household goods were left in the house after the deaths of Bonuccio, Margarita, and Junctorino in June of 1348.
titulus 3	The total value of the goods which were left in the house was estimated at 100 florins.
titulus 4	Jacopo entered the house in June 1348, after the deaths of Bonuccio, Junctorino, and Margarita.
titulus 5	Dolose Jacopo removed the goods mentioned above from this house.
titulus 6	There were *publica vox et fama* about the matters mentioned above in the commune of Batone and other neighbouring rural communes.

	Duccio asked to prove the *titulus* mentioned above by the witness.
	The messenger reported that he had presented the *titulus* to Jacopo.
Nov. 4	The judge ordered the messenger to summon Duccio to appear in court.
Nov. 6	Jacopo and Duccio appeared in court. Jacopo presented the following objection in front of the court clerk in the absence of the judge.
	Jacopo's objection: *Titulus* should not be admitted, and the testimony, based on *titulus*, should not be given, because of the imprecise formula of the written accusation and of the incompetence of Duccio as the accuser. Therefore, Duccio is not permitted to prove the contents of his accusation and *titulus*, and the trial does not have to proceed to any conviction if he proves it. Jacopo denied all contents of the accusation and *titulus*. If Duccio contests this objection, the advice of the jurist (*consilium sapientis*) must be given.
	Jacopo presented counter-allegations.
Nov. 3[58]	The judge, at Duccio's request, ordered the messenger to summon the 13 witnesses. Jacopo denied all contents of the accusation and *titulus* again, and asked for legal costs.
Nov. 6 (vespers)	Duccio and Jacopo appeared in court.
	Jacopo's objection: if the witnesses swore and answered Duccio's *titulus*, the testimony would not be legally accepted.

	Duccio asked the judge to interrogate the witness based on Duccio's *titulus* and accusation.
	The witnesses appeared in court and swore on the Bible to depose without falsehood, and excluding all hate, love, and fear.
	The judge ordered the court clerk to take the witnesses' testimonies.
Nov. 13	The judge ordered the messenger to summon Duccio.
	Duccio appeared in court and was given 20 days to proceed and to prove the contents of the accusation.

The trial proceeded with a confrontation between the accuser, Duccio, and the accused, Jacopo. It was not the judge but the accuser who had to prove the substance of the accusation. Besides this burden, there were many other elements similar to a civil trial, such as the exchange of assertions, the presentation of the allegations by the accuser, the counter-allegations by the accused, and the testimony based on these allegations. As seen above, we can confirm that the accusatorial process, which had been the main procedure in thirteenth-century Perugia, was also evident in (albeit to a small degree) the criminal court of Lucca a century later.

Now, I would like to turn to consider the possibile means of defence by defendants in criminal and civil trials. The judge always gave the defendant opportunities to contest the indictment. Such opportunities seem to have been considered as indispensable procedures for legitimating trials, as all sentences mention them expressly.

As options for defence, we can see that exceptions (*exceptiones*) were often presented in civil trials as well as rejections of the prosecution. An accused, for example, might insist on the incompetence of the judge on the present matter, the minority of the defendant, the foreign citizenship of the defendant, or the validity of the violence against *banniti* or *condemnati*.[59] In the criminal court of thirteenth-century Bologna, such exceptions were frequently presented. The fact that criminals sometimes went free owing to the effects of these exceptions prompted the jurist Gandino to lament that in such cases, the *maleficia* remained unpunished and to call for judges to be given a powerful initiative in making their the judgements.

Apart from exceptions, an effective defence by the accused was to produce a testimony for the defence (*testes ad defensam*). While in Case C, which adopted accusatorial procedures, the accuser presented allegations to prove the charges, in inquisitorial cases, the accused would do so to present points to deny the charge. The judge – or in Case C, the accused – would produce a '*contratitulus*', wherein the counter-questions were

57 The responses would have been written afterwards (probably on 29 October).

58 This date was probably a mistake by the notary.

59 For example, in a case from 1344, Katerina and Chiara, who were prosecuted for causing injury to each other, asked the judge to stop the proceedings, bearing witness to the fact that Katerina was from Florence and Chiara was German. This claim was successful, *Potestà*, 4787, [1344.3.14]: 'Katerina et Chiara [...] dixerunt et opposuerunt contra ipsas et qualibet earum procedi vel inquiri non debere calsis[causis] et ractionibus infrascriptis, videlicet quia suprascripta Katerina est de Florentia [...] in civitate Lucana stetit et habutavit per annos dues [...] pro famula Scharani barateni de Luca [...] Et dicta Chiara est tedisscha et teotonica videlicet de Alamania ...'

described and with which the judge or court clerk would interrogate witnesses, along with allegations.

An example of '*testes ad defensam*' was presented by an accused, Giovanni Donati, in a case that began on 20 July 1355. Giovanni made allegations and tried to prove them with three witnesses to deny the suspicions that he had thrown a lance at Chiccaro and wounded his leg.[60] The witnesses were examined based on the points described in the allegation presented by Giovanni and not based on suspicions, as in '*testes ad offensam*'.

5. Sentences

(1) Results of trials

Let us consider how these trials ended, using the sentence books rather than the court books. In 267 cases, 518 individuals were prosecuted from 1355 to 1356. The number of the cases of sentences in the same period is for convenience sake, that is, 289 cases, because we count some cases doubly wherein some were found guilty and others were found not guilty.

First, those who disobeyed the summons twice and failed to appear in court were banished. In 1355-1356, of 114 cases (39%), 286 accused (55%) were banished in this way. The other 223 accused (and nine accused who did not appear but were not banished) ended in one of three other routes: condemnation, found innocent, or absolved and/or otherss (e.g. being transferred to other courts).

In 1355-1356, 150 accused (in 118 cases) were condemned by judges after the examinations. Of these, 124 were convicted by their own confessions. A further 21 denied the allegations but were condemned by witnesses attesting to the charges. In Case B, although Giovanna denied the allegations, testimony proved them in part (i.e. she assaulted Landello with the piece of lime), whereupon she was found guilty and fined 12 *lire*. This fine was reduced by half in recognition of her reconciliation with Landello. Conversely, Landello was fined a reduced amount of 10 *lire* for reconciling and confessing.[61]

In 37 cases, 56 accused individuals denied the allegations and established their innocence (*absolutio*). One reason why the judge found these accused not guilty was recorded as '*non culpabile reperto*' in the sentence, meaning that the judge or accuser could not prove the allegations. In an accusatorial trial such as Case C, a verdict of not guilty meant the failure of the accusation, which in turn condemned the accuser for bringing false accusation. In Case C, the judge, after declaring Jacopo not guilty, sentenced the accuser, Duccio, with a fine of 5 *lire* on 5 December 1355.[62]

---

60 *Potestà*, 4847, fols. 15r-16v, 22v-23v.

61 As for the rule of reduction of fine by half due to peace, *Statuto 1372*, II, 121 (De pena reducenda ad dimidiam propter pacem), fol. 141v.

62 *Potestà*, 4846, fol. 175r.

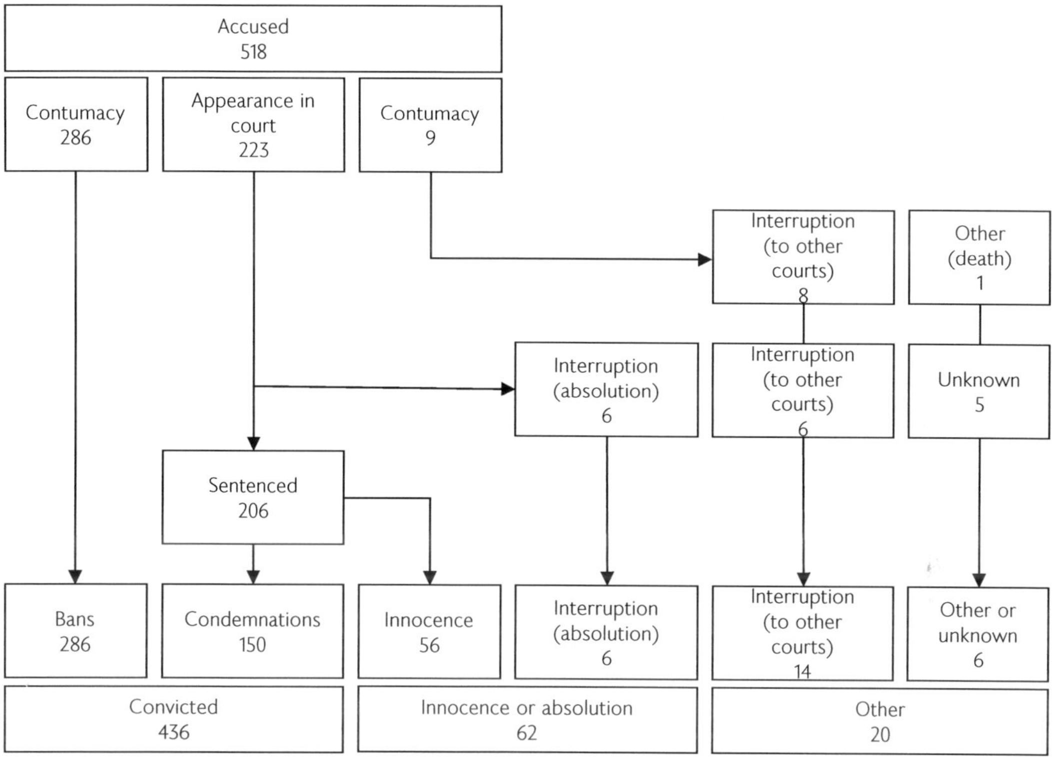

Figure 4.1: Process and results of criminal trials

This was not the only reason for a not-guilty verdict. For example, five accused were pronounced innocent because the incident in question had been domestic violence, while three others were absolved because the victims had been banished and thus were outside the protection of the commune.

Other cases were interrupted before the sentencing owing to legal technicalities. These cases are recorded in the court books, but not in the sentence books. Of these 17 cases involving 20 accused in 1355-1356, six accused (out of five of the cases) did not have to be prosecuted at all, by reason, for example, of the minority of the accused or the banishment of the victim. These cases were tantamount to innocence, and the accused were entirely absolved. Conversely, the interruption of trials for 14 accused (in 12 cases) arose because the accused were foreigners and therefore subject to the jurisdiction of the episcopal court. In these cases, the accused were not free from guilt but were transferred to the other courts.

To sum up the cases from 1355-1356, of the 518 accused, 286 (55%) were placed under ban for contumacy (in 114 cases) and 150 (29%) were condemned by the judge (in 118 cases). While under sentence of fine or corporal punishment, 62 were absolved (in 42 cases), of whom 56 (11%) were pronounced innocent by the judge (in 37 cases) and 6 (1%) were absolved by the interruption of the case due to legal technicalities (in

5 cases). Meanwhile, 14 accused (in 12 cases) were transferred to other courts; the fates of another 6 (in 3 cases) are unclear, and in one case, the accused died during the trial.

The results of criminal trials, particularly regarding the relative proportion of convictions to absolutions over the year in question, were not so different from those of the other years. For example, in 1363, of 234 accused, 80 (34%) were banished, 91 (39%) were condemned, 14 (6%) were found 'not guilty', and the trials of 29 (12%) were interrupted for various reasons. We cannot know the fates of the other 20 accused (9%).[63]

If we compare these results with those of Perugia in 1258, where only 11% of the trials ended with guilty verdicts in circumstances in which accusatorial procedures prevailed, the high proportion of convictions (80% of cases) in fourteenth-century Lucca attracts our attention. This seems to have been caused mostly by the strong initiative on the part of judges to seek attestations using inquisitorial procedure, whereas in Perugia, the main reason for absolution was insufficient evidence because of the low capacity among accusers to present evidence in court.[64]

(2) Punishment

The criminal court of Lucca in 1355-1356 imposed two types of penalty. Of the 436 convicted (*condemnati* and *banniti*), 271 (62%) were fined and 165 (38%) were sentenced to death.

The death penalty applied to serious crimes like homicide, robbery, arson, and kidnapping. Cellottoro and Bertocho in Case A were banished and sentenced to beheading. Many who were accused and prosecuted for serious crimes did not appear in court and were banished in absentia (these were called *banniti*). As we will discuss in the next section, capital punishment for *banniti* was not actually always carried out. In the records, only four people prosecuted for homicide or robbery were brought to court – probably after being caught by guards (*berrovarii*) – and were directly condemned by the judge. Of these, three were actually decapitated or hanged.[65]

As noted earlier, the period 1355-1356 saw many serious crimes, and therefore had a relatively large proportion of cases involving the death penalty. In 1363, of the 171 convicted (*banniti* and *condemnati*), fines were imposed on 131 (76%) and the death penalty on 32 (19%), apart from one instance of corporal punishment and seven unknown.[66]

63 *Potestà*, 4901, 4902, 4903, 4904.

64 Vallerani, *Il sistema giudiziario*, p. 61-62.

65 As for decapitation, *Potestà*, 4848, fol. 24r: 'die secunda aprilis mandato domini Lucani potestatis ductus fuit ad locum iustitie consuetum et dicto Michele per sententiam latam in consilio generali fuit caput amputatus seu incisum decapitus fuit'; *Potestà*, 4848, fol. 66r: 'die.xx.i junii mandato suprascripti domini potestatis suprascriptus Venturinus ductus fuit ad locum iustitie consuetum et ibi caput fuit ei amputatus'. As for hanging, *Potestà*, 4848, fol. 73r: 'die.xxvii. junii mandato domini potestatis suprascripti dictus fuit ad locum iustitie consuetum et Nicolao suspensus fuit per gulam'.

66 We know about a pronouncement of a penalty in the form of amputation of a right hand, *Potestà*, 4886-4890; ASL, *Sentenze e bandi*, 29, 30.

In fourteenth-century Lucca, financial penalties were common. Whereas Piero and six others were fined 300 *lire* for aiding a homicide in Case A, Giovanni and Landello were fined 12 *lire* and 10 *lire* respectively, for injury. As Table 3 indicates, 47 of the convicted incurred fines of 10 *lire* or less, 103 of between 10 and 49 *lire*, 47 of between 50 and 99 *lire*, 69 of between 100 and 499,[67] and five of over 500 *lire*. These amounts were already reduced from the statutory amounts by reconciliation and confession.

Table 4.3: Fine amounts in 1355-1356 (*lire*)

	PEOPLE	%
Up to 10	47	17
10-49	103	38
50-99	47	17
100-499	69	25
500 or more	5	2
total	**271**	**100**

The city statutes determined in detail the fine amount for every *maleficium* (Table 4). The trials of 1355-1356 seemed to have adopted the same amounts later prescribed in the statutes of 1372. For example, regarding bodily injury with weapons or ironware, citizens were fined up to 100 *lire* for injury inflicted on a citizen and up to 50 *lire* for a non-citizen (i.e. villagers or foreigners). Moreover, non-citizens were fined 200-400 *lire* and 50 *lire* for injuries to citizens and non-citizens respectively. Similarly, fines were set for cases of injury caused by other implements or by bare hands, or in cases of an attack to the face. Such fines were reduced by half if there was no bloodshed. The fines for threats were also fixed according to the situation wherein the crime was committed and the identity of the perpetrators and victims.

This fine structure reveals the intention on the part of the city government to treat citizens favourably and to protect them from violence. Fines were set high for crimes against citizens: 100 *lire* for villagers who injured citizens by hand compared to 25 *lire* for citizens causing harm to villagers.

(3) Arbitrium *of judges*

Let us consider the room given for the *arbitrium* of judges in their assessment of culpability.

The sentence books indicate that judges adhered strictly to the statutes when deciding fine amounts. For example, in a case of 26 August 1355, a judge fined a villager, Martino Sini, 37 *lire* 10 *soldi* for causing injury with a sword to the leg of a fellow

67 Among the 69 convicted on whom were imposed a high fine (i.e. 100-499), 40 were convicted of assisting a serious crime such as homicide.

Table 4.4: Fine amounts by *maleficium* for each situation, as prescribed in the 1372 statutes (*lire*)

SUSPECTS	CITIZENS		NON-CITIZENS (VILLAGERS OR FOREIGNERS)	
VICTIMS	CITIZENS	NON-CITIZENS	NON-CITIZENS	CITIZENS
Homicide[i]	decapitation	decapitation	decapitation	hanging
Accomplice to homicide[ii]	300	300	300	decapitation
Injury to the face in bloodshed[iii]				
with weapons or ironware	150-400	75-100	75-150	300-500
with other tools	100	50	75	150
with bare hands	50	25	25	100
Injury to the body in bloodshed[iv]				
with arms or ironware	100	50	50	200-400
with other tools	66	33	33	100-200
with a bare hand	33	16.10s	16.10s	100
Threat[v]				
with arms prohibited unsheathed	30	15	15	70
with arms sheathed or knife or stick	18	9	9	50
with a bare hand	12	6	6	25
Throwing (no harm done)[vi]				
stone, stick, iron	15	7.5	7.5	25-50
sword	20	10		100

[i]*Statuto 1372*, II, 50 (De pena facientis homicidium), fol. 27v; *Statuto 1372*, II, 51 (De pena foretani seu forensis interficientis civem Lucanum), fol. 27v.

[ii]*Statuto 1372*, II, 55 (De pena danda illi qui prestiterit interfectori vel vulneratori auxilium vel favorem in tenendo interfectum vel vulnerando sive aliter), fol. 28r.

[iii]*Statuto 1372*, II, 34 (De percussionibus et vulneribus commissis cum armis in vultu), fols. 24v-25r; *Statuto 1372*, II, 35 (De percussionibus et vulneribus commissis in vultu cum aliis rebus), fol. 25r; *Statuto 1372*, II, 36 (De pena percucientis seu vulnerantis cum manu pugno vel alio suo membro in vultu), fol. 25r.

[iv]*Statuto 1372*, II, 37 (De percussionibus et vulneribus cum armis commissis in alia parte corporis preter quam in vultu), fol. 25r-v; *Statuto 1372*, II, 38 (De vulneribus et percussionibus commissis cum aliis rebus in alia parte corporis preter quam in vultu), fol. 25v; *Statuto 1372*, II, 39 (De pena percuentis aliquem cum manu pugno vel alio suo membro in alia parte corporis preter quam in vultu), fol. 25v.

[v]*Statuto 1372*, II, 25 (De pena civis Lucani insultantis civem Lucanum), fol. 24r; *Statuto 1372*, II, 26 (De pena civis insultantis foretanum), fol. 24r; *Ibid.*, II, 27 (De pena foretani seu forensic insultantis foretanum seu forensem), fol. 24r; *Ibid.*, II, 28 (De pena foretani seu forensic insultatantis[cosi nel testo] civem Lucanum), fol. 24r.

6 *Statuto 1372*, II, 44 (De pena proitientis contra aliquem lapidem vel lignum vel ferrum vel gladum vel ensem vel aliam rem), fol. 26v.

villager, Ricco Orsi, resulting in bloodshed.[74] This fine amount had been reduced by a quarter from the statutory amount of 50 *lire* by the confession of the perpetrator.

While judges mostly adhered strictly to the statutes when imposing fines, we do find some cases which seem to be exceptional. For example, a villager, Vannuccio, was fined 145 *lire* by a judge for causing injury with a sword to the right hand of a villager, Marino, resulting in bloodshed.[75] In another case, a judge fined a villager, Luporino, 150 *lire* simply for punching (with one hand) the chest of a fellow villager, Tuccolo.[76] These fines, which exceeded those set in the statute, were determined by the consequences of the injuries. In the former case, Vannuccio's attack resulted in the amputation of Martino's finger, while the assault by Luporino, in the second case, caused Tuccolo to fall and become disabled. In fact, in these cases, the judges just seemed to follow an article of the statute, '*De percussionibus et vulneribus ex quibus aliquod membrum amissum seu debilitatum seu inutile factum fuerit*', which permitted judges to impose heavier fines.[77]

The judges imposed lighter fines than the prescribed amounts on women and minors, and the statutes expressly required the judges to exercise their discretion (*arbitrium*) in such cases.[78] In fact, a villager, Andrea, whom a judge recognised *viso aspectu* as being under the age of 16 years old, was fined only 20 *soldi* 3 *denari* for causing injury with his bare hand to the face of another villager. Although the statutory amount, prior to its reduction for confession and reconciliation, would have been 54 *soldi* (equivalent to 2 *lire* 14 *soldi*), this was very low compared with the statutory amount of 25 *lire* set for this type of crime.[79] In Case B, Giovanna, a woman from Florence, now *habitator* of Lucca, was fined only 12 *lire* (after the reduction due to reconciliation) for assault with a bare hand and for throwing a stone that hit the face of a citizen, Landello, for which the statutes generally fixed a fine of 125 *lire*.[80] Though these fines were lighter, judges were empowered by the statutes to use their discretion (*arbitrium*) when deciding fine amounts for women and minors.

The city statute of 1372 began allowing judges certain *arbitrium* to decide fine amounts for some crimes; for example, injury to the face with weapons or ironware resulting in bloodshed and injury to citizens by villagers. In a trial heard on 25 July 1355, the judge fined a villager, Piero, 300 *lire* for striking the head of a citizen, Lippo, with a

74 *Potestà*, 4846, fols. 55r-v.

75 *Potestà*, 4846, fols. 127r-128v.

76 *Potestà*, 4847, fols. 26r-v.

77 *Statuto 1372*, II, 41 (De percussionibus et vulneribus ex quibus aliquod membrum amissum seu debilitatum seu inutile factum fuerit), fol. 26r.

78 *Statuto 1372*, II, 49 (De maleficiis et excessibus commissis per minores sedecim annis vel mulieres), fol. 27r: 'Et si predicta maleficia vel aliquod predictorum fuerint comissa ab aliquo minore sedecim annis vel aliqua muliere de predictis penis mutandis et minorandis sit in arbitrio potestatis…'; *Statuto 1342*, I, 12, fol. p. 19.

79 *Potestà*, 4848, fols. 8r-9r.

80 According to the city statutes, when many crimes were committed in a case, the judge was required to impose a penalty that corresponded to the more serious crime, adding half of the fine for the other crimes, *Statuto 1372*, II, 47, fol. 26v: 'De pluribus delictis uno impetus factis'. Therefore, in this case, the fine to be imposed was 100 *lire* for the injury to the face with a stone resulting in bloodshed and 25 *lire* for hitting with a bare hand.

sword.[81] The judge, who was authorised by the statute to determine a fine between 200 and 400 *lire*, decided on 300 *lire* after assessing the circumstances of the crime.

Such *arbitrium* was not permitted in the statute of 1342. In the second half of fourteenth-century Lucca, as we will see in Chapter 6, the city government (the Anziani to be precise) permitted judges *arbitrium* to investigate and condemn extremely dangerous criminals on behalf of the commune.[82] This was similar to how the 1372 statute authorised judges *arbitrium* when imposing fines for dangerous crimes, with the ultimate intention of protecting citizens.

In other cases, we can certainly find ones wherein judges imposed fines whose amounts cannot be deduced from the statutes. It was possible that in some cases, the judges decided the fines completely arbitrarily. For example, in Case B, the judge imposed a fine of 10 *lire* on Landello (citizen) for hitting the chest of Giovanna (*habitator* of Lucca) with his bare hand. The amount, before the reductions for confession (by one quarter) and reconciliation (by one half), was the inexplicable amount of 26.6 *lire*.[83] This was lower than the statutory amount of 33 *lire*.

Despite such cases, however, the judges generally followed the rules provided by the city statutes while making a decision on fine amounts. It was mostly with the authorisation of statutes that a judge was able to fix the fines with his *arbitrium*. The statutes of the appellate court permitted convicts to appeal criminal trials only in cases where the judges imposed unreasonable fines not consistent with the statutes.[84] However, the registers of the appellate court are virtually void of actual appeals from those convicted in criminal cases.[85] This indicates that people did not recognise the criminal court and its judges as unjust in the sense of not following statutes in their determination of fine amounts, or at least not so unjust as to drive them to the trouble and expense of making an appeal.

---

81 *Potestà*, 4846, fols. 26r-v. From a 300 *lire* fine, 35 *lire* and half of 70 *lire* were imposed owing to a crime of threat.

82 This trend towards permitting judges *arbitrium* can commonly be seen in the statutes of Reggio during the fourteenth century, Carraway Vitiello, *Public Justice*, p. 157-163.

83 In another case, a citizen, Michele, was convicted of hitting the face of Narduccio, a citizen, with his bare hands. We cannot determine the original amount of the fine based on th 10 *lire* that was imposed on him after the reduction of a fine owing to confession and peacemaking, *Potestà*, 4846, fols. 133r-v.

84 Romiti, 'Lo «statutum curie appellationum»', p. 145: 'Statuimus etiam et ordinamus quod a condepnationibus Potestatis Lucani factis occasione processuum maleficiorum vel quasi, non possit appellari vd querela moveri ad dictum iudicem… nisi indictis condepnationibus summa bampni seu pene que pro maleficio vel quasi deberet imponi excederetur, in qua debuerit condepnati ex forma Lucani constituti, in quo casu possit appellari vel querela moveri ab ea summa…'. The statute of 1308 also assumed the cancellation of bans by the decisions of the appellate court, S. Bongi (ed.), *Statuto del comune di Lucca dell'anno MCCCVIII* (Lucca 1867) (hereafter *Statuto 1308*), p. 186: '…vel si in appellatione interposita ad iudicem appellationum pro Lucano Comuni vel in denuntia coram Sindico facta, in casu et modo premisso, bannita persona obtinuerit vel obtineat'.

85 We only know of a few cases wherein the decisions made in the original trial were overruled in the appellate court. For example, the marginal notes of the sentence book of 1359 show that the conviction pronounced against Puccinello in the Court of Podestà on 7 June 1359 was cancelled on 31 August 1359 owing to the decision made by the appellate court, ASL, *Sentenze e bandi*, 22, non foliation, 7 June 1359: 'vigore sententie late per dominum Nicolaum Faville de Pisa iudicem et Maiorem sindicatum Lucani communis et iudicem appellationum'.

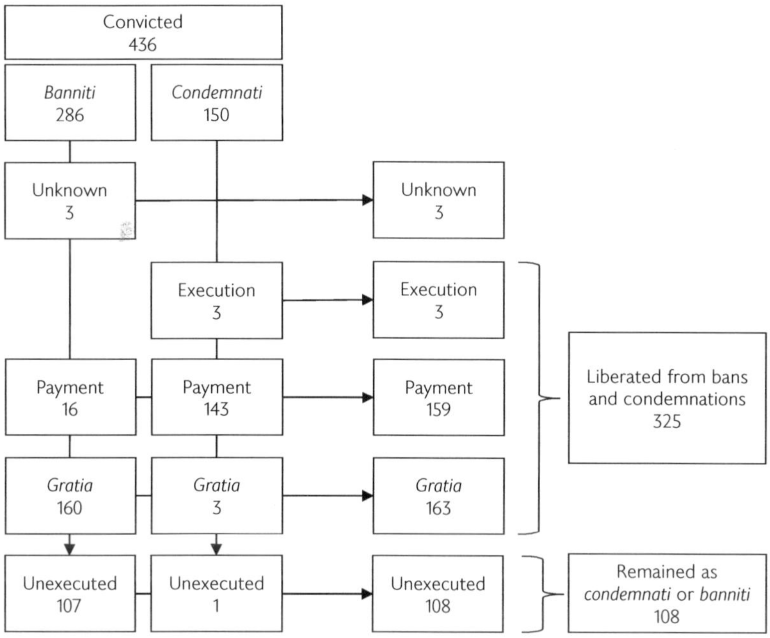

Figure 4.2: Developments after sentencing

6. Developments after Sentencing

(1) Execution of sentences

Next, let us see how cases developed after the pronouncement of sentences, considering the cases of 436 convicted (286 *banniti* and 150 *condemnati*).[86] The conviction of these individuals stripped them of the protection of the commune, making them open targets for anyone to attack them with impunity.[87]

The court clerks, after the pronouncements by the judges, had to draw up the judgement documents and send them to the custodians of the *Camera Librorum*, who were obligated to file each sentencing document in the sentence books (the *libri condemnationum* and the *libri bannorum*) for that year, so that the commune would be able to keep track of those convicted based on these books. The legal importance of the sentence books is attested by the fact that in September 1333 a member of the noble Antelminelli family, who had been banished, returned to Lucca as a rebel, where he set the communal archive alight to destroy the sentence books.[88]

86 ASL, *Sentenze e bandi*, 17, 18.

87 *Statuto 1308*, p. 196-197: 'De eo quod imbapniti pro maleficio possint impune offendi'.

88 See also Chapter 5, note 28. We can see the destruction of sentence books in other Italian cities, De Vincentiis, 'Memorie bruciate'.

The sentence books for the second half of 1355 and the first half of 1356 record 433 convicted, three fewer than are recorded in the court books. In other words, as three of the accused had been sentenced to death, and had been executed, the commune no longer had a reason to maintain a record of them in the sentence books.

In the sentence books, we often see names of convicts struck out with a line with marginal annotations, indicating the reasons why bans were removed.[89] For example, a marginal note beside the cancellation of the name of Giovanna in Case B reads:

> On 14 November 1355, the preceding condemnation of dame Giovanna was cancelled and struck out by me, *ser* Matteo del Caro of Lucca, a notary and custodian of the condemnation, due to a public certification, scripted by Nicolozi Michele of Lucca, a notary of the *Camera* of the commune of Lucca, of the payment of 12 *lire* 10 *soldi* as a fine by dame Giovanna to Fredi Martini, a *camerarius generalis* of the commune of Lucca.[90]

Therefore, Giovanna was liberated from condemnation a week after her conviction on 7 November on payment of her imposed fine and after her name had been struck from the sentence book.

In 1355-1356, 325 of those convicted (75% of the total for that period) were liberated and their names struck from the sentence books, while the names of the other 108 remained on the sentence books as *condemnati* or *banniti*.[91] This percentage is not unusual. In 1363, for example, 125 of those convicted (82% of those recorded in the sentence books) had their condemnations and bans lifted.[92]

Condemnati, who had appeared in the court and been sentenced by a judge, were distinguished from *banniti*, who had not appeared in the court and had been banished owing to contumacy. The two sentences each had their own sentence books: the *libri condemnationum* and the *libri bannorum*. For 1355-1356, the former books recorded 147 convicted, while the latter contained 286. Here let us consider these respective convictions to understand the various reasons for them and the process for liberating each of them.

---

89 The city statutes prescribed a rule for the cancellation of bans by notaries who kept the *libri bannitorum*, *Statuto 1308*, III, 76 (De forma inbanniendi et extrahendi de bapno), p. 184-188, in particular, p. 186: 'Et dicti notarii inbannitorum teneantur et debeant inbannitos pro maleficio vel quasi extrahere et cancellare de libris inbannitorum Lucani Comunis quotiens solverint in pecunia numerata…, vel quotiens deberent ipsos extrahere de banno ex fortia alicuius capituli Constituti Lucani Comunis vel Populi vel decretorum Consiliorum Lucani Comunis vel Populi vel stantiamentorum aliquorum habentium autoritatem a Lucano Comuni…'; *Statuto 1342*, I, 45, fol. 19v.

90 ASL, *Sentenze e bandi*, 18, non foliation, 7 November 1355: 'post predictam predictis anno et Indictione, die.xiiii. novembris, cassa et cancellata est suprascripta condemnatio suprascripte domine Johanne per me Matheum del caro de Luca notarium et custodem suprascriptum, quia constat mihi publica apodixa suprascripta manu Nicolozi Michele de Luca notarii introytus et exitus camere Lucani communis factis suprascriptis anno et Indictione die.xiii. novembris, Fredem Martini camerarius generalis Lucani communis habuisse et recepisse a suprascripta domina Johanna solventi pro suprascripta condemnatione libras duodecim et soldos decem bone monete'.

91 Furthermore, another three convicted, who were given the death penalty, were not registered in the sentence books. The court book notes that these death sentences were carried out.

92 ASL, *Sentenze e bandi*, 29, 30.

According to the *libri condemnationum*, most *condemnati* (146 of 147) subsequently had their convictions lifted.[93] All incurred financial penalties, and 143 of them were liberated on payment of a fine.[94] When they appeared in court, they may well have been prepared to serve a sentence. The lifting of a sentence with the payment of fines happened relatively rapidly after the pronouncement of sentences: 27 convicted paid within one month and 73 within two months. While 135 convicted had their sentences lifted within half a year, only three convicted did not pay within two years of their sentences. This high rate of payment in order to lift sentences is impressive if we consider the undeveloped police system in this period. It is possible that the various risks of remaining outside the protection of the commune pressured the convicted to pay their fines and to return under the umbrella of communal protection. Of the 69 *condemnati* who had not reconciled with their victims by the time of sentencing, 26 succeeded in doing so after their sentencing, thereby receiving a 50% reduction in their fines.

As for the *banniti* – those who were banished due to contumacy – according to the *libri bannorum*, 179 (63%) of all the 286 *banniti* had their bans lifted, while the names of the other 107 (37%) were never struck from the books. Having disobeyed the summons to appear in court, it was perhaps natural that the *banniti* also tended to default on their fines. However, it should be noted that more than 60% of *banniti* did change their minds with the intention of returning to the communal fold.

Of the 179 *banniti* whose bans were lifted, we know the reasons for 176 of them. First, 16 had their bans lifted after obediently paying their fines. More than half of these (9) did so within a year. More interesting is the way in which the other 160 *banniti* were liberated from their bans. The marginal annotations for each sentence contain indications for the reasons why each was lifted, such as on the orders of the Lucchese Anziani, the Pisan Anziani, the Pisan General Council, or the Pisan doge. I would like to turn now to focus on these political interventions as remissions, which were authorised by the city statutes and thus regarded as legal acts.[95]

(2) Gratia

In Case A, Cellottoro and the other eight accused were banished for homicide or for being accessories to homicide, respectively, and faced the death penalty or severe financial penalty as of 15 October 1355. A marginal note in the sentence book regarding this sentence reads as follows.

Cellottoro, under capital punishment:

---

93 From the other four convicted, three were put to death and one was sentenced to death, whose name, for whatever reason, remains in the sentence book.

94 The other three convicts were liberated on the orders of the Anziani.

95 According to the city statute, the notaries who kept the *libri bannitorum* had to cancel bans because of the payment of fines, decrees by the communal councils, and provisions by those who had the authority from the *commune*, that is, the Anziani, *Statuto 1308*, p. 186: 'Et dicti notarii imbannitorum… vel quotiens deberent ipsos extrahere de banno ex forma alicuis capituli Constituti Lucani Comunis vel Populi vel decretorum Consiliorum Lucani Comunis vel Populi vel stantiamentorum aliquorum habentium autoritatem a Lucano Comuni'.

Cellottoro was liberated from the ban on 15 April 1358, Indiction 11, due to the effect of a provision of the Pisan Anziani by their authority, that was decided through white-yellow ballot voting by them, in which it was stated that Cellottoro can and should be liberated.[96]

Bertocho, under capital punishment:
Bertocho was liberated from the ban on 14 March 1360, Indiction 13, due to the effect of a mandate of the General Council of Pisa, pursuant to the confirmation and the approval of a peace agreement between the commune of Pisa and the communes of the vicariate of Coreglia.[97]

Coluccino Paruei, under a fine of 300 *lire*:
Coluccino was liberated from the ban on 22 November 1358, Indiction 12, due to the effect of a mandate of the Lucchese Anziani and a payment of 20 *lire* to *Camera* of the commune of Lucca and payment of an amount to the *bargello*, Giovanni of Rasignano. This reduction of penalty was decided in the council called by the Anziani, which consulted and decided on a petition presented by Coluccino.[98]

Puccinello Butelli and Coluccino Butelli, each under a fine of 300 *lire*:
Puccinello and Coluccino, sons of Butello, were liberated from their bans on 9 May 1357, Indiction 10, due to the effect of a mandate of the Lucchese Anziani, in which it was stated that Puccinello and Coluccino could be liberated from their bans without any payment, which was decided in a council called by the Anziani on 6 April to the imprisoned brothers, Puccinello and Coluccino, in the commune's jail, under reverence for the Lord Jesus Christ at Easter.[99]

The others convicted in Case A were also absolved from their bans: Giovanni Menichelli and Giovanni Puccinello by the effect of a decree of Lucchese Anziani, as

96 ASL, *Sentenze e bandi*, 17, no foliation, 15 October 1355: 'Anno Nativitatis Domini.MCCCLVIII. Indictione.xi. die.xv. mensis aprilis extractus et cancellatus est dictus Celloctorus de dicto banno... vigore provisionis dominorum anthianorum Pisani populi... ex balia et auctoritate quam habent partitu facto inter eos ad dominos albos et giallos...in qua cavent quod dictus Celloctorus rebanniatur et rebanniri possit et debeat a dicto banno...'

97 ASL, *Sentenze e bandi*, 17, no foliation, 15 October 1355: 'Post hoc anno Nativitatis Domini.MCCCLX. Indictione.xiii. die.xiiii. mensis martii... cassus et cancellatus est suprascriptus Bertoccus de dicto banno... vigore consilii mandati generalis Pisani communis... super ratificatione, confirmatione et approbatione pactorum factorum et compositorum... nomine Pisani communis... cum aliquibus comunibus vicarie Corelie et hominibus et personis ipsorum communium...'

98 ASL, *Sentenze e bandi*, 17, no foliation, 15 October 1355: 'Anno.MCCCLVIII. Indictione.xii. die.xxii. novembris extractus et cancellatus est dictus Coluccinus de dicto banno... vigore mandati dominorum anthianorum Lucani communis... solvendo camere Lucani communis pro communi Lucano... libros.xx. bone monete... etiam solvendo et satisfaciendo ser Johanni de Rasignano... in consilio dicta die detento per dictos dominorum Antianorum super petitione coram eis porrecta per partem dicti Coluccini, consultum fuit et obtentum et cetera'.

99 ASL, *Sentenze e bandi*, 17, no foliation, 15 October 1355: 'post hoc Anno Nativitatis Domini.MCCCLVII. Indictione.x. die.viiii. mensis mai extracti et cancellati sunt predicti Puccinellus et Coluccinus filii dicti Butelli de dicto banno... secundum vigore mandati dominorum antianorum Lucani communis...in quo cavent predicti Puccinellus et Coluccinus de dicto banno cassare in totum sine aliqua solutione... quia sic in consilio detento per dictos dominos anthionos die.vi. dicti mensis aprilis fuit obtentum et reformatum, ipsis Puccinello et Coluccino exsistentibus pro dicto banno detentis in carceribus Lucani communis... ob reverentium domini nostri Yesu Christi in die paschatis resurrectionis eiusdem'.

in the case of Puccinello Butelli, and Piero and Guido by a decree of the Pisan Anziani with a payment of 50 *lire*.

When examining the council book of Lucchese Anziani in 1358, we can find a record of deliberations over the aforementioned remission of penalties for Coluccino Paruei.[100] On 28 September 1358, a petition, presented by Coluccino to the Anziani, came up for discussion in the Council of Fifty. In this petition, Coluccino requested that his fine be reduced, alleging that he had not committed a crime, as written in the indictment, and that he had reconciled with the family of the victim. He also stated that the six others convicted in the same case had already been liberated from penalties, and he claimed further that he, who had been caught by the *bargello*, now languished in prison, impoverished and on the verge of death. At the Council of Fifty, the councillor Coluccino Peri advised the Anziani to offer *gratia* liberating Coluccino from his other fines if he paid 20 *lire* to a financier and a certain amount to the *bargello* within 15 days. His opinion was unanimously accepted (no objections) and became the official advice of the council. The Anziani, according to this advice, sent an order of *gratia* to the custodians of the *Camera Librorum*; that is, the very order we see noted in the marginal annotations in the sentence book.

In the aforementioned case, the remission of penalty by a political institution was expressed as a *gratia* or pardon. In the next chapter, we will consider in detail the development and significance of the *gratia* in the fourteenth century based on an examination of the council books. Here let us see the *gratia* offered to those 165 convicted in 1355-1356 based on an analysis of marginal annotations in the sentence books.

(3) Types of gratia *and those who granted them*

First, who was able to grant *gratia*? According to the notes in the sentence book of 1355-1356, remission of sentences was granted by the Pisan authorities, who ruled Lucca from 1342 to 1368. The Pisan Anziani offered *gratia* for 64 convicts, the General Council of Pisa for 26 and Giovanni dell'Agnello, the Pisan doge who ruled Pisa and Lucca as *signore* from 1364 to 1368, offered respective *gratia* to four convicts several years after their original sentencing in 1355-1356.

Some convicts also received *gratia* from the Holy Roman Emperor Charles IV, who came to Italy and liberated Lucca from Pisan rule in 1368. His amnesty in 1369 liberated 13 of those convicted in 1355-1356 the following year, in 1370, following Lucca's independence.

The *gratia* offered by these higher external authorities lifted the penalties of 107 convicts in the sentence books. Of these, it is worth noting that 83 were convicted of serious crimes and sentenced to death. Thus, it is possible that the governors and petitioners had a mindset wherein matters of weighty judgement, such as remission of the death penalty, must be left in the hands of higher authorities.

100 ASL, *Anziani avanti la Libertà*, 39, fols. 90r-91v.

Table 4.5: Authorities granting *gratia*

	Cases
Pisan Anziani	64
Pisan General Council	26
Doge of Pisa	4
Holy Roman Emperor	13
Lucchese Anziani and General Council	42
Authorities of Pisa and Lucca	10
Unknown	4
Total	**163**

That said, Lucchese Anziani and city councillors also granted *gratia* even during the period of Pisan rule. In total, 42 convicts received the *gratia* from their own city authorities in 1355-1356. The remissions offered by the Lucchese authorities were for those convicted of relatively minor crimes: four had the death penalty lifted while the other 38 were absolved of their fines.

Ten other convicts received *gratia* granted by both the Lucchese and Pisan authorities, while four convicts received remissions from authorities not revealed by the marginal notes.

Let us consider the types of *gratia* and their context by examining the 82 *gratia* described in detail in the marginal notes in the sentence books.

First, we observe 36 *gratia* that were individually offered by authorities responding to the petitions. The Lucchese Anziani and the Pisan doge received petitions and granted *gratia* after considering each circumstance and reason written in the petition.

For these 'individual *gratia*', 15 convicts were absolved by the Lucchese Anziani, who dispensed *gratia* by analogy with the grace of God. As with the *gratia* provided to Puccinello Butelli, above, the Lucchese Anziani considered the situations of prisoners individually and granted *gratia* to the prisoners on feast days as merciful authorities.

Many convicts also enjoyed 'general *gratia*' or amnesties that freed them all from punishment. In particular, the marginal notes mention an amnesty based on a peace accord between Pisa and the communes of the vicariate of Coreglia, confirmed by the General Council of Pisa on 5 February 1360.[101] The list of convicts liberated by virtue of this agreement, preserved in other documents, indicates the absolution of 109 convicts, including 78 who were released from death penalties. Of the total convicted

101 For example, ASL, *Sentenze e bandi*, 17, no foliation, 21 October 1356: 'Post hoc Anno Nativitatis Domini.MCCCLX. Indictione.xiii. die.xv. aprilis ...dictus Bartholomeus pieri et Johannes pieri... cassati, extracti et cancellati sunt de dictis bannis librarum quingentarum ... vigore maioris et generalis consilii pisani communis ... super ratificatione confirmatione et approbatione pactorum factorum et compositorum vice et nomine Pisani communis et pro ipso communi Pisano cum aliquibus communibus vicarie corelie... et aliquibus castelanis... quod omnia bapna ipsorum et cuiusque condemnationes processiones et accusationes cassentur et cancelletur de libris Pisanis et Lucanis communis'.

in 1355-1356, 25 were remitted by this peace agreement, as in the remission granted to Bertocho in Case A. Other peace agreements, apart from the accord with Coreglia, occasioned the liberation of four people convicted in 1355-1356.

Amnesties, which may be considered as general *gratia*, absolved all convicts of their penalties. These were frequently offered upon the accession of new governors. For example, the Holy Roman Emperor Charles IV granted an amnesty in 1370, absolving 12 persons convicted in 1355-1356 of their penalties without requiring any payment. A more usual type of general *gratia* in fourteenth-century Lucca, different from the emperor's *gratia*, required those who wished to take advantage of the process to pay a certain amount as a type of tax, known as *seca*.

Among the convicted, those fortunate enough to receive *gratia* spent an even longer time as *banniti* compared with others who had their sentences lifted by obediently paying fines. Of 163 people convicted in 1355-1356, only 41 had their sentences lifted within one year, while 31 convicts were liberated between 1 and 2 years, 27 between 2 and 3 years, 8 between 3 and 4 years, 30 between 4 and 5 years, and 10 between 5 to 10 years. Furthermore, 16 convicted were finally freed after more than 10 years after sentencing, and 1 was convicted in 1382, twenty-seven years afterwards. These individuals likely anticipated an amnesty or hoped for an opportunity to present their petitions, leaving the territory of Lucca or sheltering themselves among supporters inside Lucca.

Gratia represented interventions by political power in judicial matters. While we certainly see political interventions in civil cases, these were neutral and not so influential as to directly determine the result of any judgement, as with the orders by the Pisan doge furthering summary justice, seen in Chapter 3. Conversely, with criminal matters, the political authorities did not intervene in the trials themselves but, rather, directly in the sentencing. Here the interventions were so influential as to alter the judgements themselves. Why were the political authorities permitted to intervene so directly in matters of criminal justice? With this question in mind, let us pinpoint the position of criminal justice in the communal organisation.

7. Criminal Justice and the Commune

The motivations of political authorities such as the Anziani and foreign *signore* to intervene in criminal matters may be considered to have stemmed from the desire to maintain public order and security in the territory. We will consider the motives and circumstances of *gratia* in the next chapter. For now, let us consider how such acts could be 'legally' justified, on the level not only of the city statutes but also in terms of Roman jurisprudence.[102] One answer to this question concerns the definition of convicts as a 'source of revenue' and of the legal interpretation offered by Bartolus de Saxoferrato. Incidentally, this issue of the legal validity of remissions was no trivial matter but was considered a fundamental theme actively debated by the medieval jurists.

---

102 As for the fact that the city statute allowed the political authorities grant remission of the penalties, see note 89.

(1) Those convicted as 'debtors' to the commune

The fundamental difference between criminal and civil justice concerned the parties interested in the result of a sentence. In civil justice, it was the plaintiff who won the case and obtained an amount from the defendant or the reconfirmation of their own rights, whereas in criminal justice, it was mainly the commune or the communal treasury that the convicted had to compensate for any loss incurred by disorder by paying corporal or financial penalties. The sentences of criminal justice, therefore, directly affected the finances of the commune.[103] This is why the sentence books were produced only for criminal justice. Furthermore, these books were compiled with durable material and parchment and kept under strict surveillance, which is why they have been able to survive until today.

The compilation of the *libri alfabetus* could be seen as evidence that the communal officials considered convictions as a source of revenue. An extant *libri alfabetus*, probably produced around 1360, records a list of about 2500 *banniti* and *condemnati* from 1355 to 1392 in alphabetical order by initial, detailing their names, penalty amounts (fines or corporal punishment), and dates of sentencing.[104] Convicts recorded in the *libri alfabetus* were those whose sentences had not been lifted, at least at the time of the production of this list. For example, of those convicted in the sentence books of 1355-1356, those who had had their sentences lifted and been struck from the sentence books before 1360 were not recorded in the *libri alfabetus*. The communal notaries or financial officials who started to use and keep this book around 1360 consecutively added the names of those who were newly convicted in a blank space, and then struck out the names of those whose sentences had been lifted with the payment of a fine or *gratia*.[105] With this book, the communal officials sought to control altogether the *banniti* and *condemnati*, considered as 'debtors' to the commune, so as to easily and exhaustively collect outstanding fines.[106] It can at least be said that the *libri alfabetus*, which did not concretely indicate the crimes committed, was not regarded as a tool to monitor convicts as a security risk.

The determination of the commune to collect the fines certainly seems to contradict the policy of allowing the remission of penalties. However, the main reason why the

---

103 The financial books of the *Camerarius Generalis* in the first half of 1344 shows that the amount of revenue from a fine (7162 *lire*) was 2.7% of the total income (262,407 *lire* 17 *soldi* 5 *denari*) of the *commune* in this period, ASL, *Camarlingo Generale*, 7, 8.

104 ASL, *Sentenze e bandi*, 540. The name of this book inscribed on the cover is 'Liber alfabetus vetus bannitorum inceptus anno 1355'. The number of pages containing people with initials 'A'–'X' is 98.

105 The cancellation of the names in the *libri alfabetus* corresponds to the cancellation in the sentence books.

106 Furthermore, the financial officials used their books to ensure the collection of a fine, ASL, *Camarlingo Generale*, 60 [1356], fol. 14v: 'die septima januarii, pro Johanne bianchi cive Lucano commorante in communi grangnani condepnato ex officio malleficiorum Lucani communis in libris quindecim denariorum Lucanorum bone monete in eo quod dictus Johannes armatus armis offensabilibus et defensabilibus fecit insultum et adgressuram contra Bartholomeum Amistadi de communi sancti Gemignani commorantem in communi grangnani in quo insultu et adgressura dictus Johannes cum una spata evaginata percussit dictum Bartholomeum super tabulaccio quod id Bartholomeus habebat in brachio uno ictu sine sanguine, ut in condepnatione de eo facta ex dicto officio Anno Nativitatis Domini.CCCLVI. indictione.viiii. die.xxx. decembris… Fredus de martinis Lucanus civis camerarius introytus et exitus Lucani communis habuit et recepit […] libras.xxi. soldos.xii. et denarios.x'.

political authorities could legally intervene in judicial decisions relates simply to the redefinition of those convicted, after sentencing, from judicial subjects to administrative subjects. Here, the Anziani or other political authorities, as administrative authorities, were thus within their rights to also determine financial matters, and could legally intervene, as responsible and interested parties, in altering the original judicial decisions.

(2) 'Legal' justification for gratia

The influential jurist Bartolus de Saxoferrato similarly used the logic of the redefinition of convicts in order to maintain control of political administrative power in his 'legal' justification for the political authorities to cancel or remit penalties, using and interpreting the legal principles of the Roman *Digesta*.

According to the *Digesta*:

> A provincial governor, however, does not have the power to reinstate a person whom he has condemned, since he does not [even] have the power to revoke his own imposition of a fine. What then [must he do]? He should write to the emperor if at any time proof of innocence is subsequently established for a person who had appeared to be guilty.[107]

Bartolus interpreted this as follows:

> The *podestà*, who condemned him, cannot absolve him... but must present a petition to the commune for his acquittal... In fact, he had been condemned to a fine, which must be rendered to the commune, and thus, the commune justifiably can and must absolve him. Moreover, I say the same in the case that he had been condemned to corporal punishment, this can be proceeded in the same way. I refer here to the cities that do not recognise a prince.[108]

With this comment, Bartolus replaced the provincial governor with the *podestà* and the emperor with the commune as the political authorities of the Italian city. Thus, by basing his argument on the legal principles of the *Digesta*, the *gratia*, granted by the commune or the Anziani, who were now interested parties in the judicial decisions of the *podestà*, could change from the practice *de facto* to the practice *de iure*.

According to a study by Tanzini, the Florentine jurists gave expert legal opinion on whether a penalty could be remitted. They examined the legal validity of such

107 A. Watson (ed.), *The Digest of Justinian*, vol. 4 (Philadelphia, 1998), p. 356. *Digesta*. 48.18.1.27, In criminibus: 'Praeses provinciae eum quem damnavit restituere non potest, cum nec pecuniariam sententiam suam revocare possit. Quid igitur? Principi eum scribere oportet, si quando ei, qui nocens videbatur, postea ratio innocentie constitit'. L. Tanzini, *Il governo delle leggi. Norme e pratiche delle istituzioni a Firenze dalla fine del Duecento all'inizio del Quattrocento* (Firenze, 2007), p. 197.

108 Tanzini, *Il governo delle leggi*, p. 197; Bartolo da Sassoferrato, *Bartoli Commentaria in secundam digesti novi partem* (Lyon, 1555), fol. 213r: 'Potestas, qui eum condemnavit, non potest eum absolvere... tamen tenetur dare petitionem communi, ut absolvat... Nam cum sit condemnatus in pecunia, quae debet pervenire ad commune, merito commune potest et debet absolvere. Idem dico, si esset in persona condemnatus, quia hoc potest fieri: et loquor de civitatibus quae non recognoscunt principem'.

cancellations closely, referring to legal tracts by Bartolus and others.[109] We cannot find the extent to which the problem of the legal validity of remission was recognised and discussed in Lucca, where – as seen in Chapter 3 – the relative influence of jurists was on the wane. Nevertheless, as the political administrative representatives of the commune, the Anziani, armed with the theoretical justification of *gratia* offered by the interpretation of the jurist Bartolus, would surely have been able to offer these remissions without any niggling concerns as to the validity of their decisions.

Moreover, while here we can confirm the legal validity, in theory, of the remission of penalties by political authorities such as the Anziani, other questions spring up. Why did they adopt such a policy, which was necessarily at odds with their own financial interests? Moreover, how did they select a convict to pardon, and how did they justify each decision? To consider these questions closely, we can no longer restrict our examination to the practices of the judicial courts but must turn to give careful attention to the discussions of justice in the city council.

109 Tanzini, *Il governo delle leggi*, p. 155-214.

CHAPTER 5

Gratia, the Commune, and Justice

1. *Gratia* and the Commune

Those convicted of bans and condemnations had various options after sentencing. While some obediently paid their fines in order to be released, others did not and were accordingly stripped of the protection of the commune, either legally or physically, or they complained to the appellate court.[1] Those convicted also had the option of appealing to political authorities such as the Anziani or to foreign lords for extra-judicial remissions. There are many descriptions of such petitions and decisions in favour of *gratia* in the council books of the Anziani in Lucca.

There were two types of *gratia* in fourteenth-century Lucca. One was general *gratia*, here referred to as an amnesty, which freed all convicts from punishment, either without payment or upon payment of a particular sum, a kind of tax known as *seca*.[2] This practice was also known in other Italian cities at least from the thirteenth century.[3] In Lucca from 1328 to 1342, foreign rulers often granted such amnesties during the period of their rule. For example, on 17 June 1336, the college of the Anziani, with the consent of the lord's vicar, mandated uniform rules for the remission of penalties for those who wanted to receive *munera gratiarum* from the lord.[4] The sum and the rate of the tax depended on the reason for the punishment. For example, the penalty was fixed at a flat 50 *lire* for those convicted of homicide if their victims were citizens, and a flat 25 *lire* if their victims were not citizens. For those guilty of bodily injury, the tax rate was fixed at one twentieth of the fine (12 *denari* per *lira*); and for those convicted of *maleficia* that did not have a victim, like bearing arms, the rate was one fortieth of the fine (6 *denari*

---

1 The convicted rarely complained to the appellate court in criminal cases, as seen in Chapter 4, probably owing to the limitations set by the statute. For example, the statute of the appellate court excluded appeals against the condemnation [*condemnatio*] of *maleficio* by the *podestà*, except for objections if the sums of fines imposed were thought excessive and contrary to the statute. A. Romiti, 'Lo «statutum curie appellationum» del 1331', in *Actum luce*, 23 (1994), p. 111-151, in particular p. 145. In fact, the registers of the appellate court show us that this court dealt almost exclusively with civil trials and administrative litigation. ASL., *Maggior sindaco e giudice degli appelli.*

2 The amnesty is often designated as *seca bannitorum* in the records.

3 P. R. Pazzaglini, *The Criminal Ban of the Sienese Commune 1225-1310* (Milano, 1979), p. 72-98; G. Milani, 'Legge ed eccezione nei comuni di popolo del XIII secolo (Bologna, Perugia, Pisa)', *Quaderni storici (Sistemi di eccezione)*, XLIV-2 (2009), p. 377-398; S. R. Blanshei, *Politics and Justice in Late Medieval Bologna* (Leiden, Boston, 2010), p. 460; G. Kumhera, *The Benefits of Peace: Private Peacemaking in Late Medieval Italy* (Leiden, 2017), p. 93-121; L. L. Zanetti Domingues, 'Rituali di liberazione dei prigionieri nell'Italia del Duecetno: il caso toscano tra diritto e religione', *Archivio storico italiano* 668 (2021), p. 221-257.

4 ASL, *Anziani Avanti la Libertà* (hereafter, *Anz. Av. Lib.*), 10, fols. 22v-24r: 'Nos collegium antianorum Lucani communis… presente et consentiente discreto viro domino Zanobio de Cipriariis de Florentia iudice et vicario…, ut cives et districtuales Lucani videntes et cognoscentes se a dominis nostris liberaliter assequi munera *gratia*rum ad bene agendum efficaciter animentur… stantiamus et providemus quod quelibet singularis persona…'

per *lira*), and so on. This rule of amnesty was declared in the common tongue in the street by an official crier on 18 June.[5]

Another type of *gratia*, which can be termed 'individual *gratia*', was granted in response to individual petitions. This was regularly offered under Pisan rule, above all after the 1350s. In the previous chapter, we already saw the *gratia* for Coluccino Paruei. Let us consider another example. On 21 January 1353, the Anziani submitted the petition of Coluccino Neri, a villager, to the Council of Fifty for their advice.[6] According to this petition, the *podestà* had initially found Coluccino guilty and levied a fine of 75 *lire* for injury. Coluccino humbly requested clemency and to have his fine reduced to a quarter of the original, in consideration of his reconciliation with the victim, his own poverty, and his desire to stay and work for the honour of the commune. A councillor then advised the Anziani to grant the *gratia*, which reduced the fine to one-third.[7]

Gratia were eventually standardised, spreading to other Italian cities over the course of the fourteenth century. *Gratia* were a form of lawful practice in the sense that they were legitimised by the interpretations of learned jurists, as seen in the previous chapter, as well as by city statutes. However, close consideration of the practice of *gratia* reveals their incompatibility with communal concepts of the relationship between the authorities and subjects, and highlights the problem of relying on *arbitrium*, as we shall see.

The term '*gratia*' itself was used as an equivalent for '*beneficium*' in the texts, both as general amnesty for all convicts and as individual *gratia*. *Gratia*, therefore, were defined as an authority's beneficent acts in response to a supplication by a subject.[8] In general, such policies, based on the relationship between authorities and subjects, were applied in monarchies or signorial states. While medieval French kings built their political authority by granting their grace,[9] the Italian *signori* – for example, the Visconti and the

5 *Bandi Lucchesi*, p. 34-35.

6 *Anz. Av. Lib.*, 35, fols. 6r-8r: 'Congregatis in aula minori palatii ecclesie Sancti Michaelis in Foro civitatis Lucane ad consilium detentum per dominos antianos Lucani communis… infrascriptis consiliariis de consilio quod dicitur quinquaginta bonorum virorum civium Lucanorum… pro parte ipsorum dominorum antianorum fuit in ipso consilio propositum et narratum quod coram eis exhibite fuerunt quedam petitione super quibus cum per ipsos dominos antianos sine dicti consilii consensu provideri non possit deliberaverunt ipsum consilium detinere et secundum eiusdem consilii deliberationem procedere ad consulta…' (fol. 6r). Then, the substance of the petition was transcribed in full (fols. 7r-v).

7 *Ibid.*, fol. 7v: 'ser Guido magistri karoli unus ex invitatis dicti consilii consulendo dixit super petitione predicta quod fiat dicto Coluccino *gratia* quod solvat hinc ad.xv. dies proxime futuros camerario Lucane camere pro communi Lucano recipienti tertiam parte eius quod debet pro dicto banno et facta dicta solutione de dicto banno cassetur in totum'.

8 Here, the *gratia*, as remission of penalties owing to political judgments, could extend to several other types of rulings, such as the granting of citizenship, immunity from taxation, permission for the transfer of properties prohibited by law, and the obtaining of summary justice in their favour from officials. M. N. Covini, '*De gratia speciali.* Sperimentazioni documentarie e pratiche di potere tra i Visconti e gli Sforza', in M. Vallerani (ed.) *Tecniche di potere nel tardo medieoevo. Regimi comunali e signorie in Italia* (Rome, 2010), p. 183-206.

9 C. Gauvard, *«De grace especial.» Crime, état et la société en France à la fin du Moyen Age* (Paris, 2010); Id., 'Grâce et exécution capitale: les deux visages de la justice royale français à la fin de Moyen Âge', *Bibliothèque de l'Écoles des chartes*, 153 (1995), p. 275-290.

Sforza of Milan,[10] the Della Scala of Verona,[11] Taddeo Pepoli of Bologna,[12] and Paolo Guinigi of Lucca[13] – also regularly received supplications for which they mercifully and arbitrarily granted *gratia* by means of decrees. In doing so, these rulers formed a direct relationship with their subjects and established authority over their respective dominions.

Conversely, the practice of *gratia* based on the ruler-subject relationship does not seem to have suited communal ideals because, according to the idea of the '*comune*', the government was merely a representative of the '*comune*', which was composed of citizens. In this sense, the commune was not like a monarch or *signore* in its ability to grant beneficence. Moreover, communal citizens were not defined as 'subjects' who would supplicate the *signore* but '*cives*' with the right to constitute the '*comune*'. Herein lay the incompatibility between the commune and the practice of *gratia*.

The second aspect of *gratia* was that the political authorities who took exceptional measures tended to rely on *arbitrium*. This was also incompatible with the communal mode of governance. While external rulers who granted *gratia* exercised their own discretion when modifying the judicial decisions of judges who adhered strictly to statutory laws, the communal government, controlled by the *podestà* and the *popolo* in the thirteenth century, acted in accordance with the culture of institutions and sought to legitimate its governance following jurists' advice based on the laws.[14]

The practice of *gratia*, therefore, was seemingly incompatible with traditional communal government, which was considered representative of a '*comune*' constituted by *cives* and which held the idea of justice based on laws. However, as we have seen, this supplication system and the *gratia* had begun expanding both qualitatively and quantitatively in Lucca in the fourteenth century and, as previous studies have revealed, in other communal cities, where, in many cases oligarchy had developed over the course of the fourteenth century, such as in Florence,[15] Bologna,[16] and Siena.[17]

How and why did communal governments institute the policy of the *gratia*? Close consideration of the introduction and development of this policy in communal Lucca in the fourteenth century shows how a commune freed itself from its traditional model

---

10 J. Black, *Absolutism in Renaissance Milan. Plenitude of Power under the Visconti and the Sforza, 1329-1535* (Oxford, 2009); Covini, '*De gratia speciali*'; J. Carraway Vitiello, *Public Justice and the Criminal Trial in Late Medieval Italy. Reggio Emilia in the Visconti Age* (Leiden, 2016).

11 G. M. Varanini, '«Al magnificho e possente segnoro.» Suppliche ai signori trecenteschi italiani fra cancelleria e corte: l'esempio scaligero', in C. Nubola and A. Würgler (eds.) *Suppliche e 'gravamina'. Politica, amministrazione, giustizia in Europa (secoli XIV-XVIII)* (Bologna, 2002), p. 65-106.

12 M. Vallerani, 'La supplica al signore e il potere della misericordia. Bologna 1337-1347', *Quaderni storici (Sistemi di eccezione)*, XLIV-2 (2009), p. 411-441.

13 C. Meek, '"Whatever's Best Administered is Best": Paolo Guinigi, *signore* of Lucca, 1400-1430', in J. E. Law and B. Paton (eds.) *Communes and Despots in Medieval and Renaissance Italy* (Farnham, 2010), p. 131-143; R. Marulo, *Scrivere ai potenti. Le suppliche al tempo di Paolo Guinigi* (Piombino, 2009).

14 S. Menzinger, *Giuristi e politica nei comuni di Popolo. Siena, Perugia e Bologna, tra governi a confronto* (Roma, 2006).

15 L. Tanzini, *Il governo delle leggi. Norme e pratiche delle istituzioni a Firenze dalla fine del Duecento all'inizio del Quattrocento* (Firenze, 2007), p. 23-30.

16 Blanshei, *Politics and Justice*, p. 408-497.

17 Pazzaglini, *The Criminal Ban*, p. 72-98; W. M. Bowsky, *A Medieval Italian Commune: Siena under the Nine, 1287-1355* (Berkeley, Los Angeles, London, 1981), p. 85-116, in particular p. 104; Kumhera, *The Benefits of Peace*, p. 93-121.

and assumed new features based on a new idea of justice while retaining some elements of the old. In this chapter, in order to consider this question, I would like to examine policies concerning the practice of *gratia* based primarily on council registers from three periods, namely, the dominion of various foreign masters from 1328, Pisan rule from 1342, and the republican period after 1370.

2. Amnesty under Foreign Masters

(1) Amnesties and their motivation

After the end of the dominion of Castruccio Castracani from 1316 to 1328, Lucca experienced a succession of foreign masters: Ludwig IV the Bavarian (1328-1329), Gerardo Spinola of Genoa (1329-1331), King John of Bohemia (1331-1333), the Rossi of Parma (1333-1335), Mastino della Scala of Verona (1335-1341), and the commune of Florence (1341-1342).[18] The form of government under these rulers was, in general, one of collaboration between the vicars of the respective ruling power and the college of the Anziani.[19]

A distinctive practice during these periods was amnesty, that is, the cancellation or reduction of penalties for all convicted. Despite no evidence of this type of *gratia* being in place before 1330, probably owing to a lack of documentary evidence, we can find seven records of amnesties from 1331 to 1342 27 May 1331 under King John;[20] 6 November 1333 under the Rossi;[21] 17 June 1336,[22] 8 April 1338,[23] 28 April 1339,[24] and 15 April 1341[25] under Mastino della Scala; and on 2 July 1342 under the commune of Florence.[26] The standard process of granting amnesty involved the necessary permissions being provided by the lords' ruling powers to the college of the Anziani or to the Council of Fifty, whereupon these communal authorities issued a ruling on any reduction, as mentioned at the beginning of this chapter.

Why did the lords and the Anziani grant amnesties? While their intentions were not always clearly expressed, we can deduce the background circumstances based on the preambles to the amnesties and other factors.

---

18 L. Green, *Lucca under Many Masters: A Fourteenth-century Italian Commune in Crisis (1328-1342)* (Florence, 1995).

19 For convenience, I use the term 'vicar' to refer to those who represented the lords, although each representative was named differently according to his title; for example, *vicario, luogotenente, viceagente* or *capitano*.

20 This *gratia* can be seen only on its later cancellation. *Anz. Av. Lib.*, 5, fols. 2r-v, p. 3-4.

21 S. Nelli and G. Simonetti (eds.), *Anziani avanti la libertà (Lucca, 1330-1369)*, I (Lucca, 2007), p. 328-329.

22 *Anz. Av. Lib.*, 10, fols. 22v-24r.

23 *Anz. Av. Lib.*, 13, p. 44-46 (modern pagination; no foliation).

24 *Anz. Av. Lib.*, 14, fols. 16r-18v.

25 *Anz. Av. Lib.*, 16, fols. 44r-45v.

26 *Anz. Av. Lib.*, 17, fols. 35v-38v.

First, as in the cases of the general amnesties in Siena,[27] the main motives for offering amnesties were the generation of financial profit through fines (even reduced) paid by the *banniti*, and the maintenance of social order through the social reintegration of such individuals. These motives can be seen behind the amnesty granted under the Rossi. A proposal by the Anziani on 25 October 1333, in response to which the councillors approved procedures for *gratia*, arose from a particular circumstance, namely, that public books, particularly the *libri bannitorum*, had been burned in a recent act of sedition, so that many erstwhile *banniti* could now wander freely in Lucca and its territory.[28] In the ensuing provision, made on 23 December, the Anziani and the vicar, stating that the disappearance of the books of sentences had damaged the commune of Lucca and the lord's treasury and left the city in a poor condition, declared that the names of *banniti* must be gathered from secondary evidence, such as copies of sentences, so that crimes would not remain unpunished.[29]

Another motive was to demonstrate the merciful character of the governors in order to establish their authority. The amnesty of 1338 granted under Mastino della Scala indicated that amnesty was offered so that the *banniti* would return and remain *in fede et devotione prefatorum dominorum nostrum et Lucani communis*.[30] Further confirmation of this motivation may be seen in the fact that the amnesties were granted shortly after the lords had established their dominion over the city. The amnesty of May 1331 was granted two months after King John was accepted as ruler; that of November 1333 was declared just one month after the arrival of the Rossi; and that of June 1336 was offered two months after the installation of Spinetta Malaspina as Mastino's vicar. It seems significant, then, that the government under the Rossi revoked the *gratia* proclaimed by the previous regime. On 25 October 1333, at the same council at which the amnesty under the Rossi had been proposed, the Anziani asked the councillors' advice concerning the cancellation of the privileges conceded by King John. A few months later, on 14 December, the Anziani decided to invalidate the *gratia* offered by King John. It was important for the governors that the *banniti* should be encouraged to reintegrate themselves into the commune by favour of the current regime, rather than by that of any other authority.

27 In Siena, ten amnesties were offered between 1302 and 1354. During this period, the communes set up commissions to collect money from convicts. Such commissions were also organised in times of financial emergency, Pazzaglini, *The Criminal Ban*, p. 76-80, 86-88; Kumhera, *The Benefits of Peace*, p. 93-121.

28 Nelli and Simonetti (eds.), *Anziani*, p. 321-322: '… hoc presenti anno multi libri et scripture publice et autentice… incendio, direptione seu conculcatione perierint propter quod multi imbapniti Lucani Communis confidentes quod eorum banna non reperiantur libere per civitatem et districtum evagantur…'

29 *Anz. Av. Lib.*, 5, fols. 7v-8v: '…expediat circa predicta sallibriter provideri qualiter ipsa banna et banniti… reintegrentur in vigore et reperiantur, et ne maleficia remaneant impunita… stantiamus… quod omnis illi qui reperiuntur imbanniti in libris et filzis et extractis et alfabeto camere … possint tamen solvere secam nuper inpositam per modum ordinatum…'

30 *Anz. Av. Lib.*, 13, p. 44 (modern pagination; no foliation): '…volentes in hiis propterea providere ut ipsi banpniti et condepnati *gratia*rum munera consequentes ad repatriandum et bene agendum ac perseverandum in fide et devotione prefatorum dominorum nostrorum et Lucani communis, ferventius animentur'.

(2) Introduction of the principle of a lord's power

Gratia was an extraordinary measure that cancelled or modified existing decisions made by judges based on ordinary procedures. Such measures were frequently realised not by the communal regime but by a collaborative government established between the Anziani and the vicars of the lords through which a new principle of power was introduced. Under this regime, government was considered a body that could execute whatever measures it liked, irrespective of the communal statutes. We can see this definition of the lords' power in the proclamation made on 10 July 1336 by Mastino della Scala.

Let us consider the article presented by the Lucchese, represented by the college of the Anziani, to the lords on 3 April on the arrival of Spinetta as Mastino's vicar three months before the proclamation. The college of the Anziani, in one of 13 articles, requested that Spinetta establish a regime wherein the *bonus et expertus iurispertus* was assigned to the *Maior Sindicus* et *iudex appellationum*, the ultimate arbiter to whom citizens made appeals against the decisions of all officials and judges, including the lord's officials.[31] In other words, the Lucchese were requesting an affirmation of the traditional definition of communal power, wherein the city statutes and their executor, *Maior Sindicus*, was the supreme authority, and for the lords and their officials to follow the communal principles.

In response, Mastino della Scala made a general proclamation on 10 July concerning the principles of his dominion, refusing to conform to the communal system. The proclamation prescribed that the lord's general vicar could summarily hear the complaints from subjects burdened by city officials without the need for solemn proceedings and that his decisions were, moreover, not subject to audit.[32] Here, it was the lord's general vicar, not the *Maior Sindicus*, who ranked as the supreme authority and could freely, and summarily, pass judgement.

It is certain that lordly dominance introduced to Lucca new principles of power that allowed extraordinary measures alien to traditional communal principles based on the observance of statutes by officials under the control of *Maior Sindaco*. In other words, in Lucca in the first half of the fourteenth century, extraordinary measures – of which amnesty was one – were being introduced by agencies not intrinsic to the commune,

---

31 *Anz. Av. Lib.*, 11, fols. 3r-5v, in particular fol. 4v: 'placeat… providere quod luce sit quidam bonus et expertus iurispertus, alterius quam de patria seu gente predicti Rectoris, qui sit maior sindicus et iudex appellationum et querelarum Lucani communis, ad quem possit haberi recursus et appellari de omnibus gravaminibus iniuriis et sententiis dicti Rectoris et sue curie et offitialium et omnium aliorum officialium civitate et comitatuum Lucani… Et qui rector et eius officialis, famulus et omnes alii stare debeant ad sindicatum, finitis eorum officiis et ante iuxta consuetudinem et statutum lucani communis'.

32 *Anz. Av. Lib.*, 10, fols. 88v-89r; S. Bongi (ed.), *Bandi lucchesi del secolo decimoquarto* (Bologna, 1863), p. 217-218: 'Come li dicti Signori anno facto et constituito in delle loro cictadi, luoghi, terre et territorii et distrecti loro, maggiore Officiale e Vicario generale messer Allexandro da Bologna judici, a udire sommariamente et di piano, obmesse ogni ordine et solennitade, de' gravamenti et lamentanse de' subiecti gravati, e quelli exgravare da tucte et singule cose, che contra ragione a' dicti subiecti si facesseno, o facte fusseno per li Rectori et officiali delle dicte terre et luoghi' (*Ibid.*, p. 217); 'Lo quale officiale et vicario non vogliono nè intendono li dicti Signori, che possa o debbia esser sindicato, molestato o inquietato in alcuno tempo, per alcuno modo o cagione…' (*Ibid.*, p. 218).

but rather agencies that exercised an external lordly power. These measures continued to be adopted even under Pisan rule and then after independence, when the republican system was revived.

(3) Gratia *as a 'corrective' measure on the part of subjects*

As the proclamation of Mastino della Scala indicates, the lord's inherent power was realised most visibly when assistance was requested by those subjects who had suffered 'injustice' from officials. We can confirm that amnesties did result from these subjects' requests.

One example is a request for *gratia* by the college of the Anziani, as representatives of the city, to a vicar, Spinetta, in the aforementioned 13 articles of 3 April 1336. In one article, the Anziani requested the cancellation of all penalties and impositions by means of *speciali gratia*, citing the poverty faced by many citizens who had been condemned owing to the circumstances of war.[33] Consequently, on 17 June, with the consent of Zanobio, a judge delegated by Spinetta, the Anziani were able to promulgate the rules of remission, as we saw at the beginning of this chapter.

Gratia proceedings were instigated and ultimately realised at the request of the college of the Anziani, and often following the supplications made by individual citizens to the vicar. The preamble of the provision of an amnesty issued on 8 April 1338 mentions that *banniti et condemnati* had supplicated the vicar for the cancellation or reduction of penalties so that they could come back to the city.[34] In their response to these supplications, both the Anziani and Thomasius, an agent of Guglielmo Scannabecchi, vicar of Mastino della Scala, decided to grant the amnesties. Though it is not clear from the text whether there were other supplications for remission in other cases, these two cases, at least, make it clear that the amnesty assumed the form of *gratia* wherein citizens asked the lords for help, while the lords, through their representatives, heard their subjects' requests and responded mercifully to them.

Judging from the definition provided in the aforementioned proclamation by Mastino, it must have been citizens, burdened by officialdom, from whom the lords heard and to whom they provided assistance. The presence of the lords interceding between citizens and officials as protectors of the people was particularly notable in the cases relating to the Court of Rebels (*Curia rebellium*). The functions of this office were to confiscate goods and estates from rebels and to administer them as communal property – effectively to collect, probably strictly, the loans or rents owed by rebels' debtors and tenants. On 12 April 1334, the rules of this office were revised because the severity of the Court of Rebels' dunning had occasioned much trouble and anxiety on

33 *Anz. Av. Lib.*, 11, fol. 5r: 'considerato quod multi lucani cives et comitatini pauperes banniti et condemnati sunt pro exercitibus et andatis factis in tempore preterito...dignetur ipse dominus Marchus providere quod omnia illa banna, condemnationes, sece, mutua seu imposite tollantur ex toto et pro nichilo habeantur... de speciali *gratia* specialiter cancellentur'.

34 *Anz. Av. Lib.*, 13, p. 44 (modern pagination; non foliation): 'Cum fuerit pluries suplicatus eidem domino Capitaneo pro parte bapnitorum et condemnatorum Lucani communis quod eis seca imponatur et fiat, ut redire possint ad mandata dominorum nostrorum et Lucani communis...'

the part of the citizens.[35] The new articles added that complaints could be submitted only to the vicar, who would instruct the Anziani to take measures.

We can see an example of a vicar's intervention in a trial held in the Court of Rebels based on this court's record of 1341-1342 while under the commune of Florence.[36] The inquisitorial trial started on 9 December. A citizen, Giovanni Ciomei, was indicted for holding a rebel's goods. Disregarding Giovanni's denial of the charge, officials sequestrated his goods. On 3 January 1342, Giovanni presented the court with a letter from Ghiberto, vicar of Florence. The letter transcribed in the register shows that Giovanni appealed to the vicar for help, whereupon the vicar ordered the court to absolve him.[37] On 5 January, according to the register, a court official duly did so and then returned the sequestrated goods.

This model of a lord's intervention between subjects and officials also seems to have been applicable to *gratia*, which assumed the form of 'corrective' measures that reasonably, rather than capriciously, corrected the 'unjust' decisions of officials in favour of citizens. The documents do not reveal the extent of the lords' understanding of this aspect of *gratia*. However, the aforementioned circumstances behind the amnesties – the loss of the *libri bannitorum*, which caused social and financial confusion; the return of the *banniti*, convicted under previous regimes but who now wanted to pledge their allegiance to the lords; and the poor conditions and harsh sentences passed during wartime and the supplications from subjects – represented reasonable grounds that would have induced the lords to accept that penalties imposed by officials in strict adherence to the statutes would have been too severe, and thus unjust, not in the sense of formal and legal justice but in terms of social and political justice. From the political authorities' point of view, these motivations possibly became opportunities to legitimately affect the extraordinary measures that, in a sense, would come to delegitimise the older judicial system that had been based on communal traditions. The logic of legitimating amnesties that emerged under these foreign masters whereby the ruling authorities corrected the 'unjust' decisions of local officials, became clearly evident in the individual *gratia* granted under Pisan rule.

(4) The conditions for gratia

However, one condition was imposed on this extraordinary measure, namely that *gratia* should not impinge on other citizens. On the one hand, the remission of penalties theoretically robbed the treasury (*camera*) of a source of revenue, mainly affecting the commune and the lord, though taxes were still able to contribute a certain amount of income. On the other hand, granting *gratia* risked failing to consider the victims of

---

35 *Anz. Av. Lib.*, 7, fol. 2v: '...cognito quod civibus et comitatinis lucanis, plus anxietatis et tedii materia geminatur ex aspera exactione officii Rebellium Lucani communis... ex inde magis gravatos et oppressos se sentiunt, hiis gravedinibus et oppressionibus obviare volentes...'

36 ASL., *Curia dei Ribelli e Banditi*, 7 (unnumbered folios). The trial began on 9 December 1341.

37 *Ibid.*, 'Nos Ghibertus de Foliano in civitate Lucana pro magnificis dominis et communi Florentie, capitanus generalis...volumus et mandamus ipsum Johannem [...] non debere vel posse ulterius molestari, omnes processus, inquisitiones et denuntiationes [...] cassamus et revocamus...'

maleficia, because, for example, it could cancel the penalty for injury or homicide if the convicted were to pay a certain amount of money to the communal treasury. To avoid this, the provisions of the amnesty always prescribed the obligation of reconciliation with the victim for *maleficia* involving injury or homicide.[38]

It is possible that this condition was imposed to encourage reconciliation between parties and thereby the maintenance of the social order, which Claude Gauvard found to be the case for *gratia* granted by French monarchs.[39] However, it seems to have been considered more important in Italy as a means to preserve the rights of victims. The jurists of the Visconti in Milan, who gave the *signori* legal advice, were always cautious not to damage the *ius* of other citizens when granting *gratia*.[40] The Lucchese Anziani especially hesitated to intervene in civil matters, as we saw in Chapter 2. This stance corresponded with their principle policy that the governor should not violate civic rights. In other words, the Anziani required that a convict who wanted to obtain a *gratia* must make peace with the victim, which in effect gave victims the 'right' to finally decide whether the offender could receive *gratia*.[41]

3. Individual *Gratia* under Pisan Rule

(1) Gratia *under Pisan rule*

In July 1342, Pisa gained control over Lucca after an extended struggle with Florence. Pisa then ruled that Pisa should stand as Lucca's defender and, from 1355, as an imperial vicariate. Pisa's dominion was relatively stable and long-lasting. It remained in effect until the arrival of Charles IV in central Italy in 1368. Pisa experienced several forms of government during this period: the *signoria* of Ranieri Novello, count of Donoratico Bonifazio (1340-1347); the *signoria* of the Gambacorta family (1347-1355); the commune of the *popolo* (1356-1364); and the *signoria* of doge Giovanni dell'Agnello (1364-1368). Correspondingly, the seat of governance in Lucca also changed, shifting from Ranieri Novello (1342-1347), to the college of the Anziani of Pisa (1347-1364), to Giovanni dell'Agnello (1364-1368).

During the period of Pisan rule, as far as we know from the documents, general amnesties were granted on 22 July 1348,[42] 15 June 1355,[43] 12 March 1360,[44] and 29

---

38 Ettore Verga has pointed out that the same principle applied to *gratia* of the Visconti. Ettore Verga, 'Le sentenze criminali dei podestà milanesi 1385-1429', *Archivio storico lombardo* 28 (1901), p. 96-142, in particular 123-124; Carraway Vitiello, p. 200-201.

39 Claude Gauvard, «*De grace especial*».

40 Covini, '*De gratia speciali*', p. 204-206.

41 Also, in the communal city of Siena, the condition of making peace with victims was a prerequisite of being released from a ban in times of amnesty, though in practice there were some exceptional cases in which *banniti* could be released from bans without such peacemaking, Pazzaglini, *The Criminal Ban*, p. 87-88, 93-95; Kumhera, *The Benefits of Peace*, p. 93-121.

42 *Anz. Av. Lib.*, 28, fols. 32r-v.

43 C. Meek, *The Commune of Lucca under Pisan Rule, 1342-1369* (Cambridge, 1980), p. 59, 95-96.

44 We can only find a copy of provision of the *gratia* in 1360. ASL, *Archivi Pubblici*, 39, p. 17-20.

October 1362.[45] We can see that the Lucchese Anziani sometimes asked the Pisan Anziani for the *balìa* of amnesty.[46] The Pisans in turn extended the *balìa* so that Lucca might grant *gratia,* for which the Anziani of Lucca, along with the vicar of Pisa, prescribed the rules of amnesty.

The amnesties under Pisan rule were motivated and legitimated by critical circumstances, namely, the decrease in the population in the territory of Lucca, which had been decimated by the Black Death and the disturbances of war. The preamble to the provisions of the 1348 amnesty asserted the need for the vicar and the Anziani to find a way to restore the recently devastated population in Lucca and its territory.[47] The amnesty of 1355 was granted as a measure taken to check the continuous flight of those Lucchese who feared retaliation by Pisa after the revolt against their ruler.

Under Pisan rule, another type of *gratia,* namely, individual pardons, was added to the general amnesty. As we saw at the beginning of this chapter, individual *gratia* involved the cancellation or reduction of penalties offered in response to individual petitions rather than granted under general provisions, like amnesties. Therefore, such *gratia* were exceptional measures in the double sense that the governor made individual exceptions in a limited number of cases and modified ordinary penalties on their behalf. In Siena, those seeking a further reduction of fines during periods of general amnesty or in cases involving high pecuniary penalties would submit petitions to the General Council for approval.[48] In Lucca, convicts, even those fined lesser sums, would address petitions to city government on an individual basis regardless of whether an amnesty was being offered. While such petitions had resulted in pardons previously, this practice became much more systematic during the period of Pisan rule, particularly from the 1350s. For example, we find 14 cases in 1352, 22 in 1353, 27 in 1354, 20 in 1358, 34 in 1361, 30 in 1362, and 17 in 1363, averaging 23 cases a year.[49] While individual *gratia* were offered by the Pisan authorities, as we saw in Chapter 4 from our examination of the sentence books, here I would like to pay attention to those granted by the Lucchese Anziani.[50]

(2) Procedures of individual gratia

Let us consider the procedures for granting an individual *gratia.* The first step was for convicts to present their petitions. We cannot know whether the petitioners actu-

---

45 *Anz. Av. Lib.,* 42, fols. 73v-74v.

46 Meek, *The Commune of Lucca,* p. 36. For example, the *balìa* was given to Lucchese Anziani on 27 October 1362, and thereafter they pronounced the amnesty on 29 October 1362. *Anz. Av. Lib.,* 42, fols. 73r-v.

47 *Anz. Av. Lib.,* 28, fol. 32r: 'Cum propter accidentia que in proxime preteritis temporibus occurrerunt Lucana civitas eiusque comitatus et fortia sit quam plurimum hominibus vacuata, et per rectores et antianos sit necessario providendum super viis et modis quibus civitas comitatus et fortia hominibus reparentur'.

48 Pazzaglini, *The Criminal Ban,* p. 72-98; Kumhera, *The Benefits of Peace,* p. 93-121.

49 *Anz. Av. Lib.,* 34 (1352); 35 (1353); 37 (1354); 39 (1358); 41 (1361); 42 (1362, 1363).

50 Pisan authorities occasionally ordered the commune of Lucca to remit the bans. For example, the Pisan doge Giovanni dell'Agnello ordered the Lucchese Anziani in a letter to free a convict from his ban, *Anz. Av. Lib.,* 53, p. 135-136 (an original letter on 24 October 1364). Giovanni also sometimes intervened in trials, halting the proceedings. T. Dean, *Crime and Justice in Late Medieval Italy* (Cambridge, 2007), p. 45.

ally brought their petitions to the communal palace. In the petitions, they frequently expressed the intention to come back to the city. Therefore, it seems likely that those convicted – who had been removed from communal protection – would have presented them through representatives, as we can see in cases from Siena and the kingdom of France, rather than take any unnecessary risks.[51]

The addressee of the petitions is clearly declared. According to the petitions transcribed in council records, convicts addressed petitions either to the college of the Anziani or to the Anziani and the Council of Fifty;[52] during the period of foreign rule, the lord (or his vicar) was often also addressed along with the Anziani. Thus, even under Pisan rule, citizens would ask for a pardon not from Pisa or its vicar but from the city institutions, which were naturally composed of Lucchese citizens.

It is significant that the people as subjects in the petitions implored the city councils *humiliter* and *reverenter* to reduce their penalties.[53] With reference to *gratia* offered by Taddeo Pepoli, *signore* of Bologna, Vallerani points out the logic inherent in the supplication system of the self-abjection of the supplicant and the exaltation of the addressee.[54] Thus, the continuous daily practice of *humiliter* supplication by convicted Lucchese to city councils strengthened the persistent relationship of subject and authority, between individual citizens and the city's institutions, which were composed of Lucca's citizens.[55]

Once the Anziani received a petition, they convened the Council of Fifty and proposed the petition there, as 'no provision on *gratia* can be take by the Anziani without the consent of this Council'.[56] The Council of Fifty, with additional *invitati*,[57] deliberated on individual petitions, and the councillors gave their opinions on them. In the voting process, ten members of the Anziani and the councillors of the Council of Fifty, together with the *invitati*, each put their own pellet into a white ballot box (*pyxis*) to signal agreement or a green box for disagreement. The recommendation was accepted when the motion received two-thirds of the vote, whereupon the Anziani would execute the remission by informing the notary who controlled the books of the

51 For the Sienese case, Kumhera, *The Benefits of Peace*, p. 100-113. In the kingdom of France, petition presenters mainly comprised the friends or colleagues of the convicts rather than the convicts themselves («Amis» or «amis charnels»). Claude Gauvard, 'Grâce et exécution capitale', p. 279.

52 For example, *Anz. Av. Lib.*, 35, fol. 8r: 'Coram vobis dominis Antianis Lucani communis…'. *Ibid.*, fol. 7r: 'Coram vobis dominis Antianis Lucani communis et consilio quinquaginta bonorum virorum Lucane civitate et cetera…'

53 For example, *Anz. Av. Lib.*, 39, fol. 12v: '… suprascripto domination vestre humiliter supplicatur quatinus providere et mandare dignemini quod ipso petro solvent occasione dicti banni aliquam secam Lucano communi… dictum bannum debeat cancellari'; *Ibid.*, 98r: 'Quare vestre dominationi suplicat lacrimabiliter et devote quatinus habita consideratione ad impotentiam et maximam paupertatem…'

54 Vallerani, 'La supplica al signore', p. 411-441.

55 It is possible that the addressee of the petitions in the 1350s was Lucchese Anziani, because the governor in Pisa was not a *signore* but a Pisan Anziani. Under the rule of Giovanni d'Agnello, dux of Pisa, after 1364, we can find an original letter wherein Giovanni individually ordered a Lucchese Anziani to grant the *gratia*, which indicates that the petitioners initially went to Giovanni. *Anz. Av. Lib.*, 53, p. 135-136.

56 See note 6: '…coram eis exhibite fuerunt quedam petitione super quibus cum per ipsos dominos antianos sine dicti consilii consensu provideri non possit…'

57 *Invitati* were the members who were selected directly in every meeting by Anziani. They participated in the discussions and voted in the meetings.

banniti about the decision. This ordinary process was adopted in other cases apart from *gratia*.

While the council records concisely describe this series of processes, some questions remain. The first is how a councillor's opinion, which had to be voted upon, was selected from among the various opinions expressed in the Council of Fifty. A hint is found in the council records of the previous period, which contain descriptions revealing that on 31 October 1333, three opinions were presented by the councillors deliberating the return of the sons of Castruccio, at which time the councillors voted on a recommendation by the *mandatum* of the Anziani and the vicars.[58] Here, it was the Anziani and the vicar that selected the recommendation under vote. This procedure seems to have been common in the communes wherein an oligarchic government held power, as is also evident in the statutes of Bologna for 1376.[59]

Another question about the procedures in the Council of Fifty concerns how often *gratia* were offered to petitioners. We cannot know anything about the rejected petitions because the council books only have a record of those that were approved. However, we have *minuta* from as far back as 1371, which contain drafts for every petition, even those that were rejected, and summary descriptions of councillors' opinions on them. For example, in the General Council on 4 February 1388, the petition by Michele Federico for *gratia* was considered and three councillors expressed their opinions.[60] Usually, we find the number of votes for and against written in the margins of each opinion in the *minuta*; in the case of the petition by Michele, however, there are no such descriptions. Presumably, not every opinion was able to obtain the two-thirds majority of favourable votes required for a motion to proceed.

In the *minuta* from 1371 to 1390, of the 37 petitions that were untitled in *super petitione*, councillors approved 32 of them after deliberation.[61] While we only have *minuta* from 1370, there seems to have been a relatively high probability for *gratia* to be granted, just as under Pisan rule, but petitioners were also sometimes refused *gratia* as well.[62]

---

58 Nelli and Simonetti (eds.), *Anziani*, p. 326-327: 'De mandato dominorum Cini vicevicarii et Antianorum predictorum positum fuit ad partitum dictum prefati domini Franceschini et secundum eius dictum obtentum et reformatum fuit…'

59 *Gli statuti del* commune *di Bologna*, I, 5, p. 326, 'De partitis et propositis fiendis et proponendis ac firmandis et reformandis in conscilio quadringentorum comunis et populi Bononie': 'antiani inter se deliberent quod ex dictis consciliis redditis super dicta posta eis vel maiori parti ipsorum utilius videtur'.

60 ASL, *Anziani al Tempo della Libertà*, 4, p. 18 (modern pagination; no foliation): 'super petitione Michaelis ser Federici'; 'dominus Lodovicus Mercati consuluit quod auctoritate presentis consilii prefatus Michael a dicta condemnatione sit liber dummodo offerat opere Sancte crucis cereum unum valoris duorum florenorum, et sic per notarios et custodes librorum camere sine aliqua solutione debeat libere cancellari'; 'Michael Guinigi consuluit quod soluta dimidia dicte condemnationis per eum a reliqua sit liber et sic debeat cancellari et cetera'; 'Jacobus Ronghi consuluit quod sit in totum liber et absolutum pro ut petit et sic debeat cancellari et cetera'.

61 ASL, *Anziani al Tempo della Libertà*, 4. The cases entitled in *super petitione* include various petitions for citizenship and others as well as penalty reductions. As for the petitions that were clearly specified for penalty reductions, 15 of 18 were approved in the same period.

62 In Siena, where even rejected petitions were also recorded, the General Council accepted 91.5% of petitions to mitigate fines based on an amnesty offered in 1329, Kumhera, *The Benefits of Peace*, p. 104-105.

Let us turn to those who decided whether the *gratia* should be granted. Decision-making on individual *gratia* was left exclusively to the members of the Anziani, the Council of Fifty, and the *invitati*; in other words, Lucca's citizens. Although the Pisan rector attended the Council of Fifty in the early years of Pisan rule, he did not always do so in the later years, for example, in 1363.When we consider the members of this council, it is clear that the councillors whose advice was ultimately accepted through a vote were few in number. Of the 164 cases of the *gratia* recorded in registers from 1352 to 1363, 121 were based on the advice of 16 councillors, and the top seven councillors' opinions resulted in 88 cases of *gratia*, which account for more than half of the total.[63] The advice of councillors with the title of jurist and those of notaries was adopted in only 11 cases and 42 cases, respectively, accounting for one-third. This means that the advice of legal professionals was not necessarily required for the council's decision.

Furthermore, the fact that in practice it was the advice of only certain councillors that was adopted for *gratia* brings to mind the oligarchic tendency of city institutions. The Anziani elected the members of this council and selected those councillors' opinions on which to vote. During Pisan rule, as revealed by Meek, the Pisan Anziani seemed to have been involved in the election process of the Lucchese Anziani.[64] This involvement limited the numbers of the Anziani candidates and so accelerated the shift to oligarchy. The policy of individual *gratia* could be applied based on this oligarchy; moreover, the repetitive practices of the *gratia* facilitated the concentration of power in the hands of a small group of citizens.

(3) Reasons for gratia *and governors' consciences*

a). Deliberation in council

Let us look closely at the criteria used by the Council of Fifty and the Anziani to deliberate on and adjudicate the granting of *gratia*. This is a question of the logic that representatives of the commune employed to legitimise the extraordinary measures that modified judges' legal decisions, which were based on the statutes.

First, the Council, unlike the judicial courts, was generally not a place that sought to uncover the truth. Petitioners did not adduce any evidence, such as testimonies or documents, that might prove the substance of their appeals, even in cases where they pleaded their innocence.[65] Certainly, the Anziani, in a few cases, entrusted the examination of petitions to an outsider.[66] However, in many cases, the councillors did not intend to make an intensive investigation of the facts related to the petition.

63 In total, 25 cases by Coluccio Peri, 21 cases by ser Nicolao de Ghivizzano, 12 cases by Stefano Incapestra, 11 cases by Giovanni Honesti, 7 cases by ser Guido magistri Karoli, 6 cases by jurist Bartolomeo Maulini and 6 cases by Jacopo Rapondi.

64 Meek, *The Commune of Lucca*, p. 25-28.

65 This does not seem to have depended on the secretary's omission from the written record, as we have an exceptional case wherein an *instrumentum* presented by a petitioner was transcribed. *Anz. Av. Lib.*, 42, fols. 52r-53r.

66 For example, one jurist, Bartholomeo Maurini, heard details about the circumstances of a theft from the person involved and reported that the petition was truthful. *Anz. Av. Lib.*, 37, fols. 74r-75v.

In a noteworthy case, a man convicted of smuggling wine pleaded his innocence, stating that the charge was not true because it would have been impossible for him to transport the wine via the route alleged by the charge.[67] He also stated that he was ready to prove his case in court. Nevertheless, the council decided to commute his fine from 1000 *lire* to 100 florins (approximately 425 *lire*) anyway. In other cases in which petitioners claimed their innocence, the councillors, often with a desire to compromise, also decided to reduce the fine amounts rather than examine the facts and definitively adjudicate the guilt or innocence of the petitioners.

I will now turn to the criteria on which the councillors based their recommendations and votes. We do not have any materials that directly reveal the councillors' way of thinking. Only scant descriptions of the proceedings survive in the council records, recording only the summaries of the accepted advice as follows. One councillor, considering the petition, moved that the *gratia* should be granted to the petitioner so that he could be free from condemnation.[68] Another councillor proposed that if the petitioner paid one-third of the fine within 15 days, he could be released from condemnation, and so on.[69]

Conversely, it is certain that the councillors gave close consideration to each petition as well as to the individual circumstances of each petitioner. This is shown by the fact that the rates of remission were not uniform but varied depending on the nature of the petition. As it is likely that petitioners who made a case why *gratia* should be offered would have empirically weighed up any motivations that the councillors held in high regard, we might use these petitions as a basis for presuming the norms on which the city council relied.

b). Petition theme (1): rulings that contradicted the law

The law was certainly the basis of the petitions. Petitioners routinely tried to refute the judgement of ordinary officials with references to statutory provisions. Massario Coluccini, a citizen convicted by the *bargello*[70] for injuring and killing another person's livestock, insisted on the legitimacy of his action by stating that he had harmed them because they had intruded onto his land, citing a clause in the statutes, *libro quinto capitulo xxvii posito sub rubric de dannis datis cum bestiis macellatoriis et cetera*. He asserted that given his statutory right to commit such acts, the *bargello* could not condemn him on this charge.[71] Certainly, this clause provided that those who came upon domestic animals damaging their property were allowed to harm and even kill

67 *Anz. Av. Lib.*, 35, fols. 35v-36v.

68 *Anz. Av. Lib.*, 41, fols. 130v-131r: 'Stefanus in capestra civis Lucanus unus ex consiliariis dicti consilii surrexit et consulendo dixit quod fiat dicto Ranuccio *gratia* consideratis predictis quod liberetur et cassetur in totum de condemnation predicta contrarietate aliqua non obstante'.

69 See note 7.

70 As for the criminal cases handled by the Bargello, see Dean, p. 45-47.

71 *Anz. Av. Lib.*, 42, fol. 20r: 'Et quod ipse Massarius petivit predicta fecisse vigore statuti Lucani communis libro quinto capitulo.xxvii. posito sub rubrica de dannis datis cum bestiis macellatoriis et cetera quod statutum etiam coram vobis allegat et producit. Et per consequens si auctoritate dicti statuti predicta dictus Massarius facere potuit, ser Johannes predictus contra ipsum Massarium de predictis aliqualiter procedere non poterat nec condemnare…'

them with impunity.[72] After fact-finding by two trustworthy citizens, Massario was accordingly released from penalty.

Flaws, particularly jurisdictional flaws, were often alleged as legal points to deny the legitimacy of a judgement. Petitioners often objected to being punished twice for the same crime, i.e. dual punishments imposed by the *podestà* and *bargello,* whose jurisdictions sometimes overlapped, as we shall see in Chapter 6. Such a jurisdictional flaw can also be observed in a petition by Bendinacco Pacciardi, a villager, who stated that he was punished in the Rectors' Court, which had jurisdiction only over foreigners. This villager was also punished by the *podestà* at the same time.[73]

The council gave remission to these petitioners in each case. The councillors must have been convinced that these legal flaws were a fundamental reason to render an extraordinary judgement. Here, the councillors played a role in correcting the officials' unjust verdicts according to the law. However, we also encounter cases wherein councillors would not consider the law as the absolute criterion.

For example, Antonio Baldi, a man condemned by the *bargello* with a fine of 100 *lire* on suspicion of having escaped the grasp of the *bargello*'s servants on his way to jail, stated that the *bargello* had summarily convicted him, regardless of the statutes.[74] Antonio received *gratia,* reducing his fine from 100 to 25 *lire,* from the Council of Fifty. Nonetheless, as the regulations of the *bargello*'s office allowed him to torture criminals and punish them with fines of up to 10 *lire,*[75] we know that the councillors' advice to reduce the fine to 25 *lire* was not rigidly based on the law.

In another case, a citizen who had been fined the sum of 300 *lire* by the *podestà* for causing injury by throwing stones noted that the fine should not have been over 100 *lire,* in accordance with the statutes.[76] The council decided that rather than reduce the fine to 100 *lire,* he should be freed of all penalties. Thus, the councillors recognised the importance of legal norms but did not exclusively follow them. They also relied on their conscience, which was contingent on individual circumstances, of which the law constituted only a part.

c). Petition theme (2): torture, justifiable self-defence, poverty

We can find in the petitions other elements that informed the councillors' collective 'conscience'. First, petitioners often claimed that the truth had been distorted in previous trials owing to their fear of torture at the hands of officials. For example, Barolomeo Colucci, a villager convicted of sheltering Luporo, a *bannitus,* alleged that he had only

72 ASL, *Statuto del Comune di Lucca*, 5, V, 27 (De dannis factis a bestiis macellatorum seu tabernariorum emendandis), fols. 103r-v: 'Et si bestie tabernariorum in nocte vel in die fuerint invente dannum dare, quod ille qui eas invenerit possit impune vulnerare et occidere ipsa'.

73 *Anz. Av. Lib.*, 35, fols. 8r-v: '…fieri non debet quod de uno delicto ex duobus officiis contra delinquione procedat….'

74 *Anz. Av. Lib.*, 41, fols. 122v-123r: 'dum ducaretur ad carceras Lucani communis per familiares dicti ser Johanis timens torequeri et mori in dictis carceribus, affugit de manibus dictorum familiariorum, qua occasione dictus ser Johanes incontinenti ex arrupto et de facto nullo iuris ordine servato nec aliquibus statutis Lucani communis…'

75 *Anz. Av. Lib.*, 34, fols. 63v-65v, in particular fol. 64v.

76 *Anz. Av. Lib.*, 35, fols. 22r-v: '…quia secundum formam statuti Lucani communis dictus Talentus non debebat banniri nisi in libris.C. …'

confessed his guilt on pain of torture (*tormentorum pena*) by the *bargello* and asked for liberation from prison as an innocent.[77]

In another case, a citizen named Biancuccio Franceschi, having been convicted in absentia for indirect tax fraud by the *Maior Sindaco* and fined 600 *lire*, pleaded his innocence, stating that he had not appeared in court because of fear of torture, and that his colleague, Petro, had been tortured but not been found culpable.[78]

These petitioners succeeded in obtaining *gratia*. They presented their petitions possibly in the expectation that the Anziani and the Council of Fifty would have been forced to intervene in order to help subjects through remission of penalty, considering that the truth had been distorted by officials who had threatened them with torture.

Second, we also see petitions that alleged the use of justifiable self-defence. For example, Tommasino, sentenced to death for a homicide, asked that his punishment be commuted by claiming that he had only killed his victim, a citizen named Nino, because Nino had first injured Tommasino and had threatened to kill him on the day of the homicide.[79] This petition, appended to a contract of reconciliation with Nino's brother, resulted in the reduction of his penalty to 100 *lire*.

In another case, Piero, a villager condemned to pay a fine of 141 *lire* for injuring a woman, Matilda, gave the excuse that he had struck her accidentally with his hand while trying to stop her from abusing him.[80] Consequently, the council offered to commute the fine to 40 *lire*.

Whereas such appeals on the basis of self-defence might not have received any attention from the judicial courts, the political authorities were expected by petitioners to give close consideration not only to the law but also to any extenuating circumstances that might have forced the hands of those who were convicted of crimes, and to correct decisions accordingly from a punishable crime to a pardonable crime.

A third mitigating factor, and the one most frequently cited, was poverty. This was not intended as a plea to play a rhetorical role in eliciting the councillors' compassion. Some petitioners stated that they would have no option but to become beggars because of the penalties imposed.[81] These petitions usually resulted in the reduction of fine amounts by two-thirds. We can see here the logic of supplication by which the petitioners, who might not always in fact be suffering the most abject poverty, presented

---

77 *Anz. Av. Lib.*, 39, fols. 63v-64r: 'ser Johanes... ipsum acriter tormentavit a deo quod tormentorum pena confessus fuit vera esse et inquisitione contenta et de quibus contra eum inquirebatur'.

78 *Anz. Av. Lib.*, 37, fols. 65r-66r: '... Petrus cum comparavisset fuit per dictum iudicem positus ad tormenta et acriter tortus pluribus vicibus, demum carceratus unde ipse Biancuccius monitus torturis...'

79 *Anz. Av. Lib.*, 37, fols. 66r-67r: 'Et predicta comiserit ipse Tomasius propter multas sceleratas iniurias receptas per eum a dicto Nino, et primo sicut clare scire potestis et notorium est omnibus civibus lucanis ipse Ninus... vulneravit ipsum Tomasium cum quadam guerretta ex qua percussione ipse Tomasius fuit in periculo mortis. Et postea ipse Ninus pluries et pluries minatus fuit eundem Tomasium occidere. Et finaliter ipsa die qua ipse Tomasius ipsum Ninum occidit, dictus Ninus occidere voluit ipsum Tomasium'.

80 *Anz. Av. Lib.*, 42, fols. 50r-v: '...percutere ipsam dominam Mattheldam ut cessaret ab hiis qui dicebat et faciebat contra dictum Pierum...'

81 *Anz. Av. Lib.*, 37, fols. 9r-v: '...propter eorum paupertatem ad quam deducti sunt propter eorum bannimenta predicta eorum vitam sustentare non valent sed mendicare coguntur...'

themselves as especially miserable and humble in order to exalt the governors' status as merciful authorities.

It is interesting on this point that so many prisoners among the petitioners claimed poverty. These prisoners had been convicted, had escaped and had been caught, but were unable to pay fines or secure sureties. Almost all prisoners claimed poverty, and some pleaded that they were on the point of dying in prison.[82] The Anziani and the councillors often answered these petitions by releasing them from prison on the occasion of Christian holidays, as a form of oblation. This practice, which can be seen to have occurred from the second half of the thirteenth century in different Tuscan cities,[83] was also prescribed by the 1308 statute in Lucca.[84] Under Pisan rule, however, those who would be granted individual *gratia* for release on the occasion of feast days were carefully screened on the basis of their individual petitions. Here, the rhetoric of poverty in the petitions must have awakened the councillors' conscience, calling upon their authority to soften the relative severity of the penalties for the poor and mercifully aiding their powerless and helpless subjects.

(4) Individual gratia *as a corrective measure*

We can thus find four arguments that served as grounds for motivating the Anziani and councillors to grant *gratia*, namely, legal and procedural flaws, distortion of the truth owing to fear of torture, justifiable self-defence, and poverty. These emotional and rational arguments routinely presented by petitioners sought to promote the councillors' self-image as authorities who helped subjects who had suffered 'injustice' at the hands of city officials. The governors were naturally able to alter even decisions that adhered to city statutes, or to interpret as 'injustices' those decisions based on distortions of truth by fear of torture that had been made without considering self-defence or which were too severe for paupers. Underlying these petitions is an idealised image that the supplicants seem to have drawn upon, of the authorities as enlightened rulers obligated to help their subjects by wielding their *arbitrium* fairly to set right the unjust decisions made by city officials.

The widespread use of individual *gratia* under Pisan rule shows the advanced stage of discretionary politics on the part of governors in the sense that, unlike general amnesties, exceptions were made on an individual basis, after deliberations were made on individual circumstances. This practice was widespread in the political context in which the Lucchese Anziani and the Council of Fifty handled their internal affairs,

---

82 *Anz. Av. Lib.*, 39, fol. 90v: '...et est in dictis carceribuscito procul dubio moriturus cun ipse sit pauperrimus'.; *Anz. Av. Lib.*, 35, fol. 99r: '... ut expediat ipsum in carcere mori'.

83 A recent paper by Zanetti Domingues considers the origins of oblations associated with the liberation of poor prisoners in Tuscan cities in the thirteenth century. She focuses particularly on urban religious movements devoted to assisting such people in the context of an emerging criminal justice system that led to the incarceration of an inordinate number of destitute citizens, Zanetti Domingues, 'Rituali di liberazione dei prigionieri'.

84 *Statuto 1308*, III, 76 (De forma inbanniendi et extrahendi de banno), p. 186: 'Possit etiam cancellare de banno illos qui liberati fuerint in preteritum vel in futurum a carceribus lucani Comunis et oblate Deo in Edomada Sancta secundum formam Consiliorum'.

where there was less intervention from Pisa; the socio-economic situation of the population decreased after the Black Death, and the ensuing economic and financial crisis demanded arbitrary politics. In this context, the continuous petitions from citizens motivated the city government to incorporate extraordinary measures like individual *gratia* systematically and 'legitimately'.

The use of petition was a strategic ploy from the perspective of the convicted. Many petitioners were those who had not appeared in court and thus had been pronounced as *banniti*. It seems likely that their refusal of court orders might have been owing to their sense that even if they had appeared in court to plead their innocence or claim justifiable self-defence or poverty, their arguments would not have been accepted by judges whose rulings were based entirely on the city statutes. Accordingly, they might then have chosen to approach the Anziani, who did take such justifications into account. These strategically devised petitions contributed to prompting and developing the leading citizens' decision-making according to their own consciences when governing their city and dispensing justice, even before independence, allowing them to arbitrarily adopt 'corrective' measures. In contrast, it is also certain that the widespread use of this practice accelerated a fundamental change in communal government over the fourteenth century, namely, the establishment of the superiority of politics over the judiciary through normalisation of extraordinary means.

4. Prohibition of *Gratia* in the Republican Period

(1) Gratia *in the republican period*

After Lucca's liberation from Pisan rule by Charles IV in August 1368, the Lucchese Anziani became imperial vicars over Lucca in March 1370, which effectively meant that Lucca had finally recovered its independence. This marked Lucca's entry into a new phase as a republic. The word 'res publica', used in documents of these years, referred to more than just public matters but could be substituted for the commune as 'state'.[85]

The amnesties granted from the previous period continued to be offered in the 1370s. The amnesty offered by Emperor Charles IV on 31 July 1369 was a particularly extraordinary measure in the sense that all convicts, including convicted rebels (usually excluded from such amnesties), were to be liberated, without having to pay an amnesty tax. Other amnesties were offered occasionally from 1386 to 1392. The amnesty of 1392, in particular, was granted on the authority of the college of Anziani at a time when it was dominated by the Guinigi party, which had won the factional civil war earlier that year.[86]

85 For example, in the preamble of the provision of *gratia*, G. Tori (ed.), *Riformagioni della repubblica di Lucca (1369-1400)*, II (Roma, 1985), p. 187: 'ut divino favore Respublica Lucanorum feliciter dirigatur…'. For the provision concerning justice against rebellions, G. Tori (ed.), *Riformagioni della repubblica di Lucca (1369-1400)*, IV (Roma, 1998), p. 289: 'occasione cuiuscumque maleficii vel excessus facti, tractate vel attentati contra Rem Publicam Lucane Civitatis vel in preiudicium Lucani Comunis…'

86 ASL, *Consiglio Generale*, 12, fols. 94v-95r. Here we can find the list of 100 convicts who were released.

Table 5.1: Matters considered in this section

Dates	
1368, Aug.	Freedom of Lucca from Pisan rule by Holy Roman Emperor Charles IV
1369, Jul. 31	Amnesty by Charles IV
1370, Mar. 12	Investiture of the office of imperial vicars to the Lucchese Anziani by Charles IV
1370, May 10	Proposal to the General Council about the prohibition of *gratia* for serious criminals
1370, May 10	Proposal to the General Council about maintenance of foodstuffs and *menace* against the Antelminelli family
1370, May 12	Provision concerning the banishment of the members of the Antelminelli family
1370, May 23	Provision concerning the prohibition of *gratia* for serious criminals
1370, May 30	Provision concerning a reward for those who capture members of the Antelminelli family
1370, Jun. 1	Condemnation of the members of the Antelminelli family for *crimine lese maiestatis*
1370, Aug. 1	Peace agreement between Lucca and the communes of Garfagnana
1370, Nov. 13	Proposal to the General Council to suspend the provision prohibiting *gratia* in order to offer an amnesty on the occasion of the peace agreement between Lucca and the communes of Garfagnana
1370, Dec. 24	Proposal to the General Council to cancel the suspension of the provision prohibiting *gratia* for serious criminals
1371, Mar. 10	Peace agreement between Lucca and the Antelminelli family
1371, Mar. 16	Proposal to the General Council to suspend the provision prohibiting *gratia* in order to offer an amnesty on the occasion of the peace agreement between Lucca and the Antelminelli family
1371, Apr. 11	Cancellation of the condemnation of the members of the Antelminelli family
1371, Jul. 4	Proposal to the General Council regarding the provision of 24 December 1370 and the suspension of the provision prohibiting *gratia* and *gratia* for the residents of Tirelli, a rural commune
1372, Jul.	Proclamation of a new statute including an article regarding the provision prohibiting *gratia* for serious criminals
1374, Mar. 3	Proposal to the General Council to suspend the prohibition of *gratia* to provide an amnesty for *banniti* who had fought on Lucca's side against Corrado and his men

Individual *gratia* also continued to be offered in the republic of Lucca. During this period, the General Council or the Council of Thirty-Six[87] deliberated and voted on petitions. For example, we find 23 cases of such pardons in 1370 and 18 in 1392.[88]

87 The Council of Thirty-Six was established under the Anziani, in place of the Council of Fifty.

88 A. Romiti (ed.), *Riformagioni della repubblica di Lucca (1369-1400)*, I (Roma, 1980); Tori (ed.), *Riformagioni*, II; ASL, *Consiglio Generale*, 12.

Ruling decisions from this period often in their preambles declared the protection of *libertas* as motive. This theme of *libertas* was used to legitimate *gratia*. On 9 April 1370, the Council of Thirty-Six deliberated on a proposal by 'many citizens' regarding the murders of Mone Nucci, a notary of Pistoia, and Bizocchi of Pescia, both considered enemies of Lucca by Sighinello Colucci and others. The *podestà* sentenced the murderers to be beheaded and their properties to be confiscated on 22 December 1369. 'Many citizens' proposed the cancellation of the bans for Sighinello and others, given that their *maleficia* had been motivated by '*amore libertatis et gratia rei publice*'. The councillors accepted this proposal and decided to cancel the bans.[89] The realisation of the long-cherished desire for independence may have fostered a new standard of justification in the councillors' consciences, namely, the protection of the *libertas* of the republic.

(2) A provision prohibiting gratia for serious criminals

This moral approach regarding the protection of *libertas* resulted in a new policy prohibiting *gratia* for those convicted of five grave crimes, namely, rebellion, robbery, falsehood, arson, and homicide, in cases of lack of reconciliation with the bereaved.

Evidently such prohibitions had also been applicable in the previous period.[90] At the dawn of independence, however, this policy of prohibiting *gratia* entered a new phase. In 1370, it was now clearly forbidden to grant *gratia* for such crimes as a general law; even to propose such an amnesty was now forbidden on pain of penalty. Moreover, the government might arbitrarily suspend this provision. First, let us consider how the provision was formally made.

In a meeting of the General Council on 10 May 1370, the following proposal was presented: any *banniti* convicted of homicide or rebellion from 26 March 1370 onwards could not be allowed to obtain a pardon. Moreover, those who recommended granting *gratia* for such *banniti* would be punished with a fine of 500 *lire*, thus eliminating any such prospect and allowing Lucca to eradicate crimes within its territory.[91]

On 23 May, the Anziani and six other elected officials, including three jurists and two notaries, unanimously decreed that those sentenced to death for any of the five

---

89 Romiti (ed.), *Riformagioni*, p. 277-278.

90 The amnesty under the Mastino della Scala in 1336 had made an exception for those convicted of these five crimes, preventing them from becoming beneficiaries of *gratia*. *Anz. Av. Lib.*, 10, fols. 24r. These five crimes were already considered as distinct, grave crimes, at least by the statute of 1308. S. Bongi (ed.), *Statuto del comune di Lucca dell'anno MCCCVIII* (Lucca 1867), III, 2 (*De maleficiis inquirendis, et modo procedendi super eis*), p. 132-135. At the same time, the Anziani and the lord's vicar, despite this prohibition, accepted petitions for the remission of penalties for convicts of unpardonable crimes in special cases. For example, *gratia* was granted for one man convicted of homicide even though he did not make peace with his victim, because in this case, the family of the victim stayed in the territory of his enemy. *Anz. Av. Lib.*, 12, fols. 13r-v.

91 Romiti (ed.), *Riformagioni*, p. 306-307: 'Ad tolendam facinorosis et reprobis materiam delinquendi et uti omnis spes habende gratie totaliter evanescat et Civitas Lucana et comitatus talibus maleficiis expurgetur, si in odium predictorum videtur quod nullus banditus a vigesima sexta die mensis martii proximi elapsi vel in antea bannendi pro homicidio sive proditione vel rebellione nunquam possit rebaniri vel de banno eximi; et quicumque consuluerit, dixerit sive arengaverit ipsum vel ipsos rebanire puniatur et puniri debeat de facto et irremissibiliter in libris quingentis pro quolibet et qualibet vice'.

grave crimes were, from 26 March onwards, ineligible for *gratia*, and that such condemnations had to be executed without any suspension. Moreover, anyone who proposed such an amnesty or advised the councils in contradiction of this prohibition were to be punished by the *podestà* with a fine of 500 *lire*.[92]

The proposal of 10 May 1370 and the decree of 23 May had legal significance and differed from various other decrees in that they were transcribed in full as supplementary provisions to the statutes of 1342.[93] Thereafter, the city statute that was revised in November 1370 and was finally published in July 1372 in article form, probably on the basis of these provisions, prohibited the pardoning of those convicted of the five grave crimes, and even disallowed proposals that they should be granted *gratia*.[94]

Why did the city government in this period initiate these measures? Close consideration of the background of this new policy reveals a political circumstance, namely, a rebellion by the Antelminelli family and awareness on the part of leading citizens regarding the liberty of the republic. At the meeting of the General Council on 10 May 1370, when the prohibition was proposed, the Anziani, in connection with another proposal concerning food reserves, indicated the spread of a rumour that the military forces of Bernabò Visconti had come to Tuscany and Lucca and that the Antelminelli family, particularly Alderigo, Giovanni, and Rolando, were planning to incite a revolt in Lucchese territory.[95] In fact, at that time, this influential Lucchese aristocratic family had succeeded in invading the Garfagnana area with the help of the Visconti.[96] On 12 May, the Anziani declared that the Antelminelli family and its criminal followers would be condemned to exile if they appeared before the college of the Anziani, and that if they did not, they would be convicted as rebels.[97] On 30 May, the Anziani promised a bounty of 500-3000 florins for those who could catch or kill Alderigo, Giovanni, or Rolando.[98]

The provision prohibiting *gratia*, which sought to end the *bannitis*' prospect of pardon and to eradicate crimes in Lucca's territory, can be positioned within a series of measures against this rebellion by the Antelminelli family. It was intended to demon-

---

92 Romiti (ed.), *Riformagioni*, p. 320-321: 'quod aliqua persona imbanita Lucani Comunis ad morte… pro homicidio alicuius civis vel comitatini Lucani … pro tractatu vel proditione vel rebellione Civitatis Lucane aut alicuius castri terre vel ville Lucani Communis… pro latrocinio et robaria strate, pro falsitate monete, pro incendio domorum vel capannarum, non possit vel debeat rebanniri, eximi vel liberari de tali banno… Et domini Antiani non possit vel debeant aliquo modo contra predicta vel aliquid predictorum facere vel providere vel aliquid partitum facere vel ad aliquid Consilium ponere. Et nullus possit vel debeat in aliquo Consilio proponere, consulere vel arrenghare aliquid contra predicta vel aliquid predictorum, ad penam librarum quingentarum bone monete'.

93 ASL, *Statuti del* Commune *di Lucca*, 5, fols. 183r-185r.

94 ASL, *Statuti del* Commune *di Lucca*, 6, II, 130, fol. 43r: De eo quod inbannitus in casibus infrascriptis posit rebanniri.

95 Romiti (ed.), *Riformagioni*, p. 306: 'Cum publice divulgetur et fama multiplicata continue referrat detestandum gentem armorum Bernabonis de Vicecomitibus venturam esse de proximo ad partes Tuscie et in territorium Lucanum, et Aldericus, Iohannes et Rolandus de Antelminellis tractent et operentur inducere damna, vexationes et guerram, propter que summe oporteat provideri pro defensione Civitatis et comitatus et maxime pro habendo frumentum et victualia ad hoc ut Civitas et castra fulciantur'.

96 G. Tommasi, 'Sommario della storia di Lucca dall'anno MIV all'anno MDCC', *Archivio storico italiano*, 10 (1847), p. 242-243.

97 Romiti (ed.), *Riformagioni*, p. 312.

98 Romiti (ed.), *Riformagioni*, p. 326-327.

strate a strict stance against the Antelminelli family and any of their followers who sought to rebel against Lucca. Accordingly, this provision to prohibit the remission of penalties for grave crimes, which became statutory law and had general effect, can be said to have been a political measure introduced in the infancy of the Lucchese republic against specific enemies who menaced the 'liberty' of the independent republican state.

In the sentence book of 1370, we can find the original bans against the members of the Antelminelli family. On 1 June 1370, Alderigo, Giovanni, and Rolando were condemned to death in absentia for rebellion against Lucca and its *imperator* as well as for murder and plunder in the Garfagnana by the *podestà* and *capitano*.[99] Additionally, in a deliberation on 16 July by the General Council, it was indicated that the family had been condemned for *crimine lese maiestatis* against the Imperial Majesty and against those who were administering imperial offices (likely in reference to the Lucchese Anziani as imperial vicars).[100]

(3) Suspension of the provision of the gratia

However, the marginal notes of the original sentence indicate that on 11 April 1371, Alderigo, Giovanni, and Rolando degli Antelminelli were liberated from bans by order of the Anziani and Gonfaloniere di Giustizia. This happened despite the earlier provision of May 1370 expressly forbidding the cancellation of bans for crimes committed by them. Let us consider the reasons for this reversal, which can be observed five months before their sentences were withdrawn.

On 13 November 1370, the Gonfaloniere di Giustizia, as head of the college of the Anziani, had presented a proposal to the General Council to suspend the provision prohibiting granting *gratia*, because an agreement with the communes of Garfagnana that had been made on 1 August included an amnesty for serious criminals.[101] It is possible that the communes of Garfagnana had supported the Antelminelli rebellion and that members of these communes should otherwise be convicted, such as for murder and plunder in the war. This proposal did not infringe on the provision, as it concerned not *gratia* for serious crimes but the provision itself. In response to the proposal, one councillor moved that the provision should be suspended that very day,

---

99 ASL, *Sentenze e bandi*, 42, no foliation, 1 June 1370.

100 Romiti (ed.), *Riformagioni*, p. 364-365: 'Et cum hoc sit quod predicti Aldericus et Iohannes, una cum certis aliis, tanquam rei lese maiestatis et pro crimine lese maiestatis per eos cum certis aliis comisso, contra imperialem maiestatem et contra gerentes vices imperialis maiestatis, sint et fuerint in banno missi et condemnati ex officio dicti domini Potestatis et Capitanei Civitatis Lucane et sue Curie'. This *crimine lese maiestatis* was also applied to Paolo Guinigi, who had usurped the *dominium* of Lucca as an imperial city in the *concilium* of the jurist Sozzini at the end of the fifteenth century. See O. Cavallar, '*Laesa maiestas* in Renaissance Lucca', in L. Armstrong and J. Kirshner (eds.), *The Politics of Law in Late Medieval and Renaissance Italy: Essays in Honour of Lauro Martines* (Toronto, 2011), p. 161-183.

101 Tori (ed.), *Riformagioni*, II, p. 94: 'Cum hoc sit quod plurima pacta et conventiones facta fuerunt inter commissarios Lucani Comunis et quedam communia Garfagnane et aliunde a die prima augusti proxime elapsi citra, ex quibus et quorum observantia debent nonnulli exbanniti et rebelles Lucani Comunis rebanniri et de bannis eximi ac restitui, et etiam utilissimum sit statuta et iura municipalia Lucani Comunis refici, corrigi et componi… et maxime quoddam statutum seu reformatio facta auctoritate Consilii Generalis, quod extrabanniti certis de causis non possit rebanniri…, quid placet primo et ante omnia super ipsis statutis providere, ordinare et reformare…'

which would allow the Anziani to propose their intentions with impunity.[102] This was accepted, whereupon the Anziani immediately proposed an amnesty for the rebels, as had been promised in the agreement, which was in turn approved by the General Council. Thus, the provision enacted by the decree of 23 May, making it the law of the land, was sidestepped by means of a temporary suspension less than half a year after coming into force.

Along with the agreement made with the communes of the Garfagnana on 23 November 1370, the republican government, after an attack on the territory dominated by the Antelminelli, started negotiating terms of peace with the clan. The negotiations were lengthy, but on 10 March 1371, an agreement was finally concluded in Castiglione di Garfagnana.[103] Here, the provision of 23 May 1370 that prohibited pardoning grave crimes became an obstacle to the establishment of peace with the enemy and thus to the peace of the republican state. On 16 March 1371, the Anziani, alluding to the conclusion of the agreement with the Antelminelli, proposed the suspension of this provision.[104] After the suspension, the Anziani asked the General Council to approve an article of the agreement, which promised the elimination of all judgements and trials against Alderigo's followers, including some nobles, and the return of confiscated properties. This was once again approved by the General Council.[105] It was an order from the Anziani and Gonfaloniere di Giustizia in connection with this matter that caused the notary keeping the sentence book to strike out the bans and annotate the margins of the original sentence on 11 April 1371, as mentioned above.[106]

(4) Libertas *of the republic and the sense of crisis*

Therefore, a key to understanding this policy of *gratia* was the sense of crisis felt by leading citizens at the threat of enemies from within and without. It only intensified when these citizens acquired something that they felt to be worth defending, namely, *libertas*. This sense of crisis established the provision prohibiting remissions in order to threaten 'enemies' with an exception in order to receive 'friends'. This flexible use of the provision continued. In 1374 the supporters of Corrado Wettingher invaded

---

102 Tori (ed.), *Riformagioni*, II, p. 94-95: 'cum summe sit utile statuta Lucani Comunis corrigi et renovari et iustum sit et ad honorem Comunis Lucani pertineat pacta servari…, hodie per totam diem intelligatur esse et sit generaliter et spetialiter detractum et derogatum. Ita quod domini Antiani et Vexillifer iustitie populi et Comunis Lucani sine aliquo preiudicio possint libere et impune proponere et proponi facere in presenti Consilio dumtaxat hodie, quicquid ipsi placuerit tam de rebanniendo extrabannitos…'

103 Tommasi, p. 248.

104 Tori (ed.), *Riformagioni*, II, p. 179-181: 'quod, autoritate presenti Consilii, dicto statuto, ordinamento atque reformationi intelligatur esse et sit pro hodie duntaxat detractum et derogatum…'

105 Tori (ed.), *Riformagioni*, II, p. 180-181.

106 ASL, *Sentenze e bandi*, 42, (unnumbered folios) [1370.6.1]: 'vigore mandati Magnificorum dominorum dominorum Antianorum et Vexilliferi Iustitie populi et communis Lucani, tenoris et continentie subsequentis videlicet, Nos… Antiani et Vexilifer Iustitie simul ad collegium… in observantiam pactorum pacis contracte per Lucanum communem cum Alderigo de Antelminellis… providemus et mandamus quod notarius et custos librorum imbannitorum et condepnatorum Lucani communis […] casset et cancellet Aldericum et Johannum germanos et suprascriptos filios condam domini Francischini de Antelminelliis de Luca, Rolandum condam domini Henrici […] ex bannitos Lucani communis pro malleficio'.

Lucca's territory and menaced the state's liberty. On 3 March 1374, the Anziani once again suspended the statute's provision and other prescriptions prohibiting *gratia* for penalties handed out to *banniti* for the five grave crimes.[107] Afterwards, the Anziani again granted an amnesty and re-admitted the *banniti* to the commune of Lucca. They recognised that, first, the existence of a large number of exiled *banniti* might threaten the peace of Lucca owing to incursions by armed bands and, second, that these *banniti* had fought on Lucca's side against Corrado and his men in December and January, a fact that deserved praise and proved their fidelity to the commune of Lucca.[108]

It was natural that the provision prohibiting *gratia* could be arbitrarily suspended to achieve the political purpose of protecting *libertas* as soon as it became an obstacle; it had originally been established to protect *libertas* in an excessively political environment.[109] Indeed, when the provision was initially proposed and promulgated in May 1370, it may already have been implicitly assumed that it would only apply in cases deemed highly 'necessary' or 'beneficial'. A decision on 24 December 1370 formally prescribed exceptions to this provision for cases involving political agreements to cancel a penalty.[110]

The provision prohibiting *gratia* was, therefore, a measure that contained exceptions on various levels. It made an exception of *gratia* for serious criminals, which was granted exceptionally by arbitrarily modifying sentences pronounced by judges according to the statutes. Moreover, the provisions, in exceptional circumstances, could be suspended for a day. These higher-order exceptions were motivated by leading citizens who interpreted successive political situations through the lens of a 'crisis'. Here, it was not ordinary citizens but the government which undertook responsibility for state interests

107 Tori (ed.), *Riformagioni*, IV, p. 364-369: 'quod statutum Lucani Comunis positum sub rubrica "De forma imbanniendi et extrahendi de banno", nec non statutum Lucani Comunis, cuius tenor talis est videlicet, "De eo quod nullus imbannitus in casibus infrascriptis possit rebanniri"..., hodie suspendantur et subspensa intelligantur et subspenderunt, et quod ipsis statutis... non obstantibus, possit proponi, consuli, disponi et reformari atque fieri hodie tantum licite et impune, per ipsos dominos Antianos et cives, quicquid eis videbitur etiam de his que in eis et per ea expresse sunt prohibita'.

108 From the list of *banniti* who were permitted re-entry, 49 men came from various provinces such as Camaiore and Pietrasanta. Tori (ed.), *Riformagioni*, IV, p. 365: 'considerantes quantum pernitiosa et periculosa est multitudo exbannitorum bono statui cuiuslibet Civitatis et esse posset preiudicialis et damnosa plurimum / tranquillitati Civitatis et comitatus Lucani et libertatis ipsius, maxime propter novitates noxias que indicantur de proximo de gentibus armorum in Italia existentibus... causa transeundi ad partes Tuscie et in territorium Lucanum..., quodque exbanniti infrascripti tamquam zelatores libertatis dicte Civitatis et defensionis boni status requisiti a dominis Antianis et civibus numeri sepedicti pro defensa civitatis et comitatus ac fortilitiarum Lucani Comunis et hostium offensa de mensibus decembris et ianuarii proxime preteritis, quibus per gentes inimicas domini Corradi de Wettingher alias tunc hostiliter ...'; 'quod infrascripti exbanniti Lucani Comunis e quacumque causa vel occasione etiam si essent de illis pro quibus per forma suprascripti statuti vel alterius iuris vel quomodocumque reperiatur rebanniri non possit et cetera vel eximi de banno, et alii quacumque que dici vel excogitari possit, rebanniatur, reintegrentur et rebanniti et reintegrati sint et esse intelligantur a Lucano Comuni et Lucani Comunis de omni et quocumque banno eis vel alicui eorum dato...'

109 For example, in 1388 the Anziani asked to suspend the provision of the prohibition of the *gratia*, 'pro utilitate Lucane rei publice et pro evitatione imminentium periculorum'. ASL, *Consiglio Generale*, 10, p. 546-547.

110 *Riformagioni* ed. Tori, II, p. 132: 'Et quod dicto statuto aliquo tempore vel modo in totum vel in partem derogari non possit, aut de derogando eidem proponi, consuli vel reformari ad penam..., salvo quod si quo tempore fieret aliqua pax, et pactis cuius aliqua rebannitio facienda foret, tunc et eo casu et casibus dispensari aut derogari possit libere et impune'.

by promoting new policies and which exercised great influence over the interpretation of justice. We can glimpse the state's reasoning, which induced the governors to pursue the public peace even by disregarding the laws, a reasoning that was later revealed in the thoughts of Niccolò Machiavelli and Jean Bodin.[111]

(5) Provision prohibiting gratia *and the republic of Lucca*

The provision prohibiting *gratia*, after being incorporated into the statutes in the 1370s, remained effective as a statutory law that could be used in combination with the means of its own suspension. What overall impact did this policy, introduced during the infancy of the independent republic of Lucca out of an enthusiasm for *libertas* on the part of leading citizens, have on the systems of Lucchese governance during the republican period, and what features did it engender in the commune-cum-republic of Lucca? Here I want to focus on the increasing power of the Anziani and the formal preservation of the republican system.

First, the provision prohibiting *gratia* that, at first glance, seemed to check the arbitrary power of the Anziani to grant *gratia*, in fact served to provide them with free rein through the method of its temporary suspension. This provision may thus be considered as a kind of filter that could be used to block those who petitioned the council for *gratia*. It did not cut off all prospect of *gratia*, but could be suspended to allow the passage of petitions deemed by the authorities to be useful for the protection of *libertas*. Here, it was not the council but the college of the Anziani that could validate the petitions. If the Anziani considered the petitions as beneficial enough to be accepted, they would propose the suspension of the provision and grant *gratia* with the authorisation of the General Council. The establishment of this policy represented a concentration of political power by the Anziani. In Chapter 6, we will also consider the matter of the Anziani's eventual superiority over the council.

Such discretionary politics on the part of the Anziani were never conducted openly. This serves as another important aspect of the government of Lucca, as reflected in the policies of *gratia* in this period. The Anziani, in fact, never disregarded or abolished the provision prohibiting *gratia*, merely suspended it temporarily. For example, the Anziani carefully went through the requisite legal procedures when they gave an amnesty to the inhabitants of a rural commune, Tirelli, on 4 July 1371. Here, the Anziani first had to suspend a provision prescribed on 24 December 1370 that prohibited suspending the provision prohibiting *gratia* and then immediately suspended that provision to be able to offer *gratia* to those convicted of serious crimes.[112]

Why did the leading citizens not simply abrogate the provision of prohibition? Why choose to maintain it, using such roundabout suspension procedures? One reason why they had to follow the procedures had to do with the general principles of *ius commune*, wherein laws inherently assumed value in their own right, and as such could not be

111 F. Meinecke, *Machiavelism: The Doctrine of Raison d' État and Its Place in Modern History* (New Haven, 1957).
112 Tori (ed.), *Riformagioni*, II, p. 261-262.

cancelled but only suspended or derogated, as has been explained by Tanzini in the case of Florence.[113]

This traditional approach to laws would resonate with the moral adherence to the 'maintenance of the republican form', which differed from the 'protection of the *libertas* of the republic' by leading citizens who had restored Lucca's independence as a republic. The Anziani, as leaders of a republican state, were required to respect the republican institutional structure and its governmental norms, which were based on broad political participation and observance of the statutes. This also meant that leading citizens could not be called tyrannical for disregarding the law. They felt that their own actions needed to be legitimated, at least in formal terms.

The leading citizens of the republic of Lucca can be seen as *signore* in the sense that they in fact freely proposed and granted *gratia*, citing the maintenance of the republic as their primary purpose. However, they did so by hiding their actual arbitrariness under a republican mask, as with their superficially formal observation of statutory laws. Therefore, we can say that the leading citizens tried to maintain the 'republic' in a double sense, by maintaining both its political independence and its formal character. The political practice involving the application and suspension of the provision prohibiting *gratia* was a product of the intricate efforts of leading citizens to realise this seemingly paradoxical double purpose.

5. *Gratia* in Communal Lucca

Gratia were measures that political authorities used to arbitrarily modify sentences handed down by judges in adherence to the statutes and to dispense grace to 'subjects' who had supplicated the city government. This policy would seem, on the face of it, to have been incompatible with the communal regime, which had placed great importance on the letter of the law as the logical basis for the legitimacy of rulings and which considered the Anziani as representatives of a '*comune*' composed of citizens. The widespread use in Lucca, both in quality and quantity, of *gratia* over the course of the fourteenth century, shows the manner in which the new characteristics of the commune and a new form of justice emerged, doing away or finding compromises with these communal traditions.

An important starting point in the expansion of *gratia* during this period was the exceptional power invested in the foreign masters,[114] whose intrinsic power was brought to bear by unforeseen situations and through the supplications of their subjects. Then, the Anziani and the vicars of these respective lords, making use of this power, granted amnesties to aid the subjects stifled by city officialdom.

This practice of *gratia* succeeded and was developed to the level of exception under Pisan rule. In this period, Lucca's Anziani and council, hearing subjects' appeals individually, also began remitting penalties on an individual basis. Lucca's leading citizens

113 Tanzini, *Il governo delle leggi*, p. 66-67.

114 Despite the lack of documents, it is possible that Castruccio Castracani also took the extraordinary measure.

were motivated as governors by the petitions of convicts to dispense justice with *gratia* based on their consciences, even under foreign dominion. These *gratia* always took the form of 'corrective', and thus legitimate, measures. Unexpected situations and citizens' petitions offered reasonable motivations to induce the lords or city councils to overrule 'unjust' judicial decisions, and thereby help citizens. This must simultaneously have permitted the political authorities to justifiably delegitimise, in a sense, their judicial powers, and expand the political sphere in the context of the communal government.

When Lucca regained its independence, the republican government introduced a new exceptional measure, namely, a provision that prohibited the remission of penalties for serious crimes, as well as the practice of suspending that same provision. This policy was novel in the sense that the *iusta causa*, which motivated and legitimated this extraordinary measure, was not now offered by ordinary citizens but by the political authorities. The leading citizens' idea of defending the republican state from enemies encouraged them to make exceptions regarding those who received *gratia*, and then, when it suited them, to arbitrarily suspend the provision itself. Here, it was the leading citizens who took the initiative in interpreting justice.

This evolution of arbitrary political involvement cannot be explained solely in the Lucchese context because Lucca's situation conformed to that of other contemporary cities. For example, the procedure of suspending laws began to be applied in other republican cities in the 1380s.[115] Tanzini, examining the language used in the preambles to similar provisions in Florence, Siena, and Lucca, offers the valuable insight that in addition to a shared notarial-chancery culture[116] the emergent situations routinely arising owing to military and financial difficulties, and above all after the 1370s, led citizens to break down the constraints of the traditional communal systems and act freely in response to contingent necessities.[117]The development of the policy of *gratia* in fourteenth-century Lucca coincided with the establishment of political institutions, such as the 'authorities' who offered the *gratia*, and inclined them towards policies that relied on the conscience and *arbitrium* of governors. It was possible that the practice of interpreting justice by citizens and leaders, who suppressed hidden proper interests, served to motivate and accelerate these two characteristics of politics with which the city government had not previously been entirely endowed. Just as convicts only seeking the remission of their penalties insisted that justice must not be based solely on positive law, and praised the leading citizens as helpful authorities, so those leading citizens, from a desire to protect the *libertas* of the republic, came to set the form of a more flexible justice. These strategic interpretations of justice resulted in the transformation of the characteristics of the commune.

That the figure of justice shifted inside the framework provided by the communal or republican tradition becomes clear when we look at *gratia* granted by Paolo Guinigi

115 As for Firenze, Tanzini, *Il governo delle leggi*, p. 83-87.

116 These cities commonly had a technique of governance, such as the rhetoric of notarial-chancery. In fact, Coluccio Salutati, who was appointed Chancellor of Florence in 1375, recorded the proceedings of the General Council of Lucca from 1370 to 1371.

117 L. Tanzini, 'Emergenza, eccezione, deroga: tecniche e retoriche del potere nei comuni toscani del XIV secolo', in M. Vallerani (ed.), *Tecniche di potere*, p. 149-181.

as *signore* of Lucca from 1400. During his rule, until 1430, Paolo granted amnesties and showed clemency to individual supplicants.[118] His policy on *gratia* was characterised by a simple procedure. Paolo plainly and summarily proclaimed whatever he wanted, his decrees being free from complicated procedures such as consultation, voting, or any rule that might limit his powers to dispense arbitrary judgement.[119] This clearly shows that it was the authority of the *signore* itself, rather than of the representative of a '*comune*' composed of *cives*, that formed the foundation for the legality of *gratia*.

We can see another difference between *gratia* and that of the commune in the motivation underlying *gratia*. According to the *decreta*, Paolo was explicit in his insistence that the aim of *gratia* was to manifest his generosity: *ut a pluribus eius munificentia cognoscatur*.[120] It is difficult to see from this direct description of Paolo's personal interests when carrying out an exceptional measure to modify a ruling any intent to hide his private motives or to justify his actions with any other reason. Paolo as *signore* might not have felt the necessity to legitimise his extraordinary decisions.

Having seen the *gratia* of the *signore*, we find that there is clearly a form of justice in the communal framework engraved in the council books in communal Lucca. This emerges in the descriptions of the various procedures by which *gratia* were granted, such as the proposals from the Anziani to the council and the deliberations and votes in the council, as well as in the detailed descriptions of motives used to justify *gratia*: particular circumstances (war, poverty and the disappearance of the sentence books); individual elements cited by petitions (legal flaws, distortions of the truth through fear of torture, self-defence, and poverty); and the crisis of the *libertas* of the republican state. These traces of the grounds that would justify *gratia*, such as the procedures and motives registered in the council books show clearly the characteristics of justice and the '*comune*' that constituted, at least formally, the republic composed of citizens and which, in comparison to the *signore*, were relatively constrained by *iusta causa* on behalf of the *bene del commune*.[121]

---

118 According to the study by Meek, almost 1,100 cases of *gratia* were recorded in the registers of decrees between January 1401 and October 1429. Paolo Guinigi also considered not infringing on civil rights, making it a condition of *gratia* to make a peace agreement with the victim. Here we can see a limitation, i.e. the protection of civil rights, which even the *signore* could not ignore. Meek, 'Whatever's', p. 138-140.

119 However, he continued to follow the process of fact-finding about each petition through entrusted officials, like the exactor. On the back of the supplication letters, for example, the exactor noted, 'Exactor se informet et maxime si contentus in petitione sunt vera et referat' (ASL., *Governo di Paolo Guinigi*, 33, fol. 72).

120 ASL., *Governo di Paolo Guinigi*, 1, fol. 25r.

121 It is possible that the governors could be considered *tyrannia* if they granted *gratia* without '*isuta causa*' or 'justice'. For example, the citizens of Treviso testified that the attitudes of *tyrannia* were to absolve those who committed *maleficia* or murder and to condemn many innocents, Zorzi, *Le signorie cittadine in Italia (secoli XIII-XV)* (Milano, 2010), p. 151: 'Il maestro Manfredino sarto, teste prodotto come sopra[…], disse sotto giuramento che Gherardo da Camino fu capitano della città di Treviso e del distretto già sono trent'anni e più […] e che lo vide per questo tempo e più esercitare l'ufficio capitaneale, assolvendo coloro che avevano commesso malefici e omicidi e condannando moltissimi innocenti'.

CHAPTER 6

The Commune and Politics in the Practice of Extraordinary Justice

1. The Commune and Extraordinary Justice

In the context of criminal justice in fourteenth-century Lucca, *gratia*, as *post-trial* changes to judgements, were not the only outcomes of rulings reliant on *arbitrium* that transcended strict adherence to the law. Within the *trial process* as well, trials were sometimes held summarily, without basis in ordinary procedure, and were therefore at the free discretion of judges. These were held for cases that the political authorities specified as 'exceptional'. The resultant 'summary justice', accomplished with the clause 'simply and plainly, without clamour and the form of ordinary trial procedure (*simpliciter et de plano ac sine strepitu et figura iudicii*)',[1] as prescribed in the decree issued by Pope Clement V, in the context of criminal justice, came to be applied to crimes that threatened the state and the established regime during the fourteenth century.[2]

This chapter examines what I refer to as 'extraordinary justice', namely, the sphere of trials, distinguished from ordinary criminal trials, wherein summary procedure was adopted for such 'extraordinary' cases. Incidentally, summary trials, owing to their extraordinary nature, are incompletely recorded, making it difficult to grasp the details of the actual situation from the court records. Here, based on the record books of the Anziani and the councils, I approach extraordinary justice from the aspect of the permission granted by political agencies for judicial bodies (i.e. the courts and their judges) to observe a summary procedure as well as from the complaints of defendants who received summary trials.

When investigating extraordinary justice in fourteenth-century Lucca, we notice the following two points. The first is the political nature of extraordinary justice. As an example of the introduction of extraordinary procedure, we can look to the inquisitorial trials that appeared as exceptions in thirteenth-century secular courts, which had adopted a Romano-canonical procedure. Inquisitorial trials, which enabled *ex officio* prosecution, were promoted and became established in the context of a political intention to protect ecclesiastical institutions from the heresies that appeared during the papacy of Innocent III, and in the context of promoting the ideology of

---

1 What I refer to here as 'summary justice', as summarised in Chapter 3, Part 3, are trials that aimed at 'complete cognizance'. I do not mean cases involving small sums of money or those seeking a judicial order.

2 For example, given a plenitude of power, the Visconti of Milan imposed extraordinary measures on crimes of *laesae maiestatis seu nostrae dignitatis*, J. Black, *Absolutism in Renaissance Milan. Plenitude of Power under the Visconti and the Sforza*, 1329-1535 (Oxford, 2009), p. 125-127.

the 'protection of the public' as championed by the *popolo* in the urban courts of the thirteenth century.[3]

The politically motivated demarcation of ordinary and extraordinary crimes and the application of extraordinary procedure also characterised a 'trial' that followed the summary procedure of the fourteenth century. According to Vallerani, these included the disbanding of the Knights Templar by Philip IV in 1307, which was given legal sanction by a decree of Clement V, and the 'trial' against Robert of Anjou held by Emperor Henry VII in 1313. In these cases, the conduct of the 'accused' was regarded as an outrageous malefaction (*maleficium*) or lese-majesty, an anomalous situation that by its very nature *legitimised* a 'trial' that followed a summary procedure wherein the accused was not entitled to legal protections and was denied any opportunity to offer a defence.[4]

In the extraordinary justice of the fourteenth-century Lucca dealt with in this chapter, some *maleficia* were defined by political criteria, to be distinguished from ordinary *maleficia* and subject to summary procedures. Moreover, this extraordinary justice was justified as the 'correct' justice by political reasons such as necessity and utility. Accordingly, when considering this concept, we must always devote extra attention to the underlying actions and intentions of the political authorities.

The second point concerns the relationship between political authorities and judicial authorities. The juridical environment of medieval Italian cities was not traditionally conducive to summary trials wherein judges conducted the proceedings at their own discretion. This was a tradition of the communal regime based on a balance between the political and judicial authorities that was created following the thirteenth-century *podestà* period.[5] Here, to ensure fairness and neutrality, the judiciary was entrusted to the *podestà* or *capitano del popolo* ('captain of the people'), who came from another city and theoretically did not have a stake in internal city matters. They and their judges were able to protect the 'public' with relative autonomy irrespective of the legal constraints of the city statutes. During the *popolo* period of the latter half of the thirteenth century, the autonomy of judges was jeopardised by the various decrees of the city government, which feared unchecked prosecutions by foreign judges, especially the prosecution of leading members.[6] The communal judicial system before

3 R. M. Fraher, 'IV Lateran's Revolution and Criminal Procedure: The Birth of Inquisitio, the End of Ordeals, and Innocent III's Vision of Ecclesiastical Politics', in R. I. Castillo Lara (ed.), *Studia in honorem eminentissimi cardinalis Alphonsi M. Stickler* (Roma, 1992), p. 96-111; M. Sbriccoli, '*Vidi communiter observari*. L'emersione di un ordine penale pubblico nelle città italiane del secolo XIII', *Quaderni fiorentini per la storia del pensiero giuridico*, 27 (1998), p. 231-268.

4 M. Vallerani, 'L'arbitrio negli statuti cittadini del Trecento', in Id (ed.), *Tecniche di potere nel tardo Medioevo: regimi comunali e signorie in Italia* (Roma, 2010), p. 117-147, in particular p. 117-122.

5 Regarding the coexistence and plurality of institutions in the commune, see M. Vallerani, 'Comune e comuni: una dialettica non risolta', in M. C. De Matteis and B. Pio (eds.), *Sperimentazioni di governo nell'Italia centrosettentrionale nel processo storico dal primo comune alla signoria* (Bologna, 2011), p. 9-34, in particular p. 30; E. Artifoni, 'Tensioni sociali e istituzioni nel mondo comunale', in N. Tranfaglia and M. Firpo (eds.), *La storia, 2: Il Medioevo: popoli e strutture politiche* (Torino 1986), p. 461-491; E. Artifoni, 'I governi di «popolo» e le istituzioni comunali', *Reti Medievali*, 4-2 (2003), p. 1-20.

6 As for the case of Bologna and Perugia, M. Vallerani, *La giustizia pubblica medievale* (Bologna, 2005), p. 211-275. *Tractatus de maleficiis*, by the jurist Alberto Gandino was written to seek the restoration of judges' autonomy.

the fourteenth century can be described as having been built on a balance of power, fraught with tensions between foreign judicial magistrates who sought free and fair trials and a political authority that sought to stop it from being carried too far.

When we revisit extraordinary justice in these circumstances, we begin to see how allowing foreign judges to conduct proceedings at their own discretion and disregard the law as they saw necessary during trials would not have been readily accepted by the political authorities, in terms either of overriding city statutes or of granting *arbitrium* to foreign judges. However, as we shall see, in fourteenth-century Lucca the political authorities of the commune (the Anziani and the council) granted permission to judges to conduct summary trials. What lay behind this policy of granting foreign judges *arbitrium* to conduct trials? Through the clarification of specific aspects of the emergence and the development of extraordinary justice, the latter of which was incompatible with both justice in its traditional form and the commune's governing principles, we will gain a new perspective on how justice and the '*comune*' emerged with new features.

Below, I examine the *capitano di custodia* (*ser* Scherlatto) as a foreign magistrate who came to Lucca during the period of confusion that occurred at the beginning of the Pisan rule, the *bargello*, who was tasked with maintaining the security of the territory under the Pisan rule, the *podestà*, who acted to protect the republic after the establishment of independence, and the *capitano del popolo* ('captain of the people'), who served to maintain the new regime after 1392. By paying attention to the two aforementioned issues – i.e. how the political authorities motivated and legitimated extraordinary justice, and the establishment of the political authority's superiority over judicial authority – I would like to clarify the new feature of the '*comune*' in the later fourteenth century, which was characterised by increasing political authority, as well as the process by which justice was established through the practices of political authority.

2. Captain *ser* Scherlatto's Lawsuit for the Restitution of Property

(1) Background: confiscated property and its restitution

An early example of foreign judges being allowed to conduct trials using an extraordinary summary procedure can be cited from the period shortly after the beginning of Pisan rule. On 25 August 1342, the Lucchese Anziani instructed a foreign citizen named *Ser* Scherlatto Maffei de Rasinopoli to assume the position of Lucca's captain of protection (*capitano di custodia*) and to conduct summary lawsuits involving the restitution of property on behalf of repatriated rebels. The point here is that permission to conduct summary trials was given to a *capitano di custodia* dispatched from Pisa during a period of confusion and that the scope of the trials concerned was limited to the issue of restoring the ex-'rebels' their right to property. Here I would like to review the process that led up to this permission to observe summary procedures.

Lucca in the first half of the fourteenth century experienced a period of turbulence in the form of partisan struggles within the Guelph faction (the White and Black Guelphs), the seizure of power by the *popolo minuto* – which led to the compilation of

Table 6.1: Matters considered in this section (Anz. = Anziani)

Dates	
1341, Sep. 25	Florentine rule (to 1342.7.6)
1341, Dec. 23	Anz.: instructed the Court of Rebels to preserve rebels' abandoned property
1342, Jun. 19	Anz.: complaints seeking summary trials for the restitution of property ⇒ conditional authorisation
1342, Jul. 6	Pisan rule (to 1368)
1342, Aug. 25	Anz.: complaint seeking a summary trial by *ser* Scherlatto for the restitution of property ⇒ authorized
1342, Sep. 2	Anz.: appointed *ser* Scherlatto as*capitano di custodia*
1342, Sep. 4	Grievances against summary trials for the restitution of property
1342, Sep. 21	Addendum to the decree of 1342.8.25: *ser* Scherlatto shall hold hearings *de iure et de facto*
1342, Nov. 23	Anz.: appointed *ser* Scherlatto as *conservatore* and 'administrator with respect to rebels and their property'
1342, Nov. 30	City statutes: provisions allowing *ser* Scherlatto to observe summary justice

the 1308 city statutes – the signorial rule of Castruccio Castracani, and the successive rule of multiple foreign lords throughout the 1330s. This period also saw the repeated expulsion from the city of large numbers of political *banniti* as 'rebels', followed by their return as the regime changed. The battles between Florence and Pisa that unfolded over Lucca between 1341 and 1342 and the fleeting period of Florentine control (25 September 1341 to 6 July 1342) led to a state of emergency that saw the expulsion and escape from the city of the Ghibelline faction, which was politically hostile towards Florence, as well as many other citizens seeking to escape the strife.

What arose as a legal problem, however, was the property left behind in Lucca by the 'rebels' who had fled the city. In the most cases, it was confiscated as communal property by the Court of Rebels. Three months after Florence took control of Lucca, on 23 December 1341, the Anziani, on the consideration that others were illegitimately holding the property of people who had left Lucca in the previous war, gave instructions for the enactment of the following measures. First, the property of absentees being illegitimately held must be discovered by officials of the Court of Rebels and preserved, overseein by a treasury official (*Camerarius generalis*). Second, in the event that someone might claim a right to the property, that property shall be returned by the Anziani to the one to whom it should be returned. Moreover, if it should be discovered that the property in question is that of a rebel, then it shall be confiscated by the commune.[7]

The above provisions aimed to ensure that abandoned properties would be preserved for a time and then distributed to their rightful owners.[8] In addition to those who

7 ASL, *Anziani Avanti la Libertà* (hereafter, *Anz. Av. Lib.*), 16, fols. 29r-30r.

8 According to the duty provisions of the Court of Rebels, officials of this court investigated the question of which properties belonged to absentees and rebels based on denunciations by residents, court records, the registers of

held property illegitimately, the description in the provision of 'someone [who] claims a right to the property in question' suggests the existence of individuals engaged in civil disputes with absentees who had left property behind, as well as others who possessed some sort of right to the property in question and were trying to instigate a dispute. In fact, a summary suit for restitution conducted nine months later, on 25 August 1342, by *ser* Scherlatto, Lucca's *capitano di custodia,* was a dispute between rival claimants to the rights to any abandoned property, conducted not as an administrative trial against returnees in the Court of Rebels but rather in the style of a civil trial, with an occupier claiming rights to property against a returnee.

In the final days of Florentine rule, on 19 June 1342 a complaint was raised by members of the Lucchese Guelph faction who had fled Lucca and who had been living in the Guelph territories since 1314.[9] This case, wherein the rebels and their successors sought to have the restitution of property they had held when they left Lucca, was decided *in a summary fashion,* simply by proving the fact of their former possession of the property in question.[10] The end of this complaint was appended with a statement allowing the rights holders to reserve the right to appeal in an ordinary trial. In response to this complaint, the Anziani sought advice from four people (of whom, three were jurists). As a result, they gave a decision that for properties other than those already subject to a ruling based on the jurists' advice, restitution would be conducted in a summary fashion solely by proving evidence of absence and former possession of the property.[11] While conditional, the acceptance of this summary procedure enabling the recovery of property solely by proving the fact of former possession would also be carried over into the subsequent summary justice dispensed by *ser* Scherlatto.

(2) Granting ser *Scherlatto the authority to dispense summary justice*

On 6 July 1342, Pisa gained control of Lucca under the terms of a peace agreement with Florence. A month and half later, on 25 August, based on a complaint by Lucchese citizens, Lucca's Anziani granted *ser* Scherlatto permission to conduct summary justice.[12] The citizens' complaint that motivated this permission was as follows.

---

financial administrators, and reports from rural consuls. Incidentally, a notice made in the city on 23 November 1341 stated that any person with knowledge of rebel properties must convey that knowledge to the Court of Rebels' officials within three days. S. Bongi (ed.), *Bandi lucchesi del secolo decimo quarto* (Bologna, 1863), p. 89.

9 *Anz. Av. Lib.,* 17, fols. 22r-24r. In 1314, Lucca came under the rule of the Pisan Uguccione della Faggiola, supported by Lucca's Ghibelline and White Guelph factions, meaning that those raising this complaint are presumed to have been members of the Black Guelph faction, which had been expelled.

10 *Anz. Av. Lib.,* 17, fols. 22r-v: 'omnes predicti rebelles… intelligantur repositi et restituti in omnibus et super omnibus eorum bonis mobilibus et immobilibus que possidebant tempore eorum exitus, et absentationis mostrando et fidem faciendo summarie et de facto qualiter ipsa bona possidebant dicto tempore'.

11 *Anz. Av. Lib.,* 17, fol. 23v: '… nec extendatur predicta restitutio ad bona super quibus lata esset diffinitiva sententia in contradictorio iudicio de consilio alicuius iudicis… Et quod predicta restitutio fiat summarie probata eorum absentia seu rebellione et possione dictorum bonorum tempore eorum absentie vel rebellionis…'

12 *Anz. Av. Lib.,* 18, fols. 10v-11r. Incidentally, in another provision dated the same day, the Anziani decided that *ser* Scherlatto would be permitted to conduct summary trials even regarding the restitution of movables to returnees. *Anz. Av. Lib.,* 18, fol. 11v, 'Quod ser Scherlactus possit cognoscere de rebus recommendatis tempore obsidionis'.

Ghibellines and others who had been sentenced to exile by Guglielmo Canacci degli Scannabecchi (*podestà* in 1336), Guglielmo's vicars, and other foreign lords, wished to reclaim their property left behind in the city, under the leadership of *ser* Scherlatto. They appealed that they should have their rights to possession of their property restored 'summarily, without clamour and the form of ordinary trial procedure' by *ser* Scherlatto, Lucca's *capitano di custodia*, because it was not fair and was wrong that the returnees should have to be deprived of their property in their absence.[13] However, the end of the citizens' complaint includes a proviso to the effect that the current occupiers of the property in question might also argue their own rights in another *ordinary trial*. From the opposite perspective, this proviso seems to indicate the difficulty of proving rights in ordinary trials and the ease of acquiring rights through summary justice.

This was different from the decisions taken under Florentine rule, seen previously, in that here the authority for summary justice was given to one person, *ser* Scherlatto. A decree issued on 21 September 1342 in the form of a supplement to a decree of 25 August the same year stipulated that *ser* Scherlatto could conduct hearings and make decisions *de iure et de facto*, and it empowered him to make decisions as he saw fit, any provisions to the contrary notwithstanding, for the sake of the good and peaceful state of the commune of Pisa and Lucca.[14] Here we can see an instance of a foreign judicial official being granted significant *arbitrium*.

And so the following question arises: who exactly was this *ser* Scherlatto and why was he allowed to wield such authority? Apparently, he had been sent from Pisa bearing the titles of '*capitano di custodia* of Lucca' and '*conservatore* for the good and peaceful state of the commune of Lucca and its territory', these being administrative posts second only to the vicar in Lucca under Pisan rule. His authority as the former was officially granted by the Anziani on 2 September 1342, and his appointment as the latter took place on 23 November the same year,[15] the same day that he was appointed to the position of 'administrator for rebels and their property'. While his association with lawsuits for the restitution of property will be clear from this last title, his first two positions as *capitano di custodia* and *conservatore* are the titles that best characterise the extent of his authority.

The authority that *ser* Scherlatto was granted as *capitano di custodia* included his possession of 'free and general discretion' (*liberum et generale arbitrium*) for the sake of peace in the Lucchese territory along with his mandate, together with two mounted offi-

---

13 *Anz. Av. Lib.*, 18, fols. 10v-11r: 'Quare supplicatur humiliter vobis quatenus vobis placeat stantiare et ordinare quod tales cives Lucani et alii sic reversi ad civitatem Lucanam et ad obbedientiam et mandata Lucani communis, debeant reponi summarie sine strepitu et figura iudicii per ser Scherlactum capitaneum custodie civitatis Lucane in possessionem dictorum domorum hedificiorum bonorum et terrarum, non obstantibus aliquibus stantiamentis, ordinamentis vel aliis in contrarium editis, quibuscumque salvo et reservato cuilibet possessori seu detentori dictorum bonorum, omni suo iure in alio ordinario iudicio, cum non sit equum nec iustum quod dicti cives Lucani et alii sic reverse taliter sint spoliati et privati eorum bonis in eorum absentia...'

14 *Anz. Av. Lib.*, 18, fol. 11r: 'ser Scherlactus maior officialis Lucane custodie possit cognoscere, et ea omnia decidere et terminare, et in eis procedere de iure et de facto et prout et sicut sibi videbitur et placuerit pro bono et pacifico statu utriusque communi pisarum et Luce, aliqua contrarietate non obstante'.

15 On the occasion of his appointment on 23 November, we find a record listing him as *conservatore* in order that the custodial office be strengthened. *Anz. Av. Lib.*, 18, fol. 61v.

cials, to arrest and punish *banniti*, bandits, enemies of Lucca or Pisa, and those who gave them shelter.[16] Furthermore, it was stipulated that rulings by the *capitano di custodia* could not be appealed and were not subject to audit. In contrast, in his appointment as *conservatore, ser* Scherlatto was allowed, in accordance with the sovereignty, jurisdiction, official authority, discretion, and provisions received from the commune of Pisa, to execute his duties in Lucca and its territories.[17] The reason that the Lucchese Anziani granted *ser* Scherlatto permission to observe summary procedures in lawsuits involving the restitution of property was that *ser* Scherlatto had arrived in Lucca invested with such considerable authority from Pisa.

I would also like to note that Scherlatto's use of summary procedure in lawsuits involving the restitution of property had been requested by the citizenry and then authorised by the Anziani on 25 August 1342, which *predated* his official investiture as *capitano di custodia* and *conservatore* (on 2 September and 23 November, respectively). In the complaint from the citizens, *ser* Scherlatto was already addressed as '*capitano di custodia* of Lucca', so the citizens would have been aware that he had been granted some kind of authority by Pisa.[18] However, as citizens living in the chaotic period when Pisan rule began, their call for a foreign administrator without any clear authority to be granted discretionary powers and to be allowed to adopt extraordinary measures, constituted an opportunity to expand the scope of *ser* Scherlatto's duties and authority, and at the very least provided a reason that legitimised his extraordinary activities.

The permission to observe summary justice for the restitution of property to rebels in decrees issued on 19 June and 25 August 1342 could hardly have been overlooked by those in possession of such properties and especially by those claiming the right to legal possession, as it also allowed them to hold on to the possibility of claiming rights in an ordinary trial. It seems that such an action would have required considerable labour and expense to prove one's entitlement while addressing an opponent's defence.

On 4 September the same year, at the council, it was pointed out that a large number of grievances had been brought against these two decisions under the Pisan vicar, Dino, and the Lucchese Anziani, and that countermeasures would be required, as numerous disputes and scandals could occur if they were not corrected.[19] The amendment made in response by the vicar and the Anziani, with advice from *sapientes*, was the aforementioned supplementary provision added on 21 September confirming the granting of discretionary powers to *ser* Scherlatto. While slight amendments were

16 *Anz. Av. Lib.*, 18, fols. 14r-15r.

17 *Anz. Av. Lib.*, 18, fol. 61v: 'cum baylia iurisdictione officio et arbitrio capitulis e provisionibus que quas et quos et prout et sic habet a communi pisano in civitate pisana et eius comitatu et districtu, et prout et sic in civitate pisana, ex quacumque baylia et officio capitulis et provisionibus facere et excerere potest, ita in civitate Lucana eius comitatu, fortia et districtu facere et excere possit…'

18 The first office that can be confirmed for *ser* Scherlatto in Lucca was a notice on 6 July 1342 to summon territorial communities and city block officials before the officials of roads. S. Bongi (ed.), *Bandi Lucchesi*, p. 92-93.

19 *Anz. Av. Lib.*, 18, fols. 16r-v: 'cum propter stantiamentum factum de mense iunii proximi preteriti super restitutione bonorum fienda Lucanis civibus reversis qui se absentaverunt pro parte guelfa, et propter aliud stantiamentum de novo factum super restitutione fienda reversis qui se absentaverunt pro parte gebellina, multe querele facte sint domino Dino della Roccha vicario domini contis raynerii in civitate Lucana… et multe lites proprea insurrixerint et insurgant, et multa scandala insurrgere possint nisi aliter reformentur et moderentur…'

made to the effect that summary justice would not be applied to the restitution of property to rebels from the Guelph faction, there were basically no major changes, and *ser* Scherlatto was authorised to execute summary decisions for the sake of peace in Pisa and Lucca. The importance of this September decree can be confirmed from the fact that the wording of the supplemental provision from 21 September was appended without revision to the end of the provision 'regarding the cancellation of *bannum* and the restitution of returnees' property' in the city statutes compiled on 30 November 1342.[20]

The exceptional measure of bestowing on *ser* Scherlatto, a foreign judicial official, discretionary powers regarding civil cases that also involved the rights of citizens – an inconceivable thought under the communal judicial system – could only have occurred in the chaotic period during the transition from Florentine to Pisan rule and in a sphere involving the politically fraught issue of rebels' property. Above all, the turmoil wrought in Lucchese society by the siege of Lucca between 1341 and 1342 would have been sufficiently anomalous, requiring and justifying the extraordinary measures. During the same period, further extraordinary measures were taken in the form of an amnesty on 2 July and the extinguishing of all ongoing lawsuits on 25 August.[21] The measure of permitting *ser* Scherlatto, a lone judicial official who had come to Lucca to resolve this confusion, to conduct summary trials in civil cases, can likewise be positioned as one of these emergency measures.

2. Maintenance of Territorial Security by the *Bargello*

(1) Maintaining security in territorial districts under Pisan rule

Among the chief duties carried out by *ser* Scherlatto, along with lawsuits involving the restitution of rebel property, were the arrest and punishment of *banniti*, bandits, and the enemies of Pisa and Lucca in order to maintain peace in Lucca's territorial districts. Details of his actual activities in the territory can be seen from the extant records of his convictions. Over the four months from November 1342 to February 1343, he prosecuted 74 convictions (involving 96 individuals) for crimes including the bearing of arms, gambling with dice, and the failure to denounce criminals by rural communes.[22]

Scherlatto's activities can also be seen indirectly from the records of the Anziani. A record dated 15 August 1343 describes the conviction and imprisonment by *ser* Scherlatto of a Brescia-born man named Bresciano for the crime of conspiring with Altino, a son of Castruccio, and of Ugo, a resident of the Florentine territory, for

---

20 ASL, *Statuto del Comune di Lucca*, 5 (hereafter *Statuto 1342*), V, 64 (De cancellatione bannorum et de restitutione bonorum reversorum), fols. 117r-118r.

21 General amnesty also covered rebels who would normally be exempt. *Anz. Av. Lib.*, 17, fols. 35v-38v. On the suspension of lawsuits, see *Anz. Av. Lib*, 18, fols. 8r-v.

22 ASL, *Capitano del Contado*, 1; S. Bongi (ed.), *Inventario del Reale Archivio di Stato in Lucca*, II (Lucca, 1876), p. 388. The targets of this crackdown were primarily people living in the territory. We find only a few convictions for Lucchese citizens.

instigating a fight.[23] Furthermore, on 29 November the same year we find mention of a conviction handed out by *ser* Scherlatto for an incident wherein a Lucchese citizen named Cecchorino disputed with one Coluccino.[24] From the record, unfortunately, we cannot know the nature of the procedure actually followed in the trial. Information on *ser* Scherlatto finally disappears as of 15 October 1346, when he appears before the Lucchese Anziani to tender his resignation and step down from his post.[25]

The provision investing *ser* Scherlatto with authority as *capitano di custodia* ends with the proviso that the *podestà*'s jurisdiction and duties shall not be excluded as regards the above provision, and the *podestà* shall be able to conduct hearings and punishments regarding the foregoing [security maintenance activities] in accordance with Lucca's city statutes.[26] As the jurisdiction of the *capitano di custodia* overlapped that of the *podestà*, the institution of the *capitano di custodia* served to strengthen the area of security maintenance, which had previously been executed by the *podestà* single-handedly. His dispatch by Pisa would have been a means of quelling the state of confusion immediately after the institution of its rule.

The next time information appears with regard to the *capitano di custodia* is in the context of provisions in August and October of 1352. On this occasion, the authority for maintaining security in the city and in the territorial districts that had been borne by the *capitano di custodia* in 1342 was divided, with the city being entrusted to the *capitano di custodia* as *conservatore*[27] and the territorial districts to a new foreign judicial official called the *bargello*.[28] This division of official duties was intended to establish a judicial officer specialising in maintaining territorial security. Pisa's epistolary interventions in the appointment of the *conservatore* and *bargello* seem to suggest that the reforms to the area of security maintenance were carried out under Pisan direction.

The decade of the 1350s, when the office of *bargello* was instituted, was ravaged by population decline brought on by the Great Plague, famine, and war. The Lucchese and Pisan leaders naturally paid attention to the territorial districts that served as the food supply. In 1353 and 1354, the commune of Lucca surveyed grain reserves in its territorial districts.[29] The miserable conditions in the districts are suggested by the large

---

23 *Anz. Av. Lib.*, 21, fol. 21r: 'Brescianus de Brescia condennatus in libris.cc. denariorum ex officio ser Scherlatti Capitanei custodie civitatis Lucane quia ipse sotiavit Altinum condam domini Kastruccii de Antelminellis…, et Ugo vannis de sancto Caxiano comitatu florentie contra quem proceditur ex dicto offitio quia ipse Ugo venit ad rixam cum condam Baracterio et cetera'. Then, the Anziani ordered *ser* Scherlatto's officials to release these two men at the festival of the Virgin Mary.

24 *Anz. Av. Lib.*, 21, fol. 69r: 'ipse condemnatus ex officio ser Scherlatti pro lite quam habuit cum Coluccino neri Lucano cive…'

25 *Anz. Av. Lib.*, 18, fol. 72r: 'ser Scherlactus suprascriptus existens coram dominis Antianis Lucani communis… renuntiavit dicto officio conservatorie, dicens et protestans se in eo nolle ulterius esse…'. This note has been inserted after the description of *ser* Scherlatto's appointment.

26 *Anz. Av. Lib.*, 18, fol. 14v: 'Et quod per predictam non intelligatur esse derogatum offitio et iurisdictioni domini Lucane potestatis, qui potestas possit etiam de predictis cognoscere, procedere et punire secundum formam statuti Lucani communis'.

27 Francesco became *conservatore* on 22 August. *Anz. Av. Lib.*, 34, fols. 52v-54v.

28 On 31 October, this position is held by the notary *ser* Filippo. *Anz. Av. Lib.*, 34, fol. 63v-65v. The official charged with the security of the territory is also called 'the captain of *contado*' or the 'official in charge of *banniti*'.

29 ASL, *Offizio sopra L'abbondanza*, 379.

number of petitions for tax exemptions issued by rural communes, which lamented the decline of the population due to plague and war. Another factor further exacerbating the situation in the territory was the existence of *banniti*.

Banniti hindered production activities in the territorial districts in two ways. One was caused by *bannum* sentenced by urban courts, which led labourers to leave their villages. For example, according to a complaint to the Anziani from the rural commune of San Gennaro, a dispute between families resulted in those involved being sentenced to *bannum*. Then, the families' lands had been left fallow because of their departure from their rural community.[30] The measure to combat this situation was to encourage reconciliation among the parties to the dispute and to bring them back under the protection of the law by extinguishing their conviction and *bannum*.

The second impact of the *banniti* was that they sometimes formed gangs that disturbed the peace and laid waste to the countryside. The later fourteenth century in particular, as I pointed out in the previous chapter, was a time when Lucca was being invaded by the armies of foreign powers, a circumstance wherein the *banniti* could pose a risk factor by allying themselves with the enemy. The method for dealing in such cases with *banniti* who had become outlaws was to actively seek their arrest. This was the role of the *bargello*. This is an apparent change from traditional forms of punishment based on *bannum*. Those subject to *bannum* were normally placed outside the protection of communal laws, a state wherein anyone might commit violence against their person without being charged with a crime. As such, it was a sentence that entrusted the employment of sanctions to society and its inhabitants. This time, however, rather than abandon the *banniti*, the commune began to undertake policing measures by beginning to pursue them into the territorial districts and arrest them. Here we can observe a change in the commune that took on an active character after the mid-fourteenth century.[31]

(2) Duty provisions and the authority of the bargello

The official duties of the *bargello*, who was responsible for maintaining security in the territory, were stipulated in a provision dating to 31 October 1352, which held that the *bargello* was to visit the territorial districts with his followers to arrest *banniti* as well as vagabonds, the infamous, those guilty of enormous wrongs (*enormia maleficia*), miscreants, and anyone attempting to disturb the peaceful state of the city and territorial districts of Lucca, and to bring them before the vicar and officials of Lucca

30 *Anz. Av. Lib.*, 35, fols. 9r-v: 'multi de dicto communi banniti fuerunt et sunt Lucani communis, propter que banna tam ipsi banniti et eorum familie quam eorum consanguinei et partiales et coherentes eorum se absetaverunt a dicto communi et toto districtu et fortia Lucana… et terre remaserunt inculte et devastate…'

31 It is also worth noting that such an attitude on the part of the commune was evident not only in Lucca but also in Florence during the same period, L. Tanzini, 'Costruire e controllare il territorio. Banditi e repressione penale nello stato fiorentino del Trecento', in L. Antonielli and S. Levati (eds.), *Controllare il territorio: norme, corpi e conflitti tra Medioevo e prima guerra mondiale* (Catanzaro, 2013), p. 11-30.

for sentencing and punishment.[32] This policing activity was the main function of the *bargello*.

At the same time, the *bargello* also had jurisdiction over those found gambling or bearing arms in the territorial districts. The duty provisions for the office included a detailed list of prohibited weapons and fines. In addition, the *bargello* was authorised to use torture, and was given *arbitrium* to make convictions up to a limit of up to 10 *lire* depending on the seriousness of the crime. At the end of his official duties, he had to be audited by the Sindaco.

Compared to the powers conferred upon *ser* Scherlatto as *conservatore* in 1342, the limited extent of the *bargello*'s authority is obvious. Perhaps because *ser* Scherlatto had been dispatched for the purpose of stabilising security in the immediate aftermath of the establishment of Pisan rule, he was an extraordinary figure with the authority to render judgement with *liberum et generale arbitrium* and was not subject to audit by the Sindaco. In contrast, the *bargello* of 1352 had no such characteristics; the extent of his authority was also limited to punishments of 10 *lire* or less and the office had diminished to specialising in the capture of *banniti* and others who disturbed the peace. The 1352 provision lacked the wordings available in the 1342 provision, which had been cautious of and thus restrained infringement by the *bargello* on the *podestà*'s jurisdiction. This would be proof of the *bargello*'s comparatively reduced jurisdiction.

However, while the *bargello*'s authority was largely restricted in the duty provisions, it seems that this was in fact reflective of an expansion in the scope of his actual activities. Being relieved of his official duties in the city itself enabled the *bargello* to make frequent forays into the territorial districts to conduct his policing activities. The clarification of the scope of his official duties and the limitations on his discretion in the duty provisions can be seen as evidence that the *bargello* became an increasingly productive and active presence, as well as important to the resulting need to control the high-handedness and corruption that were a consequence thereof. Moreover, as we shall see below, the *bargello* in the 1350s and 1360s had in fact become more active than before.

(3) Activities of the bargello

The activities of the *bargello* during the period of Pisan rule can be seen from registers kept for the collection of fines[33] and petitions to the Anziani for pardons (*gratia*).

---

32 *Anz. Av. Lib.*, 34, fol. 64r: 'officialis suprascriptus vigore sui officii teneatur et debeat per se et familiam suam per comitatum et districtum Lucanum sollicite ire capiendo et capere omnes et singulos bannitos Lucani communis, et etiam omnes et singulos vagabundos et infames et enormia maleficia comictentes et homines male conditionis et vite, et turbantes et turbare volentes pacificum statum Lucane civitatis et districti et contra ipsum statum obloquentes… representare seu representari et poni facere in fortiam dominorum Rectorum et officialium Lucani communis et Pisani communis luce morantium'.

33 Although only entries for revenues from fine-collection survive in the *bargello*'s register for this period, these do include references to other registers: 'A Filippo Gentilis… secundum libro ser Francisci folio.xviiii. habuit dicto anno Antelminellus suprascriptus pro Puccino Jamboni camerario suprascripto pro Lucano comuni recipienti libros quinque bone monete', ASL, *Capitano del Contado*, 7, no foliation, 13 March 1361.

The man who held the post of *bargello* from 1358 to 1363 was a notary by the name of *ser* Giovanni da Rassignano.[34] He was first and foremost engaged in the arrest and imprisonment of *banniti* as per the terms of his duty provisions. One petition to the Anziani, for example, concerned a man named Coluccino Paruei, who, as we saw in Chapter 4, had been subjected to a *bannum* of 300 *lire* by the *podestà* for abetting a murderer; it was claimed that he had been detained by the *bargello* and placed in prison, where he would now be dying of poverty.

From fine-collection registers we know that the *bargello* exercised his jurisdiction and actually made convictions. A record from 1359 reveals a total of 211 convictions for the year, 160 cases against individuals (involving 192 people) and 51 against local communities (involving 53 communities).[35] Even though details of the associated crimes are not listed in the above mentioned registers, we are able to know of the cases judged by the *bargello* only indirectly from the petitions by convicts before the Anziani.[36] Among these, we can confirm that the *bargello* issued convictions for harbouring *banniti* (5 cases), failure to denounce (1 case), bearing arms (1 case), and disobedience of orders (3 cases).[37] However, the convictions issued by *ser* Giovanni as *bargello* were not solely within the scope of these duty provisions. The *bargello* also issued convictions for cases of injuries and threat (8 cases), property damage (1 case), the killing of livestock (1 case), unauthorised land use (2 cases), and escape (1 case), all offences not included in the *bargello*'s jurisdiction as defined in the duty provisions. These were cases that rightly belonged under the *podestà*'s jurisdiction. This is the reason why we often find in the complaints from convicts instances calling for the elimination of double convictions by the *podestà* and *bargello*.

The disjuncture between the 1352 duty provisions and the actual activities of the *bargello* are further clarified in the context of fines imposed by the *bargello*. According to the duty provisions, the upper limit of such fines was set at 10 *lire*, and in fact when we look at the fine-collection register, we find many cases involving the imposition of small fines. In 1359, out of 211 cases, 89 fines were for sums of 5 *lire* or less and 78 were for sums of 5-10 *lire*. However, the remaining 44 cases exceeded the limit set by the duty provisions and some cases had fines imposed of 35 or even 50 *lire*.[38] Such cases

34 The post of *bargello* was held by *ser* Giovanni da Rasignano from 1358 through 1363. Before him, Bongi notes that Francesco Castroni was *bargello* in 1356. Bongi (ed.), *Inventario*, II, p. 388. On 8 Feburary 1354, a complaint was raised by a community that had been charged by the *bargello* for not catching *banniti*. The name of the *bargello* in this instance is not revealed.

35 ASL, *Capitano del Contado*, 4, 5.

36 Petitions to the Anziani by convicted parties seeking *gratia* for convictions and *bannum* handed out by the *bargello*, for example, accounted for 5 of a total 18 petitions brought by convicts in 1358 and 9 of the 33 brought in 1361.

37 Of these, only 'bearing arms' fell within the authority granted under the terms of the 1352 duty provisions. However, as the other cases mentioned above can also be seen in the authority delegated to *ser* Scherlatto in 1342 as *capitano di custodia* and in trials actually conducted by *ser* Scherlatto, it could be said that they fell within the existing scope of activities carried out by officials responsible for security in the territory.

38 ASL, *Capitano del Contado*, 4. A fine of 35 *lire* was collected from Lupolino Dossi on 30 April and a fine of 50 *lire* was collected in florins from the commune of Colle di Compito on 27 May.

are frequently seen in the petitions to the Anziani, as well, such as fines of 100 *lire* for charges of theft, of 40 *lire* for injuries, or of 100 *lire* for harbouring *banniti*[39]

That *ser* Giovanni's activities as *bargello* during this period violated the provisions of his duty can also be confirmed in terms of trial hearings. Moreover it is here, rather, that convicts set their sights in their appeals for *gratia*. Massario Coluccini, charged with the crime of killing another person's livestock, as discussed in Chapter 3, Section 3, appealed the conviction that the *bargello* had passed in spite of Massario' protestation of innocence based on the claim that he had killed the livestock on his land, that he was working himself, citing the provision in the statutes '*de dannis datis cum bestiis macellatoriis et cetera*'. In another example, the brothers Nucco and Lessio, charged with the crime of carrying illicit weapons, appealed by bringing a complaint that they had been convicted even though they had in fact received permission from the *bargello* himself.[40] The fact that they were convicted and not subjected to *bannum* for contumacy proves that they attended their hearing, most likely to attempt to make the rational argument presented above. Why might their voices not have been heard by the *bargello*?

Dinello, who was sentenced to a fine of 25 *lire* for harbouring *banniti*, raised an interesting argument in his petition. That is, at his trial he stated that he was not allowed to defend himself sufficiently as the law required and that *ser* Giovanni's official duties were conducted arbitrarily, such that due process and the law were not observed at all during his trial.[41] This suggests that the *bargello*'s trials did not give defendants the right to a defence, which ordinary legal proceedings would normally guarantee, which is to say that the trial was actually conducted using a summary procedure not listed in the duty provisions. Antonio Baldi, too, the man fined 100 *lire* for allegedly escaping from the grasp of the *bargello*'s servants – discussed in the Chapter 3 – had lamented that his conviction by the *bargello* was done 'abruptly and *de facto*, without respecting either *iuris ordine* or the statutes of Lucca'.[42]

A surviving register from 1372 describes the trials prosecuted by the *bargello*. While details of allegations and confessions, among other facts, are described in an abbreviated manner compared to the criminal court records of the *podestà*, it is noted that a period of time was provided for a defence, and it is shown that the procedure was carried out legitimately.[43] It is hard to say whether the truth of the *bargello*'s actual activities are

39 While it is also possible that a new provision was enacted separately after that of 1352, when we consider that the upper limit for fines is set at 50 *lire* in the revised duty provisions of 1370 it is clear that the *bargello* was in fact engaged in activities that far exceeded the remit of his official duties.

40 *Anz. Av. Lib.*, 42, fol. 54r: 'condemnatio facta fuit per dictum ser Johannem per errorem quia ipsi et quilibet eorum habebant licentiam a dicto ser Johanne portandi queque arma…'

41 *Anz. Av. Lib.*, 41, fol. 24r: 'ad plenum ut iura volunt suam defensionem non fecerit… considerato quod officium ser Johannis est arbitrarium et in processibus et aliis non servantur omnino stricta iura…'

42 *Anz. Av. Lib.*, 41, fols. 122v-123r: '[…] ex arrupto et de facto nullo iuris ordine servato nec aliquibus statutis Lucani communis…'

43 ASL, *Capitano del Contado*, 15, fol. 5r: 'Super quibus omnibus et singulis et cetera. Qui inquisiti et quilibet ipsorum coram me *bargello* personaliter constituti et cetera, respondendo dictum inquisitionem sponte confessi fuerunt et cetera, quibus datum fuit terminum ad defensionem dicta die et sequenti et cetera alias et cetera'.

shown in the activities, in line with legal procedure, that appear in the court records or in the summary procedures conveyed by the convicts' petitions to the Anziani.

However, what I would like us to note is that the complaints in petitions levelled at the injustices of summary procedure are never seen against convictions by the *podestà*, but only against those by the *bargello*. These petitions are rife with rhetorical flourishes, often exaggerating and distorting the facts. However, because petitions appealing the injustices of summary procedure are only seen against the *bargello*, the *bargello* was perceived as someone who conducted extraordinary hearings that the *podestà* did not, which at least shows an assumption on the part of the petitioners that the Anziani and councillors viewed the *bargello* in this light.

(4) Arbitrium *granted to the* bargello

The *bargello*, whose actions superseded both the duty provisions of his office and the general statutes, was ostensibly held in check by the eyes of the *Maior Sindaco*. However, the *Maior Sindaco* records appear devoid of any mention of the *bargello*.

Information relating to corrupt practices on the part of the *bargello* certainly reached the Anziani. Even in the complaints that we saw earlier, the illegality of his activities was conveyed to the Anziani, but an even graver issue was brought to the attention of the Anziani by a petition from 1352. In the petition, it was alleged that a man named Pardino had paid the *bargello* a bribe of 10 florins to release one Andrea, who had been arrested as part of an assassination conspiracy. Furthermore, it was pointed out that this behaviour had created a cause undermining justice and corrupting the *bargello*.[44]

Accordingly, the *bargello*'s excessive activities reached the ears of the Anziani any number of times. Nevertheless, the *bargello*'s extra-legal behaviour did not prove to be a major problem and this is evident when *ser* Giovanni continued to hold the office of *bargello* during this period. Here, we can assume that political powers were at work beyond the law and the powers of auditors.

It was the Pisan government and the Lucchese Anziani who pretended not to have seen the *bargello*'s activities that extended beyond his authority, and who possibly also prevented the *Maior Sindaco* from checking such activities. To achieve their original goal of establishing a position to maintain security in their territorial districts, the political authorities in both cities gave the *bargello* free rein in his activities, strongly supporting the suppression of unwanted behaviour in the districts. In other words, the Anziani and others granted the *bargello* an *implicit arbitrium*. And if the *bargello* mistakenly harassed good 'subjects' as the result of overzealous behaviour, the Anziani were able to choose good 'subjects' to save in the form of answering their petitions with *gratia*.

Therefore, the *arbitrium* that the *bargello* wielded *de facto* from the late 1350s to the early 1360s was superficially similar to but substantially different from the '*liberum et generale arbitrium*' that was *de iure* granted to *ser* Scherlatto as *capitano di custodia* in

44 *Anz. Av. Lib.*, 34, fol. 75v: 'Ipse Pardinus causa subvertendi iustitiam et ipsum Barigellum corrupendi obtulit et dedit dicto *bargello* florenos decem ut ipse Andreas detentus a dicto Barigello relaxaretur et cetera…'

1342. Whereas the latter was a judicial official who had truly acquired his own authority and conducted his activities autonomously, the *arbitrium* acquired by the *bargello* was a freedom granted *implicitly* by the city's political and administrative bodies and thus could be restricted at any time. Here we can see the feature of foreign judicial officials being strongly dependent on the city's political authorities.

(5) Expansion of the bargello's *authority in the republican period*

After Lucca was liberated from Pisa by Holy Roman Emperor Charles IV between August and September of 1368, and then through the tenure of Cardinal Guy of Boulogne from 7 February 1369, Lucca formally achieved independence on 12 March 1370 when the Lucchese Anziani accepted the title of imperial vicars by the Lucchese Anziani. The creation of the new regime had already begun on the eve of independence. In addition to the reorganisation on 2 February 1370 of the city's administrative divisions from five to three, on 16 February it was decided that one of the ten Anziani would be chosen as a Gonfaloniere di Giustizia with responsibility for such matters as accepting outside messengers and making proposals to the council.

Under these circumstances, a new provision concerning the *bargello* was issued on 11 March 1370.[45] Several changes will become apparent in comparison with the 1352 provision. To begin with, the retinue that the *bargello* was able to enlist was specified as being twenty infantry soldiers, four horses, and three riders. Under the *bargello*'s authority, the maximum fine that the *bargello* was able to impose at his own discretion was raised from 10 *lire* to 50 *lire*.[46] For crimes meriting bodily punishments, however, prisoners should be transferred to the custody of the *podestà*. Also, it was specified that the *bargello* would not be charged even in the case of someone's accidental injury or death arising in an attempted arrest, thereby allowing him to act aggressively and forcefully.

Interesting here is the specification that the *bargello* was empowered to sentence *banniti*, those committing *maleficia*, and those not obeying the *bargello*'s orders (up to 25 *lira*) 'in a summary manner and *de facto*, without heeding the strictures and the substance of the law'.[47] This is a marked difference from the 1352 provision, and we can see here a clear-cut affirmation of procedural discretion. Moreover, the *bargello* was able to carry out any and all matters entrusted to him by the Anziani, and when doing so, he could act in summary fashion, ignoring the strictures of the law so as not to invalidate the efficacy of his operations by some inadvertent mistake, and could resort to torture at his own discretion.[48] Although these powers did not extend to Lucchese citizens,

---

45 A. Romiti (ed.), *Riformagioni della repubblica di Lucca (1369-1400)*, I (Roma, 1980), p. 252-255.

46 Incidentally, in a provision concerning the *bargello* dated 7 July 1373, the upper limit for fines was increased to 60 *lire*. G. Tori (ed.), *Riformagioni della repubblica di Lucca (1369-1400)*, IV (Roma, 1998), p. 209.

47 Romiti (ed.), *Riformagioni*, I, p. 253-254: 'contra quos et quemlibet eorum procedere possit et eos punire et condepnare summarie et de facto, nulla iuris solennitate vel substantialitate servata…'

48 Romiti (ed.), *Riformagioni*, p. 254: 'Item quod possit et debeat facere et esequi omnia et singula que et prout sibi de cetero comitti contigerit per dominos Antianos Lucani Comunis. Et predicta omnia et singula sibi comissa, ut supra dictus offitialis facere et explicare possit summarie et de facto, sine aliqua solennitate vel substantialitate iuris

the limitation did not apply in the case of *banniti* or exceptional cases of individuals committed to the *bargello* by the Anziani. Now that it had become officially possible for him to act freely in this way, unchecked by the law, the *bargello* was also beyond the scope of an audit. The final wording with respect to auditing appended to the 1352 provision does not exist in the 1370 provision.

Although the matters newly stipulated in 1370, such as the sentencing of fines up to 50 *lira*, trials for those who commit *maleficia*, and summary procedures, were elements that were not set out in the 1352 duty provisions, they were frequently seen among the *bargello's* activities, as glimpsed from the petitions to the Anziani. In other words, the 1370 provision may have been formulated to encapsulate the accumulated experience of the *bargello*'s actual activities since the 1350s. However, because they were clearly stated, and especially because formal approval was given to summary procedures, they held significance as a legal endorsement of the *bargello*'s subsequent extra-legal activities. Even so, the fact that this *arbitrium* was not a sign of autonomy, as it had been for *ser* Scherlatto, is expressed in the addition of the new element of acting on the instructions of the Anziani. The *bargello* was clearly positioned here as an 'enforcer' who was subordinate to and who moved at the bidding of the Anziani.

4. The *Podestà* and the Anziani in the Republican Period

(1) Arbitrium *granted to the* podestà

The *bargello,* as a foreign judicial official, was not the only person given *arbitrium* in terms of fine amounts or legal proceedings. During the republican period, such freedom of discretion was granted by the Anziani to the *podestà* as well.

It is worth remembering that the *podestà,* unlike the more recently instituted *bargello,* was a traditional commune official. In the thirteenth century, the *podestà* had wielded political, judicial, and military authority, but in order to balance this great power the official had remained obligated to comply with the city statutes. Chapter 1 of Book 1 of Lucca's 1308 city statutes, which had been in force during the *popolo* period, was entitled 'On the oath of the Great Ruler of Lucca (*Maius Lucanum Regimen*) and his followers'. This was the oath, written in the first person, sworn by the *podestà* as 'Great Ruler' when taking office, when the *podestà* would place his hands on the statutes and

---

ita quod propter defectus alicuius solennitatis vel substantialitatis omisse vel iuris ordine non servato vitiari vel annuallari sive infringi non possint aliquo modo. Et etiam possit facere torqueri et poni ad cellam et tormentari quoscunque sibi videbitur de predictis'.

Table 6.2: Matters considered in this section and in Chapter 5, Section 4 (Anz. = Anziani; Cons. = General Council)

Matters considered in Chapter 5, Section 4	**Dates**	**Matters considered in this section**
	1368, Aug.	Lucca liberated from Pisa
Amnesty by Charles IV	1369, Jul. 31	
	1370, Mar. 11	Revision of duty provisions for the *bargello*
	1370, Mar. 12	Charles IV invests the Lucchese Anz. to the office of imperial vicars
Proposal about the prohibition of *gratia*	1370, May 10	
Provision about the prohibition of *gratia*	1370, May 23	
Condemnation of the members of the Antelminelli family	1370, Jun. 1	.
	1370, Jul. 31	Establishment of a *popolo* regime
	1370, Sep.	Unrest caused by Giovanni degli Obizzi
	1370, Nov. 9	Proposal to Cons.: Regarding the identity of the Great Ruler ⇒ the *podestà* is the Great Ruler
Proposal to Cons. to suspend the provision prohibiting *gratia* on the occasion of the peace agreement with the communes of Garfagnana	1370, Nov. 13	
Proposal to Cons. to suspend the provision prohibiting *gratia* on the occasion of the peace agreement with the Antelminelli family	1371, Mar. 16	
Pardoning of members of the Antelminelli family	1371, Apr. 11	
	1371, Apr. 17	Anz.: freedom of discretion granted to the *podestà*
	1371, Apr. 28	Supplement to the 4.17 provision: 'extra-judicially, militarily'
	1372, Jul.	city statute reforms
Proposal to Cons. to suspend the prohibition of *gratia* to provide an amnesty for *banniti* who had fought against Corrado	1374, Mar. 3	
	1374, Dec. 2	Anz.: freedom of discretion granted to the *podestà*
	1383, Jun. 29	Anz.: freedom of discretion granted to the *podestà*

pledge to rule without any impropriety.[49] And when stepping down from the position, an audit of his official duties would be carried out based on the statutes.[50]

It was properly the *podestà* to whom the Anziani granted the discretion to authorise deviations from the law. Let us review some examples, keeping in mind that this began to take place in the uncertain environment of the first days of Lucca's independence as a republic.

The first instance wherein *arbitrium* was granted to the *podestà* was with a provision issued on 17 April 1371. Entrusted with authority by the General Council, the Anziani and a committee of eighteen wise men first described their motivation to grant such a discretion as follows:

> For the good state, tranquility, and quiet of the city of Lucca and its territories, and in order that the matter to be badly used might be removed from vagabonds, and that the recklessness of scelerats might be checked by the fear of punishment, and it is clearly recognised that it would be opportune for the republic to be reinforced with new laws.

With this motivation, it was decided that the incumbent *podestà*, Francesco of Spoleto, during his term of office,

> would be able, at his discretion, to condemn and punish any crime, exceeding the sum of the fines fixed by the laws and statutes of the commune of Lucca, up to a hundred florins of gold for any crime, by taking into account the nature of the crime and the condition of the offender.[51]

Additionally, this *arbitrium* was accompanied by the proviso that it could not be rescinded, except through a vote by the Anziani and Gonfaloniere di Giustizia.[52]

While the above resolution stipulated *arbitrium* concerning the amount of a fine, a supplemental decision on 28 April 1371 also enabled the sitting *podestà* to conduct legal proceedings in a summary manner. It was designated that the *podestà*

49 S. Bongi (ed.), *Statuto del comune di Lucca dell'anno MCCCVIII* (Lucca 1867) (hereafter *Statuto 1308*), I, 1, De iuramento Maioris Lucani Regiminis et sue familie: 'Ego Maius Lucanum regimen iuro ad sancta Dei Evangelia, corporaliter tacto libro super libro Statutorum Lucani Comunis, bona fide, sine fraude vel aliquo ingenio, toto posse regere, defendere, salvare, custodire atque gubernare Lucanam civitatem, districtum, comitatum et fortiam'... An audit of duties was mandatory upon his resignation from the post.

50 In fact, the *Maior Sindaco*'s registers also record that an audit of the *podestà* was conducted. ASL, *Maggior sindaco e giudice degli appelli*.

51 G. Tori (ed.), *Riformagioni della repubblica di Lucca (1369-1400)*, II (Roma, 1985), p. 196: 'pro bono statu et tranquillitate, atque quiete Lucane Civitatis eiusque comitatus et fortie, et ut crassatoribus tollatur materia deliquendi et penarum metu scelestorum temeritas reprimatur,... ac oportuum fore dignoscitur, novis legibus Rem Publicam roborare, decernimus et ... providemus... quod magnificus et egregius miles dominus Franciscus de Spoleto, com[es] de Campello, presens Potests Civitatis Lucane, possit ad suum arbitrium condemnare et punire quemlibet delinquentem... ultra penas iuris vel statutorum Lucani Comunis... considerata qualitate delicti et conditione persone usque in summam florenorum centum auri ipsis ...toto tempore sue potestarie presenti arbitrio duraturo...'

52 Tori (ed.), *Riformagioni*, II, p. 196: 'Que autoritas et balia, arbitrium atque potestas eidem quacunque autoritate auferri, removeri, tolli, suspendi vel impediri non possit quomodocumque vel qualitercunque nisi expresse fuerit obtentum inter dominos Antinos et Vexilliferum Justitie...'

> shall be able to proceed the trials *de fact*, and extra-judicially and militarily, without the clamour and the form of ordinary trial procedure, and to execute convictions as he sees fit by his word alone, without documents, and without observing the strictures, rituals, style or even the substance of laws and statutes.[53]

Here we see that the *podestà* had been given a considerable degree of discretion. He was able to execute a sentence orally, without written form, and without having to observe ordinary legal proceedings; this act would previously have been inconceivable from the perspective of strictness and transparency in trials. The expression 'militarily' also highlights the extraordinary nature of the procedure.

After 1371, as well, the Anziani continued to grant the *podestà* discretionary powers 'as needed'. On 2 December 1374, in response to a complaint raised by the victims of crimes that 'in the silence of the night, many crimes and excesses were committed, of which it was difficult to investigate with ordinary procedures', the Anziani decided to grant the *podestà arbitrium* regarding nocturnal crimes committed from 1 October to the present. Furthermore, the *podestà* was able to conduct an investigation with use of torture based on his *ex officio* powers and the 'movement of his own mind (*proprio motu*)'.[54]

On 29 June 1383, the state of confusion caused by the recent wave of plague served to motivate the Anziani to once again grant the *podestà arbitrium*. The preamble to their provision notes that with the flight of citizens owing to fear of pestilence, the minds of devious and wicked men had been stirred to commit robbery and other *maleficia*. In response, the *podestà* and the *maior officialis custodie* (an official with jurisdiction over foreigners) were to be invested with discretionary powers for a limited period of about four months until 1 November, which drew those unafraid of God's justice away from committing *maleficia* as far as possible through fear of punishment.[55]

When we look at this series of grants of *arbitrium* to the *podestà*, which were carried out in Lucca as an independent republic, we find that such measures were each taken for a specific purpose and for a limited period. Following the establishment of the republic, their goal was to maintain security during the night and after the plague 'for the republic to be strengthened', which is the phrase mentioned in the 1371 provision. Ironically,

53 Tori (ed.), *Riformagioni*, II, p. 211-212: 'procedere possit de facto et extraiudicialiter militarie sine strepitu et figura iudicii et condemnationes solo verbo et sine scriptis facere exequi et exigere prout et sicut eidem videbitur et placebit, nulla solemnitate iuris vel statutorum, ritu, ordine vel etiam substantialitate servata'.

54 Tori (ed.), *Riformagioni*, IV, p. 571: 'Cum a pauco tempore citra ultra solitum noctis silentio commissa sint plura maleficia et excessus, ex quibus propter difficilem iudiciarii ordinis indaginem…, infeste offensorum insurrexerunt querele ultima remedia postulantes'; 'Potestas Lucanus, tam presens quam futurus, et eius curia habeant plenam autoritatem, arbitrium et baliam contra quascumque personas… inquirendis, investigandis et inveniendis, procedendi per denuntiam, accusationem et ex suo officio et proprio motu per tormenta et per omnem viam et modum quibus sue discretioni et conscientie videbitur'.

55 ASL, *Consiglio Generale*, 8, p. 547: '… advertentes fugam civium ob pestilentis morbi metum, mentes pravorum ac sceleratorum hominum erexisse ad committenda furta et maleficia perpetranda… volentes quod sivine iustitie timor non terret, saltem pene metu a malo retrahere…' A proviso to the effect that the *podestà* would not be subject to audit regarding the *arbitrium* he had been granted was appended on 22 October (i.e. 10 days before the above provision was due to expire) and extended to the following 1 January. ASL, *Consiglio Generale*, 8, p. 623: '… nec propterea sindicari debere sed penas esse suo arbitrio infligenda…'

this purpose was to be realised not 'with new laws', but through authorising deviations from the law. The *arbitrium* granted to the *podestà* to achieve this objective was limited in duration, such as for the term of the current *podestà* or for four months at a time.

As we have seen, whether implicitly or as later stipulated in his duty provisions, the *bargello* was able to exercise constant freedom of discretion in the conduct of his judicial activities. In contrast, the *arbitrium* granted to the *podestà* was not permanent but provisional. This difference was likely due to the fact that unlike the newly instated *bargello*, an officer fully subordinate to the Anziani, the *podestà* retained his original autonomy. Granting him freedom of discretion on a permanent basis would therefore have been seen to merit caution.

In the policy of granting *arbitrium* to the *podestà*, however, we can also see an attempt by the Anziani to subordinate the *podestà* to them. This strategy offered a way for the Anziani to unleash the *podestà* from the constraints of the law and have him punish *maleficia* in order to achieve their own political objectives during times that they deemed 'emergencies'. Furthermore, if necessary they would be able to strip him of the *arbitrium* they had granted at any time. By granting *arbitrium* to the *podestà*, the Anziani were not attempting to revive a regime centred on an autonomous *podestà*, as had existed in the thirteenth century, but rather to create a judicial official that could act flexibly and forcefully to achieve the Anziani's own objective of strengthening the republic. Figuratively speaking, the Anziani were attempting to transform the *podestà* who had arrived from another city on a horse symbolising the *cavalieri* into an obedient 'horse' whose reins were effectively in the hands of the Anziani.

(2) Who is the Great Ruler?

The situation wherein the governing council and the Anziani sought to subordinate the *podestà* to them as a judicial official was in practice a rejection of the communal regime that since the thirteenth century had entrusted jurisdiction to the *podestà* as a neutral figure from another city. All authority was assumed by the political authority, and this could even be considered a point held in common with the signorial regime. Did this not present a problem, however, in Lucca, which had just undertaken a new journey *as a republic*?

Having achieved formal independence on 12 March 1370, Lucca was attempting to reinstate the General Council of 180 members, which had been placed on permanent hiatus, in order to return to the *popolo*-style communal regime of the thirteenth century. Its momentum in this regard peaked with the declaration of the *popolo* regime in July 1370. On 31 July, representatives of the 'upper, middle and lower citizens' at the council decided jointly that the Anziani and Gonfaloniere di Giustizia would govern 'in the style of the *popolo* and in the name of the *popolo*' and that the nobility would be barred from the Anziani and other important posts.[56] The resulting *popolo* regime was merely

56 A. Romiti (ed.), *Riformagioni*, p. 380-382. The representatives of the 'upper, middle and lower citizens' had earlier been given full authority on 4 July by the General Council in an effort to deal with popular dissatisfaction with influential families' monopoly of the government. A. Romiti (ed.), *Riformagioni*, p. 349-353.

ideological. As Christine Meek's prosopographical study of the members of the Anziani revealed, this regime was actually more oligarchic than those of other cities of the same period.[57] Owing to a selection method wherein the incumbent Anziani had significant influence over the selection of their successors, fewer than 50 families were frequently appointed to the Anziani after 1370; the majority were from previously established and influential lineages.

In any case, Lucca in the early 1370s was ablaze with the ideology of the '*popolo* communal system'. It is surely no coincidence that the chancellor of the Lucchese Anziani at exactly this time (1370, 1371) was the humanist Coluccio Salutati, who later was appointed in Florence as chancellor, attacked the Duke of Milan in a letter, and wrote the treatise *De tyranno*.[58] A good illustration of how the conflict between this communal ideology and what was in practice a 'quasi-signorial' regime was dealt with can be found in a troublesome case stemming from the '*popolo* declaration' mentioned above.

The incident in question was prompted by Giovanni degli Obizzi, a noble who had been barred from holding office on the Anziani council and who was the leader of the Lucchese Guelph faction.[59] He came to Lucca in September 1370 and began to cause turmoil before he was eventually brought to heel by the *podestà*. Although Giovanni was tried in the Court of Podestà, herein a problem arose. On 9 November of the same year, the Gonfaloniere di Giustizia, Federico Trenta, made the following proposal to the General Council:

> A dubiety has been raised by the Court of Podestà regarding matters allegedly committed by him [Giovanni degli Obizzi]. The trial cannot be conducted by the *podestà*, because, as described in Book 1, Chapter 17 of Lucca's city statutes, jurisdiction in this matter is said to belong to the Great Ruler of the commune. Also, it is said that the Great Ruler is the worshipful Anziani and Gonfaloniere di Giustizia. It is improper that citizens hold jurisdiction or exercise their official duties over citizens. It is pleasing that the General Council makes decisions, ordains, and reforms on these and all other related matters.[60]

---

57 C. Meek, *Lucca 1369-1400. Politics and Society in an Early Renaissance City-State* (Oxford, 1978), p. 179-193, in particular p. 189-190. Most were merchants, bankers, and jurists, with few, if any, artisans from the middle and lower classes.

58 C. Salutati, *Il tratto 'de tyranno' e lettere scelte*, ed. F. Ercole, Bologna, 1942.

59 The Obizzi family, to which Giovanni belonged, was notable for being specifically prohibited in the 1372 statutes, together with the Poggio and Antelminelli families, from holding office as Anziani. Meek, *Lucca 1369-1400*, p. 183-185. He also frequently conspired against Lucca's new regime; the contemporary chronicler Giovanni Sercambi regards him as having pulled the strings of an uprising that occurred in February 1371. The uprising was a rebellion against the government of the time, perpetrated by craftsmen who were also members of the Guelph faction. G. Sercambi, *Le chroniche di Giovanni Sercambi Luccese*, ed. S. Bongi (Lucca, 1892), I, p. 204-205: 'si comprendea che la discordia nata in Luccha n'era stato principio messer Iohanni delli Opizi'.

60 Tori (ed.), *Riformagioni*, II, p. 88: 'et cum hoc sit etiam quod de his que dicuntur per ipsos esse commissa, revocetur in dubium per curiam dicti domini Potestatis, quod per ipsum dominum Potestatem procedi non possit cum dicant ex forma statutorum Lucani Comunis ad maius Regimen dicti Comunis jurisditionem huiusmodi pertinere, prout continetur in primo libro statutorum capitulo XVII, dicendo maius Regimen esse venerabile collegium dominorum Antianorum et Vexilliferi Justitie; et indecens sit cives in cives iurisditionem habere, aut hec officia exercere; quid placet dicto Consilio statuere, ordinare et reformare super predictis et omnibus ab eis dependentibus et connexis…'

Book 1, Chapter 17 of the city statutes, mentioned here, is entitled 'On punishment for those who committed culpa of inciting riots, disturbances, or arson, and on punishment for those who kindle fires in and around riots'. In this chapter, which proceeded from the 1308 statute, it is stipulated that those guilty of the aforementioned crimes shall be punished by the Great Ruler of Lucca.[61] So who was this Great Ruler? In the 1308 statute, which was influenced by *popolo* communal style, the Great Ruler clearly refers to the *podestà*,[62] who, as such, was considered to have complete jurisdiction and a true consolidated right to command in order to maintain a peaceful and unified state in Lucca and its territories.[63] However, in the 1331 and 1342 statutes, compiled under the rule of foreign lords, the term 'Great Ruler' is essentially absent. The *podestà* is no longer referred to by the title Great Ruler and is simply called *podestà*.[64] However, in Book 1, Chapter 17 of the 1342 statutes, still in effect in September 1370, most likely because it was simply left in the text unmodified, the title of Great Ruler remains in use, just as it was in the 1308 article. This is where the problem begins.

The proposal made by Federico, the Gonfaloniere di Giustizia, notes that 'it is said that the Great Ruler is the worshipful Anziani and Gonfaloniere di Giustizia'. If 'Great Ruler' is understood as the one who holds jurisdiction and the right to command, their contemporaries would naturally have understood that the Anziani and Gonfaloniere di Giustizia were the *de facto* Great Rulers. In fact, in an oath sworn on 31 July 1370 after the declaration of the *popolo* regime, Gonfaloniere di Giustizia, as the representative of the Anziani, with wording seemingly lifted from the oath of the *podestà* as the Great Ruler from past statutes, vowed to protect and govern the city and territory of Lucca.[65] However, if the Anziani and Gonfaloniere di Giustizia were the Great Ruler, then the *podestà* would have no authority to judge Giovanni degli Obizzi. This was the suspicion that the Court of Podestà conveyed to the General Council through Federico.

However, to his proposal, Gonfaloniere di Giustizia Federico added the meaningful comment that 'it is improper that citizens hold jurisdiction or exercise their official duties over citizens'. Why 'improper'? The answer is that the communal regime they

---

61 *Statuto 1308*, III, 19 (De pena illius qui commiserit culpam, unde ea die vel nocte sturmus vel aerta vel incendium fieret. Et de pena mittentis ignem in sturmo vel extra sturmum), p. 147-149. The same provision is found in the 1342 statutes. *Statuto 1342*, I, 17, fols. 11r-12r, in particularfol. 11r: 'Et quicumque causam vel eccesum commissit… condemnetur realiter et personaliter per maius Lucanum regimen…'

62 *Statuto 1308*, II, 1 (De electione Potestatis et eius modo et forma, et de feudo et familia et de sindicatu ipsius), p. 51. Bongi also indicated that *podestà* was called as maius Regimen, Bongi (ed.), *Inventario*, II, p. 304.

63 *Statuto 1308*, II, 2 (De iurisdictione attributa Maiori Lucano Reggimini), p. 54: 'Ad manutenendum honores Lucani Comunis et totius districtus, comitatus et fortie, et in pace et unione tenendum… Maius Lucanum Regimen habeat omnem iurisditionem et merum et mixtum imperium in omnes homines et personas et comunitates et universitates'.

64 The 'Great Ruler' was replaced with '*podestà*' as the name of the office. For example, a provision in the 1342 statutes that otherwise contains exactly the same wording as the 1308 provision on the oath of the Great Ruler has been renamed the '*podestà's* oath provision'. *Statuto 1342*, I, 1 (De iuramento potestatis), fol. 4r: '… Iuro ego potestas civitatis Lucane ad sancta dei evangelia corpolariter…'

65 Tori (ed.), *Riformagioni*, II, p. 385: 'Iuro ego Symon de Barga, legum doctor, Vexillifer Iustitie populi et Comunis Lucani, ad sancta Dei evangellia, corporaliter tactis scripturis, bona fide sine fraude … Civitatemque Lucanam, eius comitatum, fortiam et destrictum regere, gubernare, defendere et manutenere ad populum… cum iustitia procedere, cum effectu et potissime contra illos qui aliquo tempore ausu temerario officium Vexilliferi et Antianorum, representantium totum Lucanum populum, verbo seu facto, attentare presumerent'.

sought to build was based on impartiality and fairness and therefore did not entrust jurisdiction to 'citizens' who might hold partisan interests or render biased judgements. Instead of citizens, jurisdiction should be entrusted to neutral parties from other cities. The expression 'improper' (*indecens*) in Federico's proposal indicates his understanding that the *podestà*, as a foreign judicial official, should be installed as the Great Ruler, in accordance with communal tradition. This signal of his intentions towards the establishment of an ideological republican system was readily understood by the councillors. The opinion of one councillor, Jacopo Rapondi, which was adopted as the official view of the General Council, was as follows:

> That, from now, in this case and in future cases, by the authority of the present council, the formentioned dubiety on the statute shall be considered to have been clarified as follows. That is, in regards to the matters contained in the statutes, the Great Ruler shall always be understood as the current or sitting *podestà*. With regard to all matters in the statutes, the *podestà* of Lucca shall hold sovereignty, authority, jurisdiction, true consolidated imperium, and all manner of power to proceed, hear, condemn, or absolve and execute, and the *podestà* and his court shall be reconsidered as the Great Ruler of Lucca.[66]

This view was adopted by the General Council, becoming a legal interpretation that held lasting effect. In the margins of Book 1, Chapter 17 of the 1342 statutes, which occasioned this decision, it is still possible to find small but clear text to the effect that 'the General Council declared that the Great Ruler should be understood as the *podestà* of the city of Lucca and his court (9 November 1370)'.[67]

(3) *The ordinary Great Ruler and the extraordinary Great Ruler*

Things did not end there, however. There was a sequel to councillor Jacopo's opinion.

> With regard to the matter concerning Giovanni, although the temerity of his crime demands and requires punishment, with respect to the pleasant virtuous thing that he has done for the commune of Lucca in the past and to the love of his progeny and kinship, he shall not be convicted or punished [by the *podestà*] for the aforementioned occasion. Rather, he should be relegated or confined by the

---

66 Tori (ed.), *Riformagioni*, II, p. 88: 'quod ex nunc tam in presenti casu quam etiam in futuris intelligatur esse et prefati statuti dubitatio declarata, autoritate presentis Consilii hoc modo videlicet, quod quo ad ea que in statuto predicto continentur maius Regimen sit et esse intelligatur semper Potestas Lucanus presens vel qui pro tempore fuerit et de omnibus casibus in prefato statuto contentis, dominus Potestas Lucanus presens et futurus habeat baliam, autoritatem, jurisdictionem, imperiumque merum et mixtum ac omnimodam potestatem in procedendo, cognoscendo, condennando vel absolvendo ac etiam exequendo et in hoc et ipse ac eius curia maius Regimen Lucani Comunis penitus reputetur'.

67 *Statuto 1342*, fol. 11r: 'declaratum est per consilium generale quod maius regimen intelligatur esse et sit potestas Lucane civitatis et eius curia. Die.viiii. novembris.mccclxx'.

Anziani, and be placed at a remove 50 miles away from the city of Lucca beyond the mountains.[68]

Jacopo's opinion was a nuanced solution by communal leaders faced with a difficult challenge which came up just as Lucca was starting to be built as a republic. It seems that the leaders sought to achieve two objectives simultaneously. The first was the establishment of a *popolo* communal regime headed by a neutral foreign judicial official who would adhere strictly to the city statutes. In this regime, the governing council or Anziani, which was made up of citizens, was not allowed to conduct trials. The other was to take the necessary measures to maintain the republic and the current regime. In this case, this meant avoiding the great turmoil that would erupt with the lawful execution of Giovanni degli Obizzi, the head of the Guelph faction. These two objectives were brilliantly accomplished by positioning the *podestà* as the Great Ruler *ordinarily, but with certain exceptions*, by giving the Anziani as the Great Ruler *de fact* right to make decisions.

Such a measure, defending the republic of Lucca by using the terms *ordinarily* and *exceptionally*, can also be seen in the policy of granting *arbitrium* to the *podestà* for a limited time and purpose. The Anziani positioned the *podestà ordinarily* as a judicial official that adhered strictly to the law, but allowed the *podestà* to act on an extraordinary basis beyond the law in relation to exceptional cases, which *the Anziani deemed* to risk the existence of the republic. The same principle can be seen in the ordinary principle of the prohibition on *gratia* and of its suspension in extraordinary cases which we also saw in Chapter 5. These policies, based in ordinary and exceptional scenarios, characterised the initial phase of the republican period when the republic was re-emerging; but, despite enthusiasm for republican ideology, its survival was still uncertain.

5. The 1392 Regime and the *Capitano del Popolo*

(1) Partisan conflict and the establishment of the 1392 regime

The final scene of extraordinary justice in fourteenth-century Lucca began in 1392, about two decades after the establishment of the republic. That year, the end of the partisan rivalry between the Guinigi party and Forteguerra party with the victory of the former set in motion the establishment of an environment that would lead to the subsequent signorial rule of Paolo Guinigi. The key points here are the concentration of power in the hands of the Anziani due to political legislation along with the end of parti-

68 Tori (ed.), *Riformagioni*, II, p. 88: 'Quantum vero ad dictum dominum Johannem pertinet, quanvis sui delicti temeritas punitionem exigat et requirat quod habito respectu ad ea que pro Comuni Lucano hactenus optime virtuoseque gessit, sueque progeniei et consanguinitatis amore in nichilum occasione predictorum debeat condennari, puniri vel multari. Sed per dominos Antianos relegetur seu confinetur et ad confines ponatur ultra Alpes et longe a Civitate Lucana per quinquaginta miliaria'.

san rivalry and the appearance of extraordinary justice motivated by the maintenance of the Guinigi party 'regime'.

In Lucca, the oligarchisation of the ruling class progressed slowly, without the major party struggles observed in other cities, after the partisan conflict at the beginning of the fourteenth century. Lucca's independence in 1370, however, led to the formation of two factions within the city's ruling classes. One of these was a faction centred on the Guinigi family, which had played a leading role in the declaration of the *popolo* regime in July 1370 and was supported primarily by artisans and other non-noble citizens, while the other was a faction centred on the Forteguerra family, which was supported by jurists and noble families.[69]

These two factions clashed repeatedly over various official positions and political issues in the 1370s and 1380s, and finally the two engaged in armed conflict in 1390.[70] In February 1392, an attempt at reconciliation in a sermon delivered by a preacher was followed by the councillors pledging not to belong to any parties in the future. However, this situation proved untenable, and on 12 May 1392 the two factions gathered armed supporters from the city and the surrounding territory to stage a large battle, which left the Guinigi victorious. At the council the following day, Bartolomeo, the head of the Forteguerra party, was sentenced to death for having incited the disturbance.

After the end of the longstanding partisan rivalry, the Lucchese republic, now in the firm grip of the Guinigi party, immediately undertook the creation of a new regime. On 15 May 1392 a proposal was made to the council to the effect that, because the recent uprising had led Lucca into crisis and collapse, new legislation and the suspension of existing laws would be necessary and useful to maintain *libertas,* to restore a peaceful and popular state, and to prevent the city from falling into the same danger again[71] In response to this proposal, the Council approved the view of Michele Guinigi that all statutes and provisions should be suspended and exempted, so that the new legislation could then be enacted.

The result of this process of exempting statutes in already familiar 'emergency situations' was that 24 citizens would be organised into the *balìa* that, together with the Anziani, would have full authority to revise the statutes and rebuild the regime.[72]

---

69 In Italian cities, jurists and noble families frequently belonged to the same party. However, the close relationship between jurists and the *popolo* has attracted increased attention in recent works. S. Menzinger, *Giuristi e politica nei comuni di Popolo. Siena, Perugia e Bologna, tra governi a confronto* (Roma, 2006).

70 On the history of this partisan rivalry, see Meek, *Lucca 1369-1400*, p. 237-268.

71 ASL, *Consiglio Generale,* 12, fol. 49v: 'Cum propter novitates et graves tumultus, quibus Lucana civitas his diebus elapsis fuit exposita non sine ruine periculo… necessarium et utile sit pro reformatione civitatis eiusque comitatus fortie et districtus et pro bono pacis et concordie, et ne alias ad simile periculum veniatur sed variis animorum motibus omnis discordia evellatur providere circa ea que pro reformatione civitatis et conservatione pacifici et popularis status et libertatis ac custodia ipsius civitatis et comitatus utilia viderentur… Nec id fieri possit nisi per presens consilium dispensetur quid super ipsa dispensatione videtur, in dei nomine consulatur'.

72 ASL, *Consiglio Generale,* 12, p. 99: 'Antiani et Vexillifer Iustitie populi et communis Lucani eligant sex vel octo Lucanos cives per terzierem de quibus eis videbitur cum quibus vel maiori parte quorum habeant omnem auctoritatem potestatem et balia et liberum ac generalem plenium et absolutum arbitrium et merum et mixtum imperium … in providendo ordinando deliberando reformando statuendo et componendo tam de novo quam in iam statuta et reformata mutando corrigendo addendo et limitando'.

According to the party list left by Dino Guinigi, all 24 positions on the *balìa* were held by members of the Guinigi party.[73] Here, the 'revision of statutes' was entrusted to the emergency committee and not to professional lawmakers or jurists, and the decision did not require approval by the Council. This shows that these 'revisions' – unlike conventional revisions to the city statutes – were strongly coloured by a political and partisan character.

The *balìa* enacted several 'laws' on 26 May 1392 for the 'protection of liberty'. This had two main objectives: first, the concentration of authority in the hands of the Anziani, and second, the prevention of a conspiracy to maintain the 'regime'. Let us consider each in turn.

(2) The consolidation of power by the commissarii palatii *and the Anziani*

The key to the first point is the establishment of the *commissarii palatii*.[74] According to the new provisions, the twelve-person *commissarii palatii* (consisting of four people from each *terziere*) was formed to protect the liberty of the republic both internally and externally, together with the Anziani and Gonfaloniere di Giustizia. Externally, its main duties were to issue orders to muster armed troops in time of war; internally, they were to maintain order in the city and prevent uprisings against the republic. The maintenance of security, as we shall see, was to be carried out through the selection of a *capitano del popolo* ('captain of the people') and the revision of the *capitano*'s rulings. The members of the *commissarii palatii* were appointed for terms of six months, and their selection was guided by the Anziani and the predecessor of the *commissarii palatii*.[75]

The activities of the *commissarii palatii* can be seen from the council registers. In addition to the official duties listed above, together with the Anziani they also issued *gratia*, deterred fires and riots, deployed troops of guards to *castello* in the territory, appointed *podestà* of the territorial districts, negotiated with mercenaries, and drafted peace agreements, among other tasks. At one time, such matters would have been entrusted to the General Council or Council of Thirty-Six (or the Council of Fifty before independence) in response to proposals from the Anziani. Accordingly, the establishment of the *commissarii palatii* served to diminish the activities of these communal institutions. In fact, whereas the General Council met an average of twelve times a year over the period from 1385 to 1390, after the establishment of the *commissarii palatii* this dropped to four or five times a year. Moreover, whereas the Council of Thirty-Six had earlier been convened 20-30 times a year, this dropped to 8-20 times a year after 1392. Furthermore, deliberations at the General Council were now limited to formal and non-political matters, such as the appointment of *podestà*.

---

73 Meek, *Lucca 1369-1400*, p. 271.

74 ASL, *Consiglio Generale*, 12, p. 115-117, De electio consilio potestatem et balia commissariorum.

75 Two years' worth of candidates were chosen, and members would be selected by lottery from among these candidates every six months.

In other words, the establishment of the *commissarii palati* reduced to empty pantomimes those councils that had involved a comparatively broader spectrum of people, engendering an institutional environment wherein the Anziani and the *commissarii palatii* were able to act freely and directly without seeking the approval of the councils. This new relationship between the Anziani and the broader councils was also reflected in the process for deciding *gratia*. The revision of court sentences, as clearly stated in a 1353 proposal, had once been a matter 'which cannot be provided by the Anziani without the consent of the council'.[76] After 1392, however, the Anziani began revising the court rulings issued by the *podestà* and *capitano* without the consent of the councils.[77] More than simply subordinating foreign judicial officials to political authority, the hollowing out of the role of the councils that had formed the foundation of the commune's representative system could be said to indicate a departure from the *popolo* communal regime and the republican regime.

The consolidation of power with the Anziani and the *commissarii palatii* was accomplished for the purpose of gaining a free hand in government on the part of the Guinigi party after partisan struggle. The success of this gambit is evident from the fact that the members of the Anziani and the *commissarii palatii* were dominated by the Guinigi party at all times. This new 'regime' had no choice but to be vigilant against those who sought to oppose it and carry out policies to prevent their rebellion. This was represented by the activities of the *capitano del popolo* ('captain of the people'), instituted in a 'law' enacted by the *balìa* on 26 May 1392. This office was charged with maintaining order in the republic and, above all, maintaining the Guinigi party regime.[78] The name *capitano del popolo* is the same as that of the head of the *popolo* organisation, which had intended to protect popular interests in the thirteenth century. The choice of this traditional title seems to have been intended to recall the *popolo* period to create the impression that the new regime had been established by a 'popular' victory. However, in terms of both its institutional positioning and its actual activities, the new institution was completely different from its thirteenth-century namesake.

(3) Maintenance of order by the capitano del popolo

The principal duty of the *capitano del popolo* under the 1392 regime was to judge those who violated the new 'laws'. Particularly envisioned here were two crimes appended on 26 May 1392.[79] One of these was slandering or insultsing the republic, the Anziani, or the councillors, or speaking, in public places, any words concerning the suspension of or deviations from the statutes, or speaking words bringing disturbance or scandal to

76 *Anz. Av. Lib.*, 35, fols. 6r-7v: '...coram eis exhibite fuerunt quedam petitione super quibus cum per ipsos dominos antianos sine dicti consilii consensu provideri non possit...'

77 Regarding *gratia* by the Anziani, a reform dated 15 May 1392 stipulates that the Anziani had *arbitrium* to re-admit *banniti*.

78 ASL, *Consiglio Generale*, 12, p. 113-114, De electione officio et iurisdictione Capitanei populi.

79 In addition to the two listed below, the duties prescribed for the *capitano* also included trials for vagabonds and for individuals who solicited murderers. ASL, *Consiglio Generale*, 12, p. 108, De vagabundis expellendis et puniendis; ASL, *Consiglio Generale*, 12, p. 112, De quibusdam reformationibus veteribus per capitaneum populi observandis.

the peaceful state of the commune. Violations would result in fines of up to 10 florins.[80] The other crimes were taking up arms and participating in gatherings in Lucca or its territory, or proceeding armed towards the Anziani or a communal palace. Any of these latter acts would be regarded as conspiratorial behaviour or as uprisings in the city and were punishable by the death penalty and seizure of property.[81] The official duties of the *capitano* were intelligence activities to crack down on rebellious actions that would expose the new regime to danger, and to punish them.

The *capitano*, as a foreign judicial official, was placed under the direction of the Anziani and the *commissarii palatii*. His selection was carried out by the *commissarii palatii* and his rulings were also controlled by the Anziani and the *commissarii palatii*. The *capitano* was moreover charged with execution of orders issued by the Anziani or the *commissarii palatii*. The *capitano* was given a retinue of one expert soldier and 25 armed and militarily seasoned retainers (including four cavalry soldiers).[82]

Trials conducted by the *capitano* went beyond the frame of ordinary trials. According to his duty provisions, he was permitted to conduct proceedings summarily, *de facto*, without adhering to the laws or statutes and without documentation. The following two points, which are specified separately, are worth noting in connection with the legal proceedings conducted by the *capitano*, who also engaged in intelligence activities. One is that in order that delicts did not remain unpunished, the *capitano*, in relation to the accusations or denunciations, was allowed to conduct proceedings in an inquisitorial manner at any time.[83] This provision allowed the *capitano* to forcefully investigate suspicions of conspiracy often brought to light by accusations and denunciations. The other is that in the event that the accused was summoned and did not appear in court, at that moment he was deemed to have confessed and so be subject to *bannum*, meaning that the *capitano* would not necessarily have to summon him a second time.[84] This violated the traditional principle of Romano-canonical procedure, which required two summonses, and could be said to have been an extremely extraordinary provision that was incredibly disadvantageous to the accused.

This system, which positioned the Anziani and the *commissarii palatii* as leaders and the *capitano* (and *podestà*) as acting forces and sought to deter rebellion against the republic and the current regime, did in fact uncover many rebellions and warnings thereof. Here, let us see two examples.

80 ASL, *Consiglio Generale*, 12, p. 105, De pena obloquentium contra libertatem et pacificum et popularem statum.

81 ASL, *Consiglio Generale*, 12, p. 106, De pena inducentium seditionem seu conniurationem contra statum pacificum libertatis.

82 ASL, *Consiglio Generale*, 12, p. 113: 'Et pro suis officiis exercendis habeat et habere debeat unum milite socium probum et expertum…, et vigintiquinque familos electos et probos bene armatos et in armis expertis de quibus … quatuor equos bonos et idoneos…'

83 ASL, *Consiglio Generale*, 12, p. 107-108, De delictorum inquisitionibus: 'ne delicta remaneant impunita statuerunt quod … ideo Capitaneus populi possit etiam accusatione seu denuntia precedente vel sequente ubi et quando sibi videbitur, procedere per viam inquisitionis de contentis in denuntia seu accusatione predicta'.

84 ASL, *Consiglio Generale*, 12, p. 108, De reis citandis et contumacibus banniendis: 'Si reus criminis ex parte Capitanei populi semel citatus non comparuerit ad se defendendum, habeatur pro confesso. Et possit Capitaneus predictus reum contumacem bannire et in banno ponere in ea et de ea pena que pro delicto super quo procederetur, deberet imponi Nec teneatur predictus Capitaneus servare in ipsa prolatione bannorum formam statuti positi sub rubrica de forma imbanniendi et extrahendi de banno… ad quam secundam citationem dictus capitaneus minime teneatur'.

Late at night on 13 April 1393, Giovanni Boccansocchi and his supporters plunged the city into a state of tension when they appeared in the streets carrying weapons.[85] As he was a member of the Guinigi party, it seems doubtful that this action constituted a plot to rebel against the current regime. Nevertheless, his actions were considered a major disturbance to the peace, posing a danger of catapulting the city and the current regime into confusion. His actions contravened the provisions prohibiting armed gatherings in private homes. In addition, in the provision it was pointed out that 'popular uprisings and movements are dangerous and that swords in the hand of angry people are not easily controlled'.[86] The caution with regard to popular movements shows clear awareness of developments such as the Ciompi Revolt that occurred in Florence in 1378.The Anziani and the *commissarii palatii* eventually sentenced Giovanni to a six-month period of exile in Pietrasanta[87] 'so that his crime does not remain unpunished and that such things will not be attempted in the future'.[88]

The other example concerns a conspiracy against the Guinigi regime that was uncovered in January 1394, whose main culprits were Piero Rapondi, Niccolò di Dino, and Michele Leoni. According to what Meek has revealed from the *capitano*'s ruling, these men, who belonged to the Forteguerra party, were planning to bring back to Lucca members of the Rapondi family and other families who had been sentenced to exile. They had enlisted the support of Piero's brothers in Paris, had assembled a force from the surrounding villages, and had finally succeeded in equipping a mercenary commander, 100 spearmen, and 300 infantry.[89] However, the plan ended in failure when Niccolò Ronsini, one of the citizens they had brought into the conspiracy, ended up exposing them to the *capitano*. The three main culprits were sentenced by the *capitano* in absentia to decapitation and the forfeiture of their property. Niccolò Ronsini was likewise sentenced to death, but from the council registers we find that his death sentence was cancelled by the Anziani and the *commissarii palatii*, and he was later sentenced to exile instead on account of the revelation of the conspiracy.[90] As for the three main culprits, when we look at the rulings included in the sentence book, we find that they were later pardoned through *gratia*, freeing them from their sentences.[91]

---

85 Meek, *Lucca 1369-1400*, p. 293.

86 ASL, *Consiglio Generale*, 12, p. 289: 'periculosi sint motus et tumultuatio popularis, non enim facile regitur ensis in manibus furentium populorum… omnibus providendis non aliquis arma induat seu ad domum alicuius private persone vadat sine dominorum consensu in odium vel favorem'.

87 Marginal notation in the register mentions that the *podestà* directed Giovanni to adhere to the decision by order of the Anziani on April 15. Later, Giovanni successfully petitioned the Anziani for a pardon, enabling his early return to the city. ASL, *Consiglio Generale*, 12, p. 295.

88 ASL, *Consiglio Generale*, 12, p. 289: 'ipsorum delictum omnio non remaneat impunitum ne futuris temporibus id attentent'.

89 Meek, *Lucca 1369-1400*, p. 294.

90 ASL, *Consiglio Generale*, 12, p. 402: 'Capitaneus populi debeat supersidere in executione sententie seu condemnationis per eum ferende contra Nicolaum Ronsini et Michaelem Leonis in eius curia'; *Ibid.*, p. 403: 'Nicolaus Ronsini ex officio domini Capitanei populi captus et inquisitus causa supradicta, iuxta fidem sibi datam, sit liber et absolutus ab omni pena personali qua veniret puniendus et multandus occasione dicti tractatus… possit tamen dominus Capitanus populi supradictus dictum Nicolaum citra mortem punire multare et condemnare…' The fact that the *capitano* was granted the authority to impose exile soon after this death sentence was commuted suggests that he may have been sent to a remote location. ASL, *Consiglio Generale*, 12, p. 404.

91 ASL, *Sentenze e bandi*, 85, fols. 13r-14v.

(4) Political justice as seen through the lens of exile

Given the lack of documents, we are unfortunately unable to see the extraordinary summary procedures taken by the *capitano* from these two cases of conspiracy. Nevertheless, we do know that the final judgements in both cases were *de facto* rendered by the Anziani and the *commissarii palatii*, who directed the judicial officials. While allowing the *capitano* to perform a more repressive form of justice by granting him *arbitrium*, the Anziani stayed the execution of the *capitano*'s sentences and issued new judgements as necessary.

The most common judgement we find is exile. This measure, which we also saw in the case of Giovanni degli Obizzi in 1370, began to be issued much more frequently by the Anziani after 1392. Something common to all of those who were sentenced to exile is that if the judges had imposed sentences based in the law, they would all have been sentenced to death. A judgement of exile served to commute a death sentence and therefore seems to have been seen as a kind of *gratia*. Certainly, in the decision against Niccolò Ronsini, as indicated, his crime would not remain unpunished,[92] and imposing punishment was seen as necessary. However, if a death sentence were to have been imposed on the social and political leaders or on those who had given great service to the republic, such a sentence could present a major obstacle to the maintenance of the republic, or more precisely maintaining the 'regime', which was the original purpose of the provisions. The measure adopted in such cases was exile.

Here, we can see how the political institutions always monitored the activities of the judicial officials, and so political intentions prevailed over judicial judgements. The criteria by which the political authorities determined when to change a strict ruling based in positive law by a foreign judicial official into a sentence of exile, were not only the nature of the crime but also the political and social standing of the perpetrator, as well as his record of achievements. These criteria were deployed based on the keen political motivations of leaders who belonged mostly to the Guinigi party, rather than as something generated by the complaints of the inhabitants, which we have seen in the previous chapters.

6. Extraordinary Justice and the Extension of Politics

In Lucca after the mid-fourteenth century, the *capitano di custodia* (*ser* Scherlatto), the *bargello*, the *podestà*, and the *capitano del popolo*, all foreign judicial administrators, were permitted to conduct trials in a summary fashion, not bound strictly by legal procedures or by fines stipulated by the city statutes. This exceptional and extraordinary justice would have been difficult to imagine in communes that considered compliance with the city statutes and *ius commune* as their legal and institutional basis and so were resistant to granting such discretionary powers to foreign judicial officials. Therefore, reflected in

---

92 ASL, *Consiglio Generale*, 12, p. 403: 'ne delictum in totum remaneat impunitum et ne similia attententur'.

the creation and development of this extraordinary justice, we can see the emergence of an idea of justice and a '*comune*' tinged with a new personality.

The extraordinary justice of fourteenth-century Lucca emerged as being powerfully motivated by the 'emergencies' that arose during this period. The crises occurring in the immediate aftermath of Pisan rule in the territorial districts caused by war and pestilence, and in the republic after independence, as well as the 'regime' crisis that followed in the wake of the establishment of the Guinigi regime in 1392, encouraged the institution of 'trials' not bound by the framework of ordinary trials. However, it is important to note that these crises, certainly for all the actual political, social, and economic difficulties they entailed, were only 'crises' to the extent that they were politically perceived as such by the Anziani and other political actors; and, in some cases, such 'crises' were interpretively manufactured. For example, after 1392 the alleged 'crises' that justified the summary trials of the *capitano del popolo* were only 'crises' claimed by the Guinigi party who made enemies and took great care to maintain their regime.

The experience of this politically motivated extraordinary justice was something that was inherited by subsequent generations. The free security maintenance activities on the part of the *conservatore ser* Scherlatto were passed on to the *bargello*, who specialised in such activities in the territorial districts. While the *bargello* initially went beyond his duty provisions, implicitly observing summary procedure, this experience was codified into lawful behaviour during the republican period. The granting of *arbitrium* to the *bargello* by the governing council seems to have provided a precedent for the granting of discretionary powers to the *podestà* as well as to the *capitano del popolo* in the same sphere of security maintenance. In this way, the gradual accumulation of experience with extraordinary justice gradually led to its transformation as an *ordinary* means that could be more easily used by political institutions.

The latter half of the fourteenth century was also a period of expansion for the policy of *gratia* discussed in the previous chapter. Based on his analysis of statutes in several cities, Vallerani notes that whereas political authorities intervened in the activities of judicial officials in oligarchical communal cities, the policy of granting foreign judicial officials *arbitrium* was carried out it cities under signorial rule, seeing different trends in cities with each type of regime.[93] However, in Lucca, and most likely in other cities (i.e. if we were to investigate historical sources other than the city statutes), the policy of granting judges *arbitrium* and the policy of intervening in judges' rulings (with *gratia*) were not contradictory but coexisted, and even expanded synergistically.

The key to explaining the coexistence of these two policies lies in the changing relationship between the political authorities (the governing council and Anziani) and the foreign judicial officials. This power balance, which had previously been in a tense equilibrium, shifted significantly during this period to the advantage of the former, and the foreign judicial officials were subordinated to the political authorities. As we have seen in this chapter, *arbitrium* was granted to judicial officials for limited periods of time to achieve certain political ends, but the political authorities were always ready to rescind that freedom of discretion, or else to modify or stay the rulings of the judicial

93 Vallerani, 'L'arbitrio negli statuti cittadini', p. 117-147.

officials. The two policies of extraordinary justice and *gratia* were the opposite sides of the same coin, two perspectives on a single phenomenon that was unfolding in the cities of fourteenth-century Italy, namely the strengthening of political authority and the subordination of judicial officials.

The shift observed in Lucca in the balance between a political authority made up of citizens and a judicial authority borne by foreign citizens also took place in the republican city of Florence during the same period. In the middle of the fourteenth century, the *bargello* began carrying out security activities in the cities as a policing institution, while the *difensori* led his forces to do so in the territorial districts.[94] As in Lucca, these organisations were firmly subordinate to the Florentine governing council. In the 1380s, as the oligarchic system was becoming entrenched, the *Otto di Guardia*, which was composed of citizens, was set up under the governing council to lead a crackdown on activities perceived to be against the republic and against the regime.[95] This organisation seems to have been a counterpart to the *commissarii palatii* in Lucca. The *Otto* and the governing council were in a position to direct the actual trial by giving specific instructions on the content of their rulings to the foreign judicial officials, the *podestà* and the *capitano*. The scene of Matteo di Jacopo Arrighi arguing at the Florentine council of 1401 that 'it is not citizens but the foreign officials who are entrusted to issue convictions to citizens'[96] seems to have almost directly echoed the scene of the council in Lucca on 9 November 1370. Incidentally, it was the very same Coluccio Salutati who wrote these words in his capacity as chancellor at both councils.

In the latter half of the fourteenth century, the gathering of judicial power by a political authority, particularly the concentration of authority within a governing council composed of a few citizens, can be positioned in the context of a shift in the form of a departure from the traditional communal regime, characterised by the coexistence of and tension between independent institutions that included foreign judicial officials. Furthermore, there was a transition towards a signorial or monarchical regime wherein complete authority was held by a single political and administrative body.

How should we explain the relationship between these political and institutional changes, which became apparent during the transition from the Middle Ages to the Renaissance or early modernity, and governance techniques rooted in a new idea of justice, as with summary justice and *gratia*? Certainly, some degree of concentration of authority in the governing council and the Anziani would have been a prerequisite for the introduction of techniques of governance associated with this new justice. Nevertheless, when reviewing how extraordinary justice was introduced and developed amidst the confusion in the wake of Pisan rule, the degeneration of law and order in the territory, the external environment of the republic's establishment, and how these were all interpreted and emphasised as 'crises', we see that this new form of governance was not a *consequence* of the expansion of the Anziani's power or its

94 On the *bargello* and *difensori*, see Tanzini, 'Costruire e controllare il territorio'.

95 On the *Otto di Guardia*, see A. Zorzi, *L'amministrazione della giustizia penale nella Repubblica fiorentina: aspetti e problemi* (Firenze, 1988).

96 E. Conti (ed.), *Le «consulte» e «pratiche» della repubblica fiorentina nel Quattrocento: I. 1401 (Cancellierato di Coluccio Salutati)* (Pisa, 1981), p. 28; 'quod cives non sunt deputati ad condemnandum cives, sed Rectores forenses'.

signorial development but one that was *politically contrived*. Perhaps we can think of the practices that employed this new method of exception, which were forcibly introduced, as having functioned as a lever, a driving force to strengthen political authority or, more specifically, one that transformed medieval-style political institutions into Renaissance or early modern ones.

Conclusion

We have seen the practices implemented in the field of justice by the people of Lucca, a Tuscan communal city. Which characteristics of the commune are depicted in this book? Moreover, to what extent does the account in this book enrich or revise the conventional image of Italian medieval cities? I will discuss these questions in terms of the people's *participation* in the commune and the changes in the nature of justice that guided the commune.

The cities of medieval Italy are generally considered to have been places where concepts such as independence and self-government were valued. In such cases, the sense of *libertas* as the non-intervention of foreign powers and the notion of *libertas* connoting the republican political system of civic participation were frequently combined and exalted as republican liberty. However, historical studies conducted in recent years and the examination undertaken in this book shed light on a medieval Italian city that significantly differs from this image.

Intellectuals of the late Middle Ages, at least, considered the Italian commune to have been an imaginary political body that differed significantly from the real rulers or the assemblage of citizens. Inhabitants obeyed the orders of communal officials who were the actual representatives of the '*comune*', which theoretically comprised the residents themselves. This relationship of domination and submission between the commune and its citizens, presumed by Hobbes and Weber, existed in the minds of Bartolo and Marsilio and was a lived reality of the political and judicial system in medieval Lucca.

The conventional image of republican liberty is further undermined by the fact that an autonomous government involving the complete participation of citizens would have been a fantastical notion at the time. In Lucca, as well as in other Italian cities, the expansion of governmental authority and the prevalence of a selection process in which predecessors selected their successors meant that the right to participate in the city's decision-making process was granted to only a limited number of families. In reality, citizens who should have enjoyed civil rights as members of the urban community, held the *de facto* position of *subjects* who invariably submitted to the ruler.

However, is it really the case that ordinary people, being denied opportunities for political participation, were merely passive subjects ruled by the governing bodies and by those wielding *potentes* therein? This book reveals that inhabitants *did* participate in their commune, albeit in a manner quite different from the one envisioned by republican thinkers and conventional historians who cherish an ideal image of communal living; that is, virtuous political participation by citizens in pursuit of the *bene commune*. This mode of civic participation in the commune involved its strategic use by people pursuing their own interests. On encountering a problem, people did not completely remove themselves from the public sphere and resolve it privately; rather, they actively continued their engagement with the commune, perceiving it as a usable source of power. This is best exemplified by the ten thousand claims submitted annually to civil courts even in the small city of Lucca. This mode of participation had the effect of stimulating the commune from within, becoming a force to stir it into action.

First, people's participation primarily contributed to the word-for-word implementation of the contents of the laws and institutions established by the commune. This can be observed from the activities of citizens in the civil courts. The exception, examined in Chapter 2, was a litigation strategy for securing advantage in the courts. This practice of strictly keeping track of mistakes made by the judge or the opposing party on the basis of city statutes facilitated the faithful implementation of ordinary procedures and the legal regulations of the commune in situations where court officials merely responded passively.

Second, this participation in the commune, meaning its strategic use on the part of its people, also redefined the commune, translating it from its ideal state, which the laws invented and determined, into a different state. This was evident, for example, in the inhabitants' strategic acquisition of the judicial orders to secure the real estate we examined in Chapter 1. The commune had developed a system wherein the rights' relationships were determined based on notarial documents, and where judicial orders were issued for the assets of debtors to be forcibly transferred to creditors. However, in a society where the ownership of properties was extremely unclear, people construed these judicial orders as a means of establishing *de facto* occupancy in a manner that would be useful in subsequent conflicts over rights. By virtue of this strategic institutional reinterpretation on the part of its inhabitants, the commune took shape as a public authority that was accepted and utilised, and functioned in society quite differently to its ideal form.

Claims by people were also raised in the political and legislative sphere, as seen in Chapter 2. Here, certain instances went beyond the reinterpretation of the legal system and involved open appeals for change. Citizens' voices were being delivered to the compilers of city regulations when the city statutes were being revised; moreover, constant appeals to the Anziani resulted in the addition or revision of statutory provisions and decrees regarding when exceptions would be made. Such lobbying by the people thus served to convey to the communal leaders that existing laws were operationally 'unsuited' to the changing society and to individual circumstances and thereby allowed them to 'rationalise' laws to achieve their original purpose.

These appeals to the law by the inhabitants, beyond promoting its flexibility and 'rationalisation', also provided the judges, the Anziani, and other rulers with the opportunity to carry out activities no longer constrained by the fetters of the law. The claims seeking to simplify ordinary procedures in the civil courts outlined in Chapter 3, and the claims calling for amendments to criminal judgements based on statutes discussed in Chapter 5, are both examples of these. These claims by inhabitants had the influence to change the power structure in the institutions of the commune. The decreased willingness on the part of litigants to raise an exception, and the move towards expeditious rulings at the *arbitrium* of judges apparent in the later fourteenth-century's civil courts, created conditions that further diminished the influence of the local jurists who had, until then, served the world of civil law as agents external to the commune, thus allowing judges and, in turn, the commune they represented to seize exclusive control of civil justice. Moreover, appeals to the Anziani for pardons (*gratia*) on the part of inhabitants convicted in criminal trials served to motivate and provide an opportunity to legitimise the intervention of the political authorities in a judicial area that had previously been the exclusive province of foreign judicial officials as well as increase the authority of the governing council.

In the context of Italian cities faced with an encroaching oligarchy, the general populace was not given opportunities for direct participation in communal decision-making. However, as we have seen, people became involved in building the commune by vigorously bringing their claims forward and 'participating' actively in the commune in the manner of citizens grasping the cord in Lorenzetti's fresco. Rather than a virtuous participation aspiring to the *Bene comune*, this was something done strategically, with their own immediate interests in mind. These appeals to the commune on the part of its inhabitants could never have been neglected by the policymakers of the oligarchic government, because in the eventuality that they were not heard, the complainants would have played the hidden card of absconding from the city. In other words, an 'unconscious' creation of the commune by the inhabitants defined its dynamic character in the context of late medieval Italy.

Fourteenth-century Lucca adopted an oligarchical republican system. Communal decision-making was monopolised by an influential few, so that direct participation was beyond the reach of most inhabitants. This disjuncture between reality and the communal ideal would have been obvious to the people of the time. In such circumstances, what grounds were provided so that the orders of a commune represented by a few would be seen as consistent with justice and therefore something with which the inhabitants had to comply? In other words, what characterised the image of justice guiding the '*comune*'?

The seventeenth-century republican James Harrington once rejected the idea of Thomas Hobbes that the *libertas* of the inhabitants of Lucca under the republican system should be regarded as equal to the *libertas* of the inhabitants of Constantinople under the Sultan's rule.[1] That is, in Lucca, both rulers and inhabitants alike were subject to the law, but in Constantinople, the Sultan acted arbitrarily without bowing to the law. Therefore, the inhabitants of Lucca have more *libertas*.[2] Here, we glimpse a view linking

---

1 T. Hobbes, *Hobbes's Leviathan Reprinted from the Edition of 1651, with an Essay by the Late W. G. P. Smith* (Oxford, 1909), p. 165: "There is written on the Turrets of the city of Luca in great characters at this day, the word *LIBERTAS*; yet no man can thence inferre, that a particular man has more Libertie, or Immunitie from the service of the Commonwealth there, than in *Constantinople*. Whether a Common-wealth be Monarchicall, or Popular, the Freedome is still the same."

2 J. Harrington, *The Commonwealth of Oceana and A System of Politics*, ed. J. G. A. Pocock (Cambridge, 1992), p. 20: "… whereas the greatest bashaw is a tenant, as well of his head as of his estate, at the will of his lord, the meanest Lucchese that hath land is a freeholder of both, and not to be controlled but by the law; and that framed by every private man unto no other end (or they may thank themselves) than to protect the liberty of every private man,

republicanism with the law and despotism with caprice, a view that regards behaviour under the law as the basis for *libertas* and thus the legitimacy of governance.

In the fourteenth-century communal city of Lucca, did the legitimacy of government in fact find a basis in the law? And to what extent was the nature of justice in Lucca the same or different from that under despotic or signorial regimes?

From the discussion in this book, first, it will have become clear how the members of the government of communal Lucca, similar to the *signori*, often made decisions 'law notwithstanding'. The pardons (*gratia*) examined in Chapter 5 and the approval of summary procedures in Chapter 6 clearly show how the Anziani overcame the ordinary proceedings established by positive law and judicial rulings based therein to issue decisions based on their own 'conscience'. Even judges, as we saw in Chapter 3, started to ignore procedures stipulated by the law as they felt necessary, proceeding with their trials according to their own *arbitrium*.

The *arbitrium* relied upon and exercised by the rulers of Lucca was nothing like mere arbitrariness or caprice. As was vigorously observed by the Anziani in the preamble of their decisions, discretionary decisions had to be motivated and legitimised by *iusta causa* and *neccessitas* and linked to 'law' in the sense of a higher-order natural law. Therefore, Lucca's leaders and the commune they represented were attempting to link their actions to an idea of justice. This is redolent of Lorenzetti's personifications of the '*comune*' and of justice.

Next, I would like to summarise the idea of justice that guided the '*comune*' in terms of how the inhabitants took part in its construction and in terms of its republican trappings. These features, which are apparent in the fourteenth-century Lucchese idea of justice, also provide new insights, not found in recent previous studies, in which similarities between oligarchic communal regimes and signorial regimes are seen in the emergence of an idea of justice based on *arbitrium*.

The first issue concerns the fields and actors who motivated a shift in the logical basis of the legitimacy of rulings, from a view of laws as an absolute standard that must be strictly observed to a mindset in which positive law was *one standard among many*, and which relied ultimately on *arbitrium* and individual 'conscience'. It is concerned with the participation of various actors in the new construction of an image of justice no longer coloured by the strict letter of the law.

In previous studies of Italian cities in the late Middle Ages, it has been pointed out that political actions that diverged from the law were particularly apparent in fields relating to the interests of the state and the regime.[3] In Lucca, as well, the independence of the republic in 1370 was well timed to occasion the development of extraordinary justice in an extremely political field; the free operation of laws, such as the prohibition of pardons (*gratia*) and the temporary suspension of prohibitions, was also apparent.

---

which by that means comes to be the liberty of the commonwealth." See also M. Viroli, *Republicanism* (New York, 2002), p. 50-51.

3 L. Tanzini, 'Emergenza, eccezione, deroga: tecniche e retoriche del potere nei comuni toscani del XIV secolo', in M. Vallerani (ed.), *Tecniche di potere nel tardo Medioevo: regimi comunali e signorie in Italia* (Roma, 2010), p. 49-181; Milani, *L'esclusione dal comune. Conflitti e bandi politici a Bologna e in altre città italiane tra XII e XIV secolo* (Roma, 2003).

Therein, the goals of the political leadership to protect the independence of the republic and to maintain the existing regime, as well as the 'crisis' awareness that these actions engendered, served to motivate and legitimise discretionary behaviour and deviations from the law. Here, we can see how the 'raison d'État' featured in the subsequent ideas of Machiavelli and Bodin, in the sense of deviations from the law brought about by the political motivation to maintain the state, were appearing in the setting of *communal* or *republican cities*.[4] In this way, an aspect of the image of justice was being created by the political leadership.

However, what is evident in the shift from the image of justice austerely garbed in strict adherence to the law to one that allowed more possibility for free interpretation, is that it was not solely a field related to highly statal interests that involved the leadership. In Lucca, particularly after the middle of the fourteenth century, judgements that relied heavily on *arbitrium* began to be executed in the *normal juridical fields* of criminal and civil justice. This was evident in the case of pardons (*gratia*) and of summary procedures in civil trials. Here, a certain degree of consideration of positive law was apparent in comparison with the field of extraordinary justice. References to law can be seen among the petitions for pardons, while claims that sought compliance with the city statutes in civil 'summary justice' prompted hesitation in the free progress of judges. Even so, positive law had ceased to be the absolute standard for the realisation of justice and was becoming merely one factor in ensuring the legitimacy of the *arbitrium* that was to be ultimately relied upon.

What is distinctive about the field of normal justice is that the move away from an idea of justice based in the strict observance of positive law was motivated by the common people. Petitions from the guilty begging for the remission of their sentences were considered absolutely essential in the case of pardons, which represented an amendment to rulings made in courts based on law. In the civil courts, trials observing summary procedure by the presiding judge would be arranged by litigating parties who, facing vexatious exceptions raised by their opponents, would bring their appeals to the doge.

While it was the inhabitants who drained the colour of strict adherence to the law from the idea of justice, it was also the inhabitants who infused it with new colours. In their petitions seeking pardons, they showed what kind of actions on the part of policymakers manifested this idea of justice and, in civil trials, argued about what constituted 'complete cognizance' even in the case of summary procedures. These interpretations of the idea of justice presented on the part of the populace collided and intertwined with the interpretations of the judges and the executive college to create a raiment for an image of justice more suited to the new era.

It is worth noting that this transition in the image of justice as a result of such lobbying by the people in the context of the normal juridical field took place in Lucca in the 1350s and 1360s – i.e. during an *earlier period* than the republican era that witnessed the spread of extraordinary justice. This suggests the possibility that this shift in the logical basis of the legitimacy of rulings and in the image of justice that guided the image

4 F. Meinecke, *Machiavellism. The Doctrine of Raison d'État and Its Place in Modern History* (London, 1957).

of the '*comune*', may have had its inception in the actions of inhabitants in the field of normal justice, rather than of the political leadership in the field of extraordinary justice.

The new form of justice not fettered by the law in fourteenth-century Lucca served to weaken the distinction between the communal and signorial systems, and is consistent with the findings of recent studies focusing on commonalities between two governmental techniques. However, based on the case of Lucca, a new aspect of justice is also apparent that has been overlooked in recent research. This is a communal costume for the image of justice.

First of all, this is expressed in the procedures adopted by the political leadership when exercising their discretionary authority. Individual *gratia* in communal Lucca were carried out in accordance with procedures that involved a proposal to the council by the Anziani, then a scrutiny of the petition in council, and finally a vote. Even in situations involving added political interests, such as in connection with pardons (or the prohibition thereof) for persons convicted of serious crimes, the Anziani prohibited the granting of *gratia* or lifted such a prohibition through a provision made by the council. The Anziani, who had tremendous power, adopted this circuitous procedure to show that the justice they exercised was in line with republican council proceedings. More than anything, this consciousness is symbolically expressed in the detailed documentation of their deliberative activities. This contrasts with the way that Paolo Guinigi executed pardons with simple procedures and motivations (e.g. generous displays of excellence), but with only a few lines left in the record. Even the Anziani, who were able to seize power and present justice freely, had to explicitly declare that this justice was based on republican principles, carried out by themselves as political representatives of the '*comune*' on behalf of all its citizenry.

From the fact that the idea of justice elaborated by the political leadership of fourteenth-century Lucca was dressed in such communal garb, we can also see that the basic principle of the communal system of keeping a separation between politics and the judiciary was at least *formally protected*. Although the Anziani and the other political authorities carried out justice in substantive terms in the form of exemptions from laws, *gratia*, and exile, they always did so extraordinarily and retroactively, always with the concern of *bene del comune* as a composite bundle made up of the inviolable civil rights of individuals. And judicial authority was always entrusted to foreign magistrates, rather than to the civic political bodies. This was true even in 1392, a time when the regime was being strongly driven by political motivations; the Anziani did not conduct trials themselves. This concern with the *formal* maintenance of the communal regime, in practice, can clearly be seen in the decision to set up the office of the *podestà*, who had *de facto* been subordinate to the Anziani, as a Great Ruler.

★★★

Finally, I would like to once again underline the fact that the rebuilding of the image of justice and the image of the '*comune*' that it guided was realised through the individual practices of the people connecting the two with a cord in Lorenzetti's fresco. The practices of the people involved were never carried out consciously with the intention of rebuilding these two images. The individual inhabitants and political leaders living in fourteenth-century Lucca who appear in this book simply did their utmost to live out their own lives in the midst of the specific environment in which they found themselves.

The people who made their way to the communal palace on the north side of the piazza of San Michele in Foro each came bearing their own intentions. The voices these people lifted up to address the court and the governing council while concealing their own interests would on occasion resonate with the voices of other people. This continued to amplify with the passage of time. These growing voices then produced an idea of justice – and of the '*comune*' tied to it – that would never have entered the mind of the first utterer. The historical significance of these practices, surely unrecognised by the people at the time who lifted up their voices separately from one another at the communal palace, has here been finally revealed through an analysis of the historical sources that recorded those 'voices'.

Chronology

Dates	Events Concerning Lucca
1081	Privileges granted to Lucca from Holy Roman Emperor Henry IV
1120	First reference to consuls
1136	First reference to judgements by consuls
1178	First reference to the *Constitutum civitatis*
1187	First reference to the *podestà*
1197	First reference to the *societates populi*
1217	First reference to the public archive (*Camera Librorum*)
1255	First reference to the Anziani (as a representative body of the *popolo*)
1300	Partisan struggle between the White Guelphs and the Black Guelphs
1306	Summary justice is authorised in an edict by Clement V (*Clementina Saepe*)
1308	Oldest surviving city statutes
1314	Rule by Uguccione della Faggiuola of Pisa
1316	Domination by Castruccio Castracani (to 1328). Revision of city statutes
1328	Domination by Holy Roman Emperor Louis IV (to 1329)
1329	Domination by the Spinola family of Genoa (to 1331)
1331	Domination by King John of Bohemia (to 1333). Revision of city statutes
1333	Domination by the Rossi family of Parma (to 1335)
1335	Domination by the Della Scala family of Verona (to 1341)
1336	Revision of city statutes
1341	Domination by Florence (to 1342)
	(1341.9-1342.7) Pisa and Florence compete for Lucca
1342	Domination by Pisa (to 1368). Revision of city statutes
	(1342-47) Count Ranieri of Donoratico
	(1347-64) Pisan Anziani
	(1364-68) Giovanni dell'Agnello
1368	Domination by Holy Roman Emperor Charles IV (to 1370)
1370, Mar. 12	Charles IV appoints the Lucchese Anziani as imperial vicars
1370, Jul.	Establishment of a 'popular' system
1372	Revision of city statutes

Dates	Events Concerning Lucca
1378	Ciompi revolt in Florence
1392	Partisan conflict between the Forteguerra party and the Guinigi party
1400	Domination by Paolo Guinigi (to 1430) Abolition of the Court of Consuls
1430	Republic of Lucca (to 1799)

Bibliography

Archival Sources

Archivio di Stato di Lucca

Anziani al tempo della libertà, 4.

Anziani avanti la libertà, 5, 6, 7, 8, 9, 10, 11, 12, 13, 14, 16, 17, 18, 21, 26, 28, 34, 35, 37, 39, 41, 42, 53.

Archivi Pubblici, 13, 39.

Archivio dei Notari, 102, 103, 104, 105, 106, 108, 109, 110, 111, 112, 113, 114, 115, 116, 117, 118, 119, 120, 121, 122, 123, 124, 125, 126.

Archivio Guinigi, 73, 263.

Camarlingo Generale, 4, 7, 8, 60.

Capitano del Contado, 1, 4, 5, 7, 15.

Capitano del Popolo e della città, 7.

Capitoli, 19, 52.

Consiglio Generale, 1, 2, 8, 10, 12.

Curia dei Foretani o di S. Alessandro, 14, 15, 16, 17.

Curia dei Rettori, 3, 4, 6, 18.

Curia dei Ribelli e dei Banditi, 7.

Curia dei Treguani, 30, 31, 34.

Curia dei Visconti, 38, 39, 40.

Curia delle Querimonie, 3, 4, 5.

Curia di S. Cristoforo, 7, 9, 112, 113, 114.

Curia Nuova di Giustizia e dell'Esecutore, 25, 30, 38, 39, 40, 41.

Estimo, 2.

Governo di Paolo Guinigi, 1, 33.

Maggior Sindaco e Giudice degli Appelli, 37, 41, 42.

Offizio sopra l'abbondanza, 379.

Potestà di Lucca

Curia civile: 8, 11, 37, 58, 60, 64, 67, 82, 104, 164, 168, 174, 177, 415, 421, 422, 423, 424, 426, 427, 428, 430, 431, 432, 450, 703, 704, 705, 706, 707, 708, 709, 710.

Curia dei maleficii: 4726, 4737, 4739, 4743, 4785, 4787,4788, 4790, 4846, 4847, 4848, 4849, 4886, 4887, 4888, 4889, 4890, 4901, 4902, 4903, 4904, 5076, 5077, 5078, 5079, 5080, 5081, 5082.

Sei deputati sul reintegrare le doti, 1.

Sentenze e bandi, 13, 17, 18, 22, 29, 30, 42, 85, 540.

Statuti del Comune di Lucca, 1, 2, 3, 4, 5, 6, 7, 8, 9, 10.

Printed Primary Sources

Agidius de Fuscarariis, *Ordo iudiciarius*, ed. L. Wahrmund, *Der ordo iudiciarius des Aegidius de Fuscarariis*, Quellen zur Geschichte des römisch-kanonischen Processes im Mittelalter (Innsbruck, 1916).

Albertus Gandinus, *Tractatus de maleficiis*, ed. H. Kantorowicz, in *Albertus Gandinus und das Strafrecht des Scholastik*, vol. II (Berlin, 1926).

Bartolo da Sassoferrato, *Bartoli Commentaria in secundam digesti novi partem* (Lyon, 1555).

———, *Tractatus de tyranno*, ed. D. Quaglioni, in *Politica e diritto nel Trecento italiano. Il "De Tyranno" di Bartolo da Sassoferrato (1314-1357)* (Firenze, 1983).

Bernardino da Siena, *Prediche volgari: la predicazione del 1425 in Siena*, II, ed. C. Cannarozzi (Firenze, 1958).

Bongi, S. (ed.), *Bandi lucchesi del secolo decimo quarto* (Bologna, 1863).

——— (ed.), *Statuto del comune di Lucca dell'anno MCCCVIII* (Lucca, 1867).

Conti, E. (ed.), *Le «consulte» e «pratiche» della repubblica fiorentina nel Quattrocento: I. 1401 (Cancellierato di Coluccio Salutati)* (Pisa, 1981).

Fiumi, L. (ed.), *Regesti. Carteggio degli anziani* (Lucca, 1903).

Harrington, J., *The Commonwealth of Oceana and A System of Politics*, ed. J. G. A. Pocock (Cambridge, 1992)

Hobbes, T., *Hobbes's Leviathan reprinted from the edition of 1651, with an essay by the late W. G. Pogson Smith* (Oxford, 1909).

Latini, B., *Tresor*, ed. P. G. Beltrami (Torino, 2007).

Marsilio da Padova, *Il difensore della pace*, ed. C. Vasoli (Torino, 1975).

Nelli, S., and Simonetti, G. (eds.), *Anziani avanti la libertà (Lucca, 1330-1369)*, I (Lucca, 2007).

Rainerius Perusinus, *Ars notariae*, ed. L. Wahrmund, *Die ars notariae*, Quellen zur Geschichte des römisch-kanonischen Processes im Mittelalter (Aalen, 1962).

Rolandino Rodulphini Bononiensis, *Summa totius artis notariae* (Venezia, 1546).

Romiti, A., and Tori, G. (eds.), *Statuti e matricole del Collegio dei Giudici e Notai della città di Lucca* (Roma, 1978).

——— (ed.), *L'Armarium Comunis della Camara actorum di Bologna. L'inventariazione archivistica nel XIII secolo* (Roma, 1994).

——— (ed.), *Riformagioni della repubblica di Lucca (1369-1400)*, I (Roma, 1980).

Salutati, C., *Il tratto 'de tyranno' e lettere scelte*, ed. F. Ercole (Bologna, 1942).

Schmeidler, B. (ed.), *Tholomei Lucensis Annales, MGH, Scriptores rerum germanicarum*, t. VIII (Berlin, 1955).

Sercambi, G., *Le chroniche di Giovanni Sercambi Luccese*, ed. S. Bongi (Lucca, 1892).

Tori, G. (ed.), *Riformagioni della repubblica di Lucca (1369-1400)*, II, IV (Roma, 1985, 1998).

Watson, A. (ed.), *The Digest of Justinian*, vol. 4 (Philadelphia, 1998)

Secondary Sources

AGAMBEN, G., *Stato di eccezione* (Torino, 2003).

ARLINGHAUS, F. J., (eds.), *Praxis der Gerichtsbarkeit in europäischen Städten des Spätmittelalters* (Frankfurt am Main, 2006).

ARMSTRONG, L., and KIRSHNER, J. (eds.), *The Politics of Law in Late Medieval and Renaissance Italy: Essays in Honour of Lauro Martines* (Toronto, 2011).

ARTIFONI, E., 'Tensioni sociali e istituzioni nel mondo comunale', in N. Tranfaglia and M. Firpo (eds.), *La storia, 2: Il Medioevo: popoli e strutture politiche* (Torino 1986), 461-491.

———, 'I governi di «popolo» e le istituzioni comunali', *Reti Medievali*, 4-2 (2003), 1-20.

ASCHERI, M., 'Istituzioni e giustizia dei mercanti nel Tre-Quattrocento', in M. Del Treppo (ed.), *Sistema di rapporti ed élites economiche in Europa (secoli XII-XVII)* (Napoli, 1994), 33-61.

ARTIFONI, E., 'Il processo civile tra diritto comune e diritto locale: Da questioni preliminari al caso della giustizia estense', *Quaderni storici*, 101 (1999), 355-387.

———, 'Le fonti e la flessibilità del diritto comune: il paradosso del consilium sapientis', in Id. (ed.), *Legal Consulting in the Civil Law Tradition* (Berkeley, 1999), 11-53.

———, 'Formalismi di giuristi e di storici: un programma di lavoro?', *Le carte e la storia*, 7 (2001), 7-18.

———, 'Un nuovo registro di deliberazioni trecentesche lucchesi', *Archivio storico italiano*, 591 (2002), 79-86.

BAIETTO, L., 'Elaborazione di sistemi documentari e trasformazioni politiche nei comuni piemontesi (sec. XIII): una relazione di circolarità', *Società e storia*, 98 (2002), 645-679.

BANTI, O., '"Civitas" e "Commune" nelle fonti italiane dei secoli XI e XII', in G. Rossetti (ed.), *Forme di potere e struttura sociale in Italia nel Medioevo* (Bologna, 1977), 217-232.

BARACCINI, C. (ed.), *Il secolo di Castruccio. Fonti e documenti di storia lucchese* (Lucca, 1983).

BARTOLI LANGELI, A., 'La documentazione degli stati italiani nei secoli XIII-XV: forme, organizzazione, personale', in *Culture et idéologie dans la genèse de l'État modern* (Roma, 1985), 35-55.

BAUMGÄRTNER, I., 'Gerichtspraxis und Stadtgesellschaft. Zu Zielsetzung und Inhalt', in Arlinghaus et al. (eds.), *Praxis der Gerichtsbarkeit*, 1-18.

BEHRMANN, T., 'Von der Sentenz zur Akte. Beobachtungen zur Entwicklung des Prozeßschriftgutes in Mailand', in Keller and Behrmann (eds.), *Kommunales Schriftgut*, 71-90.

BELLABARBA, M., SCHWERHOFF, G., and ZORZI, A. (eds.), *Criminalità e giustizia in Germania e in Italia: Pratiche giudiziarie e linguaggi giuridici tra tardo medioevo ed età moderna* (Berlin and Bologna, 2001).

Il bene comune: forme di governo e gerarchie sociali nel basso medioevo (Spoleto, 2012).

BERENGO, M., *Nobili e mercanti nella Lucca del Cinquecento* (Torino, 1965).

BLACK, A., 'Society and the Individual from the Middle Ages to Rousseau: Philosophy, Jurisprudence and Constitutional Theory', *History of Political Thought*, 1-2 (1980), 145-166.

BLACK, J., *Absolutism in Renaissance Milan. Plenitude of Power under the Visconti and the Sforza 1329-1535* (Oxford, 2009).

BLANSHEI, S. R., *Politics and Justice in Late Medieval Bologna* (Leiden and Boston, 2010).

Blockmans, W., Holenstein, A., and Mathieu, J. (eds.), *Empowering Interactions. Political Cultures and the Emergence of the State in Europe 1300-1900* (Farnham and Burlington, 2009).

Blomquist, T. W., and Mazzaoui, M. F. (eds.), *The "Other Tuscany": Essays in the History of Lucca, Pisa, and Siena During the Thirteenth, Fourteenth, and Fifteenth Centuries* (Michigan, 1994).

Bowsky, W. M., *A Medieval Italian Commune: Siena under the Nine, 1287-1355* (Berkeley, Los Angeles and London, 1981).

Bongi, S., *Inventario del Reale Archivio di Stato in Lucca*, 2 vols. (Lucca, 1872-1876).

Boucheron, P., '«Tournez les yeux pour admirer, vous qui exercez le pouvoir, celle qui est peinte ici». La fresque du Bon Gouvernement d'Ambrogio Lorenzetti', *Annales HSS.*, 6 (2005), 1137-1199.

Bourdieu, P., *Le sens pratique* (Paris, 1980).

Braddick, M. J., *State Formation in Early Modern England, 1550-1700* (Cambridge, 2000).

Bratchel, M. E., *Lucca 1430-1494. The Reconstruction of an Italian City-Republic* (Oxford, 1995).

———, *Medieval Lucca and the evolution of the Renaissance state* (Oxford, 2008).

Brunner, O., *Land and Lordship: Structures of Governance in Medieval Austria* (1939; Eng. edn., Philadelphia, 1992).

Caciorgna, M. T., Carocci, S., and Zorzi, A. (eds.), *I comuni di Jean-Claude Maire Vigueur. Percorsi storiografici* (Roma, 2014).

Cammarosano, P., *Italia medievale. Struttura e geografia delle fonti scritte* (Roma, 1991).

———, 'Il ricambio e l'evoluzione dei ceti dirigenti nel corso del XIII secolo', in *Magnati e popolani nell'Italia comunale* (Pistoia, 1997), 17-40.

Canning, J., *The Political Thought of Baldus de Ubaldis* (Cambridge, 1987).

Carraway Vitello, J., *Public Justice and the Criminal Trial in Late Medieval Italy: Reggio Emilia in the Visconti Age* (Leiden and Boston, 2010).

———, 'Contumacy, Defense Strategy, and Criminal Law in Late Medieval Italy', Law and History Review, 29-1 (2011), 99-132.

Castelnuovo, E. (ed.), *Ambrogio Lorenzetti: il Buon governo* (Milano, 1995).

Cavallar, O., '*Laesa Maiestas* in Renaissance Lucca', in Armstrong and Kirshner (eds.), *The Politics of Law*, 161-183.

Cencetti, G., 'Camera actorum comunis Bononie', *Archivi* ser. II, 2 (1935), 87-120.

Cerutti, S., 'Giustiziae località a Torino in età moderna: una ricerca in corso', *Quaderni storici*, 89 (1995), 445-486.

Chabod, F., 'Esiste uno Stato del Rinascimento?' in *Opere di Federico Chabod*, II, *Scritti sul Rinascimento* (Torino, 1967), 593-604.

Cherubini, G., *Città comunali di Toscana* (Bologna, 2003).

Chiffoleau J., Gauvard, C., and Zorzi, A. (eds.), *Pratiques sociales et politiques judiciaires dans les villes de l'Occident à la fin du Moyen Âge* (Roma, 2007).

Chittolini, G., *La formazione dello stato regionale e le istituzioni del contado: Secoli XIV e XV* (Torino, 1979).

———, 'Introduzione', in Id. (ed.), *Istituzioni e società nella storia d'Italia. La crisi degli ordinamenti comunali e le origini dello stato del Rinascimento* (Bologna, 1979), 1-50.

———, MOLHO, A., and SCHIERA, P. (eds.), *Origini dello stato. Processi di formazione statale in Italia fra medioevo ed età moderna* (Bologna, 1994).

CHITTOLINI, G., '"Il privato", il "pubblico", lo Stato', in Chittolini, Molho and Schiera (eds.), *Origini dello stato*, 553-589.

———, 'A comment', in Connel and Zorzi (eds.), *Florentine Tuscany*, 333-345.

CICCAGLIONI, G., 'Dal comune alla signoria? Lo spazio politico di Pisa nella prima metà del XIV secolo', *Bullettino dell'Istituto storico italiano per il Medio Evo*, 109-1 (2007), 235-269.

COLLI, V., '*Acta civilia in curia potestatis*: Firenze 1344. Aspetti procedurali nel quadro di giurisdizioni concorrenti', in Arlinghaus et al. (eds.), *Praxis der Gerichtsbarkeit*, 271-303.

CONNEL W. J., and ZORZI, A. (eds.), *Florentine Tuscany. Structures and Practices of Power* (Cambridge, 2000).

CORSI, D., 'La legislazione archivistica dello Stato di Lucca', *Archivio storico italiano*, 114 (1956), 189-223.

CORTESE, E., *La norma giuridica: spunti teorici nel diritto comune classico* (Milano, 1962).

COVINI, M. N., '*De gratia speciali*. Sperimentazioni documentarie e pratiche di potere tra i Visconti e gli Sforza', in Vallerani (ed.), *Tecniche di potere*, 183-206.

D'ADDARIO, A., 'La conservazione degli atti notarili negli ordinamenti della Repubblica lucchese', *Archivio storico italiano*, 109 (1951), 193-226.

DE LA RONCIÈRE, C. M., *Prix et salaires à Florence au XIV*[e] *siècle (1280-1380)* (Roma, 1982).

DE VINCENTIIS, A., 'Memorie bruciate. Confilitti, documenti, oblio nella città italiane del tardo medioevo', *Bullettino dell'Istituto Storico Italiano per il Medio Evo*, 106 (2004), 167-198.

DEAN, T., 'Wealth distribution and litigation in the medieval Italian countryside: Castel San Pietro', *Continuity and Change*, 17-3 (2002), 333-350.

———, *Crime and Justice in Late Medieval Italy* (Cambridge, 2007).

DEL PUNTA, I., *Mercanti e banchieri lucchesi nel Duecento* (Pisa, 2004).

DESCAMPS, O., 'Aux Aux origines de la procédure sommaire: Remarques sur la constitution Saepe contingit (Clem., V, 11, 2)', in Y. Mausen, O. Condorelli, F. Roumy, and M. Schmoeckel (eds.), *Der Einfluss der Kanonistik auf die europäische Rechtskultur*, IV (Prozessrecht) (Wien, 2014), 45-63.

DESSÌ, R. M., 'Il bene comune nella comunicazione verbale e visiva. Indagini sugli affreschi del "Buon Governo"', in *Il bene comune*, 89-130.

DEZZA, E., *Accusa e inquisizione dal diritto comune ai codici moderni* (Milano, 1989).

DONAHUE, C., Jr., 'Procedure in the Courts of the Ius commune', in W. Hartmann and K. Pennington (eds.), *The History of Courts and Procedure in Medieval Canon Law* (Washington, 2016), 74-124.

DONATO, M. M., 'Ancora sulle "Fonti" nel Governo di Ambrogio Lorenzetti: dubbi, precisazioni, anticipazioni', in S. Adorni Braccesi and M. Ascheri (eds.), *Politica e cultura nelle repubbliche italiane dal Medioevo all'età moderna. Firenze, Genova, Lucca, Siena, Venezia* (Roma, 2001), 43-79.

———, 'Il *princeps*, il giudice, il «sindacho» e la città. Novità su Ambrogio Lorenzetti nel Palazzo Pubblico di Siena', in F. Bocchi and R. Smurra (eds.), *Imago urbis: l'immagine delle città nella storia d'Italia* (Roma 2003), 389-416.

ENGELMANN, A. (trans. by R. W. Millar), *A History of Continental Civil Procedure* (Boston, 1927).

Fenster, T., and Smail, D. L. (eds.), *Fama: The Politics of Talk and Reputation in Medieval Europe* (Ithaca, 2003).

Fissore, G. G., *Autonomia notarile e organizzazione cancelleresca nel Comune di Asti. I modi e le forme dell'intervento notarile nella costituzione del documento comunale* (Spoleto, 1977).

Fraher, R. M., 'The Theoretical Justification for the New Criminal Law of the High Middle Ages: *Rei publicae interest, ne crimina remaneant impunita*', *The University of Illinois Law Review*, 3 (1984), 577-595.

———, 'IV Lateran's revolution and criminal procedure: the birth of inquistio, the end of ordeals, and Innocent III's vision of ecclesiastical politics', in R. I. Castillo Lara (ed.), *Studia in honorem eminentissimi cardinalis Alphonsi M. Stickler* (Roma, 1992), 96-111.

Gamberini, A., and Lazzarini, I. (eds.), *The Italian Renaissance State* (Cambridge, 2012).

———, and ———, *The Clash of Legitimacies. The State-Building Process in Late Medieval Lombardy* (Oxford, 2018).

Gaulin, J. L., 'Les registres de bannis pour dettes à Bologne au XIII siècle: une nouvelle source pour l'histoire de l'endettement', *Mélanges de l'École française de Rome. Moyen Âge*, 109 (1997), 479-499.

Gauvard, C., and Chiffeleau, J., 'Conclusions', in Chiffoleau, Gauvard and Zorzi (eds.), *Pratiques sociales*, 713-720.

———, *«De grace especial.» Crime, état et la société en France à la fin du Moyen Âge* (Paris, 2010).

———, 'Grâce et exécution capitale: les deux visages de la justice royale français à la fin de Moyen Âge', *Bibliothèque de l'Écoles des chartes*, 153 (1995), 275-290.

Geltner, G., *The Medieval Prison: A Social History* (Princeton, 2008).

———, 'I registri criminali dell'Archivio Arcivescovile di Lucca: prospettive di ricerca per la storia sociale del medioevo', in Pagano and Piatti (eds.), *I documenti del tribunale ecclesiastico*, 330-340.

———, 'Healthscaping a medieval city: Lucca's Curia viarum and the future of public health history', *Urban History*, 40 (2013), 395-415.

———, *Roads to Health: Infrastructure and Urban Wellbeing in Later Medieval Italy* (Philadelphia, 2019)

Giorgi, A., Moscadelli, S., and Zarrilli, C. (eds.), *La documentazione degli organi giudiziari nell'Italia tardo-medievale e moderna* (Roma, 2012).

Giuliani, A., 'L'*ordo judiciarius* medioevale. Riflessioni su un modello puro di ordine isonomico', *Rivista di diritto processuale*, 43-2 (1988), 598-614.

Green, L., *Castruccio Castracani. A study on the origins and character of a fourteenth-century Italian despotism* (Oxford, 1986).

———, *Lucca under Many Masters: A Fourteenth-Century Italian Commune in Crisis (1328-1342)* (Firenze, 1995).

Graziotti, T., *Giustizia penale a San Gimignano (1300-1350)* (Firenze, 2015).

Grossi, P., *Le situazioni reali nell'esperienza giuridica medievale* (Padova, 1968).

———, *Ordine giuridico medievale* (Roma, 1995).

Hattori, Y. (ed.), *Political Order and Forms of Communication in Medieval and Early Modern Europe* (Roma, 2014).

Herlihy, D., and Klapisch-Zuber, C., *Tuscans and their families. A Study of the Florentine Catasto of 1427* (1978; Eng. edn., New Haven and London, 1985).

Holenstein, A., 'Introduction: Empowering Interactions: Looking at Statebuilding from Below', in Blockmans, Holenstein and Mathieu (eds.), *Empowering Interactions*, 1-31.

Jones, P., *The Italian City-State from Commune to Signoria* (Oxford, 1997).

Jansen, K. L., *Peace and Penance in Late Medieval Italy* (Princeton, 2018).

Kantorowicz, E. H., *The King's Two Bodies: A Study in Mediaeval Political Theology* (Princeton, 1957).

Keller, H. (ed.), *Pragmatische Schriftlichkeit im Mittelalter* (München, 1992).

———, 'Gli statuti dell'Italia settentrionale come testimonianza e fonte per il processo di affermazione della scrittura nei secoli XII e XIII', in G. Albini (ed.), *Le scritture del comune. Amministrazione e memoria nelle città dei secoli XII e XIII* (Torino, 1998), 61-94.

———, and Behrmann, T. (eds.), *Kommunales Schriftgut in Oberitalien. Formen, Funktionen, Überlieferung* (München, 1995).

Keller, H., *Il laboratorio politico del Comune medievale* (Napoli, 2014)

Kirshner, J. (ed.), *The Origins of the State in Italy 1300-1600* (Chicago and London, 1995).

Koch, P., 'Die Archivierung kommunaler Bücher in den ober- und mittelitalienischen Städten im 13. und frühen 14. Jahrhundert', in Keller and Behrmann (eds.), *Kommunales Schriftgut*, 19-69.

Kuehn, T., *Law, family and women: toward a legal anthropology of Renaissance Italy* (Chicago and London, 1991).

Kumhera, G., *The Benefits of Peace: Private Peacemaking in Late Medieval Italy* (Leiden, 2017).

Lazzareschi, E., 'L'Archivio dei Notari della Repubblica lucchese', *Gli Archivi Italiani*, II-6 (1915), 175-189.

Lecuppre-Desjardin, E., and Van Bruaene, A. L. (eds.), *De bono communi. The discourse and Practice of the Common Good in the European City (13th-16th c.)* (Turnhout, 2010).

Lepsius, S., '*Dixit male iudicatum esse per dominos iudices.* Zur Praxis der städtischen Appellationsgerichtsbarkeit im Lucca des 14. Jahrhunderts', in Arlinghaus et al. (eds.), *Praxis der Gerichtsbarkeit*, 189-269.

———, and Wetzstein T. (eds.), *Als die Welt in die Akten kam. Prozeßschriftgut im europäischen Mittelalter* (Frankfurt am Main, 2008).

Lepsius, S., 'Kontrolle von Amtsrägern durch Schrift. Luccheser notare und Richter im Syndikatsprozeß', in Lepsius and Wetzstein (eds.), *Als die Welt in die Akten kam*, 389-473.

Leverotti, F., *Popolazione, famiglie, insediamento. Le Sei Miglia lucchesi nel XIV e XV secolo* (Pisa, 1992).

Lombardini, S., Raggio, O., and Torre, A. (eds.), *Quaderni storici*, 63 (*Conflitti locali e idiomi politici*) (1986).

Lopez, R. S., 'The unexplored wealth of the notarial archives in Pisa and Lucca', in *Mélanges d'histoire du moyen-âge, dédiés â la mémoire de Louis Halphen* (Paris, 1951), 427-432.

Magnati e popolani nell'Italia comunale (Pistoia, 1997).

Maire Vigueur, J. C., 'Justice et politique dans l'Italie communale de la seconde moitié du XIII siècle: l'exemple de Pérouse', *Comptes rendus de l'Académie des inscriptions et belles-lettre*, 130-2 (1986), 312-330.

———, 'Giudici e testimoni a confronto', in J. C. Maire Vigueur and A. P. Pagliani, *La parole all'accusato* (Palermo, 1991), 105-123.

———, 'Révolution documentaire et révolution scripturaire: le cas de l'Italia médiévale', *Bibliothèque de l'École des chartes*, 153 (1995), 177-185.

———, *Cavalieri e cittadini: guerra, conflitti e società nell'Italia comunale* (Bologna, 2004).

———(ed.), *Signorie cittadine nell'Italia comunale* (Roma, 2013).

Mancini, A., *Storia di Lucca* (Firenze, 1950).

Manselli, R., *La repubblica di Lucca* (Torino, 1986).

Martone, L., *Arbiter-arbitrator. Forme di giustizia privata nell'età del diritto comune* (Napoli, 1984).

Marulo, R., *Scrivere ai potenti. Le suppliche al tempo di Paolo Guinigi* (Piombino, 2009).

Matraia, G., *Lucca nel Mileduecento* (Lucca, 1843).

Meccarelli, M., *Arbitrium. Un aspetto sistematico degli ordinamenti giuridici in età di diritto comune* (Milano, 1998).

———, 'Le categorie dottrinali della procedura e l'effettivita della giustizia penale nel tardo medioevo', in Chiffoleau, Gauvard and Zorzi (eds.), *Pratiques sociales*, 573-594.

Meek, C., *Lucca 1369-1400. Politics and Society in an Early Renaissance City-State* (Oxford, 1978).

———, *The Commune of Lucca under Pisan Rule, 1342-1369* (Cambridge, 1980).

———, 'I documenti del tribunale ecclesiastico di Lucca nei secoli XIV e XV come fonte storica', in Pagano and Piatti (eds.), *I documenti del tribunale ecclesiastico*, 313-329.

———, '"Whatever's Best Administered is Best": Paolo Guinigi, signore of Lucca, 1400-1430', in J. E. Law and B. Paton (eds.), *Communes and Despots in Medieval and Renaissance Italy* (Cornwall, 2010), 131-143.

Méhu, D., 'Structure et utilisation des registres de bannis pour dettes à Bologne au XIII siècle', *Mélanges de l'École française de Rome. Moyen Âge*, 107 (1997), 545-567.

Meinecke, F., *Machiavelism: The Doctrine of Raison d'État and Its Place in Modern History* (New Haven, 1957).

Menant, F., *L'Italia dei comuni (1100-1350)* (2005; Ital. edn., Roma, 2011).

Menzinger, S., *Giuristi e politica nei comuni di Popolo. Siena, Perugia e Bologna, tra governi a confronto* (Roma, 2006).

———, 'Forme di organizzazione giudiziaria delle città comunali italiane nei secoli XII e XIII: l'uso dell'arbitrato nei governi consolari e podestarili', in Arlinghaus et al. (eds.), *Praxis der Gerichtsbarkeit*, 113-134.

———, 'Forme di implicazione politica dei giuristi nei governi comunali italiani del XIII secolo', in Chiffoleau, Gauvard and Zorzi (eds.), *Pratiques sociales*, 191-241.

——— and Vallerani, M., 'Giuristi e città: fiscalità, giustizia e cultura giuridica tra XII e XIII secolo. Ipotesi e percorsi di ricerca', in Caciorgna, Carocci and Zorzi (eds.), *I comuni di Jean Claude Maire Vigueur*, 201-234.

Meyer, A., *Felix et inclitus notarius. Studien zum italienischen Notariat vom 7. bis zum 13. Jahrhundert* (Tübingen, 2000).

Menzinger, S., 'Hereditary Laws and City Topography: On the Development of the Italian Notarial Archives in the Late Middle Ages', in A. Classen (ed.), *Urban Space in the Middle Ages and the Early Modern Age* (Berlin, 2009), 225-244.

Milani, G., 'Il governo delle liste nel comune di Bologna. Premesse e genesi di un libro di proscrizione duecentesco', *Rivista storica italiana*, 108 (1996), 149-229.

———, 'Prime note su disciplina e pratica del bando a Bologna attorno alla metà del XIII secolo', *Mélanges de l'École française de Rome. Moyen Âge*, 109-2 (1997), 501-523.

———, 'Dalla ritorsione al controllo. Elaborazione e applicazione del programma antighibellino a Bologna alla fine del Duecento', *Quaderni storici*, 94 (1997), 43-74.

Milani, G., *L'esclusione dal comune. Conflitti e bandi politici a Bologna e in altre città italiane tra XII e XIV secolo* (Roma, 2003).

Milani, G., *I comuni italiani* (Roma-Bari, 2005).

———, 'Lo sviluppo della giurisdizione nei comuni italiani del secolo XII', in Arlinghaus et al. (eds.), *Praxis der Gerichtsbarkeit*, 21-45.

———, 'Legge ed eccezione nei comuni di popolo del XIII secolo (Bologna, Perugia, Pisa)', *Quaderni storici*, 131 (*Sistemi di eccezione*) (2009), 377-398.

Mineo, E. I., 'La repubblica come categoria storica', *Storica*, 43-45 (2009), 125-167.

Muzzarelli, M. G. (ed.), *Riferire all'autorità. Denuncia e delazione tra Medioevo ed Età Moderna* (Roma, 2020).

Nakaya, S., 'La giustizia civile a Lucca nella prima metà del XIV secolo', *Archivio storico italiano*, 630 (2011), 635-678.

———, 'The *Gratia* and the Expansion of Politics in Fourteenth-Century Lucca', *The Southern African Journal of Medieval and Renaissance Studies*, 22/23 (*The Late Medieval and Renaissance Italian City-State and Beyond. Essays in Honour of M. E. Bratchel*) (2012/2013), 107-134.

———, 'Organization and Use of Archival Records in Medieval Lucca and Bologna', *Journal of Western Medieval History*, 38 (2016), 95-119.

———, '*Fama Pubblica* and Informatns in the Judicial Records of Lucca in the 14th Century', in M. G. Muzzarelli (ed.), *Riferire all'autorità. Denuncia e delazione tra Medioevo ed Età Moderna* (Roma, 2020), 79-95.

———, 'Credit Networks between City and Countryside in Late Medieval Lucca', in S. Nicolussi-Köhler (ed.), *Change and Transformation of Premodern Credit Markets. The Importance of Small-Scale Credits* (Heidelberg, 2021), 117-140.

Najemy, J. M., 'Stato, commune e «universitas»', *Annali dell'Istituto storico italo-germanico in Trento*, 20 (*Atti della tavola rotonda tenutasi nell'ambito del seminario su Le origini dello Stato moderno in Italia, secoli XIV-XVI*) (1995), 245-263.

———, *A history of Florence 1200-1575* (Oxford, 2006).

Ortalli, G., 'Il procedimento per gratiam e gli ambienti ecclesiastici nella Venezia del primo Trecento tra amministrazione, politica e carità', in B. Bertoli (ed.), *Chiesa società e Stato a Venezia. Miscellanea di studi in onore di Silvio Tramontin nel suo 75 anno di età* (Venezia 1994), 75-100.

Osheim, D. J., 'Countrymen and the Law in Late-Medieval Tuscany', *Speculum*, 64 (1989), 317-337.

Ottokar, N., *The Medieval City-Communes* (Firenze, 1933).

Padoa Schioppa, A., 'Il ruolo della cultura giuridica in alcuni atti giudiziari italiani dei secoli XI e XII', *Nuova rivista storica*, 64 (1980), 265-289.

———, 'Sul ruolo dei giuristi nell'età del Diritto Comune: un problema aperta', in D. Segoloni (ed.), *Il Diritto Comune e la tradizione giuridica europea. Atti del Convegno di Studi in onore di G. Ermini* (Perugia, 1980), 155-166.

———, 'Note sulla giustizia milanese nel XII secolo', in *Milano e la Lombardia in età comunale. Secoli XI-XIII* (Milano, 1993), 66-70.

———, 'La giustizia milanese nella prima età viscontea (1277-1300)', in *Ius Mediolani: studi di storia del diritto milanese offerti dagli allievi a Giulio Vismara* (Milano, 1996), 1-46.

——— (ed.), *Legislation and Justice* (Oxford, 1997).

———, 'Profili del processo civile nella Summa artis notariae di Rolandino', in Tamba (ed.), *Rolandino e l'Ars notaria*, 583-609.

———, 'La coscienza del giudice', in Id. (ed.), *Italia ed Europa nella storia del diritto* (Bologna, 2003), 251-292.

———, *A History of Law in Europe. From the Early Middle Ages to the Twentieth Century* (Cambridge, 2017).

Pagano, S., and Piatti, P. (eds.), *I documenti del tribunale ecclesiastico di Lucca nei secoli XIV e XV come fonte storica* (Firenze, 2010).

Panella, E., 'Dal bene comune al bene del comune. I trattati politici di Remigio dei Girolami', in *Politica e vita religiosa a Firenze tra '300 e '500* (Pistoia, 1985), 24-25, 100.

Pasciuta, B., *In regia curia civiliter convenire. Giustizia e città nella Sicilia tardomedievale* (Torino, 2003).

Pasquini, L., 'La rappresentazione del bene comune nell'iconografia medievale', in *Il bene comune*, 489-515.

Pazzaglini, P., *The Criminal Ban of the Sienese Commune 1225-1310* (Milan, 1979).

Pennington, K., 'Innocent III and the Ius commune', in R. H. Helmholz et al. (eds.), *Grundlagen des Rechts: Festschrift für Peter Landau zum 65. Geburtstag* (Paderborn, 2000), 349-366.

———, 'Introduction to the Courts', in W. Hartmann and K. Pennington (eds.), *The History of Courts and Procedure in Medieval Canon Law* (Washington, 2016), 3-29.

Perani, T., 'Pluralità nella giustizia pubblica duecentesca. Due registri di condanne del comune di Pavia', *Archivio storico italiano*, 619 (2009), 57-89.

Piccinni, G., 'Il sistema senese del credito nella fase di smobilitazione dei suoi banchi internazionali. Politiche comunali, spesa pubblica, propaganda contro l'usura (1332-1340)', in Id. (ed.), *Fedeltà ghibellina, affari guelfi. Saggi e riletture intorno alla storia di Siena fra Due e Trecento* (Pisa, 2008), 209-289.

Pinto, G., *La Toscana nel tardo Medioevo. Ambiente, economia rurale, società* (Firenze, 1982).

———, *Toscana medievale. Paesaggi e realtà sociali* (Firenze, 1993).

Polica, S., 'An Attempted «Reconversion» of Wealth in XVth Century Lucca: the Lands of Michele di Giovanni Guinigi', *Journal of European Economic History*, 9 (1980), 655-707.

Poloni, A., 'Il ricambio dei ceti dirigenti delle città comunali italiane nel Duecento: nuove osservazioni sul caso pisano', *Archivio storico italiano*, 601 (2004), 415-451.

———, 'Fisionomia sociale e identià politica dei gruppi dirigenti popolari nella seconda metà del Duecento. Spunti di riflessione su un tema classico della storiografia comunalistica italiana', *Società e storia*, 110 (2005), 799-821.

———, 'Strutturazione del mondo corporativo e affermazione del popolo a Lucca nel Duecento', *Archivio storico italiano*, 613 (2007), 449-486.

———, *Lucca nel Duecento: uno studio sul cambiamento sociale* (Pisa, 2009).

———, *Potere al popolo. Conflitti sociali e lotte politiche nell'Italia comunale del Duecento* (Milano, 2010).

PUNCH, D. (ed.), *Il cartulario del notaio Martino. Savona, 1203-1206* (Genova, 1974).

RUBINSTEIN, N., 'Political Ideas in Sienese Art: The Frescoes by Ambrogio Lorenzetti and Taddeo di Bartolo in the Palazzo Pubblico', (1958), in G. Cappelli (ed.), *Studies in Italian History in the Midle Ages and the Renaissance, I, Political Thought and the Language of Politics. Art and Politics* (Roma, 2004). 61-98.

———, 'Le allegorie di Ambrogio Lorenzetti nella sala della pacee il pensiero politico del suo tempo', (1997), in G. Cappelli (ed.), *Studies in Italian History*, 347-364.

REINHARD, W. (ed.), *Power Elites and State Building* (Oxford, 1996).

ROMANO, D., 'Quod sibi fiat gratia: adjustment of penalties and the exercise of influence in early Renaissance Venice', *The Journal of Medieval and Renaissance Studies*, 13 (1983), 251-268.

ROMITI, A., 'Il processo civile a Lucca. La curia appellationum (1331)', in *Lucca archivistica storica economica* (Roma, 1973), 152-162.

———, 'Lo «statutum curie appellationum» del 1331', *Actum luce*, 23 (1994), 111-151.

———, 'Archival Inventorying in Fourthennth-Century Lucca: Methodologies, Theories and Practices', in Blomquist and Mazzaoui (eds.), *The "Other Tuscany"*, 83-109.

SALVIOLI, G., *Storia della procedura civile e criminale*, P. Del Giudice (dir.), *Storia del Diritto Italiano*, III-1 (Milano, 1925).

SBRICCOLI, M., *L' interpretazione dello statuto. Contributo allo studio della funzione dei giuristi nell'età comunale* (Milano, 1969).

———, 'Legislation, Justice and Political Power in Italian Cities, 1200-1400', in Padoa Schioppa (ed.), *Legislation and Justice*, 37-55.

———, '"Vidi communiter observari". L'emersione di un ordine penale pubblico nelle città italiane del secolo XIII', *Quaderni fiorentini per la storia del pensiero giuridico*, 27 (1998), 231-268.

———, 'Giustizia negoziata, giustizia egemonica. Riflessioni su una nuova fase degli studi di storia della giustizia criminale', in Bellabarba, Schwerhoff and Zorzi (eds.), *Criminalità e giustizia*, 345-365.

———, 'Giustizia criminale', in M. Fioravanti (ed.), *Lo stato moderno in Europa. Istituzioni e diritto* (Roma, 2002), 163-205.

———, *Storia del diritto penale e della giustizia. Scritti editi e inediti (1972-2007)*(Milano, 2009).

SCHIERA, P., 'Legittimità, disciplina, istituzioni: tre presupposti per la nascita dello Stato moderno', in Chittolini, Molho and Schiera (eds.), *Origini dello stato*, 17-48.

———, 'Il Buongoverno melancolico di Ambrogio Lorenzetti e la costituzionale faziosità della città', *Scienza e politica*, 34 (2006), 93-108.

SIMONETTI, G., 'Il Collegio degli Anziani nei primi anni delle dominazioni straniere', in Nelli and Simonetti (eds.), *Anziani avanti la libertà (Lucca, 1330-1369)*, I (Lucca, 2007), 17-31.

Simonde de Sismondi, J. C. L., *Storia delle repubbliche italiane dei secoli di mezzo* (Capolago, 1831-32).

Skinner, Q., *The Foundations of Modern Political Thought* (Cambridge, 1978).

———, 'Ambrogio Lorenzetti: the Artist as Political Philosopher', *Proceedings of the British Academy*, 72 (1986), 1-56.

Smail, D. L., 'Common Violence: Vengeance and Inquisition in Fourteenth-century Marseille', *Past and Present*, 151 (1996), 28-59.

———, 'Notaries, Courts, and the Legal Culture of Late Medieval Marseille', in K. L. Reyerson and J. Drendel (eds.), *Urban and Rural Communities in Medieval France: Provence and Languedoc, 1000-1500* (Leiden, 1998), 23-50.

———, *The Consumption of Justice: Emotions, Publicity, and Legal Culture in Marseille, 1264-1423* (Ithaca, 2003).

———, 'Aspects of Procedural Documentation in Marseille (14th-15th Centuries)', in Lepsius and Wetzstein (eds.), *Als die Welt in die Akten kam*, 139-169.

———, 'Violence and Predation in Late Medieval Mediterranean Europe', *Comparative Studies in Society and History*, 54 (2012), 1-28.

———, 'Debt, Humiliation, and Stress in Fourteenth-Century Lucca and Marseille', in B. Sère and J. Wettlaufer (eds.), *Shame between Punishment and Penance. The Social Usages of Shame in the Middle Ages and Early Modern Times* (Firenze, 2013), 247-262.

———, *Legal Plunder. Households and Debt Collection in Late Medieval Europe* (Harvard, 2016).

Spagnesi, E., 'L'insegnamento di Baldo degli Ubaldi a Pisa e Firenze', *Atti e memorie dell'Accademia toscana di scienze e lettere La Colombaria*, 69 (2004), 127-155.

Stern, L. I., The Criminal Law System of Medieval and Renaissance Florence (Baltimore and London, 1994).

Storchi, C. S., 'Compromesso e arbitrato nella *summa totius artis notariae* di Rolandino', in Tamba (ed.), *Rolandino e l'Ars notaria*, 329-376.

Tabacco, G., 'La storia politica e sociale. Dal tramonto dell'Impero alle prime formazioni di Stati regionali', in R. Romano and C. Vivanti (eds.), *Storia d'Italia, II: Dalla caduta dell'Impero romano al secolo XVIII* (Torino, 1974), 1-274.

Tamba, G., 'Per atto di notaio. Le attestazioni di debito a Bologna alla metà del secolo XIII', *Mélange de l'École Française de Rome*, 109 (1997), 525-544.

———, *Una corporazione per il potere. Il notariato a Bologna in età comunale* (Bologna, 1998).

——— (ed.), *Rolandino e l'Ars notaria da Bologna all'Europa* (Milano, 2002).

Tanzini, L., *Il governo delle leggi. Norme e pratiche delle istituzioni a Firenze dalla fine del Duecento all'inizio del Quattrocento* (Firenze, 2007).

———, 'Diritto e giustizia nelle città tardomedievali: recenti contributi della storiografia europea', *Archivio storico italiano*, 617 (2008), 549-559.

———, 'Una pratica documentaria tra sovrabbondanze e silenzi: i Regolatori e le scritture d'ufficio a Firenze tra XIV e XV secolo', Lazzarini (ed.), *Reti Medievali*, 11.

———, *Dai comuni agli stati territoriali. L'Italia delle città tra XIII e XV secolo* (Noceto, 2010).

———, 'Emergenza, eccezione, deroga: tecniche e retoriche del potere nei comuni toscani del XIV secolo', in Vallerani (ed.), *Tecniche di potere*, 149-181.

———, 'Costruire e controllare il territorio. Banditi e repressione penale nello Stato fiorentino del Trecento', in L. Antonelli and S. Levati (eds.), *Controllare il territorio: norme, corpi e conflitti tra Medioevo e prima guerra mondiale* (Catanzaro, 2013), 11-30.

TIRELLI, V., 'Sulla crisi istituzionale del comune a Lucca (1308-1312)', in *Studi per Enrico Fiumi* (Pisa, 1979), 317-360.

———, 'Il notariato a Lucca in epoca basso-medievale', in M. Montorzi (ed.), *Il notariato nella civiltà Toscana* (Roma, 1985), 241-309.

TOMMASI, G., *Sommario della storia di Lucca dall'anno MIV all'anno MDCC* (*Archivio storico italiano*, Tomo X) (Firenze, 1847).

TORI, G., 'Coluccio Salutati, Chancellor of the Republic of Lucca, and the Problem of the Minute di Riformagioni Pubbliche (1370-71)', in Blomquist and Mazzaoui (eds.), *The "Other Tuscany"*, 111-122.

VALLERANI, M., *Il sistema giudiziario del comune di Perugia. Conflitti, reati e processi nella seconda metà del XIII secolo* (Perugia, 1991).

———, 'Movimenti di pace in un comune di Popolo: I Flagellanti a Perugia nel 1260', *Bollettino della deputazione Umbria di storia patria*, 101 (2004), 369-418.

———, 'Il comune come mito politico. Immagini e modelli tra Otto e Novecento', in G. Sergi and E. Castelnuovo (eds.), *Arti e storia nel Medioevo*, vol. iv, *Il Medioevo al passato e al presente* (Torino, 2004), 187-206.

———, *La giustizia pubblica medievale* (Bologna, 2005).

———, 'Tra astrazione e prassi. Le forme del processo nelle città dell'Italia settentrionale del secolo XII', in Arlinghaus et al. (eds.), *Praxis der Gerichtsbarkeit*, 135-154.

———, 'Consilia. Un progetto di schedatura archivistica della consulenza giuridica in età comunale', *Le carte e la storia*, 12-1 (2006), 24-29.

———, 'Procedura e giustizia nelle città italiane del basso medioevo (XII-XIV secolo)', in Chiffoleau, Gauvard and Zorzi (eds.), *Pratiques sociales*, 439-494.

———, 'Modelli di verità. Le prove nei processi inquisitori', in *L'enquête au Moyen Âge: études réunies par Claude Gauvard* (Roma, 2008), 123-142.

——— (ed.), *Quaderni storici*, 131 (*Sistemi di Eccezione*) (2009).

———, 'Premessa', *Quaderni storici*, 131 (*Sistemi di Eccezione*) (2009), 299-312.

———, 'La supplica al signore e il potere della misericordia. Bologna 1337-1347', *Quaderni storici*, 131 (*Sistemi di eccezione*) (2009), 411-441.

——— (ed.), *Tecniche di potere nel tardo Medioevo: regimi comunali e signorie in Italia* (Roma, 2010).

———, 'L'arbitrio negli statuti cittadini del Trecento', in Id (ed.), *Tecniche di potere*, 117-147.

———, 'Consilia iudicialia. Sapienza giuridica e processo nelle città comunali italiane', *Mélanges de l'École française de Rome. Moyen Âge*, 123-1 (2011), 129-149.

———, 'Comune e comuni: una dialettica non risolta', in M. C. De Matteis and B. Pio (eds.), *Sperimentazioni di governo nell'Italia centrosettentrionale nel processo storico dal primo comune alla signoria* (Bologna, 2011), 9-34.

Varanini, G. M., '«Al magnificho e possente segnoro». Suppliche ai signori trecenteschi italiani fra cancelleria e corte: l'esempio scaligero', in C. Nubola and A. Würgler (eds.), *Suppliche e "gravamina". Politica, amministrazione, giustizia in Europa (secoli XIV-XVIII)* (Bologna, 2002), 65-106.

———, 'Aristocrazie e poteri nell'Italia centro-settentrionale dalla crisi comunale allguerre d'Italia', in R. Bordone, G. Castelnuovo and G. M. Varanini (eds.), *Le aristocrazie dai signori rurali al patriziato* (Roma and Bari, 2004), 121-193.

Viroli, M., *Republicanism* (New York, 2002).

Wickham, C., *Community and Clientele in Twelfth-Century Tuscany. Origins of the Rural Commune in the Plain of Lucca* (Oxford, 1998).

———, 'Gossip and Resistance among the Medieval Peasantry', *Past and Present*, 160 (1998), 3-24.

———, *Courts and Conflict in Twelfth-Century Tuscany* (Oxford, 2003).

———, *Sleepwalking into a New World. The Emergence of Italian City Communes in the Twelfth Century* (Princeton, 2015).

Zanetti Domingues, L. L., 'Rituali di liberazione dei prigionieri nell'Italia del Duecetno: il caso toscano tra diritto e religione', *Archivio storico italiano*, 668 (2021), 221- 257.

Zorzi, A., *L'amministrazione della giustizia penale nella Repubblica fiorentina: aspetti e problemi* (Firenze, 1988).

———, 'Contrôle social, ordre public et répression judiciaire à Florence à l'époque communale: éléments et problèmes', *Annales ESC.*, 5 (1990), 1169-1188.

———, 'Ordine pubblico e amministrazione della giustizia nelle formazioni politiche toscane tra Tre e Quattrocento', in *Italia 1350-1450: tra crisi, trasformazione, sviliuppo* (Pistoia, 1993), 419-474.

———, '*Ius erat in armis.* Faide e conflitti tra pratiche sociali e pratiche di governo', in Chittolini, Molho and Schiera (eds.), *Origini dello stato*, 600-629.

———, 'Politica e giustizia a Firenze al tempo degli ordinamenti antimagnatizi', in *Ordinamenti di giustizia fiorentina* (Firenze, 1995), 105-147.

———, 'Negoziazione penale, legittimazione giuridica e poteri urbani nell'Italia comunale', Bellabarba, Schwerhoff and Zorzi (eds.), *Criminalità e giustizia*, 13-34.

———, 'La cultura della vendetta nel conflitto politico in età comunale', in R. delle Donne and A. Zorzi (eds.), *Le storie e la memoria. In onore di Arnold Esch* (Firenze, 2002), 135-170.

———, 'Pluralismo giudiziario e documenazioni: il caso di Firenze in età comunale', in Chiffoleau, Gauvard and Zorzi (eds.), *Pratiques sociales*,125-187.

———, *La trasformazione di un quadro politico. Ricerche su politica e giustizia a Firenze dal comune allo Stato territoriale* (Firenze, 2008).

———, *Conflitti, paci e vendette nell'Italia comunale* (Firenze, 2009)

———, *Le signorie cittadine in Italia (secoli XIII-XV)* (Milano, 2010).

———, 'Bien Commun et conflits politiques dans l'Italie communale', in Lecuppre-Desjardin and Van Bruaene (eds.), *De bono communi*, 267-290.

———, 'Justice', in Gamberini and Lazzarini (eds.), *The Italian Renaissance State*, 490-514.

——— (ed.), *Le signorie cittadine in Toscana. Esperienze di potere e forme di governo personale (secoli XIII-XV)* (Roma, 2013).